CHUCK HODELL, PHD

Introduction to
Instructional
Systems Design

Theory and Practice

ATD Press is an internationally renowned source of insightful and practical information on talent development, training, and professional development.

ATD Press
1640 King Street
Alexandria, VA 22314 USA

Ordering information: Books published by ATD Press can be purchased by visiting ATD's website at td.org/books or by calling 800.628.2783 or 703.683.8100.

Library of Congress Control Number: 2021930885

ISBN-10: 1-95215-712-9
ISBN-13: 978-1-95215-712-7
e-ISBN: 978-1-95215-713-4

ATD Press Editorial Staff
Director: Sarah Halgas
Manager: Melissa Jones
Community of Practice Manager, Learning Design: Eliza Blanchard
Developmental Editor: Kathryn Stafford
Production Editor: Hannah Sternberg
Text Design: Shirley E.M. Raybuck
Cover Design: Rose Richey

Printed by BR Printers, San Jose, CA

This book is dedicated to my mother, Ann Juanita Kelton Hodell. She was a lifelong teacher and sadly passed away when I was 12. The memories of her teaching fifth grade in the classroom, nursing at the local nursing schools and hospital, and working as a swimming instructor in the summer all sit on my shoulder in every aspect of my career as an author, educator, and mentor. She selflessly and tirelessly attempted to make the life of every one of her students better. While the memories have faded, the call to service as a teacher remains eternally strong thanks to her indelible mark on my life and work.

Contents

Introduction

The world of instructional design is an exciting place to live and work.

Teachers, trainers, instructors, and in fact everyone who is associated in some way with learning has a home in the field of instructional systems design (ISD). Whether you teach and design your own courses or facilitate learning using already prepared courses, there is substantial value to learning the fundamentals of this incredible field and having a working knowledge of its essential elements of analysis, design, development, implementation, and evaluation (ADDIE).

Instructional designers are responsible for course designs from early childhood to PhD-level programs and everything in between. Every learning experience falls within the structure of this science of how learning takes place and how to best create learning environments that foster knowledge and mastery.

Many have never heard of instructional design because it is the almost silent partner that supports the process of designing, implementing, and evaluating learning experiences. In much the same way that the driver of a battery-operated luxury car never thinks about materials science engineering and battery design, students taking courses never think about how their learning experience was designed. The countless hours of analysis and design that take place long before a course is implemented are largely unknown partners in the learning process.

The more you dig into the world of instructional design, the more you discover that this field has been around in one form or another since the first learning events took place in our distant past. The science of learning transfer until recently had no name and no identity. But it certainly existed, and the same forces that are in play in the modern world of online learning were influencing learning from the very beginning. The difference is that now we have spent years studying how learning takes place and have learned in a variety of ways how to make learning exceptionally efficient and powerful.

The prominent scholars and scientists who have provided the foundational, theoretical, and operational elements for instructional design may be less well known than those in other fields, but that is part of the mystique of this work and the science behind it. Does the fact that everyone knows about the incredible discoveries of Albert Einstein and Thomas Edison make their work seem more important or more relevant than instructional design? It can be argued that learning touches everyone in some way. All of us have either taken courses, been involved in learning experiences, or benefited from learning transfer in our lives. Learning is the currency that paves the way to understanding, skills, and progress.

Who Is This Book For?

This textbook is for everyone interested in the field of ISD, including novice and intermediate-level instructional designers and those working in affiliate areas of study. There is no assumption of previous ISD knowledge; that is why we start in section 1 with the basics of learning and learning transfer, work through the ADDIE model of ISD in section 2, explore distance learning and social media in section 3, and examine workflow and other advanced concepts and practices in section 4.

The field of instructional design is so complex and varied that no single textbook could ever hope to cover every aspect of ISD. It is for this reason that this textbook seeks to hit the basics of both theory and practice to provide a sound foundation of knowledge and skills that can be enhanced and expanded as a designer gains experience. To put this in ISD terms, we are seeking to provide the prerequisites that every instructional designer needs to get started and become both informed and conversational in the basics of the field.

This text also provides the path for learners to create their first work products to use as examples in a portfolio of their ISD knowledge. Where many other texts stay in the theoretical world, we provide both theory basics and pathways and examples of instructional design artifacts that are created every hour of every day in the real world of instructional design.

What Will You Learn?

As a reader of this text, you may be here for a quick overview of ISD and to gather some basic background information on the field, perhaps to judge whether you have any interest in working in the world of the instructional designer. Others may be taking an entry- or intermediate-level academic course in instructional design for credit at one of the colleges and universities that use this text. It is also possible that you are participating in a continuing education course in ISD offered by ATD or a local community college. This text can also be used for teaching apprenticeship instructors how to be better teachers and course designers. Each of the sections and chapters is designed to offer learners a different slice of ISD basics. It is important to know and remember that every topic is presented from the perspective of instructional design and its usefulness for instructional designers.

Section 1

Our first section visits the theoretical foundations of ISD, starting in chapter 1 with the story of how instructional design has evolved over thousands of years, from the first learning interactions to today's world of distance learning. In this chapter we start with defining learning itself; you will learn about the eight generations of learning transfer and why these play a key role in the practice of ISD.

In chapter 2, we then dig into learning theory and how all of us learn and retain new material. Along the way we visit the building block theories of learning, from behaviorism to constructivism.

Chapter 3 is an exploration of the adult learner and how this population learns best. We look at both generational learning and adult-learning challenges. There is also a discussion of learning disabilities and how these affect designing for adults.

ISD models and specifically the ADDIE model of instructional design are first explored in chapter 4. The Successive Approximation Model (SAM) and other models are also discussed so that a strong base of knowledge is provided for building courses and projects in ISD.

Section 2

In the second section, we drill down into the five primary elements of instructional design work, specifically analysis, design, development, implementation, and evaluation. Some will refer to this as the ADDIE model of ISD, but in reality these are the five clearly definable areas of work that take place in course design and projects. Each of these elements of instructional design contain specific tasks and outcomes and when combined represent the modern practice of ISD.

In chapter 5 we look at the incredibly interesting and complex world of analysis. Without analysis, the work of an instructional designer is based more on luck than on reliable data and information. There is no acceptable substitute for analysis in any instructional design process, and many designers consider this element of ISD to be the very foundation of everything else in the practice of instructional design.

Chapter 6 explores the element of ISD that is essentially the guiding or managing function in instructional design. The term *design* is the foundation of ISD both as a name and as a professional practice. Instructional designers do in fact design learning, and in this chapter we visit all of the many aspects of this ISD element from the perspective of a practicing designer.

In chapter 7, we cover development, the element in ISD where the design takes shape and the materials and tangible elements of a course become real. Development is also the time when pilot testing and preliminary quality control kick in. In many ways, this is the busiest and most demanding time for a designer, especially when working with subject matter experts.

Chapter 8 brings us to the implementation aspects of course design and involves the designer actually delivering a course to learners. We begin our discussion of evaluation in this chapter because designers will almost always have evaluation of mastery as part of a professional course design. This is also the time for serious quality control tools to be implemented, and we cover quality rating rubrics, which are used in implementation to ensure that a course is well designed.

In chapter 9, we enter the world of evaluation at a very detailed level. As instructional designers, we are not just interested in evaluation of mastery for learning, which is of course a prime aspect of evaluation, but we also engage in the evaluation of the design product as it relates to design plans, lesson plans, and objectives. We also review the performance agreement principle and its role in designing courses and ensuring that learners are evaluated in the most authentic way.

Chapter 10 closes this section with a detailed look at behavioral objectives. Outside of the design work, very little is known or appreciated about how objectives are written and the complexity of what goes into designing and writing these instructional design essentials. We look at the four objective domains and learn to write both short-form and long-form objectives as well as distinguish between terminal and enabling objectives. The concept of evaluating content mastery is also introduced.

Section 3

As you progress in your instructional design career, the role that technology plays in design is inescapable. Distance learning, social media, and the associated software and applications, like the learning management system (LMS), will play an increasingly important role. All learning is built from the framework of ISD, but each learning approach requires a different set of instructional design skills and tools; technology-based learning is prime among these requirements.

We begin this section with a look at distance learning and its long and proud history in instructional design in chapter 11. You may be surprised to learn that distance learning has been around for well over 100 years, and that the recent increased use of the term is not just identified with the modern use of computers and software in learning and course design. There are four generations of distance learning, and the evolution of the process is key to designing digital courses. The role of social media in learning and instructional design is also discussed.

Much of the work now designed and implemented in formal learning environments takes place with the help of an LMS. This software interface is integral for the distribution of courses from K–12 to doctoral work, and literally millions of learners are this second online and learning using these systems. Chapter 12 is a primer on these systems, and we discuss some basic design characteristics that affect instructional designers as they work with these applications.

In chapter 13, our final chapter in this section, we look at the incredible world of social media from the perspective of an instructional designer, its history, and the advantages and challenges of designing with social media for implementation within different population and content areas.

Section 4

In our final section, we spend time with some practical, and in some cases advanced, aspects of ISD. The process of designing learning involves many aspects of managing projects and allocating resources, like any professional endeavor, and having an efficient workflow is key to keeping any project within deadline and budget.

Workflow is the foundation of professional projects, especially in instructional design. You can have the best design skills in the world, but you need to have a process to get projects to completion. In chapter 14, a generic workflow model is presented, which allows you to shape your own approach to managing learning projects, or any kind of project for that matter.

In chapter 15, we enter the world of upper-level ISD work with a look at criticality and then deeper consideration of content mastery. Criticality is a process used in instructional design to determine which content best fits the goals of a learning course and project. Many times, there is much more content to cover than time allows, and this is the process you use to objectively determine which content is most useful for a learning project.

In chapter 16, we discuss competency-based instructional design, the process of designing courses based solely on the content and what it demands for mastery of specific skills. This approach in ISD is found most often in detailed and specific skills programs that demand demonstrated mastery beyond just a simple overview of the content. You will see this approach in learning for professionals in healthcare, emergency services, apprenticeship, the military, and other demanding design environments.

Chapter 17, the last chapter in this section, presents a vital area of instructional design—migrating classroom and other traditional forms of learning to digital and online platforms. Whether this means putting a classroom college course into an LMS or migrating a K–12 classroom into an online environment, there are certain elements of this process to consider from the design side of the equation.

As you can see, the work of instructional design is a fascinating and sometimes complex endeavor, and it is almost impossible to learn about this field without spending some time with the basics and the more advanced elements of the process that most instructional designers work with on a daily basis. It isn't possible to cover every aspect of ISD in one textbook because the field is so expansive and varied, but basic elements of this profession are covered here in great detail.

Enjoy this journey into the world of instructional design and prepare for a professional career unlike any other.

Theoretical Foundations of ISD

CHAPTER 1

The Journey to Instructional Systems Development

KEY CONCEPTS

- Sharing skills and knowledge as an inherent part of life
- Learning as a process
- Learning in formal and informal settings
- Eight generations of learning transfer
- Instructional design as a systems approach to curriculum development
- Instructional design as both science and art
- Impact of programmed learning and the advent of scaling of teaching
- Criterion testing and standards for evaluation of mastery
- Interlocking knowledge and skill areas required of an ISD practitioner
- Infinite landscape of ISD careers

CHAPTER OBJECTIVES

At the end of this chapter, the learner should be able to:

- Define learning.
- Describe the process of learning transfer.
- Define instructional systems development.
- List one key feature of each of the eight generations of learning transfer.
- Give examples of the scope of the field of ISD.
- Define *systems approach*.
- Define *programmed learning*.
- Cite two examples of how criterion-referenced testing has impacted learning transfer.
- List several knowledge areas and skills required of instructional design professionals for competence and mastery.
- Describe the range of careers available to instructional designers.

In every corner of our world, for as long as there has been intelligent life on this planet, people have been teaching skills and passing on knowledge to others, from a fire to going on a successful hunt, to today's world of unlimited hashtags. Civilization has always revolved around learning and sharing information in one form or another. Life is learning in every conceivable way.

Through the centuries, the art of teaching has been marked by a number of different formats and advances in the efficiency and reliability of learning transfer. It is not too simplistic to say that without learning, knowledge, and skill transfer, all of us would still be struggling to make fires and hunt dinner with little progress in anything else. This is because each new level of knowledge builds on what has taken place before; without the process of learning transfer, we have no bridge to new discoveries. It can be argued that there is really no new information in the world, just the process of discovering the knowledge we didn't previously know. We then combine it with already established information to create something we consider new.

Through eight generations of learning transfer, from demonstration to digital technology, the process of both teaching and learning design has matured considerably, and we now enjoy the most reliable methods and practices for preparing instruction we've known yet. This formalization of the process of curriculum design has brought us into the age of instructional systems development (ISD).

For each new learner there has to be at least one teacher. While the specifics of the teacher-learner relationship have materially changed with the advent of each new generation of learning transfer, there is no escaping the truth that teaching is both timeless and universal. In this chapter, we look at the history of learning, the generations of learning transfer, and the foundations for the practice of what we now label *instructional design*.

Learning Is a Process

The passing of skills and knowledge has always been a process. It can be argued that humans, at the very beginning of our existence, acted mostly on instinct when learning new ways to obtain the basic informational elements of life. A need prompted a response, which then became the basis for learning a skill. After repeated similar situations and outcomes, learning of some sort took place and became the foundation for any knowledge that followed. This is a reasonable proposition, but really holds together only when speaking of the earliest interactions of life. At some point, instinct had to give way to learning and transmission of this knowledge to others. While instinct certainly lives in all of us, the maturation of informational transference has been a steady and progressive process to what we have in the modern world of learning.

However, there has still been much discussion about the relationship between instinct and learning. Abraham Maslow, who developed a needs hierarchy that we look at later in the book, argued that instinct is in fact learning. Oscar Oppenheimer (1958) disagreed, suggesting that instinct is not the same as learning and that something more has to take place for instinct to evolve into learning. If this is true, our instincts must be supplemented by some vehicle in order for learning to transfer from one person to another. Today, there is universal agreement that instinct is but one of a million data points that each learner uses to process and then store new information through the process of learning.

Given what we know today, it is reasonable to assume that the earliest forms of skills enhancement came from both instinct and experience, which then fostered sharing of this information. Being cold would trigger a hunt for warmth, both clothing and shelter. Hunger would lead to hunting, fishing, and gathering available roots and berries. And, as each new challenge offered insights into the best way to perform any of these skills, passing on this knowledge would become an incremental process, which started with the validated skills and then built each succeeding layer of improved revision based on the previously tested knowledge.

Survival was unquestionably the most important priority in early human history; even before the existence of formal language, skills that helped in this struggle were being passed from one person to another. Sometimes this was the older passing to the younger. This could be as elemental as finding the safest shelter for the night or finding sustenance for meals. It is also probable that the skills needed for a person to survive a traumatic experience, like defending oneself against an animal attack, would also probably be passed on to those who had not yet had this life-threatening experience.

Defining Learning Transfer

There are any number of definitions for the term *learning transfer*; we define it as the action of a learner processing and storing knowledge or skills obtained from

No matter
how learning
is presented,
it still requires
stimulus and
response.

another source. This other source may be another person or medium, such as a book or electronically distributed information. You may also see this represented by the term *training transfer*.

The formal adaptation of the construct of learning transfer is rooted in the work of Edward Thorndike, who deemed it "transfer of practice" (1916); this also set the foundation for connectivism, which we review later. Thorndike wrote, "The sciences and arts arose by the impetus of wants, and continue in their service" (Richardson and Slife 2013). This suggests that learning has its roots in the needs of the learner, and no matter how learning is presented, it still requires stimulus and response. This is a common theme in modern learning theory.

The Generations of Learning Transfer

The process of passing knowledge and skills from one person to another has several milestones from inception to the present day. Each of these periods represents a turning point in the incremental growth of the learning transfer process. It is fair to say that none of these periods was heralded at the time as significant, but the benefits of time and reflection have proven that there exist several important points of departure from previous ways of transferring knowledge.

Perhaps the easiest way to begin thinking about learning transfer and the process of instructional design is to put the practice into a context of generations of learning transfer. Each of these generations has characteristics that reflect the practices and processes generally thought to have existed during each of these periods of time. After the first generation, which is essentially everything before the use of pictures and drawings for communication, there is an obvious milestone that marked the advent of a new generation.

While these generational periods are dynamic, both beginning and ending based on larger historical and societal influences, they give a clear context of how the process of learning transfer moved from one accepted norm to the next. Each generation after the first used the previous one as a foundation for the advances that were taking place. This highlights one of the most prominent aspects of instructional design, which is that the basics still exist and that advances in the field are more enhancements and improvements than a complete replacement of these basic principles.

The eight generations of learning transfer are more symbolic than anthropological. Each is a distinctive point of reference to a time when new ideas arose that impacted learning transfer in a fundamental way. These are the eight generations of learning transfer:

- **First Generation:** Demonstration
- **Second Generation:** Pictures and Drawings
- **Third Generation:** Written Language
- **Fourth Generation:** Printing
- **Fifth Generation:** Distance Learning
- **Sixth Generation:** Analog Technology
- **Seventh Generation:** Social Sciences
- **Eighth Generation:** Digital Technology

Let's take a look at each generation and discover how each of these periods had a significant influence on what exists today in ISD.

First Generation: Demonstration

The first generation of learning transfer could easily be called "doing what comes naturally." At this first, binary, and naturalistic stage of learning, everything was essentially based on instinct. It was show one, do one—or in ISD terms, demonstrate one and perform one. If one couldn't hunt or gather food, one probably didn't eat. Hunger was the motivation, and survival was the real test of performance.

At first, humans collaborated in small groups to forage, which was the beginning of creating joint goals and of the simplistic sharing of information by "pointing and pantomiming" (Tomasello 2014). This should be considered the first effort at sharing knowledge interactively, with one person communicating important content with another, using fundamental vocalizations, which might have been enhanced by pointing or gesturing.

The first verbal communications used single-syllable words, such as *ha*, which might have meant *air; va*, which might have meant *water;* and *ta*, which seems to have indicated an inanimate object (Cordall 2019). One can imagine an animated conversation transferring knowledge of birds (*ha*), fish (*va*), and perhaps a rock (*ta*) between two of our early ancestors.

Hunting, shelter construction, and fire building were learned skills, either from personal experience or from a lesson from someone with more knowledge. That knowledge was skillfully, yet almost instinctively, handed down from one generation to the next, first by demonstration and later supplemented by oral dissemination and visualization of skills.

Self-education, mostly among children, was the standard for hundreds of thousands of years. Schools as we know them today are a very recent development. In fact, before the advent of agriculture approximately 10,000 years ago, play and work were indistinguishable from each other. Children were given "almost unlimited freedom to play and explore on their own" (Gray 2008) because this was considered the way that children learned naturally.

The hunter-gatherer life was a skill-based existence that was not considered labor intensive or even work; it was considered in today's context to be play. The skills and knowledge necessary to exist in this environment were supported by initiative and creativity and not necessarily hard labor. It was a challenging way to live, with education evolving as the product of need, both for sustenance and for life itself. In instructional design terms, this population learned through trial and error and probably would have been confused by any suggestion of formal education as a concept.

This all changed with the onset of agriculture and the labor-intensive nature of work; the resulting civilizations required more permanent places of dwelling and long hours of repetitive, back-breaking labor. There was no time for play and informal discovery, and civilization turned a corner in how education was both perceived and practiced.

Every learning experience from the beginning of time required some form of instructional design. At first, it was simply show and tell. Someone hunted; others watched and learned. Practice and feedback were the glue that made the learning stick, and with each new combination of teacher and learner a new generation of refinement was added to this accumulation of knowledge. Trial and error were incorporated into the incremental progress within each skill, and the seemingly modern engagement of best practices had its genesis in these early teachers and learners.

Second Generation: Pictures and Drawings

The earliest forms of lasting communication were probably cave drawings. It wasn't until 73,000 years ago that abstract drawings were made at Blombos Cave in South Africa (Henshilwood 2018). Oddly enough, one of the glyphs appears similar to the hashtag symbol we find in rampant use in social media today. It is this evolution to drawings that marks the second generation of learning transfer, since learning could now be enhanced by more permanent visuals.

According to Christopher Henshilwood, an archaeologist from the University of Bergen, the Blombos Cave drawings show that "what they could do with symbols is, for the first time, store information outside of the human brain. And that is a major advance" (Guarino 2018). The reason this is important to learning transfer, and clearly a generational marker, is the fact that knowledge was now being stored, in this case on the wall of a cave for others to see and learn from. No longer were humans passing knowledge and skills only through first-person actions; we now have a concrete example of how they passed their knowledge in a way that was permanent.

Third Generation: Written Language

The first known language preserved in writing is often considered to be either Egyptian or Sumerian. Egyptian language can be traced back to the writings found on tomb walls dating from around 3,250 BC. These writings belong to the "Manito-Semitic family of languages" and contain the first known "instance of a complete sentence" (Allen 2012).

Sumerian was written in cuneiform script, and it is thought to date to around 3,000 BC. It is an interesting language with six vowels, and is considered an agglutinative language, which has no inflection when spoken.

Written language is a turning point in learning transfer because this more permanent form of communication is incrementally more complex. It certainly lasts longer than simple oral communication and allows for information to be as permanent as the means of recording it. Rather than being more instinctive, as oral communication tends to be, writing takes more thought and intent and represents a more cognitive approach.

Fourth Generation: Printing

Most scholars credit Johann Gutenberg with inventing the printing press in 1436, although some say the Koreans may have predated him with movable copper type printing in 1392. In either case, the practice of writing and distributing information in written form has been with us for roughly 600 years. Gutenberg's incredible accomplishments have a very interesting link to instructional design. He was trained within the goldsmith guild of the times and he also taught the printing process to his friends, making him both a product of instructional design and an instructional designer himself. Little did he realize that his invention would someday be the single largest distribution method of instructional material that has ever existed, challenged only recently by digital systems.

Fifth Generation: Distance Learning

The concept of distance learning generally accepted and practiced today originally appeared in a 1833 advertisement in a Swedish newspaper for a composition course offered through the mail or post, as it was then called (Simonson and Seepersaud 2019). This was quickly followed in 1840 by Englishman Isaac Pitman offering shorthand lessons via the penny post. As we will see in a later chapter, distance learning has come a long way in the intervening years, but the end product of the process has remained relatively the same, offering learners an alternative to attending in-person courses.

With the appearance of a model that removed the necessity of the direct, real-time involvement of a teacher, learning transfer turned a significant corner. It is doubtful that anyone at that point would have predicted that this conceptual model would become the mainstay of learning that it is today. However, it is these seemingly small changes in approach and thinking that build the foundation for much greater and more impactful ways to teach and learn. It is important to remember that these early offerings in distance learning didn't rely on technology for their implementation. Yet as advanced technology has entered our lives, we continue to see how one breakthrough in practice supports and encourages the next.

Sixth Generation: Analog Technology

Whether you consider the first telephone call (in 1876) or the first radio broadcast (in 1896) to be the first example of technologically distributed information, it is obvious that the late 19th century served as a significant turning point in the ability of humans to communicate information.

These analog forms of communication were the first real glimpses into the way that technology could enhance learning transfer. The major innovation was that communication of information could take place at a distance through analog transmission of voice or data. Distance learning as a concept could now be offered by technology, exponentially expanding the opportunity for one teacher to reach large numbers of learners in real time at multiple locations.

And, while Alexander Graham Bell's first voice transmission to Thomas Watson wasn't by any stretch a learning moment as defined today, it did prove that gathering a teacher and learners in one spot was no longer required. Humans can use technology to communicate at a distance. This is the very essence of how learning transfer progresses incrementally based on milestone events that at the time seem unrelated to ISD.

Later, more significant digital technology, specifically the computer, would usher in a new age of learning transfer (the eighth generation). The distinction between the two generations is related to how the technology was used in learning transfer, with the sixth generation being more one-directional and the eighth being more bi-directional.

Seventh Generation: Social Sciences

The challenges of preparing millions of people for their roles in World War II advanced the complexity and sophistication of training and instructional design. Psychologists and the training and education communities worked together to lay the foundation for what is now known as instructional systems development. This early and critical period in ISD's history witnessed a more effective design of training materials as well as new approaches to selecting trainees based on the psychological principles of finding the best fit between learner abilities and available job classifications.

This period marked the beginning of a formalization of instructional design and the recognition that learning, curriculum design, and mastery are much more complex concepts than previously thought. This partnership of subject matter experts, psychologists, and training professionals provided a number of foundational building blocks to the then-emerging field of ISD. The most important of these were a recognition that curriculum design was in fact a science as well as an art, and that mastery could be both objectively measured and used as a design element.

For example, Robert Reiser points out that aviator training during World War II led to an excessive and unacceptable failure rate, so testing was developed that "examined the general intellectual, psychomotor, and perceptual skill" of aviation candidates, allowing a much better selection for training. This approach was then generalized to other positions. The results were impressive, as reflected in the considerably higher percentage of successful trainings that took place. It was during this period that figures such as Robert Gagné and Leslie Briggs rose to lead the fledgling ISD movement and exhibited considerable influence in the design of training materials (Reiser 2001).

The publication of Gagné's *The Conditions of Learning* and *Psychological Principles in Systems Development*, at least partially based on his military work during WWII, were significant in the history of the field. His later collaboration with Briggs and Walter Wager on *Principles of Instructional Design* (1974) is now considered a classic text in the field. It was also during this time that Gagné's Nine Events of Instruction took root and established a solid psychological road map for designing learning.

Eighth Generation: Digital Technology

It is fair to say that the largest leap in the use of technology for learning transfer came with the introduction of the personal computer and digital communications. There were varying rollouts of this concept, beginning with the IBM 5100 in 1975 and the Apple II in 1977. Both opened the door for affordable home computers that were more likely to be used for learning than the hobbyist computers, which had appeared first and were somewhat expensive. As production increased and the costs dropped, more computers were appearing in the home for both children and adults to use and enjoy.

ROBERT MILLS GAGNÉ

Robert Mills Gagné was a Massachusetts native who became part of the group of psychologists that came together during World War II to create the foundation for the study of instructional design as we know it today. The necessity of finding efficient ways of training hundreds of thousands of learners opened the door for research into how training can be delivered in a way that fits how students best learn. It was Gagné who promoted the concept of learning hierarchies, which later evolved into the scaffolding and sequencing of skills from simple to complex when designing courses. He correctly suggested that skills are learned best when based on the mastery of preceding skills. It was also Gagné who transformed the study of instructional design from an art to a science with the integration of a systems approach to course design. The Nine Events of Instruction is a perfect example of his systems approach to learning. He obtained a PhD from Brown University in 1940 and retired from Florida State University after previously serving on the faculty at Penn State, Princeton, and the University of California, among others.

What really made this digital technology come to life for knowledge transfer was the development of the internet. On December 6, 1967, the Department of Defense allocated $19,800 for the "design and specification of a computer network" (*Congressional Digest* 2007), and four months later, ARPANET (Advanced Research Projects Agency Network) evolved into what we now know as the internet. The effort got more expensive a year later, when $563,000 was invested in the design and construction of a system to link computers at the University of California–Santa Barbara, the University of California–Los Angeles, Stanford Research Institute, and the University of Utah. All of this was foundational to what we now use for state-of-the-art learning transfer.

The Path to Instructional Design

The system for both improving content and sharing skills is the basis of instructional design. Each succeeding generation of learning transfer sits on the shoulders of the learning that preceded it. The fact that education and training courses are designed and delivered every second of every hour of every day in a constant cycle of information-sharing highlights the never-ending cycle of knowledge flow. This is true for every level of learning transfer, from pre-K exploration courses to doctoral-level courses in astrophysics.

The teachers in today's world share many of the same qualities as our distant teaching relatives; they both found a way to transfer knowledge and skills at a level necessary to ensure learning mastery. Complex fields of science and engineering are really no different at their core from hunting and fire building when it comes to the process of teaching and the design of lessons. The only real differences are the complexity of the content and the choices available for implementation.

Since the mid-1980s, the educational environment has begun a slow but steady journey into technological delivery of learning in its unlimited forms. Classrooms are now considered legacy educational environments by some, and a small group believes that this current wave of technological learning transfer could lead to even more advanced systems that will be implanted in learners.

Instructional design has no preferences when it comes to choices made in the design process, like decisions about classroom or online implementation. It requires only that rigorous attention is paid to all aspects of the design process. This is where the importance of instructional design comes into play. There is a formal and proven way to design learning that incorporates all possible variables.

REFLECTION

The generations of learning transfer highlight how the process of learning is built on a framework of existing communication styles and technologies. From simple utterances to instantaneous digital communications, learning has always been at the forefront of the use of innovative technologies.

- As you look into the future, how do you think learning will change in the next five, 10, and 25 years?

- Will we ever see a time when learning will not require any of the customary learning elements, like classrooms and teachers?

Just as most of the learning transfer of our distant relatives was completely carried out informally, today, most learning transwer is still carried out in less formal settings like home schools, retail stores, shop floors, repair facilities, sports fields, and anywhere two people are together working through challenges and finding solutions. In the fascinating world of informal learning, right this minute new employees are watching and listening to more tenured colleagues to learn the ropes and imitate the skills required of their new position or responsibilities, all without any formal classroom setting.

The difference between the excellent and the mediocre in most of these learning experiences is that without instructional design knowledge, most courses are essentially best guesses at how to transfer learning. Little is done in the way of analysis and even less is attempted at measuring mastery. This is where instructional systems development enters the picture.

Instructional Systems Development (ISD)

ISD is a systems approach to designing and implementing training. Think of it as the rocket science of learning design. There is a significant difference in how well learning and retention take place when knowledge transfer is directed by a trained instructional designer. There exist today courses and programs in ISD at most major colleges and universities, and organizations have significant ISD training and certification programs. You will see ISD defined and referenced in a number of different ways, including the following:

- Instructional Systems Design (ISD)
- Instructional Systems Development (ISD)
- Instructional Design (ID)
- Systems Approach to Training (SAT)
- Instructional Systems Approach (ISA)

All variations mean essentially the same thing and are often used interchangeably.

ISD is used by education and training professionals worldwide, and it is estimated that more than $83 billion a year is spent on designing and implementing training (*Training* magazine 2019). With this much money being spent, organizations want the very best training product available, and the only way to ensure this level of quality is by using a professional and proven design method.

Every day you hear about training in the news, and more often than not it is related to an absence of training or to training programs that are not effective at teaching content at the level of mastery required for learners. Every time a train, plane, bus, or truck is involved in a serious accident, one of the first culprits raised is a lack of training. This is the same for law enforcement, the military, and civil and emergency services. Without training, and more specifically the correct training, there is eventually going to be a problem. In some situations, the results of this lack of training are minor and may cause either inefficiency or loss of revenue. In other cases, lives are lost, and reputations and credibility are severely and sometimes permanently damaged.

Training is always one of the first things reviewed in federal investigations by the National Transportation Safety Board in the search for the cause of an accident. Did the pilot have training on the emergency procedures when an engine failed? Did the engineer know the speed limit for a specific section of track? Did the bus driver have training in driving on snow-covered roads? These and thousands of other similar inquiries all go back to one basic and inescapable question: "Was there sufficient training and evaluation in this situation for the pilot/engineer/driver to avoid or prevent this accident?" Even if the initial answer is no, a more in-depth investigation will often lead to a root-cause discovery related to training.

In most civil lawsuits filed against an organization relating to an accident or other liability, one of the prime areas of litigation is directly related to the quantity and quality of training required by an organization and if involved employees received and passed these courses. Questions also relate to the course content, employee requirements and work practices, how often and how long ago employees took a specific series of courses, and how well they did in evaluations of mastery.

The world of professional training and education is an enigma to the uninitiated. As consumers of the product for most of their lives, they are blissfully disengaged from the process of designing and delivering instruction. The minutiae of how all of this happens rarely invokes any thoughtful reflection by the end user except on the extremes of excellent and awful. The rest is simply consumption.

This is no different from thousands of other elements of daily life that we have come to accept without any thought about how they happen or why. Consumers of our educational products focus on their role as the student and are less likely to think about instructional design than about what to have for lunch.

> Every time a train, plane, bus, or truck is involved in a serious accident, one of the first culprits raised is a lack of training.

By anyone's reckoning, the training industry and instructional design are formidable fields of study and practice, and the formalization of learning transfer has never been more important. Tight budgets and ever-increasing requirements for courses in every field demand more efficiency and professional skills. It is not acceptable to simply offer courses; there has to be a system that supports both evaluation of mastery and documentation of impact. Dollars spent must be justified, and knowledge increases must be documented.

With such investments, organizations want to make sure they are getting the best training available; that doesn't happen by accident. It is the direct result of highly qualified instructional designers working with teams of subject matter experts and other professionals to design, develop, and implement this training.

The issues of course design and evaluation of learning in K–12 and higher education always make their way into discussions of both the competency of our school-age children and our competitiveness with the rest of the world. If American test numbers are lower than those of other comparable countries around the world, we essentially have an instructional design problem to address.

ISD is the energy behind medicine, law, accounting, and countless other occupations that require specified levels of education and some form of licensure or

TRAINING INDUSTRY FACTS AND FIGURES	To better provide the context for how large the training field has become, let's look at some statistics from the 2019 ATD *State of the Industry* report:

- The average organization spent $1,299 per employee, per year on learning.
- The average employee was involved in formal learning for 34 hours per year.
- Traditional, face-to-face learning accounted for 54 percent of learning hours.
- Self-paced online learning logged 22 percent of hours.
- Virtual or live online learning accounted for 11 percent of learning hours.
- Organizations in software, information, broadcasting, and telecommunications spent the most per employee at $2,184 per year.
- Manufacturing spent the least, on average $487 per employee.
- The average cost for each learning hour implemented was $78.
- The largest percentage of training content was for managerial and supervisory training at 14 percent.
- The lowest percentage of training content was for sales at 5.5 percent.
- Technology-based learning accounted for 43 percent of learning hours.
- Self-paced online learning was most likely to be accessed by a laptop computer, at 81.1 percent utilization.
- On-the-job learning was emphasized highly or very highly by 55 percent of organizations.

even yearly refresher courses. None of this exists without professionally designed courses, programs, evaluations, and other peripheral elements to establish standards and ensure subject mastery by those we trust with our lives, our money, and our livelihood. This is no small task, and professional instructional design is behind all of this work.

The difference between the programs that engage the professional instructional design process and those that are created by nondesigners is not always obvious. However, programs and courses designed by instructional designers will benefit from the rigor expected within the field and generally are considered to be state-of-the-art products.

> The world of professional training and education is an enigma to the uninitiated.

ISD Practices and Principles

There are four guiding principles and points of practice that help explain the professional foundation of instructional design. While not all-inclusive, this is a good overview of the basics of ISD from a practitioner's point of view.

1. The ISD Process Is a Constant

One of the most valuable assets that ISD brings to the practice of instructional design is that the process of instructional design doesn't change based on decisions made for any individual design issue. Whether a designer chooses online, in-classroom, asynchronous, or distributed implementation doesn't in any way impact ISD as a process. These decisions are based on a number of design elements that are explored in the analysis phase of the ISD process.

This timelessness of ISD means several important things to a designer and to organizations. First, no matter when a designer learns and practices the ISD process, the process doesn't change. It also means that whatever new technologies make their way into the instructional landscape, they can be easily incorporated into an instructional program. The idea of "keeping current" as used in ISD simply means keeping up with the trends in various aspects of analysis, design, development, implementation, and evaluation—not the process used to make these necessary design decisions.

2. ISD Is Without Bias

The neutrality of the ISD process is vital to its effectiveness as a system. It must not contain any inherent bias or preconceived notions. This is vital when an instructional designer is making important decisions about various aspects of a course design, including implementation choices and other non-content-related areas. For example, analysis may show that a population can read only at a fifth-grade level, but a designer decides that the materials for the course will be written at a high-school level, because the participants are adults and should be able to read at that level. This is a major mistake and, frankly, unprofessional.

It is possible to see bias enter instructional design when a popular new technology is promoted as the best way to reach a specific population. This was the case in the beginning of each new approach, such as online learning and social media. Some designers will attempt to make any new approach work, and in many cases the technology is not yet mature enough to be used effectively. A good example is the early adaptations of e-learning, where courses were designed with large graphics and other audio and video features that couldn't be used by anyone with anything less than very fast internet access, but most potential learners were using dial-up access. They were a major flop in most cases and really brought home the point that a technology has to mature to be considered for most design work.

ISD has no preordained way to solve a specific design issue. Every decision evolves from gathering and analyzing data. The system guides the process, and the variables inform decisions. If the best choice is a classroom-based course, then a designer should not attempt to make it work using social media.

3. ISD Is Not Technology Dependent

It seems that every new technology or learning model spawns a new approach to implementing instruction, and these are almost always no different from the last big thing in education and training. Multimedia, distance learning, social networking, and tablet computing all have a place in effective instructional programs. However, the process of designing curricula is not impacted by any of these technologies. ISD guides a design decision; it never makes one, although the choices should be pretty obvious after analysis is completed.

4. ISD Self-Evaluates

One of the basic axioms of the ISD process is, "If you are having a problem with a specific ISD design task, it is likely because there is something wrong with the design." Simply put, design problems are usually at fault when the design process stalls. A designer may struggle with writing a lesson plan and making the content work with the population. This is not because of a lack of skill in the designer; it is because the population is probably not well defined or is too diverse for the design approach.

For example, including five-year-olds in the same class as adults in content areas like art or music appreciation is almost impossible due to the obvious differences in learning styles, attention spans, and motivation. If the objectives are not related to building a bond between the populations, then separate them into two courses and design for each population separately.

Another example is when a designer can't write objectives for a very simple content area. Closer examination reveals that the course is actually a conference seminar where participants simply attend and do not in any practical way participate. A designer can never write behavioral objectives for this type of event because there is seldom real learning taking place and students can't be evaluated. The choice then becomes either to admit that this session is not training and do not try to design a course around it, or to upgrade the course to something real that offers lasting instructional value.

ISD's Theoretical Foundation

As you will learn later in this book, there are numerous ISD models and approaches that are available for study and adoption in the world of instructional design. But you will probably find after some investigation that almost all of these are based on the ADDIE model. Some practitioners like to tinker with these basics, but they are generally doing so at the risk of eroding or confusing the foundations of the profession.

Like every branch of science, instructional design started with commonsense approaches to teaching and later looked to theoretical models to shape the foundations of the field. The most prominent and field-tested ISD model is ADDIE, which is an acronym for the five elements of the model: analysis, design, development, implementation, and evaluation. Several hundred other instructional design models exist, the most notable being Rapid Prototyping, Dick and Carey, Kemp, SAM, Transactional, Gerlach-Ely, Hannafin-Peck, and ASSURE.

With the advent of online and technology-enhanced learning delivery, many other models have emerged, including ADDIE-M and IDM-DT (Schoenfeld and Berge 2004). In all, there are enough ISD models for every designer to find something they love and something they hate about each of them. In the end, models are only a place to start, and no single model covers all of the unlimited variations of content and learners that exist in the world of instructional design.

In chapter 4 we will cover several of these ISD models, but the important take-aways for designers are that there is a scientific foundation to instructional design, that the process of learning and storing data in long-term memory has been studied for years, and that to this day it is still the subject of much research and discussion.

Just as in physics or any hard science, there are both theoretical and applied practitioners within the field of ISD. This is a perfect and encouraging state for the field to be in, and it highlights the fact that ISD is as dynamic as any science. There isn't always consensus on every aspect of instructional design, but there are very lively discussions about many of the important elements of ISD and how to make the process more efficient and learner friendly. Every day is a new day in the world of instructional design.

Systems Theory and Instructional Design

ISD is by its very nature a system. Ludwig von Bertalanffy is widely regarded as the one who brought systems theory to the attention of the scientific community. His focus initially was on biology and what he considered a "systems theory of life" (von Bertalanffy 1926), which later evolved into what is now known as General Systems Theory, or GST (Drack 2009). He built on the principle that "the whole is always greater than the sum of its parts" and further defined it as a complex of elements in interaction (von Bertalanffy

SYSTEMS THEORY

Systems theory and instructional systems development are inseparable concepts because they both evolved from the work of Ludwig von Bertalanffy and his belief that the world is dynamic and contains integrated elements that influence one another constantly. Bertalanffy began with the view that living organisms are constantly taking in and releasing energy in what he termed "flux equilibrium," meaning they were constantly changing. Gagné took this interrelatedness concept one step further and suggested that learning and teaching are also dynamic and that changes in one element of the learning equation would impact every other element in the process. He reasoned that the system of learning must represent the dynamic properties of the variables like content, process, and learners. From there, the impact on ISD is considerable. The system of designing instruction must reflect the requirements for learning based on ensuring that the inputs of content and learning environment match the best learning approaches for students to reach mastery. Instructional systems are in fact a reflection of the system of learning that occurs naturally in all students.

1945). From here the definition becomes more complex, with the notion that the more that is known about each element in a system, the more it can be made predictive. In instructional design parlance, the more we know about learners, subject matter, and expected outcomes, the better we can design courses. The term *systems approach* is commonly used to describe instructional systems development.

Systems theory in ISD is directly tied to the fact that there are crucial elements within every variable, like population and content, that have the potential to significantly impact one or more of the other elements. For example, we have quickly defined a population of learners based on the simplest demographic data points of age and income and decided that they will be defined as millennials working in service trade occupations. If we had performed even the basics of analysis, we would have learned that this population is in fact composed of doctoral students in academic programs. The lower income was based on the fact they are living on student loans and scholarships, and while they are millennials, they are still not making the expected levels of income. In this system, the element of income changed and therefore impacted any potential course design.

Programed Learning and ISD

Well before the advent of computers and the internet, instructional designers were looking for ways to improve the implementation of teaching tasks by automating the processes of teaching and evaluation of mastery. Most consider Sidney Pressey to be the first to move this idea to reality, since he wanted to change the way teachers used their time so they "could do more real teaching" (Pressey 1927). Initially, his testing machine actually interfaced with learners and evaluated mastery by presenting a series of questions and scoring the answers. This then evolved into a teaching machine with the addition of a device that prevented a learner from moving on from an incorrectly answered question until it was answered correctly. The assumption, from Pressey's view, was that immediate feedback and remediation would enhance the ability of a learner to retain the correct answer in long-term memory. Even B.F. Skinner credited Pressey with initiating the discussion of the importance of immediate feedback in instruction design (Day and Skinner 2019).

REFLECTION

The field of instructional design is often referred to as a systems approach to curriculum development. This means that the many elements of learning are all interdependent in some way for both the design and implementation of courses. There are inputs, processes, and outputs that are identifiable in each instructional design project.

- Given the universality of systems in our lives, do you think that learning to be a systems analyst is a skill that can be applied to any profession or aspect of life?

- Are there any situations where systems do not have any impact?

This early experimentation with programming learning had several significant impacts on instructional design. First, the revolutionary instructional concept of moving the art of teaching from a human being into the world of automation was the precursor for today's world of asynchronous learning programs in formats such as online and distributed learning. If one could envision learning coming from a source other than a teacher, there is no limit to how far this might progress. Almost 100 years later, we have only touched the surface of how far these early concepts may evolve as technology expands and learners find these types of communications second nature. It is also important to note that Pressey was living in an era when the assembly line process was coming of age after its invention by Henry Ford in 1913. A culture of improvements in productivity was happening across many elements of society. Within this context it would seem reasonable that the practice of teaching would be revisited and any perceived inefficiencies would be addressed.

The second impact of programmed learning was the practice of teaching and evaluating mastery in a behavioralist's mindset. Skinner is considered by many to be the architect of behaviorism and is probably best associated with the Skinner Box and his teaching machines. While Skinner is the one who receives the most credit for advancing this work, he was first drawn to this academic arena after reading John B. Watson's book *Behaviorism* (1925), in which he described psychology as the "science of behavior" and discussed how it was possible to predict and influence behavior. This eventually led to Skinner's work on operant conditioning, which he believed led to mentally healthy individuals being able to manipulate and thereby control their environment.

The third influence of programmed learning was the ability to scale up implementation to any required level. This was demonstrated in WWII as millions needed to be trained in thousands of different content areas, and finding teachers and materials to cover all of these learners was simply impossible under the old classroom approach of each teacher starting at the beginning with each course. It was now feasible to design and then duplicate and distribute courses and materials to many learners of different ability levels.

The fourth element of programmed learning that still thrives today is the practice of standardized testing, both pre- and post-course, to best ensure both learner mastery across a population and the ability to best fit measured knowledge and skill for each individual to a specific trade or learning pathway.

Criterion-Referenced Testing (CRT)

Robert Glaser introduced criterion-referenced measurement in 1963 (Glaser 1963), and it expanded the field of evaluation into previously untested waters. Criterion-referenced tests and the associated results are thought to indicate expected behaviors of a learner based on the outcome of a specific evaluation. For example, a learner who scores higher than another learner is said to have greater potential based on the evaluation results. In its simplest form, it is a binary process with answers being either correct or incorrect.

The philosophy and utilization of CRT helped establish the use of standards for both analysis and evaluation of mastery. This building block for the way ISD evolved and is still practiced sets the foundation of all forms of determination of mastery.

How This Works in Practice

For the purposes of this discussion, let's say you have just been given the responsibility to teach a course in onboarding new employees for your organization. You have three months until the first offering of the course and you have been told you can expect to have 15–20 new employees to teach. Your client is allowing four hours of implementation time for the course. At this point, the average instructor might gather some materials, map out an outline of the important topics, and start designing a slide deck with the information they want to teach. This is how almost everyone starts as a designer, and in many cases, this is the workflow that is followed for any course on any topic until teachers become students of instructional design.

It doesn't usually take significantly more time to design using ISD for a short course like this, but there are several ways that ISD prompts a teacher or designer to ask and answer a series of basic questions that if answered and acted on will improve any course design. For example:
- Is there a problem that can be addressed by designing a course?
- What specifically are the expected outcomes from the perspective of the organization?
- What specifically are the expected levels of mastery for the course of each learner?
- Exactly what content is required to be covered?
- What extra content would be nice to cover if there is time?

- What does my population of learners have in terms of skills, attitude, language, level of education, and so on?
- What are the prerequisites for a learner to take the course?
- How will I measure whether a learner reaches mastery?
- Who is qualified to teach this course?
- What is the budget for design?
- Will I have access to SMEs (subject matter experts) for content validation and scope?
- Which type of delivery system is best for this population (online, blended, or classroom)?

While this is just a very abbreviated list of the basic questions that an instructional designer or a teacher might ask at the beginning of a course design project, it includes the highlights of what is important to consider. This may seem overly complex or perhaps simplistic to you at this point, but this is the very essence of ISD. You have to gather information and data, make design decisions about critical course elements, prepare materials, implement the course, and then evaluate mastery and course efficiency.

While all of this becomes second nature after a while, having a methodical approach and procedures for the design process takes some time to learn and practice, just like any new skill. And, the more you practice each of these skills, the more you realize the complexity of the relationship between learner, content, and delivery system.

Professional Practice of ISD

Every instructional designer should be aware of the generally accepted standards of knowledge and skills that act as the foundation of their work. These areas of guidance are extremely useful as a designer starts and matures in the field of ISD. Since there is a seemingly endless variety of different roles that a designer might play, a set of common points of practice provides the best place to start in acquiring and building professional skill.

There are different ways to think about these skills and knowledge, and each designer's distinct view of these will be based on past experience and other forms of acquired capabilities. Some previous knowledge and skills are rather easily migrated, while others are elements that should be reviewed and retained as necessary.

For example, there is a variety of specific knowledge and skills to assess for instructional design competence and mastery. These include knowledge and skill in design models and processes, such as ADDIE and SAM; knowledge of needs assessment approaches and techniques; knowledge of instructional modalities, such as classroom learning, blended learning, gamification, and mobile learning; skill in eliciting information from subject matter experts; knowledge of formal and informal learning experiences; skill in designing blueprints, schematics, and other visual representations of learning and development solutions; and knowledge of methods and techniques for planning, designing, and developing instructional content (ATD 2019).

Instructional design capabilities include all the basic elements of modern curriculum development, including demonstrated skill in analysis, design, development, implementation, and evaluation. Designers must be able to design products that integrate the most appropriate learning strategies to ensure high levels of learner mastery and knowledge transfer.

Not only do designers need to be able to look at populations and design cutting-edge courses, they also must be able to find the best fit between populations of learners and course delivery options. Training and facilitation capabilities demand that the latest learning approaches, which include distance learning, online learning, technology-enhanced learning, blended learning, and other new approaches to implementing training, are considered and used if found to be the best choice for a specific situation.

It is almost impossible to work as an instructional designer and not be involved with technology in some way. A designer must have the ability to identify, review, and select from an incredibly wide range of technologies in the design of instruction. The key to any technology decision is knowing what works best for the learner; it is imperative that a designer be able to make informed recommendations on every aspect of technology in learning.

Types of Careers in ISD

Today, there are literally hundreds of thousands of people worldwide working in ISD-related careers. Some are actually called instructional designers or ISDs and have very clearly delineated roles and responsibilities. The vast majority are teachers, trainers, facilitators, instructional technologists, subject matter experts, or human resource professionals, but there are hundreds of other titles that relate in some way to designing and implementing courses. Most of this latter group would not consider themselves instructional designers or may have never even heard of the term before. The reason for this unfamiliarity with the process is the fact that anyone who has shared information with others usually considers the process commonsense or something that comes naturally. The reality is that this is a process that has to be learned and practiced to be accomplished at a level of competency expected in today's world of high tech and mass distribution of knowledge.

Instructional design is a dynamic field of work and study. Let's take a quick look at some very common activities and see if you think they are related to instructional design:

- Coaching a sport
- Being a scout leader
- Managing a fast food restaurant
- Teaching K–12
- Being a college professor
- Having a YouTube channel
- Being active on social media
- Mentoring new employees
- Cooking a holiday meal with the family
- Volunteering at a local charity
- Writing an op-ed piece for your local paper
- Appearing on Channel 9 as the weather presenter
- Running for political office
- Helping an inexperienced friend change a flat tire

Now, imagine yourself as the person participating in any of these activities and think about how you are demonstrating the skills of an instructional designer. If you are coaching a sport, you are constantly, sometimes imperceptibly, passing on your knowledge and skills relating to performance of the sport. If you inspire and encourage your players, you are probably a positive influence in passing on knowledge and skills. If you are a bully and have a negative attitude about other teams, referees, and other aspects of the environment, you are also designing instruction, but with a different, negative outcome.

Let's say you are the Channel 9 meteorologist and you are giving the weather report on the evening news. You say something that is new or reinforced knowledge about weather every time you are on the air. For example, you say the barometer is falling, and snow or a thunderstorm is on the way. We now know that a falling barometer means changing weather. Next, you say that the

CAREERS IN INSTRUCTIONAL DESIGN

Careers in instructional design can have many titles and cover an almost infinite landscape of different responsibilities. Here is a short list of typical job titles within the field. What they all have in common is the foundation of instructional design at the core of each required skill set.

- 3D Multimedia Designer
- Associate Learning Designer
- Bilingual Instructional Designer
- Communications Designer
- Content Designer
- Content Developer
- Content Writer
- Corporate Learning Curriculum Analyst
- Course Developer
- Curriculum Designer
- Curriculum Developer
- Data Science Instructional Designer
- Developer and Trainer
- Digital Instructional Designer
- Digital Learning Multimedia Designer
- Educational Services Designer
- Education Technologist
- E-Learning Course Developer
- E-Learning Developer
- E-Learning Instructional Designer
- Front-End Developer
- Graphic Designer
- HR Instructional Developer
- Information Developer
- Instructional and Visual Designer
- Instructional Content Designer
- Instructional Design Analyst
- Instructional Design Architect
- Instructional Designer
- Instructional Designer Consultant
- Instructional Developer
- Instructional Graphic Designer
- Instructional Media Designer
- Instructional Project Manager
- Instructional Systems Designer
- Instructional Technologist
- Instructional Trainer
- IT Assessment Designer
- Junior Instructional Designer
- Junior Technical Writer
- Knowledge Management Instructional Designer
- Language Arts Instructional Designer
- Learning and Development Manager
- Learning and Development Specialist
- Learning and Performance Instructional Designer
- Learning Experience Designer
- Learning Manager
- Multimedia Designer
- Online Course Writer and Designer
- Online Instructional Designer
- Presentation Designer
- Sales Instructional Designer
- Security Training Specialist
- Senior Instructional Designer
- Simulation Learning Designer
- Technical Instructional Designer
- Technical Writer
- Training and Development Specialist
- Training Developer
- Training Specialist
- Visual Designer
- Web Developer

spring equinox arrives on March 19, another bit of new information. In times of bad weather, countless folks are hanging on every word and learning something every day.

Cooking with the family is a bounty of new information and skills for the younger participants. How many times have you heard someone say that they fixed "Grandma's potato salad" or "Dad's favorite grilled chicken?" Yes, they most likely learned from watching someone or copying a recipe. This is instructional design at its most basic level—passing on knowledge in a seamless form.

While ISD is probably not even recognized as being in play in these situations, let's look at how a little instructional design assistance would make the transfer of knowledge more efficient.

Let's take our coaching example and dig a little deeper. Let's say as a coach you want to teach the most basic passing skills in soccer. Instead of asking each player to simply kick the ball to another player, you first tell the kids that you are going to demonstrate the skill of passing and that they will be able to do this at the end of the lesson. You then do it several times so that everyone can see what you are doing. You then explain in very basic terminology what is happening. You then ask each player to pass the ball to another player, and after each kick you offer feedback on performance and offer tips to assist with any problems that may exist. You close the session by asking each player to individually kick and then pass the ball, and then you offer a final evaluation of their mastery with suggestions for improvement as necessary.

You first told the kids what they were going to be able to do after the lesson. You then demonstrated the skill. You added more detail with an explanation. You had each student practice the skill and offered detailed feedback and mentoring. You then closed with each student by having them demonstrate mastery in an evaluation. This is the nucleus of ISD at work. By using sound principles of ISD, the difference in mastery for our soccer students is considerable.

See how this works? Even when we aren't aware of our influence and teaching efforts, they are taking place. ISD moves this to a level of taking the most of each learning situation and turning it into something both observable and measurable, and, probably most importantly, something that can be duplicated and taught at scale from one to a million or more learners.

Summary

Learning has been a part of humanity since before words were spoken or even before the earliest forms of language or drawing were part of day-to-day life. What has changed in time is how learning is transferred. From basic, nonverbal communications to today's digital domains of social media and smartphones, the process of sharing knowledge and skills has changed only in the sophistication of the process of both teaching and designing instruction. Instructional systems development is the magic that makes learning transfer as efficient and as effective as it is in today's world of education and training. Instructional systems development is the professional field that combines the best of learning theory and practical, scientific approaches to solve real-world training challenges.

CASE STUDY 1

An organization is investigating the option to add a full-time instructional design department to improve training practices and materials. There are two distinct points of view within the organization.

One group thinks this is a waste of time because nothing new has really happened in training approaches in years, and all of the rush to online and blended learning is just hype and doesn't really add anything new to the process.

The other group thinks that instructional design is the wave of the future and is practiced in some form by all of the top companies. They are anxious to begin an online asynchronous program for employees to use for many different types of instruction.

As an independent third party brought in to clarify the options, what would you say to this organization concerning the state of the practice of instructional systems design?

CASE STUDY 2

A medium-sized community college is proud that it is considered a college for working adults. It has applied programs in the skilled trades, culinary arts, retail, and hospitality. Its decisions relating to course and program implementation and faculty are focused on the traditional education model of hands-on courses taught in the classroom by experienced faculty.

DISCUSSION QUESTIONS

1. How is learning different today from 50,000 years ago as it relates to how a student receives and processes information?

2. When reviewing the eight generations of learning transfer, which is the most impactful on the learning process?

3. What will likely be the ninth generation of learning transfer?

4. Does technology change the way people learn?

5. Which instructional design knowledge, skills, and abilities are the most important to the work of instructional designers, and why?

6. How is using a systems approach to designing curricula different from any other methods?

7. Is there ever a time when someone is neither a teacher or a learner?

With a younger instructor pool now starting to teach in most programs, there is pressure to have more formal course materials, newer teaching technology like digital whiteboards, and the ability to communicate with students via social media.

As the instructional designer tasked with answering these concerns, what approach will you take to address the call for newer approaches? Will you use the generations of learning transfer or systems approaches to course development in your response? What else do you think is important to consider and present as supportive information?

CASE STUDY 3

A community organization is requesting the assistance of an instructional designer to review its several short courses in suicide prevention focused on underserved communities like veterans and single parents. It has traditionally designed its own courses rather than use packaged courses from larger national organizations since it felt they seemed too commercial and not as personal.

The executive director has asked you to visit a board meeting and talk about ISD and how an instructional designer can impact the effectiveness of the organization's courses, yet allow for the level of personalization and local community it is seeking.

What will you say and what examples will you use to make your case for a professional ISD approach that can meet all its course needs and still address its concerns?

Learning Theory Through the Lens of ISD

KEY CHAPTER CONCEPTS

- The science of learning theory
- The link between psychology and learning
- The several different theories of how learning takes place, including:
  - Behaviorism
  - Neo-behaviorism
  - Cognitivism
  - Constructivism
  - Connectivism
  - Socioculturalism
- Cognition as a process
- Metacognition and the process of learning to learn
- Cognitive psychology and its role in instructional design
- The several major differences between pedagogy and andragogy
- Maslow's Hierarchy of Needs
- Bloom's Taxonomy
- Gagné's hierarchy of learning and its role in ISD
- The design differences between teacher- and learner-centered learning approaches
- Learning styles
- Gardner's multiple intelligences and instructional design
- The rule of 3s and the rule of 7s and their place in ISD
- Thiagi's alternative view of the laws of learning

CHAPTER OBJECTIVES

At the end of this chapter, the learner should be able to:

- Define learning theory.
- Describe the key elements of the psychology of learning.
- List the key components of the following learning theories:
  - Behaviorism
  - Neo-behaviorism
  - Cognitivism
  - Constructivism
  - Connectivism
  - Socioculturalism
- Define *cognition*.
- Define *metacognition*.
- Define *cognitive psychology*.
- Describe the differences between pedagogy and andragogy.
- List the key elements of Maslow's Hierarchy of Needs.
- Describe the purpose of Bloom's Taxonomy.
- Describe the different levels of Gagné's hierarchy.
- Describe the difference between teacher- and learner-centered learning approaches.
- Present an opinion on the value of learning styles for adult learners.
- Describe the key elements of Gardner's eight multiple intelligences.
- Describe why the rule of 3s and the rule of 7s are related to ISD.
- Describe the key points of Thiagi's Laws of Learning.

One of the fundamental building blocks of instructional systems development is the study and practice of how learning and mastery occur in students. Without a thorough grounding in learning theory and its application, ISD would lack credibility. It is impossible to design without knowing how learning is transferred. Just as in most professional disciplines, there are honest differences in the way practitioners approach these theories and how they apply this information in ISD. The beauty of this discussion is that each legitimate theory has something to offer instructional designers. Each learner has a unique set of learning needs and capabilities, and it is the responsibility of an instructional designer to use all available resources to find learning solutions. As a professional in the world of instructional design, you will mix and match most of the approaches in this realm and decide what works best for each unique situation.

The Science of How Learning Takes Place

Since adult learning became a professional field of study in the early 20th century, the discussion among scholars has revolved around how adults learn. Theories abound, and there is seldom any agreement on which one best addresses every facet of adult learning. Instructional design and adult learning are no different from any other field of science where there are honest disagreements at numerous levels. You see this in physics, biology, medicine, and every other professional endeavor where there is more than one point of view. With this in mind, we stipulate that there is no single overarching and universally accepted theory of adult learning. As time goes forward, new theories will evolve, and this is a healthy and encouraging fact of life in our field. For now, as you review the information in this chapter, just keep an open mind for each theory and approach and fit the information into your repertoire.

Before we begin a review of the different types of learning theories, it is important to define the term *learning* as we use it in this text. The formal definition of *learning* found in most dictionaries focuses on the acquisition of knowledge and skills in any manner or form. By this definition, the source of learning may or may not be the result of something that involves the instructional design process, such as a formal course. For our purposes as instructional designers, learning is any change in behavior, regardless of the source of the knowledge or the way it is transferred. So, by our definition, any knowledge or skill acquisition that takes place as the result of the instructional design of a course, mentoring program, or other designed experience is within our scope.

In its most basic terms, learning is the input, processing, and storage of knowledge and skills. You will also find that short-term and long-term memory play a part in whether learning sticks or hides away forever in one's memory. Then we add practice and feedback to the equation, and we begin to see that this seemingly simple process is, in fact, complicated and learner-specific. When we add the individual learning capabilities of each learner, whether they have learning disabilities or other potentially interfering issues, then the path to learning gets very complicated.

This discussion does not include the myriad forms of informal learning that take place organically. The nature of informal learning will be discussed later in this text, and the connection will be made between certain types of informal learning and their stimuli in the learning environment. For our discussion here of learning theories, we are focusing on programmed and directed learning experiences. The complicated world of designing informal learning experiences will be covered in a later chapter.

As we journey through the learning models and approaches, we'll start with a generally accepted framework for the learning process. It is important to remember that every theory and model of practice looks at the process of designing and supporting learning in different ways. Some learning theories use more formal and strictly defined parameters than others. It is important to look at these theories as a foundational background to your design. In most cases, they don't provide much in the way of practical points of design that we can follow, but they do offer ideas and approaches that should be part of the larger volume of foundational ideas that each designer calls on.

As an instructional designer, your personal philosophy and approach will probably be a melding of many of these ideas. In the end, however, it is important to remember that each population, content area, and implementation-mode combination will demand a slightly different design approach, and strict adherence to one or another model is self-limiting at best and not good practice in most design scenarios. Always keep an open mind and review each new theory and approach as they become known to you.

As you will see, each learning theory has its own strengths and weaknesses. Many designers favor one or another theory. Behaviorists like to design behaviorist courses and constructivists like to design constructivist courses. Designers sometimes find themselves stuck in a learning theory rut. This is a much more complex process than it appears on the surface, because the variables are infinite and most folks have grown accustomed to the traditional school setting with teachers and classrooms. Those traditionalist learning environments still exist, but the world is changing, and testing new teaching waters requires a thorough knowledge of how learning takes place.

Learning Theory

Without a detailed working knowledge of the most studied learning approaches, it is almost impossible to design and implement any instruction. It is not so much that we use these theories as step-by-step guidelines for the design process; it is that without the context of these theoretical approaches, we have no general overarching conceptual theme as we design. There are many ways to begin the categorization of learning theories, but a basic overview was introduced by Susanne Wilson and Penelope Peterson of the National Education Association (2006) and consists of the following learning approaches:

- Cognitive
- Social Cognitive
- Affective
- Neurophysiological
- Behaviorist

For this text, we concentrate on the learning theories most prevalent in the practice of ISD, specifically behaviorism, neo-behaviorism, cognitivism, constructivism, and socioculturalism. At all times, remember that these theories are best utilized as background and foundational information and are meant to serve as a foundational philosophy rather than a specific set of guidelines for course design.

Let's look at the theoretical basics that serve as the foundation for our review of learning theories.

Cognition

While often defined as simply the processing of information by a learner, cognition is so much more, and its implications in instructional design are key to even the most basic course design strategies.

Digging deeper into cognition or the act of learning, you must consider the roles of encoding and decoding as they apply to the brain. Encoding is the input of new information into the brain. Decoding is how the new information is processed and compared with information already stored in memory. This becomes even more complex when we introduce concepts like common currency and narrow and wide versions of encoding. The study of neural science is an ever-expanding field of discovery, and it is beyond the scope of most designers' work to try to keep up with all of the latest thoughts. Just remembering that neural activity involves encoding and decoding is the most important aspect of this for instructional designers.

Metacognition

Metacognition is cognition about cognition, or thinking about thinking. For the instructional design practitioner, one of the most important aspects of metacognition is that it is a key to learner retention of content. In a learning environment, metacognition enables a "teacher's questions . . . [to] eventually become the questions that students can ask themselves" (Larsen 2009). Many believe that cognition can take a learner only so far and that the act of working with others, be it a teacher or other students, brings a learner to a state of metacognition.

Larsen (2009) takes this further and explains that metacognition makes "the difference between what the learner can do independently (actual development) to what the learner can do given the support of the teacher (potential development)." In instructional design this means that there are times when discussing and sharing information with a group or a teacher is more likely to expand cognition and lead to higher levels of achievement and mastery. Metacognition is closely aligned with Lev Vygotsky's work on the zone of proximal development (ZPD). We will explore this more as we dig deeper into Vygotsky's work and the ZPD shortly.

Cognitive Psychology

You can't review learning theory without looking at the larger context of cognitive psychology. Most scholars would define it as the scientific study of the mind (Gallatly and Braisby 2012). Given that definition, it quickly becomes obvious that learning and learning theory are foundationally linked to the many luminaries of the world of psychology, like Sigmund Freud, Jean Piaget, B.F. Skinner, Ivan Pavlov, Abraham Maslow, Carl Jung, Elizabeth Loftus, and John Dewey.

With this large group of theorists, it is easy to get lost in the details of each approach to learning. This is a perfect time to work through some of these theories and talk about how they actually work in the day-to-day practice of designing courses. Let's explore each of these theories from the perspective of an instructional designer, paying close attention to the details of each approach that directly impact the design process.

Behaviorism

When the study of psychology was first introduced, and the opinion of the general public was considered a key to its acceptance as a true science, psychologist John Watson believed that only with some form of "objective observation and scientific measurement" (Clark 2018) would the public be convinced. This construct would be key to the foundational logic of behaviorism. Most now identify the philosophy of behaviorism as the stimulus-response theory of learning.

Behaviorist theory proposes that "learning occurs when an individual responds favorably to some type of external stimuli" (Clark 2018). In its most basic form, this suggests that learning is more about receiving new information than actually storing the new information in short- or long-term memory. It completely ignores the role of retention in learning and how content is stored and later recalled.

Behaviorism is tied to the concept of conditioning, when a learner has a response to a stimulus. Ivan Pavlov's classical conditioning and B.F. Skinner's operant conditioning are the two most prominent types, but others do exist. In the world of instructional design, conditioning might best be described as the process of a learner being able to master content based on planned reinforcement within the designed learning space.

There are generally considered to be two kinds of conditioning: classical and instrumental. In classical conditioning, learning is associated with reinforcement and sometimes punishment to change or influence behavior. In instrumental conditioning, the learner acts in a certain way before there is any reinforcement.

Conditioning is further divided into escape and avoidance conditioning. In escape conditioning, learners will be conditioned to escape a negative stimulus. In avoidance conditioning, learners are conditioned to respond to actions prior to a negative stimulus. Olson and Hergenhahn (2016) observed that "research involved with just classical and instrumental conditioning leaves out vast areas of human experience."

Classical conditioning is best linked to Pavlov and his now-famous work with dogs. Pavlov was able to show that, with conditioning, a dog could be expected to salivate at the sound of a bell as well as at the presentation of food. To reach this response, a bell was sounded immediately before food was given, and the dog would respond by salivating even without the presentation of any food.

One interesting facet of Pavlov's work is that no conditioned response will last forever; he termed this *extinction*. In the case of his dogs, he would continue to ring the bell without any corresponding food distribution and the conditioning response would quickly cease to happen.

Skinner, on the other hand, was able to condition rats to voluntarily press a lever by rewarding them with a pellet of food each time they did it. This concept is called *operant conditioning*. The interesting side note of Skinner's work is that operant conditioning can be guided by both positive and negative stimuli. Behaviors can be modified by reward and punishment; it doesn't take much imagination to see how this works in reality. We have all been subjected to positive and negative consequences as the result of a specific behavior.

If you were to classify behaviorism in terms of the relationship between teacher and learner, you might call it more instructor-centered than learner-centered, because the learner is seen as nondirective of the process and generally participates at the direction of the teacher. The teacher both provides the content and governs rewards and any negative reinforcement throughout the learning experience. It can be argued that most educational environments before the advent of technology were more behaviorist in design than any other approach. As an example, awarding grades as a result of a learner's mastery is an obvious form of both positive and negative reinforcement.

The most common and obvious elements of behaviorism in instructional design include lectures, application and feedback exercises, the memorization of content, and evaluations that are based on recollection of content.

Behaviorism has found its way into many of the practices we currently see in instructional design.

Neo-Behaviorism

All psychological theories, as they are reviewed, tested, and otherwise discussed, are often revised and updated by new theorists adding their thoughts. As the 1950s approached, there was a new effort to expand the behaviorism view of learning. American E.C. Tolman demonstrated that even Skinner's experiments had more in-depth information to offer by showing that rats could "remember and use facts" (Faruji 2012).

Neo-behaviorism is best defined as an extension of behaviorism since it "acknowledges that operant and classical conditioning together do not completely determine behaviors" (Faruji 2012). Clark Hull further added to the complexity of this process by moving from the stimulus-reward theory argued in behaviorism to a stimulus-organism drive-reward theory. This addition is based on the concept of habit strength, which proposes that the more a stimulus is rewarded, the stronger the response in the learner will be.

This neo-behaviorist learning philosophy was supported by research that proposed that habit strength was real and that the process was more complex than just a simple response. It was proven that the more repetitive the response, the more closely one could associate the stimulus. It also framed the learner as having the ability to display a level of selectivity, rather than just a reflexive stimulus response to events in their environment.

To take this a step further, neo-behaviorists argued that it takes more than conditioning to elicit a behavior. In fact, it was recognized that "conditioning involves a cognitive element" (Faruji 2012). Another important construct was habit strength, defined as "the degree to which a particular stimulus and a particular response are associated." Specifically, "the more often a response has previously been rewarded in the presence of the stimulus, the greater is the habit strength and the more likely the response is to occur" (Faruji 2012). This concept of reward and future performance is one of the more interesting aspects of neo-behaviorism.

Hull was the first to link motivation and other internal characteristics to performance. He suggested that there were an additional three levels of complexity and variables to consider when looking for a response to occur:

1. **Organism drive:** an internal motivation for behavior
2. **Stimulus intensity:** the rate or amount of any given stimulus
3. **Incentive:** the intensity and speed of a reward

All of this was foundational for the later cognitive framework of connectionism.

Cognitivism

Cognitive behavioral theory (CBT) is "a psychotherapeutic approach to solving problems concerning dysfunctional emotions, behaviors, and cognitions through a goal-oriented, systematic procedure" (Lee and Edget 2012). It sees the process of learning as inexorably linked to memory, specifically long-term memory, since it is required for learning to persist and act as the foundation of additional learning. Cognitivism can best be defined as a learning theory that "emphasizes the role of mental activities in the learning process and includes actions such as thinking, remembering, perceiving, interpreting, reasoning, and problem solving" (Clark 2018).

The 1950s saw the advent of cognitivism as the gold standard in learning theories. During this period, Jean Piaget and Robert Gagné, giants of modern learning theory, took center stage. Active participation by learners became the focus of both research and practice, and the age of schemata began. In psychology, schemata are a unit of information such as a word or a concept, like a specific color. Learners were now seen as functioning cognitive cerebral computers capable of taking new information and comparing it with known information to create new schemas, or schemata.

Piaget was a renowned Swiss psychologist who had completed his doctoral degree at 22 years old and soon after started his work on children's cognitive development after consulting with Alfred Binet (Ghazi 2016). He is famous for his cognitive development theory, and also brought the notion of learning scaffolding or stages to the world of psychology. His work stands as a foundation for all aspects of learning; some scholars even divide the timeline of theories of cognitive development into "B. P. (before Piaget) and A. P. (after Piaget)" because of the impact of his work on the field (Barrouillet 2015).

Piaget (1964) describes four periods of cognitive development:
1. Sensorimotor Period: birth to 24 months
2. Preoperational Period: years 2–7
   ◦ Symbolic Substage: years 2–4
   ◦ Intuitive Substage: years 5–7
3. Concrete Operational Period: years 8–11
4. Formal Operational Period: 11 through adulthood

Each of these periods has specific sets of expectations and observable behaviors that help determine if learning in an individual is within expected ranges. While Piaget's focus was on juvenile cognitive development, all adults travel through these periods as they grow. In cases where analysis shows that a learner or group of learners is experiencing cognitive challenges, it is often helpful to look and see at what point their development was hindered or not achieved.

A.J. Malerstein and Mary Ahern, writing in the *American Journal of Psychotherapy*, then further applied this theory to adults, describing three basic character organizations: symbolic, intuitive, and concrete (operational). They theorized that the symbolic adult is "concerned with attachment to others"; the intuitive adult is most concerned with "getting, having, and being"; and the concrete, operational adult is "concerned with function, control of function, and social roles or codes." These classifications are an interesting view on how the adult mind functions; Malerstein and Ahern noted that "the majority generally use social cognition that is typical of either the Intuitive or the Symbolic Stage" (1979).

Constructivism

Constructivism means that learning is best achieved when a student takes new information and "constructs" their own meaning of the content based on their existing knowledge, attitudes, and experiences. This mitigates the influence of a teacher and assumes that no conclusions are presented to the student. For example, if a student is studying political science and is looking at the data from a recent election, they would be expected to draw their own conclusions of the results based on what their experience and other knowledge sources tell them.

To take this a step further, a constructivist learning approach portrays the learner as both engaged and exhibiting control of the process of learning (Clark 2018). This works best when building from a foundation of existing knowledge within the learner. One assumes that this type of approach is more likely to be used in higher-order learning situations once basic knowledge of the content has been entrusted to memory.

Kevin Clark (2018) proposes that these types of activities are usually associated with constructivism:

- Discovery learning
- Collaborative learning
- Case studies
- Research projects

- Flipped classrooms
- Modeling and coaching
- Problem-based learning

Psychologist Elizabeth Murphy (1997) originally proposed several examples of "constructivist learning characteristics," which were expanded by Jeanne Schreurs and Roza Dumbrayveanu to include these learner-centered approaches (2014):

- Reading about a selected topic on the internet and discussing it with other learners and with the teacher.
- Searching for and presenting a real-world example of a selected topic.
- Contacting an external domain expert to talk about a selected topic, reporting on it, and exchanging that knowledge with other learners of the team.
- Searching for additional knowledge, including scientific articles covering the topic.
- Preparing and writing a team paper reporting on the project results.
- Solving a real-life problem by discussing the problem, searching for the required knowledge and methods, discussing it with experts, and reporting on the solution.
- Presenting learner reaction in an article based on one's previous knowledge.
- Reporting via a 400-to-500-word essay by each team of learners, explaining their interpretation of and reaction to their colleagues' postings.
- Creating a wiki (structured by the teacher) about a selected topic, as a team activity.
- Participating in a discussion session (real or virtual) and sharing knowledge and vision.
- Preparing a group presentation or task about a selected topic, sharing the reports with other learners and assessing their input.

The theorists usually associated with constructivism are Jerome Bruner and Lev Vygotsky. Bruner is known for his work on discovery learning, and Vygotsky is linked to social development theory and the zone of proximal development (ZPD).

The ZPD emphasizes the role of a group or community of learners since "everyone in the group would contribute greatly to the collective success, by sharing their past experiences and prior knowledge" (Nguyen 2017). The idea that the sum is greater than any individual element comes into play. The ZPD also emphasizes the point that each learner brings their own unique set of values, experience, and motivation and should be incorporated in the learning experience as both an individual and as part of a community of learners.

Vygotsky (1978) defined the ZPD as "the distance between the actual developmental level as determined by independent problem solving and the level of potential development as determined through problem solving under adult guidance or in collaboration with more capable peers." In his view, it was necessary to provide learning before cognitive development could be expected. This would be manifested with the assistance of those with more knowledge or experience.

One parallel construct from Vygotsky's work is the teaching method most commonly known as scaffolding. One way to look at scaffolding is that "practice, rather than simple observation," (Welsh 2017) is the preferred method for moving learners to mastery. You are building knowledge and skills by scaffolding mastery of successive layers of information. This is supplemented by the application of timely feedback in which "problem demonstration is followed by an opportunity for students to imitate, working in groups, to solve a similar problem" (Welsh 2017).

Constructivism is very popular in the e-learning design community and is often preferred firmly and passionately over other approaches.

Connectivism

First proposed by George Siemens in his 2004 article "Connectivism: A Learning Theory for the Digital Age," connectivism correctly points out that all of the preceding theories on learning were initiated and studied before the influence of digital technology. With that in mind, Siemens went on to suggest that the inclusion of chaos theory and other similar views (Steffens 2015) in the learning theory discussion would provide a more realistic and relevant construct for learning in the digital age.

You are building knowledge and skills by scaffolding mastery of successive layers of information.

Among the principles suggested by Siemens (2004) are:
- Learning and knowledge rest in the diversity of opinions.
- Learning is a process of connecting specialized nodes or information sources.
- Learning may reside in nonhuman appliances.
- Capacity to know more is more important than what is currently known.
- Nurturing and maintaining connections is necessary to facilitate continual learning.
- Ability to see connections among fields, ideas, and concepts is a core skill.
- Currency (accurate, up-to-date knowledge) is the intent of all connectivist learning activities.

- Decision making is itself a learning process. Choosing what to learn and the meaning of incoming information is a process that continually shifts to adjust to current reality. While there is a right answer now, it may be wrong tomorrow due to alterations in the information climate affecting the decision.

One important belief that Siemens (2004) also shared is that "behaviorism, cognitivism, and constructivism do not attempt to address the challenges of organizational knowledge and transference." This can be interpreted to mean that learning is more than the process of knowledge and skill attainment, that in fact all learning takes place in an environment that impacts the process. This directly relates to some very fundamental elements of learning predigital technology, in that learning is no longer considered linear once you add online courses, social media, and any of thousands of other contextual influences on the learning process. Learners are now inundated with information from social media and other digital sources, and very little of it is received within the context of learning in a course.

An element of the connectivist movement that has gained phenomenal interest and popularity are massive open online courses, or MOOCs. After more than a decade of maturation and improvement, MOOCs are now offered by many colleges and universities. Nearly 1,000 universities now offer some form of MOOCs, with almost every major university, such as Harvard, Stanford, and MIT participating (Class Central 2019).

Sociocultural Learning Theory

Learning that happens in a predominately social or community setting falls within the definition of sociocultural learning theory. First appearing in the 1990s, it is based on the notion that learning and sociocultural influences can't be easily or successfully separated. Specifically, language "can never function independently of its sociocultural context" (Dąbrowska 2019). For example, in sociocultural learning theory, language cannot be taught in a vacuum; providing the contextual framework of how a language engages with those communities speaking it provides great success at mastery.

One way to look at this would be to consider language training with the options of immersion or isolated, singular learner engagement. It would seem logical that immersion training, where a learner is both physically and emotionally tied to the language, would offer benefits not available to the learner sitting at a computer in isolation to learn. This would also include any learning content that is tied to a specific point of reference.

REFLECTION

Behaviorism and constructivism are two popular learning approaches that view the process of learning in different ways. Behaviorism leans toward guided and structured learning events, while constructivism supports a more student-centered approach to building learning events.

- In the practice of building courses, what factors will you consider as the key elements of deciding if a course lends itself more to behaviorist or constructivist design approaches?

- Are there times when both or neither of these two approaches might be the best choice?

Apprenticeship is one example of the benefits of sociocultural learning. If an apprentice in the field of masonry learns only in a classroom, they might master the skills to a level of acceptable performance, but a key component—the integration of the skills with the work—is missing. Working outside brings issues of weather, noise, and commuting to a specific, often variable work location. There is also the issue of socialization within a trade or working environment. Apprenticeship is as much about learning the landscape of a career and how to perform, communicate, and support the working environment as it is the skills themselves.

Andragogy and Pedagogy

In 1968, Malcolm Knowles proposed that there were distinct learning approaches for adults and children. This discussion continues to this day, and it is important to present both pedagogy (the study of teaching) and andragogy (the study of teaching adults) as part of our discussion of learning theory. As instructional designers, we accept that different populations of learners have their own unique set of characteristics, one of which is certainly age. We explore andragogy and Knowles's work in detail in chapter 3 on the adult learner.

The term *pedagogy* comes from the Greek *agogos*, which means "leader." A *paidagogos* was the person who led students to school and back and was also involved in some forms of education relating to manners. This then evolved into the term *pedagogue*, which means "teacher."

Since pedagogy didn't specify the age of the recipient of the education, until Knowles introduced his principles of andragogy, all teaching was considered to belong under the title of pedagogy. There is still some discussion concerning whether andragogy applies to all age groups and still falls under the pedagogical umbrella. However, most now consider andragogy as a legitimate theory with its own value in partnership with pedagogy.

Over the years, a number of teaching approaches have adopted the pedagogical naming structure, including signature pedagogy, prison pedagogy, deliberate pedagogy, innovative pedagogy, pedagogy of hope, pedagogy of solidarity, proleptic pedagogy, courageous pedagogy, and even geeky pedagogy. Since this foundational term is so widely used, it has a tendency to be considered more a synonym of teaching than a robustly academic or theoretical concept. For our purposes in instructional design, we use the term *pedagogy* sparingly, and only when we are speaking of teaching as a holistic term and not necessarily one specific theory of learning.

Signature Pedagogy

Signature pedagogy finds common ground between the K–12 and adult learning worlds and is an approach to higher education to "prepare students to practice a profession" (Boitel and Fromm 2014). This is usually seen in programs for law and medicine, where the examples given are rounds in medicine and the Socratic method in law. This is also true of skilled trades apprenticeships, internships, and many other structured applied programs.

The overriding approach used in signature pedagogy is that "students learn and that professionals use habitual methods by which they connect and integrate theory and practice" (Boitel and Fromm 2014). Another way to say this is practice makes perfect. Medical professionals learn best practices from both observing and performing examinations and treatments. Lawyers in training observe and practice courtroom behaviors and permissible ways of speaking and presenting information. A masonry apprentice observes a skilled journeyperson apply the 3-4-5 method to establish a 90-degree angle on a layout, then tries it solo.

Maslow and Learning: The Hierarchy of Needs

It is impossible to think about learning theory without a review of the importance of Abraham Maslow's Hierarchy of Needs. This 1943 seminal work in psychology brings an important element of context to when and why learners may or may not do well with mastery. The five levels of this hierarchy are shown in Figure 2-1.

Figure 2-1. Maslow's Hierarchy of Needs

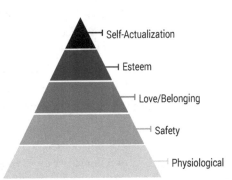

He further defines the first four as deficiency needs and the final as a growth need.

To be more specific:

1. **The Deficit Principle:** If a need is not satisfied, it generates tension, motivating action toward satisfaction. This assumes a satisfied need does not motivate; also, unmet needs are assumed to predominate (Maslow 1970, 293).

2. **The Prepotency Principle:** The needs must be met in their ascending order, and only after each lower-stage need is at least partially met can the next higher-stage need be pursued (Maslow 1982).

3. **The Progression Principle:** Physiological needs, such as food, shelter, and warmth, must be met before a person will look to needs further up the pyramid (Maslow 1982).

Maslow's work is the first time we see a considerably more complex picture of the relationship between the learning environment and the learner and its impact on learning transfer. The generic interpretation of the student's role in the process of learning has now expanded to include degrees of preparedness and motivation. Once we move from thinking that the student is a fixed and immovable object in the process, we become enlightened to the fact that learning is indeed more than just the transmission of knowledge; it is in fact at least a two-factor process that relies on the student receiving and processing knowledge as well as on the distribution of data.

One criticism of Maslow's work is that cultural and spiritual influences and priorities are not reflected in the model. Bouzenita and Boulanouar (2016) write that "a model of a hierarchy of the different needs like Abraham Maslow's can therefore not give credit to the reality of the interaction between material and spiritual aspects of the human being in different life situations, even if the spiritual aspect was to be named first." For an instructional designer, this requires that the hierarchy must be expanded to include the domain elements of culture, language, and societal influences.

Any hierarchy of needs that ignores or minimizes expected external factors on learning must be reimagined to be valid in practice. These externals are always important considerations, and it is hard to envision any principles of practice in instructional design that don't incorporate the expectation of variables based on regional, social, cultural, and spiritual influences.

Maslow modified his thinking and the model over the years, and this has created some interesting discussions. His most recent version prompted Mark Koltko-Rivera to write that "the later model places the highest form of human development at a transpersonal level, where the self/ego and its needs are transcended. This represents a monumental shift in the conceptualization of human personality and its development" (Bouzenita and Boulanouar 2006).

Another way of thinking about this concern is that placing transpersonal at the top of the hierarchy is saying, in essence, that most—if not all—learning takes place at the lower points in the hierarchy in actual practice. This is interesting because most scholars define transpersonal as "development beyond conventional, personal or individual levels" (Scotton 1996), which would indicate that moving to the top of the hierarchy requires participation by more than one person. If this is true, then one could now leap to the conclusion that the highest levels of learning can be achieved only in groups. Then, both the anthropologists and social scientists would have to reimagine learning as a process. Needless to say, the conversation continues.

Bloom's Taxonomy

Benjamin Bloom's Taxonomy is a framework for thinking about and designing behavioral learning objectives. While we will talk in much more depth about Bloom's Taxonomy in our later chapter on objectives, there are three key theoretical points to discuss regarding learning theory.

The first important element of Bloom's work is the idea that learning—and, more specifically in the case of instructional design, objectives—is not all equal. There is a continuum of cognitive complexity that ranges from simple to challenging. At each point on the continuum is the assumption that a learner has mastered the less complex prerequisite knowledge or skill before being able to engage more complex content. This is extremely useful in analysis when trying to determine a population's skill and knowledge level before deciding where to start with new content. It works equally well in instructional design to make sure that a design contains the appropriate level of challenge for learners.

The second impact Bloom's Taxonomy has on ISD is that the approach of scaffolding skills and knowledge within a course is based on the idea that there are clearly identified levels of cognitive challenge. Instructional designers using Bloom's Taxonomy as a guide to writing objectives will have available

> One could now leap to the conclusion that the highest levels of learning can be achieved only in groups.

a framework of verbs to use in writing objectives with the clear intention of scaffolding knowledge and skills for learners to progress from one level to the next of content mastery.

The third thing to consider with Bloom is that using the taxonomy as a basis for course objectives has proven to be better for higher-order thinking. This is true since the taxonomy allows for a comparison between different levels of difficulty and ensures that a designer's intent relating to complexity of behaviors and content is being honored. Weiser and Fittipaldi (2019) showed that "a significant increase in higher-order thinking" was achieved using Bloom's Taxonomy. In the world of instructional design, higher order thinking is generally described as either creative thinking or critical thinking. Specifically, it has been defined as "the ability to extract past thoughts and experiences and combine them into novel ways" (Saeedinejad et al. 2018).

Gagné's Hierarchical Model

Robert Gagné is a prominent figure in the practice of instructional systems development. We will discuss many aspects of his work, most importantly his Nine Events of Instruction, later in the text, but his work on the hierarchy of learning is also important. His view was that learning must be placed in a hierarchy from simple to complex to move students to mastery.

Gagné looked at designing curricula that were "established by learning . . . arranged in a hierarchical fashion whereby one task depends on a previous learning of a more simplistic one" (Lawson 1974). This corresponds to the view that scaffolding learning was a requirement for mastering increasingly more complex content.

Gagné also had thoughts on the domains of learning, which we will later review in the chapter on objectives. These are his five domains of learning (1972):
1. Motor skills, which are developed through practice.
2. Verbal information, the major requirement for learning being its presentation within an organized, meaningful context.
3. Intellectual skills, the learning of which appears to require prior learning of prerequisite skills.
4. Cognitive strategies, the learning of which requires repeated occasions in which challenges to thinking are presented.
5. Attitudes, which are learned most effectively through the use of human models and "vicarious reinforcement."

Humanism

The importance of self-esteem and motivation within learners is the center point of humanism. It was first introduced by Carl Rogers and Maslow, who felt that "students need to be encouraged to make the most of their learning opportunities" (Pugsley 2011). This was in response to what some observed as behaviorism leading to more programmed, teacher-led experiences and perceptions of learners as end users and not necessarily full partners in the learning process.

Teacher-Centered Versus Learner-Centered Learning Approaches

There is much discussion among designers when it comes to the differences in approach between teacher-centered and learner-centered course designs. Some will argue that all courses should be learner-centered since it allows a student to guide the process and gives them a sense of ownership. Others contend that learners need to follow an instructor in areas that require precision of process with content that relies on established research and data, such as the sciences and math. Let's now look at each and see how each one evolved.

Teacher-Centered Learning

Most early forms of education and many present learning transfer events are considered teacher-centered learning. This is because the teacher directed most, if not all, of the process, and students were largely the recipients of information. The learning was largely programmed, and mastery of the content was the overriding aim of the process. There was little if any recognition of an individual student's life experience, demographics, or other learner variables.

In teacher-centered learning environments, all students are expected to learn at the same rate, and they are all assumed to be equally prepared and motivated to participate. One example of this is the large lecture hall in any college or university that hosts course after course of a basic science curriculum that is offered to meet the core requirements for the five general education credits required for most degrees. In these learning environments, a lecturer, usually a professor, will go through the required material and then test students on the content. This is a bit of a stereotypical scan of the process, but it highlights the fact that there is a place for this type of approach, and the less-than-favorable tone applied to teacher- or instructor-led courses is sometimes misplaced.

Learner-Centered Learning

When the student or learner is seen as the focus of the implementation process, it can be considered a learner-centered learning approach. Constructivism has learner-centered learning at its heart and has assisted in the transformation of learning to include that which takes place outside of the classroom.

The core of learner-centered learning is the use of learning outcomes or learning objectives. All activities and the role of the teacher are anchored to these objectives. And, perhaps more importantly, the assessment or evaluation of mastery is tied to the objectives. The acronym LOLALA (Schreurs and Dumbraveanu 2014) represents the alignment of the elements of:

- Learning Outcomes
- Learning Activities
- Learning Assessment

With this direct link between objectives and assessment we are reminded of the term *performance agreement*, which is used often in instructional design. When both the objectives and evaluations of mastery are directly correlated, performance agreement is reached and there is more than reasonable assurance that learners will be assessed on legitimately linked objectives and evaluations. This is one of the key design philosophies in ISD and is covered in more detail in the chapter addressing the writing of objectives.

The differences between teacher- and student-centered approaches can be summed up in a binary fashion; teacher-led learning is more lecture than discussion and student-centered learning is more discussion than lecture. There are many variations of this difference in styles, and this is somewhat simplistic, but it serves as a guide for designers. As with most macro attempts at differentiations, the detail is much more complex, and the reality is that most courses have some element of both these styles.

You will hear this discussion at times when a course or program is seen to be too autocratic in approach. The lecture with 50 projected slides is not always entertaining, and there is a temptation to classify this type of learning as less successful than other options. However, there are content and learning populations that will have no option but this approach. Very technical and complex content will need to be presented in an orderly and directed manner. It is difficult to imagine a course in basic computer programming offered in any other way.

Learning Theory Implications for Instructional Design

Now that we have explored the most prominent learning theories, it is time to place these in the context of the work of an instructional designer. What do each of these theories mean in practice, and what kinds of learning techniques are generally associated with each theory?

Table 2-1 presents a generalized look at the way each theory plays out in the real world of instructional design. There are some obvious differences in approach to designing. Many times designers are likely to design a course and then determine that it has elements of one or more of these theories in the design. Very few designers actually look at these theories first and then make choices about a design approach.

Table 2-1. Comparing Learning Theory Approaches for Instructional Design

Learning Theory	Learning Approach	Best Application	Teacher Centered	Learner Centered
Behaviorist	Conditioning	Lectures	X	
Neo-behaviorist	Conditioning plus habit strength	Application Feedback	X	
Cognitivist	Scaffolding	Active learner participation		X
Constructivist	Learner sets own direction	Discovery learning		X
Connectivist	Nonlinear	MOOCs	X	X
Sociocultural	Community	Language and culture		X

The Neuromyth of Learning Styles

Generations of teachers, trainers, and instructional designers have been taught that learning styles are an important part of learning and student mastery. Learning styles are best defined as the practice of designing and teaching to one of three methods of ingesting information: visual, auditory, or kinesthetic. However, this popularity is largely based on opinion and not research. As Knoll (2017) states, "Although learning style has garnered widespread acceptance in the educational community, there is a distinct lack of empirical support for the meshing hypothesis."

Research has shown that courses for children were most likely to be based on learning styles since "those who worked with younger children were more likely to interpret learning styles in an essentialist way" (Nancekivell et al. 2020). You often hear a teacher say that they need to have more visuals in a lesson or that a specific group of content areas needs to always be taught kinesthetically. It has been estimated that 80 percent of American K–12 teachers and 93 percent of British K–12 equivalent teachers at one point believed that "learning style is important to student learning" (Knoll et al. 2017).

While some suggest that people are predominately visual learners, it is unclear at best that receiving and processing information visually is actually the most efficient way to move information to long-term memory. Recent research has shown that visual short-term memory (STM) "can store information for a few seconds, is limited in its capacity, and depends critically on conscious processing" (Huang 2020). This would suggest that the common wisdom concerning learning styles, specifically related to visual learning, is suspect at best.

One of the larger issues associated with a learning styles design approach is cognitive overload. To be more specific, Mayer and Moreno (2003) define cognitive overload as happening when "the processing demands . . . may exceed the processing capacity on the cognitive system." The reason for this is that designing a course for a specific learning style means that the majority—if not all—of the information will be visual, since it is estimated that 65 percent of learners could be defined as visual learners. This stream of only visual information could quickly overwhelm learners and actually hinder mastery because the designer has created a cognitive overload.

Bolisani, Scarso, and Padova (2018) note that "the larger and older a group, the more likely the impact of cognitive overload." This suggests that the more traditional use of learning styles design approaches in legacy learning environments, which include traditional classroom groups, might be especially damaging to learners.

There is a fair amount of discussion about how learning styles became so well entrenched in the design and teaching communities, and many believe it comes from a lack of real understanding about how learning takes place. In fact, it is clear that there has been very little thought on the part of advocates to really explain why they believe that learning styles are a legitimate element of learning. To be more specific, Nancekivell (2020) writes that "even though learning styles are categorized as a neuroscience-based myth, no prior work, to our knowledge, has investigated whether or how people believe learning styles are instantiated in the brain."

Westby (2019) presents four ideas about why there has been such a blind acceptance of learning styles, specifically:

- There are genuine differences among students in how they learn, and these differences can impact their learning abilities. A person over six feet tall will likely find it easier to master basketball skills, but that does not mean the person has a kinesthetic learning style.
- Students do learn better when they can relate what they are learning to prior experience or an interest.
- Learners have preferences in how they like to learn; they may prefer to learn by watching video, but that will not impact how well they learn.
- There is mixed evidence that using a variety of media, such as using audio with visuals, may work—not because it appeals to different learning styles, but because it keeps learners engaged.

Harold Gardner, who is famous for his multiple intelligences work, called learning styles theory "incoherent" (2013), and there has been little since to change the notion among most educators and designers. Like many seemingly logical observations, the truth is much different from the perception.

For instructional designers, learning styles serve very little purpose except in specialized design scenarios for very specific populations. The most important element to consider when designing is to make sure that the objectives and evaluations of mastery are directly aligned to the skills and knowledge that a learner will be expected to meet after a course. The best designs are seamless to the learner in terms of what is expected of them. You learn to ride a bike by riding a bike. You learn to bake a cake by baking a cake. Don't confuse learners with psychobabble like *learning styles* in your designs.

> There are genuine differences among students in how they learn, and these differences can impact their learning abilities.

For instructional designers, learning styles serve little purpose except in specialized design scenarios for specific populations.

Multiple Intelligences

In 1983, Howard Gardner published his book *Frames of Mind: The Theory of Multiple Intelligences*, and nothing has been the same in learning theory since. Gardner went well beyond the antiquated notion of an IQ score somehow summing up an individual's intelligence and abilities. He reasoned that there are at least eight specific elements of intelligence that need to be considered to understand the sum of how a person learns.

Gardner's eight intelligences are:
- Linguistic
- Logical-mathematical
- Spatial
- Bodily-kinesthetic
- Musical
- Interpersonal
- Intrapersonal
- Naturalist

Thomas Armstrong goes even further and suggests that each of Gardner's multiple intelligences has an "essential nature":
- Linguistic intelligence: word smart
- Logical-mathematical intelligence: number and logic smart
- Spatial intelligence: picture smart
- Bodily-kinesthetic intelligence: body smart
- Musical intelligence: music smart
- Interpersonal intelligence: people smart
- Intrapersonal intelligence: self smart
- Naturalist intelligence: nature smart

From an instructional design perspective, the multiple intelligences tell us that each course needs to be reviewed for the possible design implications that address learning and mastery in more than just the traditional IQ or single intelligence approach. In many cases, this is directly tied to how a designer determines that mastery should be evaluated. For example, within any of these intelligences, would it not be a more realistic and valid determination of mastery to evaluate within the intelligence and not just use a traditional quiz or test process that requires choosing one of several options or expanding in writing on a topic? If teaching music performance, wouldn't it be better to evaluate mastery of the performance or a discussion of a performance? In dance, would it not be better to have a rubric of dance steps and positions than a simple true-and-false evaluation? This is simplistic, but very telling when it comes to making informed and defensible choices in determining mastery. The more complex the content and population, the more a designer needs to consider how multiple intelligences might impact learning.

Marketing and Memory

While it might seem to be a stretch to bring a discussion of marketing into the study of learning theory, there are actually two areas of marketing that have almost identical goals in instructional design. The rule of 3s and the rule of 7s are both foundational elements of marketing, and, somewhat surprisingly, both describe the mechanics of how information can be formatted and presented in a way that aids memory. Marketing wants the end user to remember a product or service, and ISD wants a learner to store content in short-, then long-term, memory. There's really not much difference in the hoped-for results.

The rule of 3s has been used for years in marketing to force buyers to focus on a single aspect of a product to more easily nudge them toward a purchase. One aspect of this approach is that limiting a message to three points or elements clears out the competing environmental noise that tends to distract and misdirect a buyer's focus. It is also thought that repeating something three times indicates importance and forces the mind to pay more attention.

The rule of 3s in ISD has some very important elements that relate directly to how a learner moves information from short-term to long-term memory. In the revised version of Gagné's Nine Events, which we will study later in the text, you will see that elements five, six, and seven are titled Application Feedback I, Application Feedback II, and Application Feedback III. This is because practicing content three times and receiving feedback on performance three times moves the content to short-term memory, then ultimately to long-term memory. Not only are we using a version of the rule of 3s, we are ensuring that what is stored in memory is in fact the correct version of what was taught. The wisdom of this approach is pretty obvious when you see learning approaches that don't allow practice or provide any feedback. It is extremely easy for a learner to think they have mastered content, only to later find that

The more complex the content and population, the more a designer needs to consider how multiple intelligences might impact learning.

> Repeating something three times indicates importance and forces the mind to pay more attention.

their interpretation of the content was incorrect. It is much more difficult to unlearn content than it is to design correctly in the first place and provide application and feedback to a learner to ensure memory storage is accurate.

The rule of 7s in marketing states that a potential customer must be exposed to a product at least seven times before they are moved to purchase. That is why all of us suffer through the exact same commercial at least seven times. It makes sense, and it has proved to be true. In ISD it has a slightly different meaning.

While we just saw how the rule of 3s helps move information into learner memory, the rule of 7s is more directly related to how we design learning events. If we fail to have at least seven elements in our learning approach, we may be jeopardizing the prospect of mastery for a learner. As an example, in Gagné's Nine Events, the nine learning process elements are all directly linked to our content and expected mastery. From gaining attention in the first element, to closure in the ninth element, the learner is constantly guided by this road map to mastery. This schematic journey through learning to mastery is seldom if ever noticed by the learner, but it is the most effective way to design efficient and productive courses.

While our marketing colleagues have a somewhat different goal in their use of these two rules, there is no denying that the hoped-for outcomes are similar in intent. Sales by memory or mastery by memory are essentially the same outcome with a slightly different goal. Consider these two rules as you design learning, since both are proven approaches to memory management by design of process.

Thiagi's Laws of Learning

Sivasailam Thiagarajan—or Thiagi, as he is best known to the ISD community—has proposed 14 Laws of Learning. They are an extremely interesting way to look at learning theory through a different lens. All of Thiagi's work centers on the practical side of the application of learning theory, which is helpful to us as instructional designers because we spend most of our time in the real world.

Laws Applicable to Adult Learners

The following laws are particularly relevant to adult learners.

Law of Previous Experience
New learning should be linked to (and build upon) the experiences of the learner.

Check the entry level of the participants. Remind yourself that adults bring a variety of rich experiences to the training session. Design activities to ensure easy adjustments to fit different entry levels and to incorporate relevant experiences.

Law of Relevance
Effective learning is relevant to the learner's life and work.

Use simulations and role plays to strengthen the link between the learning situation and the real world. After a training activity, debrief the participants and discuss strategies for applying what they learned in the game to their real-world context.

Law of Self-Direction
Most adults are self-directed learners.

Don't force everyone to participate in every activity. Identify training objectives and let participants select among different resources and activities to learn at their own pace and according to their personal preferences. Involve participants in setting training goals and selecting appropriate types of learning activities.

Law of Expectations
Learners' reaction to a training session is shaped by their expectations related to the content area, the training format, fellow participants, and the trainer.

Some learners are anxious about mathematical concepts and skills. Encourage them with intriguing puzzles and short-cut techniques. Other learners feel uncomfortable about making fools of themselves in public while playing games. Establish ground rules that reward risk taking among participants. Demonstrate nonjudgmental behavior by applauding participants for their effort.

Law of Self-Image
Adult learners have definite notions about what type of learners they are. These notions interfere with or enhance their learning.

Reassure participants about their ability to learn new concepts and skills. Motivate them to attempt challenging tasks. Ensure frequent and early successes by

If we fail to have at least seven elements in our learning approach, we may be jeopardizing the prospect of mastery for a learner.

making initial tasks simple and by progressing in small steps. However, avoid patronizing participants with simple, trivial tasks. Incorporate learning tasks at different levels of difficulty in your activities.

Law of Multiple Criteria

Adult learners use a variety of standards to judge their learning experiences and accomplishments.

Encourage participants to choose personal standards and scoring systems. Provide different ways to "win" in your activities. In simulations and role plays, keep scores related to different criteria. During debriefing, discuss alternative criteria for measuring participants' performance.

Law of Alignment

Adult learners require the training objectives, content, activities, and assessment techniques to be aligned to one another.

Create a training situation that closely resembles the job situation. Teach and test for the same content, using similar strategies. Make sure that the scoring system used in your training activities rewards the mastery of the training objectives.

Laws for the General Public

These laws apply to all human beings, from infancy to old age.

Law of Active Learning

Active responding produces more effective learning than passive listening or reading.

Intersperse lectures and reading assignments with active-learning episodes such as quizzes and puzzles. Provide participants with ample opportunities to respond by asking them questions, encouraging them to ask questions, answering their questions, and questioning their answers.

Law of Practice and Feedback

Learners cannot master skills without repeated practice and relevant feedback.

Don't confuse understanding a procedure with the ability to perform it. Invest ample time in conducting activities that provide repeated practice and feedback. Make sure that the training activities incorporate immediate and useful feedback from peers and experts. Use rating scales, checklists, and other devices to ensure that the feedback is objective and useful.

Law of Individual Differences

Different people learn in different ways.

Use training activities that accommodate a variety of learning styles. Make sure that participants can respond by writing, speaking, drawing, or acting out. Encourage and permit participants to learn individually, in pairs, and in teams.

Law of Learning Domains

Different types of learning require different types of strategies.

Learn to recognize different types of training content and objectives. Don't use the same type of activity to teach different types of training. Use suitable designs to help participants achieve different training objectives related to concepts, procedures, and principles.

Law of Response Level

Learners master skills and knowledge at the level at which they are required to respond during the learning process.

If your training activity requires participants to merely talk about a procedure, don't assume that they will be able to apply it in their workplace. If you want participants to solve workplace problems, the learning activity should require them to solve problems. Avoid trivial, closed questions with rote-memory answers in your training games. Challenge participants with authentic situations that require innovative solutions.

All Creatures Great and Small

These laws apply to all animals, including white mice, pigeons, dolphins, and people.

Law of Reinforcement

Participants learn to repeat behaviors that are rewarded.

Make sure that training activities provide several opportunities for earning rewards. Require participants to make frequent decisions and responses. During the initial stages of training, reward even partially correct answers.

Law of Emotional Learning

Events that are accompanied by intense emotions result in long-lasting learning.

Use training games, simulations, and role plays that add an emotional element to learning. Make sure that emotions don't become too intense and interfere with learning. Make sure that participants don't learn dysfunctional behaviors because of intense emotions. Debrief participants after emotional activities to reflect on their feelings and learn from their reactions.

Summary

Instructional design is a complex and challenging field of study examining how learning and mastery take place in learners. Each designer must have an incredibly thorough knowledge of learning theory and application to be able to design courses and programs at a level of professionalism now considered the standard in the field of ISD. The study of Maslow and Gardner aids in adding an extra dimension to the world of learners and the instructional design process, because they define learners beyond the simplistic analytic parameters like demographics and educational levels.

CASE STUDY 1

Let's imagine that you are alone and have been lost in the woods for a day and are understandably very hungry. It is cold and getting dark, your cell phone battery is dead, and you think there are wild animals in the area. As an instructional designer who has knowledge of Maslow's Hierarchy of Needs and Gardner's Multiple Intelligences, you resort to your training to think about how best to approach your situation.

What would you list as your priorities?

How would you rank them from highest to lowest based on Maslow's hierarchy?

Is one of the multiple intelligences more important or useful to you in this situation?

How would you, as an instructional designer, frame a solution for your predicament?

CASE STUDY 2

At a recent faculty meeting held at a large liberal arts college, a debate began between faculty who believe learning styles are an essential element of course design and another group that feels equally as strongly that learning styles are a neuromyth and that they should not be considered an essential element of new course designs. The discussion continued until the dean asked that a committee be formed to review the current research on learning styles and report back at the next meeting on its findings.

The dean has assigned you as the chair of the new committee since you are the lead instructional designer for the college.

How will you approach this assignment, and what are your views on the question of whether learning styles are a legitimate consideration in instructional design?

CASE STUDY 3

A small start-up curriculum development company has recently secured a contract with a manufacturing firm that specializes in producing personal protective equipment (PPE) for first responder and healthcare industry clients. It has been forced into rush production of N95 face masks using newly acquired equipment that requires training for operators that is specific to the new equipment.

Up to this point in the history of the company, learning the operation of new equipment was done by training one lead operator and then having this individual perform on-the-job training over a period of time to train the other operators. This is not possible now since the demand requires almost instantaneous skilled operation of the new equipment.

There is resistance to the suggestion by management that all operators be trained at the same time, since this is seen as infringing on the established hierarchy of managing learning using lead operators as trainers.

As the lead instructional designer for the curriculum development company, how will you use your knowledge of learning theory and the differences between learner-centered and teacher-centered design approaches to provide a learning solution that fits the needs of the organization and also addresses the concerns of the lead operators?

CHAPTER 3
The Adult Learner

KEY CONCEPTS

- Andragogy
- Age as a determinate of adult learner populations
- Differences between adult and child learners
- Adult learning principles
- Generational learning as a design consideration
- Addressing adult learning challenges
- Designing for adults with learning disabilities
- Determining how adults learn best

CHAPTER OBJECTIVES

At the end of this chapter, the learner should be able to:

- Define adult learning as a distinct area of interest in ISD.
- Determine the age of adulthood for ISD purposes.
- Compare how adults and children learn.
- List examples of adult learning principles.
- Define the term *generational learning*.
- Describe at least three adult learning challenges.
- Describe the impact of adult learning disabilities on instructional design.
- Describe at least five methods for teaching adults.

In this chapter, we are going to explore the world of adults as learners and the unique design elements to consider when designing for this population. There is never a one-size-fits-all approach in ISD that is authentic or accurate, and this is no more true than when designing for adults. Not only are the issues of motivation and existing knowledge perplexing at times; you must also be aware of the learning challenges and disabilities that many adults face as learners. The work of Malcolm Knowles and other prominent theorists has paved the way for how we approach adults as learners. In this chapter we will look at all of the factors that influence how adults learn and the design implications for each.

The Study of Adults as Learners

The study and practice of looking at adults as a unique population in the learning process began as a distinct field of study with Malcolm Knowles and came to be formally known as andragogy. Since Knowles's work first appeared in 1968, the design community has learned much about how to best design for this population.

Before the latter half of the 20th century, the issue of children passing into adulthood was largely seen as a natural and routine process, with teens finishing school and moving into traditional adult roles of work and raising families. Or as Swartz, Hartmann, and Rumbaut (2017) write, "All of these goals and milestones accomplished, they would fairly quickly settle into the regular, routinized world of adult life." Around the time of Knowles's work, because adulthood has come to be viewed as much more complex, "it has become clear that the process of becoming an adult or taking on the roles usually associated with adulthood is not nearly so quick, easy, normative, or typical."

Just as the process of looking at what constitutes adulthood has become more complex, the world of instructional design has become exponentially more sophisticated as it has become obvious that adults need to be viewed through more than one lens. Factors like occupation, socioeconomic standing, education level, and motivation are equally telling. Another influence that is often discussed is generational identification. Boomers and millennials are often portrayed as having different values, approaches to work, and maturity levels. Then when you add Gen X, Gen Z, and other designations, the picture becomes muddled. Some argue it makes little difference in terms of instructional design. Others argue it makes all the difference. We will discuss the topic of generations later in this chapter.

Should andragogy rise to the level of a learning theory?

Knowles's view of the adult learner included the feeling that adults needed to be in adult learning situations and should "feel accepted, respected and supported" (Knowles 1980). This raises some legitimate questions about an adult's journey from the world of K–12 into the world of adult learning. Do approaches need to be different from the childhood educational experience to have any chance of success with an adult learner? Are we doing enough to make adult learners feel accepted, respected, and supported?

Another common and still debated question with andragogy is whether characteristics of adults are "characteristic of adult learners only" (Merriam 2001). For example, some challenge the notion that adults and children are motivated differently; others question whether children are capable of directing their own learning. This highlights the importance of performing a thorough analysis of any population to make sure that the learning characteristics of the group are accurately reflected.

Some experts question whether andragogy should even rise to the level of a learning theory. Merriam notes that "at first the main point of contention was whether andragogy could be considered a 'theory' of adult learning." Anne Hartree wrote that he felt that andragogy might be more "a model of assumptions about learning or a conceptual framework that serves as a basis for an emergent theory" than a theory on its own (Merriam 2001). While this can be debated with some vigor on both sides, there seems to be little to remove the theory classification from andragogy.

Who Can Be Considered an Adult?

One of the first points of discussion—and at times disagreement—when having a conversation about adult learners is defining an adult. Is this strictly an age determination or do we look at other factors such as education level, living status, or course content?

Age would seem to be the first consideration for determining who qualifies as an adult learner. Some argue adulthood begins at age 18; others are convinced it is 21 years old. The age of maturity or majority, as it is sometimes called, is different depending on both your location and the nature of the definition. Sometimes it is a legal point, and at other times a policy criterion determines adulthood.

Regulations like drinking age, voting age, and age of consent further cloud the definition. If a couple can get married at 16, are they not adults? What about the ability to purchase a house or car? You can join the military at 17 and file for bankruptcy at 20. If we simply go by the common terminology of age of majority, most learners reach adulthood between 18 and 21 years old.

While we can certainly determine a legal age of adulthood by different rules and regulations, the study and practice of instructional design demand that we think about this pseudo-mystical line of demarcation differently. Many designers look at moving out of the K–12 learning environment as a point of departure because it is so clear cut. Others look to the content of a course to determine learning approaches and adult learner considerations. Then you can add higher education, apprenticeship, and continuing education participants as adult learners. In the end, the real determination of learning approach and the fitness of adult learning principles falls to the person analyzing the learners and their environment and creating the learning.

In this text, we will consider adult learners as individuals of post-high-school age, generally over age 18. This designation serves only as a point of reference in the most general terms, because the real determination of course design approach, like all things in instructional design, will be based on the learner, the content, and implementation choices.

Adult Learning Principles

The center point of Malcom Knowles's work is what he called his core set of adult learning principles (2005). These six principles serve as a starting point in our discussion of how best to design learning for adults:

- The learner's need to know
- Self-concept of the learner
- Prior experience of the learner
- Readiness to learn
- Orientation to learning
- Motivation to learn

Let's look at these individually and explore the implications for instructional design.

The adult learner really wants to know the why, what, and how.

Need to Know

One thing we know for sure about adult learners is that they expect to be fully informed about any learning experience they participate in. However, there are variations based on learning environments and content. In mandated learning situations where a student is required to attend, the adult learner really wants to know the why, what, and how concerning their participation because the choice to attend is not their own.

This need to know sits at the heart of what a designer needs to think about and plan for with adult populations. When we look at Gagné's Nine Events of Instruction, we see that the first three elements are gaining attention, direction, and recall; each of these helps explain in great detail the why, what, and how that Knowles addresses. Once an adult learner completely processes the environment and is given information on what they are doing, what they will be required to do, and how this fits into their life, it is much easier to present new content and move a learner toward mastery.

As an instructional designer, never make assumptions about what adults require in terms of information relating to process. It is important to make clear early in the implementation why a course is being offered and how the learner will benefit from participation. Always design with the idea that adults are partners in the process and not just end users. This really improves the chance that an adult will participate actively and reach mastery. Designs need to include having the conversation with adults about the why, what, and how elements.

The biggest mistake a designer can make is to treat adults like kids in the learning space. The best visual to represent this intrinsic adult feeling is to imagine a room full of adult learners being forced to sit in chairs designed for kindergarten kids. It is uncomfortable and awkward, and the fight-or-flight instinct it triggers blocks any new learning that might have taken place in a properly prepared learning environment and approach. Psychologists tell us that the fight-or-flight instinct is a stress response to being in something that can be terrifying to an individual. Forcing an adult into an uncomfortable learning situation can be terrifying for them, and to some extent almost all adult learning scenarios have the potential to be stressful for learners.

Adults Need to Be Respected

Adults like to feel like they are in control of their environment. It is fair to say that the many failures associated with adult learning courses can be attributed to not honoring an adult's need to feel like they are an individual and that they have some control in the process of learning. An overwhelmed and frustrated adult learner is never going to perform anywhere near their potential in these situations. As Knowles (1998) points out, the adult learner needs to be "autonomous and self-directed" and anything less has the potential to impact participation and mastery.

Adults Expect Learning to Be Based on Their Life Experience

When we discuss an adult learner's previous experience in the context of instructional design, we are truly addressing every facet of a learner's life. Adults, as both individuals and learners, have traveled a life journey that is full of experiences and emotion, both positive and negative. From childhood, adults have accumulated life experience, knowledge, and skills in a way that is unique to each of them. As adult learners, this life knowledge is carried into the learning experience in both expected and unexpected ways.

> The biggest mistake a designer can make is to treat adults like kids in the learning space.

For example, an adult learner who did not do well in K–12 or perhaps didn't finish high school may well bring vivid memories and emotions from those experiences into the learning moment. When you add the number of adults who have undiagnosed learning disabilities, you start to appreciate the challenges that some adult learners face even entering a classroom or participating in an online course.

According to the Learning Disabilities Association of America (2020), 85 percent of adults with learning disabilities have "a reading disability, or dyslexia." It is also possible to see adult learners with dyspraxia that has remained hidden and undiagnosed. These types of hidden disabilities are often not addressed or acknowledged at any level, and may leave a learner with a dread of anything that even hints at a formal learning situation. Some adults who resist participating in learning simply don't want to be exposed to the prospect of failing as a learner again.

Beside the issues associated with learning disabilities, adult learners bring the totality of their life experience to any learning event. One of the worst mistakes an instructional designer can make is to assume that education level is the only determinate of an adult learner's knowledge and skills. In the age of media saturation and seemingly endless access to information, adults absorb incredible amounts of metadata. Add to this an adult's occupational and avocational skills and knowledge, and it becomes clear you must start any design process by determining the level of content-related prior experience a learning cohort or population brings to the learning experience.

Adult savants are not uncommon participants in adult learner populations. This is especially true in adult populations that might generally be considered as functioning at the lower end of the educational achievement continuum and that are not traditionally considered particularly academic. *Savant syndrome* is the term used to describe when a person is able to achieve remarkable accomplishments despite mental or physical challenges. Kim Peek, the inspiration for the movie *Rain Man*, is one example.

This unexpected learner characteristic is common in nonsavant learners, too. It is possible to see iron workers who can tell you as much about the requirements for a building's framework in skyscrapers as some architects, as well as EMTs and paramedics who can diagnose and stabilize a critical care patient as quickly as a physician. Jumping to the conclusion that a degree or other formal certification is the only indicator of achievement or learning is a risk most seasoned instructional designers would never take.

Adults Need to See the Connection

"Ready, set, go, learn" is easier said than done when it comes to adult learners and their ability and willingness to participate in learning experiences. There is a degree of complexity in this discussion that can't be overlooked from the perspective of instructional design. For an adult to participate and succeed in learning, they must see the connection to their life and goal. Abstract learning is rarely considered useful by adults.

Design failure in this area may result in learners demonstrating boredom or other attitudinal signals that they are lacking the motivation to participate at required levels or even to complete a course. They may not engage in the learning in any meaningful way, because they fail to see the connection to their interests or needs. A designer must make an obvious connection between course content and learner need.

Adults Need Goals and Objectives

One durable aspect of adult learning is that adults expect to reach specific goals and objectives in a learning environment. For instructional designers, this means that course objectives need to be specific and written in a way that ensures that learners can picture themselves benefiting from the newly learned skills. Simply thinking that participation in a course is the goal for an adult learner is not likely to lead to any tangible success for a course or program.

One way to think about this from the design perspective is to consider the difference in design approaches, such as learner-centered or instructor-centered courses. Learning orientation is focused on a passive developmental approach that focuses on "developing skills and mastery," while performance orientation is "focused on demonstrating skills and mastery" (Harvey et al. 2019). This is an important distinction, since learning orientation is (for many learners) a safer space to occupy if one is concerned about performance and evaluation of mastery. Performance orientation is almost mandatory on most tactile and skill-based content.

As a designer considers these two approaches, writing objectives for learning orientation will focus on the process of developing skills, and writing them for performance orientation will move the discussion of skills to the actual application of skills. For most adults, the actual performance of a skill is considered the most important choice, although there may be a learning prerequisite to practice and master specific skills.

As this relates to goals and objectives, adults want to see some tangible benefit to their investment of time and energy in a learning experience. To ask an adult to learn about a skill is seldom as powerful as saying that a learning experience will provide the opportunity to learn how to perform a skill.

Adults Need to Be Motivated to Learn

There is one area of adult learning that is almost universally accepted, and that is the belief that adults learn best when they are motivated by seeing a demonstrable outcome that supports their goals. The goals are as varied as the individuals involved, but job advancement, enjoyment of a new hobby, academic achievement, self-improvement, and licensure are just several examples. Because of this, instructional designers need to be sure that motivation is centered in their thinking about course elements.

> Adults must feel like they are the reason the learning is taking place in order to become instrinsically motivated.

Lambert and McCombs argue that "it is part of human nature to be curious, to be active, to initiate thought and behavior, to make meaning from experience, and to be effective at what we value" (Lambert and McCombs in Wlodkowski 2003). This engagement must be supported and encouraged in adults to be successful.

This motivation is more involved than just a learner feeling good or bad about participating in a course. Adults must feel like they are the reason the learning is taking place in order to become intrinsically motivated. To put it a different way, Jennifer Rogers (2007) writes, "This may be why adult learners so often take refuge in the idea that what we are learning is really meant for someone else." Adults who are the least bit insecure or feel forced into a learning situation may never feel like they are the focus of a course unless they are made to feel welcome and as if they are the reason the course was created in the first place. One of the most important design features for adult learners is making sure this takes place in implementation.

The issue of "fit" is not unique to adults, but its importance is probably more acute with this population. Adults want to invest their time and resources wisely. If something doesn't seem to be within their focus of interests, the course will be viewed negatively and this will impact participation.

Raymond Wlodkowski is well known for his work in the area of motivating adults; in his article "Fostering Motivation in Professional Development Programs" (2003), he lists four motivational conditions for culturally inclusive teaching:

- **Establishing inclusion:** Creating a learning atmosphere in which learners and instructors feel respected by and connected to one another
- **Developing attitude:** Creating a favorable disposition toward the learning experience through personal relevance and choice
- **Enhancing meaning:** Creating challenging, thoughtful learning experiences that include learners' perspectives and values
- **Engendering competence:** Creating an understanding that learners are effective in learning something they value

Culture in this context is the culture of the shared learning experience and encompasses the inclusivity that one expects in professional educational offerings.

Generational Learning

Much has been made of the differences in generations concerning almost every variable in life. From music to money, one generation is perceived to be different than another. As we look at adult learners, it is prudent to explore the role of generational differences in instructional design.

There are as many different generational designations as there are theorists with an opinion, but most essentially fall within these five generations:
· Traditionalists: born 1925–1945
· Baby Boomers: born 1946–1964
· Gen X: born 1965–1979
· Millennials: born 1980–2000
· Gen Z: born after 2001

You will also hear different generations identified as:
· Centennials
· Thirteeners
· G.I. Generation
· Silent Generation
· New Boomers
· Lucky Few
· Good Warriors
· Hard Timers
· New Worlders

The differences in these are mostly based on someone's interpretation of the characteristics of a certain age group. Stereotypes, often incorrect at best, are a common feature of this discussion. For example, the generation that is older than yours is always backward and stuck in the past. The generations younger than yours don't have a good work ethic and never get off their smartphones. So it goes. The reality of generations is that most analytic elements are based more on environment and existing knowledge than any age distinction by generation.

For the purposes of instructional design, generational classifications are only one subset of data that builds the profile of a learning population as analysis is performed. There are as many learning populations of mixed generations as

REFLECTION

Malcolm Knowles paints a thorough picture of adult expectations of learning. They expect to be partners in the process of learning and to be able to leave a learning experience with skills they can use immediately. They need goals. They also want to be respected and to not waste any of their time.

· Given these six adult learning principles, what are the special considerations instructional designers must include in course design approaches?

· What types of approaches should be considered, and are there approaches that will almost certainly not be well received by adult learners?

those with a majority of one generation. Exceptions are the obvious designs for age-specific populations. For example, a series of courses on how to apply for Social Security probably isn't something that millennials are going to line up to take until they are retirement age.

There are generational characteristics that may influence design work. You may find in your analysis that a population of millennials might be more engaged in group work than boomers, or you might find the opposite with gen Xers. Your favorite icebreaker might completely irritate half of your students based on their generation. And motivation is one area of analysis for instructional design that might show differences in generational identity based on life experience and present need.

One of the most popular discussions concerning generational differences is in the area of technology-enhanced learning. There is a general feeling that digital natives, or learners who have never known a time without digital technology in their lives, are more likely to accept and flourish with digital learning modes like online courses. Recent research shows that this is not necessarily true. According to Lai and Hong (2015) in the *British Journal of Educational Technology*, "Findings . . . do not support the notion of a unique learning style or preference for the current generation of young people." So, while the common feeling among educators might be that a certain generation is more likely or more willing to use technology in learning, and that older generations are less likely to use technology, it is not universally true.

In some areas of training, millennials are by far the most dominant generation. As we mentioned earlier, the most common definition for the term is adults born between 1980 and 2000. One example of the impact of having a majority millennial population is the U.S. Army. In 2019, the total active duty force in the army was 470,623 people. Of this number, 410,308 were millennials (Trent 2019). That equates to 82 percent of this population falling in the ranks of millennials. Let's see how this impacted the army's training approaches.

With changes in need and a sobering recognition of its majority millennial population, the Army chose to move to a system that "must have an adaptive development and delivery system not bound by brick and mortar" (Trent 2019). To further meet the needs of the population and the military, this new approach needed to be capable of sustained adaption. This is a significant departure from the standard classroom approach used in the past. And this is not just within the military; across the board there is a new dynamism in training approaches.

One can argue that new approaches are less about generational preferences and more about the impact of media and technology on the learning landscape. If technology had advanced to this level of development in the 1950s, would baby boomers be different learners than they are described today? Any answer to this is conjecture at best, but it highlights the fact that generations are not always the most important element of a population when designing instruction for adults. It is simply too easy to apply stereotypes to any group without substantial research.

Adult Learners and Competing Priorities

One of the most important elements of adult learning that seems to remain somewhat of a mystery is the fact that adults have an incredible number of competing priorities when participating in learning experiences. This might seem an obvious requirement, but few course designs actually allow for the flexibility necessary for some adults to participate at a level that supports success.

For higher-education adults, from a strictly statistical viewpoint, employment is a major competing priority. According to Strom, Paris, and Strom (2011), 45 percent of four-year college students work more than 20 hours a week, and 60 percent of two-year students work more than 20 hours a week, with "one third over 35 hours a week." They also noted that "only 10 percent of [students] referred to boredom or difficulty understanding the content of classes" as reasons they left school. That means many priority challenges for higher-education students are related to trying to work while in school. This in no way negates competing priorities of personal and family issues, financial stress, and unexpected health concerns.

Within non-higher-education populations, an endless variety of competing priorities exist. As with the higher-education community, work and personal issues are always part of the equation. For adults who are participating in in-house courses, we need to look at an additional set of competing priorities, including workplace politics and social issues. These can sometimes be very subtle, like someone having too much work to complete on deadline to participate in a scheduled course. There are also the problems associated with mixing cohorts of both managers and reporting employees. Situations such as these can mute motivation and hinder participation depending on the course content and work environment.

REFLECTION

It is often said that learners of different generations learn differently—that being a 21-year-old learner is different than being a 70-year-old learner. Gen X, gen Z, boomers and millennials are all completely different learners from an instructional design perspective.

• Do you believe that learners of different generations are demonstratively different when it comes to considerations in course design?

• Do you think any differences can be addressed in the course design process in a way that does not require different courses for each different generation?

From an instructional design perspective, issues like these are major players in design decisions if the impact is universal across a population. Busy learners are going to be checking their smartphones and drifting off mentally to think about what is waiting for them instead of focusing on a course. A tainted workplace political atmosphere often results in limited participation by nonmanagers if the expression of opinions and examples is part of the course design.

Adult Learner Design Challenges

In any discussion of adult learners and the role of an instructional designer, it is mandatory that the issue of learning challenges and disabilities be addressed in a way that ensures that all learners are served to the best of our abilities in the process of course design and implementation. There are millions of adults with both diagnosed and undiagnosed learning challenges who are members of the populations we work with, and designing instruction for them is an important aspect of our work.

Learning challenges and disabilities have occasionally been misrepresented to portray these adult learners as somehow deficient in their ability to participate successfully in courses. This is seldom true. Instructional designers have an incredible opportunity to serve these learners with designs that recognize the issues, respect their individual situations, and encourage their participation and success. All of this must be done without bias, stereotyping, or condescending approaches.

Adult learners, more than younger learners, are challenged in ways that are not obvious or easy to address. Many adults learn to mask these issues and ignore opportunities for formal learning experiences. The reality for many of these adult learners is that negative or unproductive learning experiences—at any point in their lives, from birth to adulthood—have impacted their attitude and motivation in new learning environments. This can be exponentially negative in adults who experienced little if any success as a learner in the K–12 world of education.

Estimates put the number of people suffering from developmental learning disabilities at 5 to 15 percent (APA in Aro et al. 2019). The most common of these are reading disabilities. These adults are less likely to seek higher education after high school or to voluntarily participate in formal learning opportunities. They are also more likely to pursue vocational education options (Eloranta et al. 2019).

Addressing reading fluency has shown to "have significance for adult-age employment" (Eloranta et al. 2019). And, since many course designs are associated with vocational training in one form or another, a designer should be vigilant in assessing if, and to what degree, reading challenges exist in a population.

When designing for adult populations, it is critical that the analysis phase of the design process include a very thorough scan of issues associated with both learning challenges and learning disabilities.

One of the most prevalent challenges that many learners face as they age is hearing loss. Most estimates put the number of individuals with learning disabilities and hearing loss at 40 percent (Emerson et al. 2012). Some believe this number may be considerably higher. In the simplest terms, hearing loss impacts social interaction, comprehension of course content and materials, and learning process communications, and may lead to learner frustration and even depression.

Learning Disabilities

Trying to define the term *learning disability* would seem to be an easy task, but the more you explore the issue the more you find that a one-size-fits-all-situations definition doesn't really exist. Legal definitions vary, but usually relate to "significant impairment of intellectual functioning; significant impairment of adaptive/social functioning; and age of onset before adulthood" (Webb and Whitaker 2012). The key point of challenge to these types of definitions is that the determination of any impairment of intellectual functioning is based on a formal IQ test. Generally accepted practice is that an IQ of less than 70 represents intellectual impairment.

Most of the adults with severe learning disabilities, described as having IQ impairment, are a subpopulation that is generally not a group designers will work with unless designing something specifically for that group. Rather, more often than not an instructional designer will encounter adults with more subtle learning disabilities. It is these hidden or less obvious learning disabilities that can usually be identified in the analysis process and addressed in most course design scenarios. To say the least, the continuing discussion in the field concerning IQ testing and results is drawing little in the way of agreement on the definition of the construct.

While the characteristics of adults with learning disabilities vary widely, there are some observable elements that might be apparent during analysis that serve as an indication that further inquiry is necessary. For example, adults who struggle to read, write, or perform basic math problems might be the subject of more analysis. This is also true when a designer finds that remembering information, following instructions, and other associated tasks are a challenge for learners. Positive characteristics of adults in these populations may include problem-solving skills, compensatory strategies, persistence, empathy, and outgoing personalities.

Now let's look at some of the more common challenges that an instructional designer might find in adult learners with learning disabilities.

Post-Traumatic Stress Disorder (PTSD)

One of the many learning challenges found in adults is post-traumatic stress disorder, or PTSD, as it is commonly called. As an indicator of the persistence of this in adults, it is estimated that more than 18.7 percent of Vietnam veterans suffer from PTSD at some point in their lifetime, with 9.1 percent presently suffering from the disorder (Burriss et al. 2008). Military populations are not the only groups to suffer from PTSD. Law enforcement, paramedics, firefighters, physicians, nurses, teachers, and almost anyone who has had a traumatic episode in their life are at risk for PTSD.

PTSD often impacts memory, and learners can exhibit trouble concentrating. The American Psychological Association defines it as "an anxiety problem that develops in some people after extremely traumatic events, such as combat, crime, an accident, or natural disaster" (APA 2020). Horwitz (2018) describes it as "a distinct memory-related syndrome resulting from exposure to trauma—rather than a generalized syndrome that is highly interrelated with other diagnostic conditions." Horwitz also states that "Freud came to believe that hysterical conditions arose from memories that were grounded in unconscious fantasies, not in real events." This indicates that there was a period of time when the symptoms of PTSD were not considered something to be addressed in the same way as they are now. So little thought was given to this as it related to designing instruction. The new attitude toward and acceptance of the learning challenges that may be associated with PTSD offer instructional designers an opportunity to build learning that supports this population.

With this in mind, an instructional designer needs to be prepared to use the analysis data to determine if there is a potential for students to react to different aspects of a course in implementation from the perspective of suffering from PTSD. If PTSD is identified in a population, the designer can consider which approaches may work best in terms of building a safe learning environment. While the study of PTSD is beyond the scope of this text, as with other learning challenges in adults, a designer must be aware that this exists and work with professionals to find the best fit between the population and the content and implementation options.

Autism Spectrum Disorder (ASD)

ASD is "a lifelong neurodevelopmental disorder that is clinically defined by impairments in social interaction and repetitive and stereotyped behavior" (American Psychiatric Association 2013). While this impacts only about 1 percent of the population, it represents one of many issues that fall under the general category of learning challenges.

Adults with both diagnosed and undiagnosed ASD are members of some of our design populations. Many are mildly impacted in the process of learning and function within any expected continuum of ability. Whether recognized in analysis or by other means, these students may or may not present significant challenges. There are, however, certain elements of this population that a designer will need to address.

Some—but certainly not all—adults with ASD may exhibit "slow task completion," which is often related to "verbal fluency," an indicator of cognitive processing speed. This can be characterized as "slow and accurate" (Johnston et al. 2019). It is possible that there also may be mood disorder, depression, varying degrees of cognitive function, and "comorbid mental health difficulties" (Burns et al. 2019).

This is a field of continuing study and interest, and any of these listed impacts are not consistent across this population. As with all things analytic, it is necessary to gather as much information as possible for the design approach.

Asperger's Syndrome

Asperger's Syndrome is a developmental disorder, which means that people are born with the condition. It is not a mental illness, as it is sometimes incorrectly labeled. Adults with Asperger's generally exhibit behaviors such as "appearing self-centered or selfish and having difficulty in interacting with other people" (Hagland and Webb 2009). They often have one specific interest on which they focus their attention. They are able to remember great detail about their favorite topic and, when engaged, are very capable of talking for a long period of time about it.

For the purposes of instructional design, some people with Aspergers have "problems with the understanding of language . . . especially if sentences are long or complicated" (Hagland and Webb 2009). It is also possible that they will struggle with short-term memory and attention. All of these are keys to designing for this specific type of learner, whether in groups or as a single student in a larger population.

Attention-Deficit/Hyperactivity Disorder (ADHD)

ADHD has been a recognized issue for more than 200 years and impacts an estimated 4 to 5 percent of adults (McGough 2014). It does not appear to favor any specific demographic group and is not "a function of intellectual ability" (McGough 2014). There are elements of ADHD that can impact adult learners.

Adults may display mood disorder, anxiety disorder, substance abuse, and intermittent explosive disorder (McGough 2014). The degree to which you can design for a general population with ADHD participants is a more complex issue than designing for an identified cohort containing only ADHD participants. As with any design-related analysis work, it is critical that subject matter expert guidance be incorporated into the design process with this population.

The Role of the Instructional Designer

It is beyond the scope of a designer to make a diagnosis or attribute any behavior to a specific learning challenge. However, it is not uncommon to have some degree of these challenges in a population of adults. The experienced designer will consider this information as they work through the design process. There are designers who seldom or never have courses with populations that fall into this category. There are also programs that may traditionally incorporate design considerations for these populations in a prominent way.

One obvious design concern is when courses and programs might illicit some level of emotional response to the content or delivery mode. Since some of the challenges adults face are well hidden during normal, day-to-day activities, being exposed to a learning experience as a member of a learning cohort might be stressful enough to bring some buried behaviors to the surface. There are times when the design must include directions to the facilitator or coding in the programming of e-learning courses that provides support to learners who need assistance. This could be in the form of an easy exit if necessary or providing emotional support as required.

There are now many governmental and political safeguards and guidelines that act to support the opportunities for adults with learning challenges. For example, the United Nations has the Conventions on the Rights of Persons With Disabilities (CRPD). The United Kingdom has the Disability Discrimination Act. Canada has the Canadian Human Rights Act. The United States has the Americans With Disabilities Act (ADA) and the Health and Human Services Section 508 requirements for website content.

Additionally, there are numerous state and local requirements for serving those with disabilities relating to employment. Once someone is employed, they may also need to be trained, both in vocational skills and every other aspect of employment, like safety. It is also important to realize that our discussion of disabilities, as instructional designers, may have a focus on physical challenges and learning challenges.

It is never the responsibility of an instructional designer to diagnose or treat any condition. However, it is the role of a designer to find approaches for working with populations and learners who need assistance within the scope of their work. It is the same for any of the thousands of laws that govern the treatment of adults with challenges. It is not unusual for some projects and course design teams to include both legal and medical subject matter experts who offer their expertise in these situations.

In higher education, almost all universities and colleges have some form of student disability services that support and encourage the participation of all students, staff, and faculty. These are often in response to legislation like the Americans With Disabilities Act (ADA) and the Rehabilitation Act of 1973. *Reasonable accommodation* is the term often used in this context and refers to the process of both identifying and addressing any qualifying disabilities. This has an immediate and profound impact on the work of an instructional

> It is never the responsibility of an instructional designer to diagnose or treat any condition.

designer, since both the course and the course implementation environment are subject to analysis and remediation based on each scenario.

The ADA also has an impact on licensing and examinations through its Title II and Title III authorities. These have a direct impact on instructional design since the development of evaluation instruments for licensing is a common ISD task—not to mention the fact that courses designed to assist in the taking of examinations also fall within the role of instructional design. Specifically, Section 36.309 of the DOJ regulations requires examinations to be administered so that the results "accurately reflect the individual's manual, or speaking skills" (ADA 1992). The ADA was amended in 2008 with the passage of the ADA Amendments Act, written "to carry out the ADA's objectives of providing 'a clear and comprehensive national mandate for the elimination of discrimination' . . . by reinstating a broad scope of protection to be available under the ADA" (ADAAA 2008). Yingling (2011) states that this allowed "individuals who had 'learning disabilities' that substantially limited a major life activity were entitled to reasonable accommodations on licensing exams under the ADA."

Additionally, Section 508 of the Rehabilitation Act requires that federal agencies "ensure accessibility and usability by individuals with disabilities" (U.S. Access Board 2020) for information and communications technology (ICT)-related facilities. The Health and Human Services Department says that this section is based on the following statistics (Erickson et al. 2012):
- 6.4 million people in the United States have a visual disability.
- 10.5 million people in the United States have a hearing disability.
- 20.9 million people in the United States have an ambulatory disability.
- 14.8 million people in the United States have a cognitive disability.

There are a number of requirements for meeting 508 compliance, and any designer working within these guidelines will need to stay current with the law. While much of the impact for 508 guidelines is related to noneducational access, the same guidelines generally apply to online courses, evaluations, and other associated technology-based design features. These guidelines are also required for grants and other federally funded efforts.

Designing for Adults

The first, obvious caution on this topic is that there is no one-size-fits-all solution for any of the variables in the practice of instructional design. We will look at a range of things to consider with the knowledge that there is a continuum of approaches, and the foundational elements presented here will always need fine-tuning as you design for each specific adult population.

Here are five adult learning truths that can be useful for instructional design:
- Adults hate to waste time.
- Adults need to see the connection to their work and life.
- Adults want to use any new skills or knowledge immediately.
- Adults use their previous experiences as their foundation in learning.
- Adults may not have done well in previous learning efforts.

10 Ideas When Designing for Adult Populations

While there are countless variations of design approaches for any population, there exists a solid set of core ideas to consider when working with adult learners. All of these are time-tested and serve as foundational design options for adults.

Treat Adults as Adults

While this seems like an incredibly obvious adult learning guideline, it isn't always as simple as it may sound. Many teachers and designers without the benefit of any formal ISD experience or training often fall back into teaching and designing as if adults were still attending high school or earlier grades. Sometimes this is done by using outdated and stale learning methods like lecture-only presentations or having adults sit at a school desk for hours at a time. It can also be related to the attitude of the course and not having a conversation with adults but instead just being patronizing or worse.

Adults deserve respect in this process if for no other reason than they are participating in a course. For some adults, simply taking a course is frightening, and for others it brings back unpleasant memories of other educational experiences. Respecting and acknowledging these feelings is required with this population.

From an instructional design perspective, ensure that any design for adults respects the learners and addresses any significant motivational or prior experience issues that are identified in the analysis phase of the design process.

Make Learning Immediately Useful and Relevant

It is not too radical to say that everything an adult is taught should be immediately useful to them. This perception of immediacy in value isn't optional. Even though some courses and content don't lend themselves to this sense of immediate value, there are design approaches that address the specifics that a learner can be given to make the leap between their initial impression and the potential for usefulness. When an adult learner begins participating in a course, it is required that this be part of the very first contact.

There is always a way to design a course that makes the value and immediacy of return known to the adult learner. Let's take the example of an onboarding training for new employees. Most adults likely want to just get going and meet their co-workers and start their job. If the design includes a short initial overview of the value of the time invested, it brings focus and builds motivation. One way to do this is to point out that timesheets, vacation requests, and other HR elements are going to be covered and that it will save each of them valuable time when it comes to actually using them. This is also a great time to have a more seasoned employee share experiences with the organization and how it has impacted their life. Both these design approaches will go a lot further in building community and usefulness of content than having a boring lecture on these issues.

Honor Each Adult Learner's Life Experience

If you have 25 adult learners participating in a course, it is very likely that you have about 625 years of life experience if your population only averages 25 years of age. If your average is 50, you have 1,250 years of experience. As a designer, to simply ignore this incredible asset to your design is foolish. Experience in adults is earned and not just a passive statistic. Not only must you design to include this experience, but you may also at times have to design to overcome negative life experiences to move learners to mastery.

This double-edged sword of experience can easily be turned to positive from negative. And, conversely, if a course is designed poorly, the experience can move learners from positive to negative. An essential element of your analysis is to determine where a population lies on the continuum of positive and negative experiences related to the content. This isn't always obvious, but it must be determined if there is any hint that there are issues.

Don't Waste a Single Second of an Adult Learner's Time

With adult learners it is "get in and get going"; don't waste one second of their time. Don't use a clever icebreaker that takes half the course time, or make adults sit through long, boring introductions.

Be Creative in Design Approaches

Never fall back on the easiest design approaches, which are generally lecture related, unless they are absolutely necessary and supplemented with some form of interactivity. Adult learners want to be part of the process, not just the end user or, in worst-case scenarios, those who simply endure the experience.

Don't Create "Old School" Courses

Old school may be fine for music or a choice of clothes for a reunion, but there is very little appreciation of old school for learning experiences with adults. The classroom of their K–12 experiences is not a top choice for adult learners. This may be based on negative memories of inadequacy or failure. It can also become a learning environment that is neither creative nor current. The return to lecture-and-listen approaches doesn't score many points with adults.

Design Learning Using Packets of Individual Episodes

Adults learn best when taught using short packets of information. Sometimes these are as short as one word or sentence. An effective packet of information is always less than several minutes in length. Interspersed with these individual learning episodes are discussion, practice, feedback, and other interactive elements.

Use Immediate and Frequent Feedback

Never design for adults without including a mechanism for immediate and frequent feedback by a teacher, a peer, or an electronic learning component. Not only is this important in terms of engaging and holding an adult's attention; it is also a proven component of moving information to storage in cognition in the correct form. Without this element of design, adults will be bored and restless, and—worst of all—they may store incorrect information by making assumptions about the knowledge and skills taught to them.

DISCUSSION QUESTIONS

1. As an instructional designer, how would you decide what age designates an adult learner from other possible classifications, like K–12?

2. How, as an instructional designer, do you consider the concept of andragogy when designing for adult learners?

3. Which of the adult learning principles do you think is the most important when designing for adult learners?

4. How does the generation of a learner impact the way they learn or how they should be taught?

5. As an instructional designer, how would you address learning challenges in the course design process?

To demonstrate this point, think about a time when you heard information in a class, on TV, or on social media and you incorrectly remembered the information chunk because there was no feedback on what you heard or saw. If some form of feedback and evaluation of the quality of the transmitted data is integrated into a course, the learner will almost always have remediation on any incorrect or misinterpreted information. The new information will then be stored as intended, and future learning will rest on a firm foundation.

Make Learning an Adventure

It is no overstatement that learning as an adventure is more successful than static and boring learning environments, especially for adults. If it doesn't seem new and interesting, adults may not engage at the same level as is possible with creative design approaches.

Create Supportive Ongoing Learning Resources

Continuous learning in adults requires a plan for post-learning-experience support systems. These can be as simple as online resources or as sophisticated as regular updates and communications. Adults like to feel like their investment in learning, even when mandatory, is more than a one-off experience. Lifelong learning means adults like to stay engaged in the process past the initial implementation.

Chapter

In this chapter, we explored the world of adults as learners and the unique elements that instructional designers need to consider when working with this population. There is never a one-size-fits-all approach in ISD that is authentic or accurate, especially when designing for adults. Not only are the issues of motivation and existing knowledge perplexing at times; you must also be aware of the learning challenges and disabilities that many adults face as learners. The work of Malcolm Knowles and other prominent theorists has paved the way for how we approach adults as learners. This chapter considered various factors that influence how adults learn and the design implications for each of these influences.

CASE STUDY 1

You have been assigned the responsibility to design a series of courses for a small contractor who is working on a program to assist in transitioning employees to retirement. The organization sees a need to address the many issues associated with moving from full-time work to retirement, including healthcare, finances, emotional-transition issues, and other common challenges.

The population specifics are:
- Age 55–70
- Blue-collar and white-collar workers
- Some are military veterans, police officers, and emergency services members, like paramedics
- Various degrees of financial security, from no retirement savings to rather large retirement accounts

There is no direction from the organization on course design or delivery modality.
- What are the issues that you will be looking at in the analysis of this population of adult learners?
- What are your recommendations for implementation, in the classroom, blended, or online?
- Are there any issues with the population that you think might create some learning challenges?

CASE STUDY 2

A small community college is receiving negative Level 1 evaluations in an applied program in culinary arts. The population is mostly second-career adults over 35 who are transitioning from jobs in manufacturing that have been eliminated at local companies.

As a contractor in ISD focusing on addressing problems in courses and programs, you have been asked to evaluate the situation and make recommendations.

Your subsequent review of the evaluations shows a common theme of learners feeling like they are not being respected, and that they are being treated like they are 18-year-olds just out of high school with no life experience.

Given what you have learned from the evaluations, what recommendations will you make to the college concerning ways to improve both the courses and their relationship with participants in this program?

CASE STUDY 3

A local nonprofit that provides support for children suffering from chronic, non-life-threatening illnesses is thinking about expanding their programs to adults. It wants to write several grants to seek state and federal funds for the planned expansion of services. It presently offers short courses to the children in areas such as building self-esteem and creating self-help skills.

You are a volunteer at the organization who is also seeking a master's degree in ISD from a local university. The organization recently learned of your academic work and has asked you to help write the grant, specifically how the organization will address the needs of adults as opposed to its history of working with children.

In thinking about the new population and the history of serving children, what are your suggestions and recommendations for moving the program's focus and courses from children to adults? How will you make the case in the grants that the shift to adults has been well researched and the courses will be redesigned to serve this different population?

CHAPTER 4

ADDIE and Other ISD Models

KEY CONCEPTS

- ISD models are the scientific foundation for instructional design
- The ADDIE model of ISD
- SAM and other models practiced in ISD
- The three truths of ISD models
- ISD models are not a road map for course design processes

CHAPTER OBJECTIVES

At the end of this chapter, the learner should be able to:

- Define the structure and uses for an instructional design model.
- List the five elements of the ADDIE model.
- Compare and contrast ADDIE with SAM and at least two other ISD models.
- List the three truths concerning ISD models.
- Explain why ISD models are not meant to be a road map for instructional design projects.

Theoretical models for the practice of ISD go back to the work of Robert Gagné, Jerrold Kemp, M. David Merrill, and other instructional design notables from the first generation of ISD practitioners from WWII to the early 1970s. These models evolved as part of the formalization of the process of designing curricula and were seen as a way of bringing credibility to the emerging field that we know as ISD. It was reasoned that if there were models for the interpretation of the complexities of relativity and psychiatry, the field of instructional design also needed a platform of scientific methodology to explain and legitimatize its practices. As an illustration of the power of models in general, and ISD specifically, many employers require knowledge of ADDIE or one of many other ISD models as a basic requirement for employment.

You will also often hear instructional designers talk about the fact that they use ADDIE or another ISD model when designing. This usually happens during presentations, or it is written into bid proposals. To an even greater degree, it is now considered a litmus test for a designer to have specific knowledge of and experience with at least one ISD model.

In this chapter, we start our examination of ADDIE and other ISD models by taking a look at what models of any science or practice are designed to accomplish. To first define a model, it is necessary to establish the framework for what a model actually is and what it provides to the study and practice of any field of endeavor.

How Models Evolve

Systemicity is the underlying basis for evolving theoretical models. This is because models at their heart are systems, and each element of a model should show how it relates to the other elements within a defined system. Condillac wrote in 1771 that "a system is nothing other than the disposition of the different parts of some art or science in an order where all these supports each other mutually" (Cardey 2013). It is also likely that any model will contain presumptive and assumptive elements that can be reviewed and examined at length with varying degrees of agreement. At times it seems as if everyone sees something different in a model.

Linguist Yves Gentilhomme (1985) provided an inventory of what he saw as the properties of a system for modeling language. This provides a framework for looking at any model, in our case ISD models. The three basic elements (revised for our use) are:

- **Identification:** The model must be identifiable as a single object:
  - Only one idea
  - Able to be named
  - Must be distinguishable from other systems
  - Must be distinguishable from its environment
- **Structure:** The model has an internal organization that can be studied
- **Interdependence:** Each component of a model must have a relationship to the other elements

This systems approach to modeling fits nicely with ISD, since instructional design is considered a systems approach to designing curriculum. Within that framework, each ISD model is a representation of a system for the process of instructional design, and each model is developed using a systems approach to each of a model's different elements. It is comforting to know that the idea of modeling systems goes back many generations, and the use of modeling in ISD is another indication of the science of the practice of instructional design.

Another term that helps establish the foundational construct of models is *mind mapping.* A mind map is "a comprehensive, visual and graphical intellectual tool that allows one to organize and better express ideas and creative concepts" (Jablonski 2017). The key words in this definition are *visual* and *graphical.* Being visual and graphical not only helps to make an approach look legitimate but also aids in the study and practice of a model.

Most formal definitions of a model will point to the fact that the concept of modeling should provide an "accurate theoretical description in order to understand or explain" if used as a transitive verb (Collins Online English Dictionary) and not as a noun as it is typically used in ISD. It is meant to provide the framework for replicating all or part of a model's elements. The visual elements of a model represent the relationship of one element to the others in a way that enhances understanding of the way they interact. So, in a hypothetical model, element A is connected to element C, but not to element B except through element D. A picture is worth many chapters of a textbook.

Specifically, ISD models are intended to provide a visual and theoretical road map to define and describe a specific design philosophy and its terms of practice. If a designer follows a specific model and builds workflow activities that reflect the model elements, it is much more efficient to then work through each new design project. It is easy to define each step in the procedure and to determine milestones and evaluation points that will work in most situations. This makes each new project a little less daunting, so the design team can focus on the specifics of each content, population, and implementation choice and not worry about reinventing the ISD wheel with each new assignment.

Common ISD Model Elements

All these models evolved to be vehicles for both explaining and predicting a specific process, in our case the design of instruction. ADDIE very nicely captures the ISD process in a rudimentary, though descriptive manner, and at some level it also is predictive of what is necessary in the process of designing instruction. Some misinterpret the model to suggest that you perform the five elements in a linear pattern, starting with analysis and ending with evaluation. However, a strict conformance to that rendering of the model will usually result in a very simplistic design process with little in the way of dynamic responsiveness to the inevitable complexities and unique aspects of each project.

As we review the five elements of the ADDIE model, be aware that this is only meant to provide a foundation for the design of instruction. It is not meant to be an operational road map to success in the practice of ISD. Which is to say, while we talk about analysis being one of the five building blocks of ISD, we are not prescribing how that will best work within your specific puzzle for each project, with distinct variables in content, population, budget, and other key areas. We will talk about those specifics later in the book. Think of this overview as a look at the guiding principles of ISD rather than the operational steps in the practice of professional instructional design.

To further reflect on the nature of models in ISD, Gustafson (1991) suggested that there is also a taxonomy of instructional design models. It is reasoned that as a science, ISD models needed to classify each operative element and combine them into a system for the design of courses. Given this approach, each model fits into one of three specific focuses:

- Classroom
- Product
- Systems

ISD Models

You can't have a discussion of ISD models without evoking the names of Robert Mager, Benjamin Bloom, Robert Glaser, Jerome Bruner, Robert Gagné, Leslie Briggs, and Jerrold Kemp; all influenced the evolution of the field. ISD from the late 1960s onward saw a creative and impressive stream of ideas that fostered each of the following approaches, which almost always ended up becoming models.

Among the better known ISD models, and the ones that we will review in this text, are:
- ADDIE
- Rapid Prototyping
- Kemp
- Dick and Carey
- ASSURE
- SAM

Each of these has its unique features and approaches. However, once you break them down into component features, all have the elements of analysis, design, development, implementation, and evaluation somewhere in the mix, regardless of what it might be called in a specific model. As we look at ADDIE and a select group of other models, the wisdom of these models and their learned creators becomes incredibly clear.

ADDIE

The most famous and most commonly discussed ISD model is ADDIE, which is an acronym for the five elements of analysis, design, development, implementation, and evaluation (Figure 4-1). Developed by a team at Florida State University in the 1970s, it was originally designed for use by the U.S. Army but was later adopted by all the military services. It is now universally accepted as the standard used by the majority of designers who claim a preference for one ISD model.

The model was originally called SAT (Systems Approach to Training) and later became ISD (Instructional Systems Development). Over time, ISD went on to be the standard nomenclature for the work generally performed in producing courses, and ADDIE became the name for the theoretical model for ISD.

There are critics of the ADDIE model; that is to be expected when you consider the scope of the ISD practitioner landscape and the need to create niches for new academics and research. Some will argue it is too old and some will argue it is too detailed. It is also considered by some to be too linear and too rigid. Others say it doesn't work for technology-based learning or online course development. A very small group even suggests that any models for ISD are unnecessary, since it just requires some common sense to design courses.

These discussions are healthy, but frankly there is no other model that does a better job of representing the work that takes place in the practice of ISD at a macro level. Specialist models work very well for some designers and design processes. Designers should review all the models and find the best fit for any specific project.

Figure 4-1. ADDIE

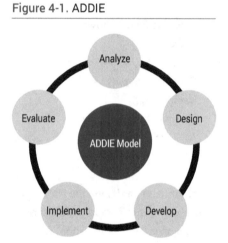

Analysis

Analysis is theoretically the first, or entry, stage of ADDIE, and is considered the data-gathering element for this model. Here, instructional designers assemble all the information they can possibly gather about content, populations, delivery systems, methods, and budgets before they consider anything else. In this model it is assumed that analysis is the first step and that it takes place in each instructional design process, which unfortunately is not always true.

Design

Design is the blueprinting stage of instructional systems, during which instructional designers create the blueprint for a project with all the specifications necessary to complete the project. During this stage, instructional designers write the objectives, construct course content, and complete a design plan.

Development

Materials production and pilot testing are the hallmarks of development. At this stage, most nondesigners not working directly on a project, begin to see progress. Everything from lecture notes to virtual reality is brought from design to deliverable.

Implementation

The most familiar of the elements is implementation. At implementation, the design plan meets the learner and the content is delivered. The evaluation process that most designers and learners are familiar with takes place in this element. Evaluation is used to gauge the degree to which learners meet objectives and facilitators or technologies deliver the project.

Evaluation

Evaluation shouldn't be listed last in the ADDIE model since it takes place in every element and surrounds the instructional design process. Evaluation is the process of determining both mastery of learners and the quality of a course design. Generally, there are four basic types of evaluation, sometimes erroneously called levels, with many more layers of evaluation possible in any given scenario.

ADDIE Model Tasks

To frame the ADDIE model in operational terms, it is useful to view the key steps in each phase from an instructional designer's perspective. We will be covering each ADDIE step in greater detail later. Until then, let's look at the primary functions of each element.

Analysis
- Frame the challenge, problem, or need as tangible action items.
- Determine if each is an instructional or a noninstructional issue.
- Forward noninstructional items to appropriate resources for resolution.
- Evolve strategies for instructional issues.
- Perform the necessary analysis processes to gather data.
- Determine needed resources.
- Draft a budget and timeline.
- Obtain sign-off.
- Evaluate all analysis elements.

Design
- Draft a design plan as your blueprint for the project:
  - Rationale
  - Objectives
  - Population profile
  - Course description
  - Learner and facilitator prerequisites

REFLECTION

ADDIE is considered by most instructional designers to be the gold standard in ISD models. Others disagree and think it is too dated and rigid to be useful in the practice of instructional design. While there are several hundred ISD models that have been presented over the years, ADDIE still maintains its status as the one model everyone seems to know.

- If ADDIE didn't exist, what model would you design or use as an instructional designer?

- Is it possible that ISD could exist just fine without any theoretical underpinning, like a model, to present instructional design in foundational terms?

- ○ Evaluation strategy
- ○ Deliverables
- Evaluate all design elements.

Development
- Draft the lesson plans:
  - ○ Gaining attention
  - ○ Recall
  - ○ Content
  - ○ Application Feedback I
  - ○ Application Feedback II
  - ○ Application Feedback III
  - ○ Evaluation
  - ○ Closure
- Draft the materials (where applicable).
- Draft online content (where applicable).
- Pilot test (as applicable).
- Modify as necessary based on pilot-testing evaluation.
- Evaluate all development elements.

Implementation
- Move project to active status.
- Evaluate (Kirkpatrick Levels 1–3):
  - ○ Reaction
  - ○ Learning
  - ○ Behavior
- Modify as necessary based on evaluation.
- Evaluate all implementation elements.

Evaluation
- Review all five ADDIE elements continuously.
- Revise evaluation process as necessary.

Rapid Prototyping Model

As one could assume from the name, the rapid prototyping ISD model "is intended to reduce the time and cost of a traditional ISD approach" (Daugherty et al. 2007). Some think this is the way all design should take place, and it has even been called a "paradigm shift in understanding the nature and purpose of the field of instructional design" (Tripp and Bichelmeyer 1990). This model is based on the fact that certain elements of the ADDIE model and ISD design process are very quickly decided and become boilerplate for future similar designs. Since this model is less linear than ADDIE, it encourages working with already established design decisions in the areas of implementation modes and materials and then building new content on these available modular design elements.

One example of the use of RP is the process of migrating traditional classroom courses to an online environment. While the content of a course will likely remain the same, the delivery methods and packaging of the content will be more streamlined and allow for a level of boilerplating of the design process, which allows for a very productive course build once the prototype is tested for fit and quality. This is incredibly important as thousands of universities and large organizations move their extensive libraries of classroom courses online using one or more learning management systems (LMS). With this approach, the major variables in course design are largely reduced to the content and other course-specific materials. A designer will work with the instructor and any subject matter experts to quickly migrate courses online. This assumes a stable population and an available source of content and materials.

Figure 4-2. Rapid Prototyping Model

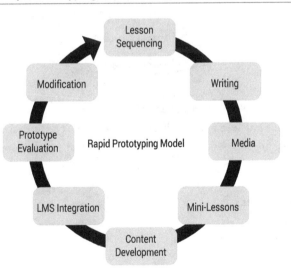

Kemp Model

Jerrold Kemp's ISD model is one of the more interesting approaches to designing curricula. In a world of ISD practitioners who take great comfort in, and occasional criticism for, being linear in thinking and workflow, Kemp's system is completely circular (Figure 4-3). Unlike in ADDIE or most other models, a designer can start a project from any of the nine elements of this model. It also allows a designer to skip certain elements if they aren't required for a specific project.

Figure 4-3. Kemp Model

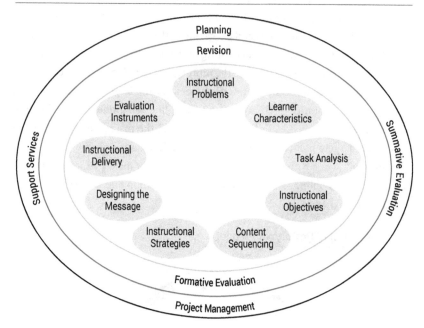

You will find the Kemp model practiced in some language-related course design projects since it is seen to be easily adapted for their specific design needs. This stems from his work at Indiana University and San Jose State University for 30 years in their instructional development programs.

The nine elements are:
- Instructional problems
- Learner characteristics
- Task analysis
- Instructional objectives
- Content sequencing
- Instructional strategies
- Designing the message
- Instructional delivery
- Evaluation instruments

Also included in the model are these elements:
- Planning
- Revision
- Summative evaluation
- Formative evaluation
- Support services
- Project management

This model is a very complex example of the early thoughts on ISD and how a model should represent all the possible process elements necessary to design instruction. The fact that a designer could theoretically start at any of the elements causes some confusion, since an experienced designer would never start with evaluation instruments or content sequencing, for example, before determining objectives and learner characteristics.

Dick and Carey

This ISD model saw wide use during the earlier years of the formal practice of instructional design. Consisting of 10 elements, it roughly follows the ADDIE model. Some see it as "rigid and cumbersome" (Yavuz 2007), and it is certainly a behaviorist design model linking the stimulus of course material with the response of learning the content.

Figure 4-4. Dick and Carey Model

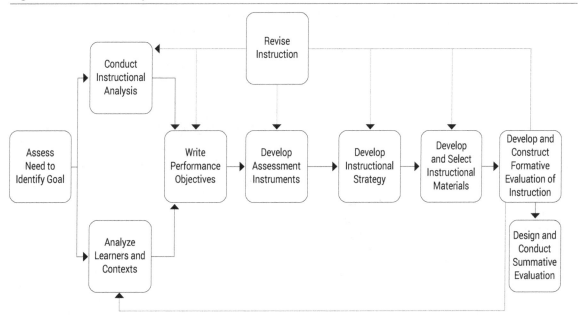

If you look closely at Dick and Carey, you will see all the ADDIE elements with the addition of several specific process areas that would normally be part of any design process but that are highlighted in this model for emphasis. You will see this in many models, including the ASSURE model we will look at next.

ASSURE

The ASSURE model of ISD is the work of Robert Heinich, Michael Molenda, and James Russell. It first appeared in 1989 in their textbook *Instructional Media and the New Technologies of Instruction*. As the title of the textbook suggests, this model is focused on the inclusion of media in instructional products.

The six elements of the model are:

- Analyze learner
- State objectives
- Select methods, media, and materials
- Utilize media and materials
- Require learner participation
- Evaluate and revise

Figure 4-5. ASSURE

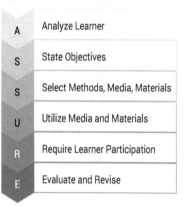

This model is similar to ADDIE, with the addition of the more detailed elements like "utilize media and materials" and "require learner participation," which are assumed to be done using any ISD model. This model simply makes a point of highlighting the use of media and electronic learning support approaches.

SAM

The Successive Approximation Model of ISD is the result of the work of Michael Allen and was first published in the 2012 book *Leaving ADDIE for SAM: An Agile Model for Developing the Best Learning Experiences.* Allen suggests that the model "is well suited to small projects." It is designed to address the four criteria of Allen's "ideal process model":

- The process must be iterative
- The process must support collaboration
- The process must be efficient and effective
- The process must be manageable

SAM is divided into three elements, which are the preparation phase, the iterative design phase, and the iterative development phase. Each of these three phases is subdivided into more detailed process elements. While it has three basic elements, two less than ADDIE, if you look at the details of the sub-elements it actually contains all of the ADDIE elements. Again, it is another variation of the original ISD model.

Figure 4-6. SAM

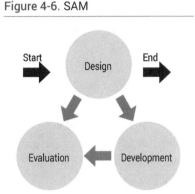

The SAM model is a streamlined design approach that some may find more resonant with their workflow demands, especially in online learning. As with all ISD models, it is up to the designer to decide what works best for a specific design situation.

Comparison of Six ISD Models

As you review Table 4-1 comparing the five generic ISD elements with the six most commonly referenced models, there is an obvious symmetry between each model and the generic construct of instructional design. It is up for interpretation whether rapid prototyping includes the evaluation element and if SAM includes analysis and implementation within their separate frameworks. Assuming that both include analysis and implementation, only worded or interpreted differently, what you will find is that each model has all of the five generic elements, sometimes named something different.

Table 4-1. Comparison of ISD Models

	ADDIE	Rapid Prototyping	Kemp	Dick and Carey	ASSURE	SAM
Analysis	X		X	X	X	
Design	X	X	X	X	X	X
Development	X	X	X	X	X	X
Implementation	X	X	X	X	X	
Evaluation	X	X	X	X	X	X
Other		X	X			

The differences are largely in the actual practice of using a model as a framework for workflow and other design project specifics. Many design elements in these models are more process features than actual model elements. For example, the Kemp model element of instructional strategies would seem to be more of a by-product of the process and not a specific process point. Other examples of this include the elements of writing, modification, and mini-lessons in the rapid prototyping model, which can easily be interpreted as process elements and not model elements.

For instructional design professionals, the practical side of this discussion is that most designers will use the individual model elements in a workflow that best suits each organization, designer, and specific combination of design requirements, including content, population, and instructional strategies. In reality, each designer and design project has its own unique model of ISD for that particular set of requirements.

When it comes to explaining the ISD process to an audience that does not have familiarity with instructional design, such as a client group or those writing a proposal or grant, most designers will use the ADDIE model as a basis. The uninitiated have little, if any, interest in the subtle differences between ADDIE and SAM and only want to know that there is some theoretical construct for the process of designing instruction. Almost everyone has heard of ADDIE, and it just makes things easier to keep it simple for the nondesign community. More experienced and knowledgeable clients and managers may want to dig deeper into a specific project's approach, and it pays to think about and plan for the inevitable questions concerning design approaches.

The Purpose of ISD Models and Three Simple Truths

For as long as ISD has been a professional endeavor, there have been various theoretical models that attempt to represent the way ISD is structured. From the original ADDIE model to SAM, Kemp, Dick and Carey, ASSURE, rapid prototype, and hundreds of others, these models have assumed an almost mythical status.

In reality, while models play an important role in the education of an instructional designer, their impact on the day-to-day practice of ISD is generally best described as foundational. It is wonderful for the design community to review these, usually as they learn the design process. It allows for the study of the theoretical basis for each model's approach.

ISD models by their very nature represent ideas, speculation, and hypotheses that are generic, loosely defined frameworks. They present a foundation of theoretical elements reflecting some level of predictive power. To have any chance of being useful in general situations, these ideas must be enacted very close to the prescribed values in a model. Additionally, most models are replicable only within a limited range of variables and, at best, to a modest level of precision.

To use the example of analysis, which is an element of most ISD models in some form or another, we find that the operational reality is often very different from the linchpin status often afforded it in a model. In professional practice it is often not funded adequately, if at all, and is not the primary concern of most designers in the way that most ISD models would suggest. In some situations, analysis takes weeks or months and is funded to a desired level. In many other projects, analysis data is assumed to already exist, and little in the way of resources is allocated. In still other projects, there is simply no analysis process beyond that which takes place when writing objectives or designing a lesson plan. The idea that it must be performed first and is the foundation of all design work is sadly not universally the reality in the practice of ISD.

The popularity of ISD models, and the importance some designers place in them, has its origins in the hope that there exists one universal approach, technique, or procedure that reins in the complexity of instructional design and that provides a logical, manageable, and replicable road map to success in every situation. As you would expect, the silver bullet for ISD doesn't exist. In fact, one of the primary reasons that experienced instructional designers are in such high demand is their ability to aggregate a very complex instructional design process filled with countless variable elements into a finished product, the path to which is based on a loose interpretation of instructional design models.

The reason for this disconnect between ISD models and the all too practical realities of professional instructional design is based on three simple truths that seasoned designers know exist in the practice of ISD:
· No two design projects are ever the same.
· No one designs in a perfect world.
· One design process never fits all scenarios.

Let's look at each of these in more detail to explore these ideas.

No Two Design Projects Are Ever the Same

Ask anyone working in the world of instructional design and they will probably say that they have never worked on two projects that were exactly the same. There are always variables, including timing, budget, available resources, and availability of subject matter experts, that make each project distinct. If you attempt to align any project with a model, you will likely never go beyond labeling project tasks with a specific model's elements. Because I use ADDIE as my model, you will probably be able to find elements of analysis, design, development, and evaluation in various aspects of my work, but ADDIE never really drives the workflow; that is the privileged domain of specific project demands.

No One Designs in a Perfect World

Models assume that every aspect of the design process is bound for perfection and that projects never encounter anything approaching the common realities of modern instructional design. Models lack the flexibility to face the unknown that is waiting just ahead on the schedule. The day-to-day challenges of professional instructional design have never and will never be something that a model can predict. That is unless we have a model with the critical element of "stuff happens."

No Single Design Process Fits All Scenarios

This final truth is often the Achilles heel of any ISD model. If we believe that our first two truths are accurate, there is little rational possibility that any model could ever promise to reflect a course design process and workflow in anything more than generic terms. It is the skill of an instructional designer that pulls all of the various design elements together regardless of the appearance of working within a template to complete a project. There is no greater folly than the notion that the assembly line mentality works in professional design projects. There are certainly similarities, and a workflow process is always recommended, but the sum of design variables is never the same from project to project.

ISD Models Are Just Models

The very real world of detail and precision in the instructional design process can never be more than loosely reflected in a theoretical model like ADDIE. Models are best used to explain the ISD process to the uninitiated, or to represent our work in a five-minute overview to stakeholders and clients or in an RFP for a project.

Like Einstein's $E=mc^2$ in the field of theoretical physics, the theoretical models in ISD suggest a starting point for the discussion of how this foundational knowledge may lead to practical applications. Just as there is a tension in science between the theoretical and applied science professionals, ISD is in the same position with a tension between the modelists and the practitioners. To be sure, this is a healthy discussion, but most practitioners rely more on their years of experience than the best of theories once they are actually working in the field. Years of trial and error and experience with increasing numbers of variables are the real foundation of the practice of professional instructional design.

While some may wish that there is an all-encompassing ISD model that joins all conceivable design work elements into a simple checklist for success, there exists no realistic mechanism for this to happen beyond the skills of an instructional designer. So, let all of the ISD models simply play a role in your thinking about your work and don't let them be your day-to-day guide in the sense that everything you do somehow falls within a model's constraints.

Summary

Every aspect of instructional design rests on a solid foundation of research followed by generations of application and refinement by design professionals. ISD models are one of the most compelling elements of the practice of instructional design, and almost all professional design work starts with the knowledge of these models. The most studied of these models is ADDIE; however, there are literally hundreds of ISD models that have been presented and promoted over the years, each with their unique thoughts on how to practice instructional design. As enlightening as these models appear, the seasoned designer will find that these are only the starting point for the practice of ISD and will modify these design elements to fit a specific project's needs.

REFLECTION

Every course and project presents different challenges based on the unlimited variables that exist in every learning environment, from populations to content. As ISD matures as a science, the practice of instructional design is constantly being influenced by new technologies, new learning environments, and changes in life and culture that were completely unpredictable.

- Is it possible for a designer to incorporate all of the unpredictable variables, like a worldwide pandemic, natural disasters, and other societal shifts, into a working ISD model that allows the design process to address every shift in specifics as it appears?

- Will designers be required to move from the relatively safe space of using models to a completely free-form design approach that allows fluid shifts in design as required by individual circumstances?

DISCUSSION QUESTIONS

1. What is the most important aspect of ISD models for a professional designer?

2. Are models in ISD representative of the fact that instructional design is a systems approach to preparing courses? If so, how do they reflect systems thinking on learning?

3. Is the ADDIE model too simple or too complicated?

4. When reviewing all of the ISD models in this chapter, which most closely aligns with your thoughts on what an ISD model should look like, and why?

5. Is there ever a time when a model can be used as a template for designing courses in ISD?

CASE STUDY 1

Your design group has a new client who has never worked with professional instructional designers. The client thinks that designing courses is easy and that it doesn't take a professional designer to do this work. The client is questioning why someone would need an advanced degree to do this work.

Specifics:
- Small marketing company
- 80 employees in five states
- Need five sales courses for new products
- Previous courses were designed and taught by a senior vice president with no ISD or education experience
- Previous courses were not well received and considered a waste of time by employees

Given what you have learned in this chapter about ISD models and the extensive scientific background of the field of ISD, what will you say to your new client about the value of having professional designers and well-designed courses based on scientific study and practice?

CASE STUDY 2

You are the lead instructional designer for a large biotech firm that designs and offers hundreds of courses every year. All the designers in the department have at least an undergraduate degree in education or instructional design. Several designers have advanced degrees in the field.

The organization has recently promoted a manager in the human resources department to lead your department and to determine if there are any efficiencies that can be gained by designing courses in a more streamlined way, since course design is very expensive given the design team's education and experience. The new manager has no experience in training or instructional design but mentions ADDIE and SAM as examples of efficient ways to design courses.

How would you explain the relationship between ISD models and the real world of instructional design?

Is there a way to be more efficient and reduce costs by strictly following an ISD model?

CASE STUDY 3

You are a PhD student in a program in the department of education at a large private college. Your research and dissertation are focused on the modernization of educational design approaches and how to address real-world design challenges that exist in the ISD community.

You have decided that there needs to be a new ISD model to address the modern practice of ISD.

What will your model look like and what elements will it contain?

The Five Elements of Instructional Design

CHAPTER 5
Analysis

KEY CONCEPTS

- Analysis as the first step in instructional design
- The who, what, where, when, and why of analysis
- NOP analysis as a first step in the analysis process
- Five different types of analysis commonly used in ISD
- Root-cause analysis
- Population analysis
- Task analysis
- Worst-case scenario analysis
- Instructional strategies for how learners will be taught
- Half-life in ISD
- Unintended results analysis
- Analysis paralysis

OBJECTIVES

At the end of this chapter, the learner should be able to:

- Define the process of analysis.
- Define the reason for the five Ws of analysis.
- Describe the NOP analysis process.
- List at least five types of analysis used in instructional design.
- Define *root cause analysis* in ISD.
- Define *population analysis* in ISD.
- Explain the process of task analysis.
- Explain the reasons for worst-case scenario analysis.
- Define *instructional strategies*.
- Define *half-life* as it is used in ISD.
- Define *unintended consequences*.
- Describe analysis paralysis.

Analysis is the single most important activity in the practice of instructional design. Without it, there is little in the way of reliable information and data upon which to competently perform any aspect of instructional design. It is impossible to decide even the most basic question of whether training or designing a course is the best way to address a perceived training need. Nothing can replace analysis, and you can't ignore it. It is impossible to work in this field without mastering this process. Analysis is inseparable from the work of an instructional designer. No model of ISD exists without analysis in some form.

Outside the ranks of professional instructional design, making the case for the importance of analysis can be difficult with groups who think that it is overrated and largely unnecessary. It is sometimes thought that a project doesn't need much analysis work because everyone (supposedly) already knows the population, content, and other variables that analysis explores. Nothing could be further from the truth, but that doesn't diminish the pressure to skip or abbreviate the analysis element in ISD.

This leads many designers to try to find ways to perform analysis that don't appear expensive or time consuming. Sometimes, there is no budget or time allocated for any significant analysis work. This process is important enough that designers must on occasion perform analysis on their own rather than attempt to design a project without the information.

Regardless of the environmental challenges presented by tight budgets and less-than-convinced outside interests, the work of analysis must be addressed one way or another. As we work through the many facets of this powerful ISD process, its value and the ways to make the work both efficient and effective will become clear.

In your role as an instructional designer performing analysis, you are operating as a detective working to solve a crime. In our case, the crime might be poor performance, lack of updated safety training, or a chronic customer service problem. In every course design process, there are unknowns and questions to answer, and you are always presented with clues about what you need to do and how you are going to get there. Your design instincts may be strong, but you need to have facts to back up your hunches. Imagine that you will have to testify in the court of instructional design to prove your approach and methods. Given that scenario, you are going to want to gather and analyze everything you can get your hands on in this process.

In instructional design, analysis is the first element of the ISD process and provides the data necessary to accurately determine need, goals, populations, and numerous other foundation points, which form the basis for a course design project. The analysis process involves taking the time and effort necessary to gather and mine data to establish a reliable foundation of information from which to perform other, more detailed work. Without the analysis process, there can be little confidence that any decisions made in the design are based on fact. As we journey through this chapter, you will review not only the reasons for the importance of analysis, but also the various ways it is performed in instructional design.

The Five Ws in Analysis

First you will want to start with the who, what, where, when, and why of every aspect of your design variables. For example:

- Whom do you need to work with to gather your data?
- What happened to bring this situation to the point of needing a training program?
- Where and how is the training going to be implemented?
- When does this have to be completed and what is the budget?
- Why should this project even be started?

As you ask yourself these questions, begin to frame how you will gather the data you need to feel confident that you are sufficiently informed (Figure 5-1).

Figure 5-1. Questions for Analysis

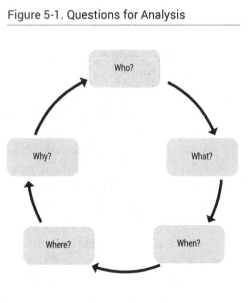

In the analysis stage, instructional designers can never know too much. Curiosity is the first analytic skill that belongs in a designer's toolkit. It is impossible to ask too many questions; to continue the detective theme, ask yourself if you have uncovered every fact and talked to every important player in your course design process.

Need, Outcomes, and Population Analysis (NOP Analysis)

When you are first beginning the analysis process on a specific project, you need to define the basic elements that are the foundation for everything else you do when designing. NOP analysis fulfills the functions of addressing need, outcomes, and population in one relatively easy process. If you do nothing else, you should perform a NOP analysis. This process is obviously not as in-depth as other types of analysis we will be reviewing shortly. It is just intended to set the context and define the scope of a project. A designer can perform a NOP analysis in a very short period of time. While the follow-up work in analysis, if performed, is much more detailed and time consuming, NOP allows a designer to determine the environment and make sure that everyone involved in a project is on the same page right from the start.

The first NOP function, need, can be either the easiest or the most challenging part of getting started. *Need* in instructional design is defined functionally as the reason you are beginning the instructional design process. If you are unable to clearly and distinctly identify a need, then not much else is going to matter. Need is sometimes based on a mandate, such as a licensure requirement for 80 hours of classroom courses before a student can take a specific examination to qualify for a professional position. Need can also be defined as a perceived or documented lack of knowledge in a workforce, or an unacceptable level of productivity or performance. In fact, need can be almost anything if it is identifiable and able to be addressed by a course or program.

Some instructional designers believe that training is the only solution to any problem identified in an organization. They will insist that everything from employee morale to profitability can be improved by a course. Sadly, that type of attitude is sometimes counterproductive and has led to billions of dollars of unnecessary training. The reality of this process, and the reason that NOP analysis is so important, is that a small percentage of problems do not require training solutions. In fact, there may not be any training problems at all. You may face serious problems down the line if you don't take a small amount of time up front to dig into the reason for the impression that training is needed.

There are some needs that cannot be fixed with training. For example, low wages, miserable working conditions, and the lack of proper equipment are not suitable reasons for training. There are solutions for these issues, and an instructional designer can suggest performance improvement methods to solve them. No instructional designer wants to end up designing the equivalent of a course titled "500 Jobs Better Than Yours" for an unhappy workforce. The cardinal rule when performing analysis in ISD is always: Accurately determine if there is a training solution before providing one. If you can't define a need and at least outline an operative solution to address the need, this is the time to stop and regroup and make sure everything is as it appears on the surface.

Outcomes is the second NOP element and represents several specific design considerations, including organizational goals, learner goals, and methods of evaluation of mastery. These are considered goals rather than objectives because they don't cover the more detailed, behavioral level (we will cover objectives later). This is the 1,000-foot view of what an organization wants to accomplish and what the finished project will represent to it.

From a designer's perspective, outcomes can be a very tricky guessing game if you don't ask the correct questions and dig deep enough to find out what is actually going on. An organization might want to make sure employees are competent in a new software system or know how to initiate basic HR functions like vacation and sick time requests. The organization might also just want employees to feel appreciated, and the actual outcomes are more affective in nature than teaching a skill or providing knowledge. Both are legitimate, but each is very different in terms of design approach and process, and the failure to determine and agree with a client on this basic tenent of the design can end up being catastrophic.

The *P* in NOP analysis represents *populations*. This analysis element, in a quick preliminary overview, allows a designer to acquire a general sense of what a population looks like in design terms. Does this population generally seem like they would benefit from the intended course or program? Is it possible the population in question is too large and mixed to have learners benefit universally from a single approach, making multiple implementation modes more appropriate?

Population overviews in NOP are also a reality check to determine if there are any learning challenges or disabilities in a population. Since every variable in a population will have the potential to influence the design process, the NOP will give an early indication that something might have to be analyzed a little deeper. Age, education, technology competence, and attitude are the common elements to keep on a designer's analytic radar.

REFLECTION

The NOP analysis process is often used informally by instructional designers to set a framework for each course or project. This process can be as informal as "napkin note-taking" with a smartphone or pad, or as detailed as using a set of specific points of interest that serves as the basis for the more detailed analysis work that usually follows.

As a designer, you have determined that you will not be given any formal budget or time to perform analysis to design a course. However, you know that failing to perform some level of analysis may result in poor design and potentially poor performance of the course.

How can you see yourself using an NOP analysis in this situation? Do you feel there are times when an NOP analysis is enough to get the data you need to design?

NOP analysis is a quick, one-time overview to jump-start analysis and make sure there isn't something missing at the macro level that needs to be addressed. This can assist in budgeting and bids, but it is also an excellent exercise to conduct with clients, managers, or other decision makers who are not on the design team to narrow any areas of misunderstanding or confusion. This is an excellent time to start the discussion about making sure that there actually is a training solution to the perceived problems or needs.

Types of Analysis Used in ISD

Let's look at a few of the most often used types of analysis in more detail. Population analysis, root cause analysis, and task analysis always finish at the top of the list of daily-use analysis methods and are often supplemented with any of a variety of other methods based on the needs of the designer. It is fair to say that each designer will need different approaches for each unique blend of challenges as they get started with the analysis process:

- Root cause analysis
- Needs analysis
- Job/task analysis
- Population analysis
- Technology analysis
- 360 Environmental analysis
- Constraints analysis
- Front-end analysis
- Organizational will analysis
- Unintended results analysis
- Worst-case scenario analysis
- Unknown unknowns analysis
- Content choice analysis

Population Analysis

In the practice of instructional design, analysis of the population of learners is not optional. Gathering and confirming every aspect of a learning population is required before making critical decisions about objectives, delivery modalities, and evaluations as well as other questions that can arise in the design process. This process requires skills that might seem intuitive on the surface but require countless hours of practice to perfect, because the variations within each population are countless.

The biggest mistake designers make in this area is to ignore this process, even if it only means verifying data that you have been given or seeking clarification in areas that seem to conflict.

What a Population Analysis Tells a Designer

Population analysis is distinctly different from other types of analysis since the focus is on the relationship between the individual and the project being designed. This being the case, we look for specific types of data that give us keys to this relationship. For example, we need to know the present level of content mastery in a population, the relationship between that mastery and the proposed content, and the best way to implement the content with a specific population. However, in many projects that is only the beginning. We may also need to know about motivation, language competency, cultural norms, learning styles, and other variables.

Many non-designers associated with a project say there is very little value in performing a population analysis unless there is a recognized set of issues that exist within a population. Without taking the time to check, there is no way for a designer to discover, acknowledge, and address population variables. Designing a course in workplace communications would suggest that a careful look at the target population is necessary, because the content relates directly to a population's ability to communicate with one another. But the same issues can exist in a new employee orientation or a course in retirement planning within an organization, and might be ignored because the importance of population data isn't as obvious.

There are certain basic sets of data that you will need to gather and consider as you review a population. The order of importance for these is different for each project and may actually change during the design process, depending on the environment and volatility of the content or design.

The Population Report

It is not unusual for designers to struggle with writing a population report even when they have gathered all the necessary data and performed all reasonable forms of population analysis. The problem may arise from the context they use as the foundation for their report. From an ISD standpoint, the analysis report is always a snapshot of a population at the time the process takes place. It is intended to represent the present truth and not the hoped-for future population.

One powerful way to start a population profile is to imagine you have your entire population in one place and you can see each member clearly. You can see their key data related to education, motivation, present knowledge, and demographics. Within this context, it is easier to visualize the reality of a population and resist the urge to fall back on stereotypical preconceived concepts of a population.

Wording should be in the context of what presently exists, such as:

- This population ranges in age from 18 to 25 years old.
- This population is approximately 33 percent male and 67 percent female.
- Everyone in this population has documented at least a high-school-level education, including those with a GED.
- Motivation in this population is mixed based on the fact that both labor and management employees will be taking this course. Some members of this population don't want to participate and think this is a waste of time. Others are looking forward to the opportunity to express their opinion in a nonjudgmental and risk-free environment. Percentages of opinion in either camp are difficult to gauge based on the present available data.

It is also appropriate to mention when you don't have sufficient data for any important aspects of the course, which may influence design decisions. This absence of data is usually reported in ways similar to these:

- While this population is generally thought to have no opinion on the content in this course, there is no reliable data to confirm or deny that impression.
- Reading level is difficult to determine in this population since no benchmarks or reliable first-person data is presently available.

It is also very important not to write a population profile as if you are looking for an ideal learner or setting prerequisites for the course. Those details are best handled in the rationale and prerequisite sections of a design plan, which we cover later in the text.

Content Mastery

One of the first criteria that a designer needs to determine is the anticipated level of content mastery for a population before a course is implemented. This is easy if there is no minimum level of mastery required for participating in a course, but that is seldom the reality. Even open-enrollment or community participation courses have some expectation for pre-course mastery, even if it is a seemingly obvious element like basic language skills or literacy at a certain grade level.

It is often necessary for a designer to perform a skills analysis to determine content mastery in a specific population. In other situations, it may be acceptable to review general population data available through numerous sources. In either case, you can't start working on content issues and design until you actually know where to start. In this process, you can use tools like the content mastery continuum, which we will review in a later chapter.

Population Demographics

All designers are familiar with the importance of demographic data sets, including age and educational achievement level. However, there are times when more sophisticated demographic data is necessary. The process of gathering this data requires a systematic approach to analysis. A designer needs to determine what, if any, demographic variable may impact course design.

Many population members consider personal data privileged, and may be hesitant to share much with a designer. Information like gender, marital status, income, cultural background, religious affiliation, and language skills may be difficult to gather with any degree of accuracy beyond general observation. There may be opportunities to obtain this data from third-party sources if you honor all legal and ethical concerns and restrictions. HIPPA and FERPA are but two of the federal laws that regulate the gathering and handling of data, and as a designer you must always honor those restrictions.

Motivation and Attitude

How a population views a content area or their participation in a course is almost always invaluable information for an instructional designer. With so much training and education now considered mandatory, motivation and attitude play an increasing role in course design.

If a course is in a content area that is considered personal or is something that is uncomfortable for a learner, a designer needs to know how a population will react to the learning environment and the content before the course is implemented. Diversity and workplace behavior are often content areas that require an attitude scan among the population to determine underlying issues. You have to design measures to neutralize or deal with unpleasant or controversial issues within a course and not leave the facilitator with the responsibility of dealing with potential problems on the fly.

Language and Culture

Instructional design projects are not confined to one language, culture, or other demographic marker. An integral element of analysis in ISD is to determine if any of these variations will be significant enough to impact the design process.

For example, sometimes the seemingly minuscule impact of translation can have a big effect on implementation and the timing of a course. Simultaneous translation takes less time than consecutive translation; a course that lasts four hours in one language for a native-speaking population can easily take six or more hours if consecutive translation is used since it requires everything to be said twice, once in language A and once in language B.

Cultural aspects of a population must be identified in the analysis process to ensure that issues related to respect and familiarity are incorporated into the course design. No designer wants to make a simple mistake in materials or interaction that violates cultural norms, which would then immediately invalidate an entire course or program. It is mandatory that a designer honors any and all cultural elements.

Choices in Implementation

Every population of learners has different views on how they want to participate in courses. Some learners want to be online, while others may prefer the classroom. Some may want to use social media, while others may want to work in groups. Others may want to have synchronous online learning, while a majority think anytime, anyplace better suits their availability, and opts for asynchronous online learning. All these options need to be analyzed for fit with each population of learners. There are times when the implementation is fixed to one type or another, such as always classroom or always online, in which case a designer must determine any negative impacts of these immovable limitations on a population. In other instances, analysis results defy conventional logic and provide designers with data that can save a project if they implement it in a way that is most appealing to a majority of a population.

For example, a very high-tech corporate population, working remotely around the world, was thought to prefer online learning since they worked in a high-tech environment and delivery was relatively simple and cost effective given the technology already in place. A population analysis, however, showed that this population was relatively bored with using technology for this purpose and wanted the opportunity to learn with others in a classroom environment. The end product was a traditional facilitator-led series of courses that was very well received and actually proved to be significantly less expensive to produce and implement. Without the population analysis, the project could have run into significant motivational issues that would have negated most of the potential for success.

Technology and Distance Learning Acceptance and Use

Distance learning has arrived on the learning landscape and is growing in impact, even though it is not the answer for all populations and courses. As the previous example shows, not even high-tech populations necessarily want distance learning options for training. However, environmental influences like pandemics and the inability to travel to traditional learning sites like classrooms are increasingly driving distance learning to be at least an option in most training situations.

The ISD process doesn't have an opinion on how a course is implemented; the data and analysis will drive this discussion. However, it certainly has a role in determining what works best for a specific population and content area. The process of determining this fit starts with a population analysis that includes gathering data related to distance learning attitudes and access issues.

Attitudinal data that relates to preferences in learning implementation can easily be obtained. Important questions about when and where the training takes place must relate directly to the options available. If, in an office environment, learners are required to take a course during work hours, they may prefer a classroom setting. If they are expected to take a course on their own time, they may prefer an online option. Be sure to run through the entire spectrum of options to accurately measure population preferences.

Other Relevant Population Data

Just remember, there is something unique about each population. Sometimes these are minor elements that have no real bearing on a project's future, and other times the smallest points will have a major impact. It is also not unheard of for things to change or suddenly appear in a population as a project moves through design and development. A diligent designer will continuously scan the population for anything that might have been overlooked or ignored in the analysis process.

How to Conduct a Population Profile

It is important early in the population analysis process to establish which issues may influence the project's success. A simple rubric works fine for this step. For each element that may have an influence on the process, the designer will say whether or not it could affect the outcome of the project, why, and whether they can do anything about it.

The designer should analyze each of these issues with one question in mind: "Can this element affect the outcome of this project?" For each element, the designer should ask if it has the potential to cause success or failure. Motivation and incentive issues alone can sink a well-designed training project. If the answer is yes, this element can cause success or failure, the designer must address why, and what they are going to do about it.

Conducting a population analysis can be a complex undertaking, but there are some very simple steps any designer can follow to ensure at least a basic profile of any population.

Gather and Review the Demographics of Your Target Population

Demographics are the nuts and bolts of your population, and there is little in the way of opinion-based data in this section of your analysis. The types of demographic data you need depend on your design, but generally they include census-like data that relates to age, gender, ethnicity, culture, income, location, and education. Often this data is included in a survey given to the population to complete. This data is generally easily obtained, but there are times when one or more of these data areas are considered too personal, too invasive, or unnecessary by the population, and you may have to either gather data from a secondary source, like organizational or regional data or estimate as best you can. There are times when the process of gathering this data, itself can be considered invasive by a population, and you may decide to forgo the formal data collection process and replace it with a more observational approach.

Gather Data Related to Attitudes, Values, and Opinions

Knowing how a population feels about a certain content area or situation is sometimes vital to a population analysis. If you are working on a course for a troubled workforce, knowing why population members feel a certain way is key to building a course-based solution. There are design projects that will sink or swim based on this data. In other populations and design projects, this attitudinal information has limited value. For example, do you really care if a technician enjoys replacing a part in a sophisticated piece of electronic equipment if there is no viable option for making it more enjoyable?

There are various methods available to gather this information, including surveys, interviews, and focus groups. There is a tendency to find more affective data through the more personal and one-on-one analysis methods of interviews and focus groups. Surveys, usually anonymous, are of value for larger populations or where the element under discussion is less personal or closely held.

Consider the Affective, Cultural, and Environmental Issues

When working on a design project for a population that is unfamiliar to you, or one that is geographically or culturally new to your experience, pay special attention to the environment in which the population resides. A designer can't ignore the seemingly insignificant points of data that appear without first determining their value and importance to a population. Issues that arise might be as simple as starting time and classroom seating, and while they might not seem important to a designer on the surface, if a course is implemented using only assumed knowledge, unintended negative consequences could impact success.

Several, but not all, of the factors designers need to consider include:

- **Religious and spiritual influence:** It is important that designers consider prayer times and other activities that might conflict with training times.
- **Gender interaction:** Cultural expectations around gender and gender segregation might create challenges in designing group activities such as role-play exercises.
- **Attendance and timing issues:** Many countries are more polychronic (time is fluid) than the Western monochromic attitude, which expects extreme punctuality. Starting at 8 a.m. might mean starting sometime after 8 a.m. in some cultures.
- **Evaluation techniques:** Some learners might be hesitant to offer opinions or criticism of one another or to question a facilitator.
- **Appropriate materials:** Designers must consider participants' views about how materials represent them, especially graphic representations. The manner of dress and types of activities shown in materials must be acceptable to the target population.

REFLECTION

Population analysis is one of the foundational requirements in all instructional design work. The degree to which it is performed and the level of effort and data gathered are unique to each course design and project. Some designers work with one population for many courses and don't really feel the need to revisit a population with each new design. Others argue that even a cursory review of a population is necessary for each course design.

As you look at population analysis and the role it plays in ISD, what is your feeling about the importance of this process? Do you think there are times when it is unnecessary? Do you feel that there is ever a perfect population with little variation in any of the key metrics you are interested in as a designer?

- **Working days and hours:** In many areas of the world, the normal workweek is not Monday to Friday. Variables like this occur within the individual countries and populations represented in a typical cohort of learners. It is also imperative that training is not scheduled or even considered during national or regional holidays.

Gather Everything Else

A professional instructional designer is always looking for that extra data set that will provide a key bit of information that will add value to the analysis process. Many times, these moments are unexpected or unsolicited, yet enormously important to the design process. It is not unusual for a designer to learn about something critical to a design based on an overheard conversation or a quick review of an organizational newsletter or publication. Don't be afraid to gather every bit of information that comes your way and review it for hidden nuggets of data.

Ultimately, this type of attention to population variables leads to a comprehensive training project that reflects the needs of the population and helps ensure a good start to the design plan. It is important that every element of a population study be reviewed and considered in the design process.

Root-Cause Analysis

The first task for a designer is to identify the need and determine the root cause of any problems that may exist. Sometimes the need and root cause are relatively easy to uncover. At other times, they may take some digging to reveal. Designers must listen carefully to what they hear and use logic to test each potential issue.

Organizations are inundated with data that they must collect to satisfy local, state, and federal requirements. If they want to participate in quality assessments like ISO 9001 and similar programs, they are constantly gathering data. And, while the quantity of the information necessary for these needs is increasing, the training responses to many of the needs identified are still not up to what is expected or required. Okes (2019) points out that "much of the training that is provided is too high level and philosophical, or is focused on creative rather than analytical problem solving."

When working to find the root cause of an issue, it is important to remember that very few problems result from one very obvious issue. Most problems are much more complex than that; Parker (2017) notes that "complex, serious, or pervasive problems are rarely the result of a single event or failure. Frequently a 'perfect storm' of several causes forms to create an ideal environment for the failure to occur." When looking for a root cause, don't stop at the first information uncovered and assume it represents the entire spectrum of elements that support the creation and growth of an issue.

Many professionals performing work on root-cause analysis use some form of the Five Ws system. And, once they identify the issues, the proposed answers to the issues are then repeatedly subjected to the question, "Why will each solution work?" You may also hear this called the fishbone technique (Baum 2019) since it is often diagramed this way.

It is important to point out that even when a need appears to have an instructional solution, that might not be the best solution. That assessment might be made on the basis of symptoms and not the root cause of the problem. Just as in medicine, treating the symptoms seldom cures the illness.

Worst-Case Scenario Analysis

One of the most powerful, and sometimes most valuable, analyses in the workflow of instructional design is to look at all of the things that can go wrong with a course development project. While this may seem to be a process that isn't all that enjoyable, it does allow everyone to dig very deeply into a project's variables and see what might be in the process that can cause problems. The value of this analysis comes from the fact that knowing something might happen makes it easier to plan for and provide backups or alternative plans as necessary.

For example, a team might use a flipchart or text stream to list the things that could go wrong in a plan. Things that often come up are implementation issues like lack of technology in classrooms or unreliable staff, such as instructors. Many times, difficulty working with subject matter experts (SMEs) or lack of support from managers can impact the process. Today, health issues like the COVID-19 pandemic impacting choices in implementation require that a backup plan be established.

There is also the psychological benefit of placing everyone's fears on the table and discussing them. Price (2011) calls this "the general propensity to try and anticipate the uncertainties of life." If a designer doesn't exercise the human desire to have some confidence in decisions and approaches, it is possible that valuable time will be lost later when events occur that could have been planned for if discovered early. How many times have we heard someone say, "I knew that was going to happen, but I didn't say anything"? This type of analysis is the mechanism to allow a complete airing of any issues and dig deep enough in the variables to at least anticipate challenges before they appear.

Conducting a Task Analysis

Even though it is such a fundamental tool of the instructional designer, task analysis is often done poorly or given little preparation time. In fact, it is not as simple as one might assume. Four levels of detail exist in a task analysis: job, task, skill, and sub-skill, as shown in the following section.

Task Analysis Examples

These are examples of task analysis for a first responder and a customer service representative in a retail environment:

- **Job:** First Responder
  - ◦ **Task:** Responding to a reported fire in a single-family residence.
  - ◦ **Skills:** Safe driving, reviewing available information from the dispatcher or CAD, wearing appropriate safety gear, assessing scene on arrival, notifying dispatcher and command officer of findings, addressing the situation until completed.
  - ◦ **Sub-skill:** Communication with other first responders and dispatchers and the specific safety requirements for this type of dispatch situation.
- **Job:** Customer Service Representative in Retail Environment
  - ◦ **Task:** Addressing and solving a customer complaint.
  - ◦ **Skills:** Actively listening to the customer's concerns, asking clarifying questions, finding a resolution to the customer's concerns.
  - ◦ **Sub-skill:** Sensitivity to customer's concerns, knowledge of products and policies, creative problem solving, and a supportive and reassuring tone of voice.

Some instructional designers spend most of their professional life working in situations that require them to follow technical task-analysis procedures. Imagine trying to perform a task analysis on a job like that of manager of an energy-producing nuclear reactor. That job involves numerous tasks that must be replicated exactly the way they are engineered because a misstep in the task analysis could put people's lives in jeopardy. Consider what would happen if a task analysis missed a key step in a safety procedure. As a result of that omission, employees might not receive training for a specific problem that might occur. No training probably means diminished effectiveness in dealing with the problem.

In most cases, these three steps are a great way to begin the task-analysis process from the perspective of an instructional designer:

1. Define the target of the analysis: Whom are you going to work with? What titles or responsibilities do you want to analyze?
2. Choose the methodology: Will you use task analysis, focus groups, or other methods of analysis?
3. Select the analysis subjects: Choose the best candidates for analysis. Typically, these are the people who actually do the work and are considered the best at it. It helps to work with several individuals who are struggling with a task so designers can see why they are having trouble.

Task-Analysis Field Visit

One of the best ways to learn the art of task analysis is to go into the real world and give it a try. This isn't nearly as difficult as it may seem at first. Designers actually perform task analysis many times a day without thinking about it. A good example might be standing in line to use an unfamiliar ATM. As people work their way up the line, they are actually doing task analysis as they watch those in front operate the machine. Each time one person performs an operation, people in line are observing and remembering how it is done.

As an instructional designer, it is often extremely valuable to place yourself in the role of the potential learner to find out what it feels like to be in a position of not knowing what to do. For example, if you're designing courses for a regional transit agency, make a point of using the automated fare card or token machines to determine if there are any obvious problems for the uninitiated. This point of practice might become obvious quickly if you purchase a fare card without a problem, but can't get it to work in the entry turnstile. You discover there are no markings on the card showing how to slide it through the reader. A designer should always put themselves in the position of being a learner whenever possible.

How Will the Training Be Delivered?

Instructional designers need to determine the distribution methods and instructional methods they will be working with early in their planning, sometimes before really starting the project. It is essential that these two elements be in place before designers get too involved with the design phase. Since both of these variables impact every aspect of a final design, the earlier a discussion and decisions can be made about these issues, the more a designer can concentrate on the nuts and bolts design issues, including objectives and evaluation tasks. There are times when the distribution or instructional approaches, or perhaps both, are determined by a client or other pre-design constraints.

Instructional Strategies

Instructional designers make choices that determine how their learners interact with the subject matter. The designer's tool of matching innovative distribution methods and instructional methods is important. This choice is important because "instructional strategies can help create synergies through relationships between the student and faculty, student and their peers, and student and the process" (Hill and Conceição 2020).

Instructional methods are techniques that designers use to link objectives with learners. Lectures, group discussions, and case studies all serve as the link between the learner and subject matter, much the same way a book or webpage links information with the end user. Distribution methods are the ways designers deliver the instructional methods. Proper matching of distribution and instructional methods and platforms also saves time and energy, both for the designer and the learner.

We should first look at the foundational concept of instructional methods and review the four primary relationships that exist between teachers and learners:
- **Direct Instruction:** Teacher-centered and controlled process of delivering instruction.
- **Indirect Instruction:** Shared information processing involving teacher and learner.
- **Experiential Instruction:** Focuses as much on the process of learning as on the actual content.
- **Independent Instruction:** A learner directs their own course of study under the guidance of a teacher.

Direct Instruction

- **Structured Overview:** This is often referred to as the bullet-point approach and is generally a very basic presentation of content.
- **Demonstration:** In this strategy, a teacher simply demonstrates a process, skill, or procedure for learners. It can be enhanced by dialogue and an opportunity for questions and answers.
- **Lecture:** This is the process of one or more instructors disseminating information to learners. Instructional designers typically use lectures only in combination with other methods. They might use them alone if they have an inspirational facilitator and want to inspire learners. Otherwise, learners will be fighting back yawns and hunger pains while a facilitator is lecturing. With lectures, it is important to have in place the design elements of clear time limits as well as liberal use of visuals or other stimulators.
- **Online Lecture:** This can be designed and produced in many ways, but the general format is to record a presenter delivering a lecture. If the production budget and technology are available, it can be enhanced by visuals like slides, charts, and graphic-pen-generated drawings, transcripts, and notes.
- **Drill:** Keep doing it, doing it, doing it. Drills are used extensively in computer-based training. For example, many programs require learners to enter words or numbers numerous times to complete a sentence or math problem.

Indirect Instruction

- **Case study:** This method moves the learner up the cognitive ladder and requires decisions, either in a group or singularly. Case studies are great ways to provide instruction in cognitive skills like negotiating, facilitating, reasoning, and constructing solutions. Instructional designers must be careful to ensure that the cases are relevant to their learners. If the cases are out of the learner's contextual framework, they are not likely to hold the learner's interest. It is vitally important that the instructor provides complete case studies, not just bits and pieces of a case. Incomplete information can easily turn a case intended to illustrate a marketing challenge into a case solved by the company giving employees two weeks of additional vacation every year. For example, a case study might say that employees were working without any days off, but it might fail to mention that the extra work was because the office was being moved to another building. If the case study doesn't provide complete information, readers may think the problem is overwork, and settle on the solution of extra vacation.

- **Critique:** This is a modified case study approach that requires determining the strengths and weaknesses of a situation or process, then finding a solution. An annual review by a boss is a valid instructional method.
- **Discussion:** In this context, discussion is directed, follows another activity, and creates the environment for interactivity. The discussions may be held by large groups, small groups, buzz groups, or teams. Generally, the discussion should not involve groups of more than than 25 or 30 learners. If size is an issue, the group should be broken down into workable chunks. It is important that instructional designers prepare both the facilitator and learners before any discussion starts so they know what they will be discussing and why. Without direction or preparation, the group may wander off the subject.
- **In-basket:** Learners participate by working through a pile of data sitting in front of them, usually on a desk. They have to make decisions about each item, and the results offer a snapshot of their ability to solve problems. This method usually incorporates a degree of role-play and case-study methods.

Experiential Instruction

- **Role play:** In role plays, learners enact the roles of people placed in various situations in an effort to closely match training with the real world. Role plays are a great way of placing learners in the action of solving a problem or practicing a skill. Instructional designers must be mindful of any issues that could cause problems if they use role playing with a group of introverts or a population facing some physical or emotional challenges. Designers must take the time to prepare both the role and scenario descriptions as well as precise instructions for learners and facilitators.
- **Brainstorming:** This method asks learners to build experience into creativity by developing ideas on a specific subject with other colleagues. It can be tough to pull off and sometimes even tougher to design because it is freewheeling. Brainstorming sessions should never last more than 10 minutes, and facilitators should be given enough ideas for refocusing if the group becomes lethargic. Designers need to accept the fact that brainstorming may backfire on the facilitator and that these sessions have the potential to have a negative impact on the success of the project if the process gets bogged down with political or emotional responses. For example, a group that is working to find new ideas for a marketing campaign may end up blaming engineering for never having the right product available when the market peaks. It becomes important, therefore, that a facilitator be prepared to nudge the group back on track and away from a negative ending.

- **Simulations:** Practice, practice, and more practice. Simulation is one of the best methods for getting learners to practice a skill, process, task, or procedure. It is also great for psychomotor skills. Simulations are the process of performing a task in a safe environment. They are especially helpful for dangerous or expensive tasks. Psychomotor objectives are exercised in simulations because there is no chance of damaging expensive equipment or injuring a participant in a dangerous procedure.
- **Gaming:** Gaming is the process of placing participants in the position of having multiple choices to make in an exercise that borders on real life but provides the safety of a simulation. Just as video games simulate some level of reality, gaming provides the same safe environment without subjecting participants to the dangers of actually performing a task. Some of the best gaming is sophisticated and reaches the limits of technology. Many military applications are right at the corner of reality and surrealism.
- **Critical incident:** This method is used in many training areas that challenge the ability of a learner to react quickly to a problem. Essentially, this is a version of a case study, but it leaves out some of the key data. Airline pilots are subjected to critical incident methods when they simulate flights that develop problems. The extensive use of flight data recorders has allowed the advancement of this method in transportation training.

Independent Instruction

- **Job aid:** This training method pays great dividends in many projects. Job aids are any material that workers keep at hand for easy reference—such as a printed form, cheat sheet, or procedures manual—that contains information on a concept or skill. Since our memory is often unreliable, it is useful to have something in hand that supports the concept or skill involved. Job aids can many times stand on their own and not require any class or technology time to implement.
- **On-the-job training:** On-the-job training (OJT) is probably the most often used instructional method. Some organizations realize they are using it, but others often don't. OJT is intended to be mentoring in its purest form. Instructional designers must ensure that this method does not preclude the use of others.

Other methods that are related directly to technology are computer-based training, multimedia, interactive TV, teleconferencing, groupware, virtual reality, and employee performance support systems (EPSSs). Chapter 11 describes web-based instruction.

Instructional Methods to Avoid

There are several instructional approaches you may want to avoid:

- **Technology first:** This is a common temptation when a new technology becomes popular and there is very little reason to support it being used in training or education. Always ask yourself the design question, "Does this support learning?"
- **Time killer:** This method is usually little more than groups discussing a topic or subject matter with little or no direction by a facilitator. It is typically used to kill time and offers little, if any, instructional value.
- **Directionless learning:** This less-than-productive method usually begins with a statement from the facilitator that the group will decide together what they will be learning. This may have some limited usefulness in ongoing groups, but it generally signals that there has been no planning or instructional design before the course. If the choice is among several instructional paths that have already been prepared, that is fine. Without the planning for options, this method is an abandonment of instructional design principles.
- **Theory boredom:** When complex information and theory need to be taught, the method should be more than just endless talking by one individual. Adults need to have both the context and the background information on why something is important to learn. Visuals and any change of tone or presentation, like drawing on a whiteboard or flipchart, is better than just talking. Make the case for how this information fits in the larger context of a topic and why it is key to mastery of the content.

Types of Distribution Methods

Several distribution methods are widely used for training. The ones presented here are just a starting point for the discussion:

- **Captive audience:** Otherwise known as classroom training, this is the most common way to administer training. It consists of one or more learners with one or more facilitators in a single location using no technologies.
- **Technology enhanced:** This is the name for training that makes use of an overhead projector, a slide projector, or a laptop or computer projector. One or more technologies assist in the implementation of the course.
- **Technology facilitated:** This is referred to by several hundred different terms such as multimedia, computer-based training (CBT), e-learning,

and virtual reality. This method is delivered with the technology, learner, and perhaps a facilitator in one location, with the technology serving the dominant role in facilitation.

· **Distance learning:** This term describes the method in which learners are at one or more different physical locations than the source of the instruction. Teleconferencing is an example of distance learning.

· **Distributed learning:** Home study courses are an example of this method. Training is distributed by a process, such as by mail, that is not related to the implementation.

Other distribution methods include cable television, satellite television, thumb drives, CD-ROM, email, extranet, internet, intranet, local area networks (LANs), simulators, voicemail, and wide area networks (WANs).

Learning technologies may be synchronous or asynchronous. Synchronous learning assumes that the learning and the facilitation take place at the same time. A good example is a chat room on the internet. Everyone is participating in real time, and learners are usually expected to participate at a set time, much as in a regular training course. Asynchronous training allows late sleepers and night owls to participate in training. Learners have a choice of when they participate as one benefit of the technology. Learning is sometimes implemented as an email system or a forum on a computer server.

Half-Life in ISD

One of the most fascinating aspects of instructional design is the fact that work from so many other fields of study has a home in the practice of ISD. One of the best examples of this is the fact that an important aspect of physics is also directly applicable to the analysis process in instructional design when generalized from its original use.

Since the inception of the atomic age, most of us have become familiar with the term *half-life*. It refers to how long half of the atoms in a radioactive substance will continue to emit radiation before they disintegrate into another element. For cesium-137, it is about 30 years. In training and instructional design terms, we are interested in how long it takes for the content, software, delivery system, or other key aspect of a course or program to become obsolete, or at least require updating. It is seldom 30 years like cesium-137; it is more likely to be hours or days for some aspects of many course designs.

While some instructional designers might think that the issue of half-life is a small or even esoteric issue in the design process, experience has shown that ignoring this aspect of course design can date a course and even a large program after a very short period of time. There are numerous examples of courses being implemented today that rely on cloud-based data that is updated every time a course section is run. There are even updates between morning and afternoon sessions in some courses. Examples include programs in environmental science, firefighting, emergency medicine, emergency management, and any other content area you can work with as a designer that contains constantly changing data. As part of any analysis process, take the time to review half-life issues before making any important design decisions.

Technology Half-Life

When thinking about the half-life of technology, learning management systems, apps, and software, you really need to be careful about the implementation issues related to certain design choices. We may be in the age of 5G mobile data access in some areas of the world, but there are areas that still have dial-up access to the internet. Every technology eventually becomes stale and at some point outdated. End-user technology, like operating systems, isn't updated universally by users, and older versions of an app or software might not work with every intended learner.

For example, the half-life of a legacy technology like VHS tape was probably five years or less given the move to DVDs. Now, consider the upgrade to Blu-ray and eventually cloud-based streaming. The same can be said for almost any technology you might decide to use today. It will certainly not remain dominant forever, and it seems that each new generation of technology is viable for a shorter period. This also includes LMS software, since this is a key factor in many web-based technology choices. This obsolescence is particularly noticeable in computer- and web-based instruction. It is not uncommon for the design project to outlast the technology. A designer may, for example, design a computer-based training project on the basis of a certain hardware and software platform that could easily be at least a generation old when it is implemented.

As you consider the half-life of your technology, several key points are probably necessary for you to think about:
- How long has the technology been available?
- Is it a new version of an existing technology or something entirely different?
- What is the typical upgrade and versioning time span?

- Is it growing in usage or lagging behind other similar technologies?
- Is it compatible with current systems?
- Does it contain the features you need in your anticipated course products?

For hardware technology, you will need to consider some of these issues:
- Are there video and screen display variables, such as size and resolution?
- Is it compatible across all required hardware platforms?
- Does it support social media with interactive video and other required features?
- Are there memory storage issues, such as how programs and apps are loaded on a system?

Content Half-Life

The same half-life approach is critical to content. You must determine how long the content in a course or program remains stable before it needs to be updated. In some courses, the half-life might be less than a day and it is necessary to have dynamic programming to allow for databases to be searched for updates on a per-use basis, which might be once a day or once a week depending on how often the course is delivered. Content in this category might be linked to statistical data like hospitalizations, monetary exchange rates, stock quotes, sunrise and sunset, or other constantly changing data points that are critical in a course.

In some topic areas, the useful life of the data is measured in years. This is the case with basic sciences, math, and other well-grounded content areas. This also applies to some soft-skill areas like basic communications and leadership, although influences like social media and any future technologies can necessarily influence course content, too.

It is important to note that this does not apply to all data, but only enough of it to render the training suspect or dated. It may only take one incorrect element of the subject matter to ruin weeks of work by a designer.

To prevent this from affecting a design, designers should ask the following data-decay rating questions for each element of the project that may be affected. As seen in Table 5-1, respond with a rating from 0 to 5 (lowest to highest):
- How critical is the data to the success of the training?
- How likely is it that the data will change?
- How easy is it to update data internally?
- Can learners or trainers easily obtain updated data?

Table 5-1. Data-Decay Rubric

	Data Point	Rating (0–5)
How critical is the content?		
How likely is the content to change?		
How easy is the data to obtain?		
Can learners and facilitators easily update data?		

If the analysis of the decay rating ends up being near the low end of the scale, designers should consider a process that allows for updating. This can be as easy as providing a webpage for updated information or distributing data sheets as necessary. In either case, designers should not assume that a completed project will rest comfortably on the information provided, unless they have determined that to be the case.

Other Common Problems Addressed in Analysis

As a designer works through the details that are almost always part of analysis, they also find that different challenges will often come to the surface as data and information are gathered. Not every project will require these additional analytical approaches, but many will, and having a background in these areas will make things more obvious as you work through the analysis process.

Too Much or Too Little Content

Instructional designers rarely have the luxury of exactly matching the amount of content with the time available for implementation. It is common for designers to have three days of content for a two-hour implementation requirement or 20 minutes of content for an eight-hour window. The first consideration is criticality. This is the most thorough way to determine content choices.

If your time or budget doesn't allow for a formal criticality review, another effective way to solve the "too much content" issue is for the designer to call a meeting of all stakeholders in the training and marshal all the facts and data possible about the training.

At the meeting, the designer should take the following steps toward a consensus on the content:

1. Cluster the data into topic areas.
2. Rank the topic areas.
3. Assign priorities to the data within each topic area.
4. Decide which topics and subtopics cannot be eliminated.
5. Review all topics and subtopics for redundancy.
6. Combine and eliminate subtopics as necessary.
7. Estimate timing on the topic areas and on each subtopic.
8. Map out a project plan and outline each topic with the subtopics underneath it.
9. Delineate the topics and subtopics with time indications so it is obvious which ones will remain using different options.

If too little content remains, designers should review what they have to make sure they aren't missing something. If nothing is missing, they should try breaking the topics down into smaller chunks to see if it is possible to include more. It may also be possible to shorten the implementation time. It is never a good idea to waste a learner's time. Everyone can tell when instructors are stretching content. Designers need to offer realistic expectations for keeping this problem from surfacing.

When Training Is Mandated

Mandated training is an exception to some design approaches since the course or program may be initiated in the absence of the normal analytical design process. Rather than initially determining if a course is built on a platform of need, it may simply be designed based on a legal, organizational, or other type of mandate. For example, a safety course might be mandated by a local ordinance even though employees have already completed a similar course that meets all of the legal requirements. Another example is a court-ordered requirement to take a safe driver course after so many driving violations, even though the violations were not related to a lack of knowledge of the laws. All of these situations require that a designer make sure the usual analysis of available data is performed to ensure that there are no missing elements that impact design.

Designers should think about these specific questions before they move to the design stage with mandated training:

- Has it been determined that there really is a problem, gap, or need that can be addressed?
- Have any problems, gaps, or needs been classified as either training or non-training?
- Do you have enough data gathered to make these determinations?
- Do you have clarity concerning the need for the mandated course?
- What does the target learning population think about having to participate in this training?

One of the most important aspects of designing mandated courses is to determine the motivation issues associated with learners in these courses. Are they on board with taking a course, or should a designer expect some pushback and lack of interest in participating? This information will impact choices in interactivity and consensus building as it relates to how a course is implemented.

Unintended Results Analysis

On the surface, this might be something that most designers never even consider as they work through analysis. However, each new population, unit of content, and learning environment provides new opportunities to create unintended consequences for learners, organizations, and instructors. This is one area of analysis that can save the day in the design process. Let's look at one example that supports this type of analysis.

A designer is asked to prepare a course to deal with the issues of workplace culture as they relate to unprofessional behavior by managers and team leaders in a large for-profit organization. The organization's board of directors expects complaints to fall off and disappear as a result of employees being mandated to attend and complete the course. After doing some quick analysis of data from similar organizations after they implemented such programs, it becomes obvious that there will be a jump in reported cases of unacceptable behavior because the reporting process will be made clear and employees will heed the organization's vow to investigate and act on any valid complaints. If a design were to be evaluated based on the expectation of an immediate decrease in the number of cases reported, there could be some serious repercussions. By performing an unintended results analysis, the designer is able to prepare the organization for the immediate uptick in reports without blame being assigned to the quality of the course.

Fuzzy Logic in Analysis

In 1975, Dr. L.A. Zadeh of UC Berkeley introduced the concept of fuzzy logic to the world. In its most basic form, the concept illustrates that most human reasoning is not very precise at all, but is usually more approximate in nature. Another term usually associated with fuzzy logic is *approximate reasoning*.

It is also true that findings based on limited analysis and data gathering are less accurate than findings based on higher levels of analysis and data gathering. It is logical to assert that analysis that takes only one day will be less accurate than analysis that takes five days if we can stipulate that each day is equally rigorous in terms of work performed. This is an important aspect of fuzzy logic: the more data gathered, the more reliable the data becomes, until at some point you pass a threshold to attain reliability. This will differ for each distinct analytic effort.

The often-used axiom "paralysis by analysis" is definitely not true if there is some level of greater detail being achieved in the analysis process. From my experience, the paralysis comes from the decision makers and not from the analysis process. You can overthink any aspect of ISD, but it is almost impossible to gather too much relevant data in analysis. The decisions are usually made by budget and time allotted rather than level of achievement in the process of analysis. It is within this conceptual framework that some very important mistakes in ISD can potentially be made when analysis is either assumed or given little effort in course development.

Approximate reasoning happens when designers make assumptions or allow stereotypes or other simplistic conclusions to exist as part of an analysis process. One of the most often-used examples of this, including by Zadeh, goes as follows:

Most men are vain—Socrates is a man—therefore is it very likely that Socrates is vain.

Now let's apply this approximate reasoning to an instructional design analysis data point:

People working at a minimum wage job usually have a high-school education or less—my population is working at minimum wage for the organization that is my client—therefore it is very likely that this population has a high-school education or less.

See how this works? In this example, which is not that uncommon a population in a project, we are allowing ourselves to believe the myth concerning education level based on a faulty premise. In some populations, minimum wage is being paid only because the job is an internship, and the population actually has a minimum of an undergrad degree and sometimes a graduate degree or higher. Internships sometimes offer only a stipend, so this logic would allow you to arrive at the faulty conclusion that the population probably has an even lower education level; again, a faulty conclusion.

Let's try another example.

Immigrants working in America can usually speak English—a population under analysis is mostly immigrants—therefore it is very likely that my population speaks English.

This is another faulty assumption that will sink a course before it even starts implementation. You can make no guesses about basic, yet vital, data like language skills. There are populations of learners in large metropolitan areas that may speak 25 or more different languages. To make the assumption that all learners speak English would be a horrible design mistake. Having this data will often change the shape of a course design. Multiple first languages in the population and other variables can also significantly increase the budget for a project.

Jumping to assumptions without enough data is a very dangerous occupational tactic that will often prove to be at the very least faulty and at worst damaging to a designer's reputation. This happens countless times with everything from demographics to motivation. Designers quickly settle on a shaky data point only to find out later that they missed the reality by a large enough margin to impact a project. Every time you work on the analysis element of a project, remember fuzzy logic and the clarity that more data offers you when designing.

Chaos Theory and ISD

Another example of the way that instructional design benefits from other areas of science is the idea that meteorological software designed for predicting weather patterns also helps plan for the unknowns in course design and implementation. If left to chance, many of the best instructional design projects might suffer unnecessary challenges that could have easily been avoided with a very short application of chaos theory.

Chaos theory was first introduced by Dr. Edward Lorenz in the early 1960s. A mathematician and meteorologist, he programmed a computer model to predict weather patterns and make weather forecasts for events like hurricanes more precise. This was completely unheard of at the time. Surprisingly, the more he ran the software using different data strings, the more he noticed that weather data predicted different things based on where and when he entered the data. For example, if he entered data for a weather system off the West Coast of Africa and ran it for results, he would get one prediction. If he ran the data from the same system once it had reached the middle of the Atlantic, he got a different prediction. Anyone who follows the weather during hurricane season is very familiar with the relatively unpredictable nature of these storms, even as little as 24–36 hours into the future. And, from this observation, chaos theory was born.

Edward Lorenz best explained the theory as, "When the present determines the future, but the approximate present does not approximately determine the future."

Smith (in Reed 2016) wrote that "chaos systems exhibit sensitive dependence, determinism and nonlinearity," which indicates that even the most stable system or data are subject to incorrect or unpredictable outcomes. For instructional designers, the truth of chaos theory is that we can never expect to predict the outcomes of our work to a level of complete precision. Even our best work must be seen in the context of chaos and the possibility that something may have changed in our analysis from the time of our data input to the time of design and implementation.

This is a reminder that our assumptions must also be accompanied by a revisit of analysis data and an updating of design approaches and other related design process outputs, like materials, if changes warrant.

Analysis Paralysis

One aspect of analysis that every instructional designer must recognize and avoid is the tendency to want to make sure that every possible molecule of data has been sourced and every possible outcome has been considered. When it becomes impossible to move a course or project forward because of a lack of decisions based on too much conflicting data, you have analysis paralysis. Some use this term too freely, and a small minority of professionals actually fall in love with the term and use it to imply that any analysis is too much analysis.

The reality of instructional design is that there are times when some level of paralysis will enter into your work. It may evolve from one or more of the following reasons:

- The data from analysis is not consistent and therefore deemed unreliable.
- There are limited or unavailable resources to gather the necessary data.
- No one has the authority or political will to make a decision.
- There is little to no support for the project.
- The context or environment of the project has materially changed.
- Analysis results are questioned or deemed incorrect.
- The project was designed to fail or never move beyond the fact-finding stage.

The key questions to ask if you fall into this situation are:

- Have all of the data and information necessary to complete analysis been gathered and reviewed?
- Are there opinions from all viewpoints present in the data?
- Is there any bias or prejudice in the data?
- Are there any constraints that keep the analysis process from being completed?
- Are political or other non-data issues holding up a decision?
- Should the project have ever been initiated?

Possible solutions include:

- Come to a consensus and move to design.
- Table the project until later.
- Do more analysis based specifically on areas of disagreement or questionable data.

There are times when nothing will move a project forward, and it becomes obvious that it is time to regroup and make some higher-level decisions about how to proceed. There is no shame in having to put things on hold, and it is certainly better than ignoring the dissonance and moving ahead with a project that is doomed to be second-guessed. Always take your losses early if they are coming.

Using Key Performance Indicators

Key performance indicators, or KPIs, are goals and objectives that are not directly related to the instructional design aspects of a course or project. They are primarily used to set performance goals and establish specific, measurable milestones and deadlines for established performance indicators. To relate KPIs to instructional design more specifically, you will find these to be one of the more reliable measures to use in gauging return. In the context of the analysis element and workflow, they serve the very useful purpose of attaching specificity to the expected outcomes, and must be based on numerical data.

KPIs may be used in a vertical micro-context, such as a weight-loss program within a business that has a goal of seeing every participant lose 5 percent of their body weight over a six-month period. At the macro level, this same business, which has several programs, a KPI may be reaching a 20 percent year-over-year increase in sales.

Let's look at one way to think about this in ISD terms and how a design will see this process play out.

A client is seeing an uptick in complaints related to a live chat feature on its website that is designed to address basic customer service and repair concerns without requiring items to be returned or replaced. In theory, this chat function should reduce unnecessary repairs and returns of its products since many complaints are related to the operation of the products and not to any actual product defects.

The company is experiencing a 23 percent negative satisfaction rating for the chat function as reflected in post-use surveys. There is also an increasing level of social media chatter about poor service by the company, which seems to be directly tied to frustration with the chat customer service representatives. At the present time, the people participating in the chats from the company are repair techs who have no training or experience in customer service or operating the chat software.

As the instructional designer for the company, you have been asked to prepare a course for the chat staff about basic customer service roles and how to operate the software. As part of the discussion, you have been asked to prepare KPIs to measure whether the training is effective and to set goals and milestones for the project outcomes and impact.

After doing research and looking at the numbers for similar companies in terms of product and chat features, you have determined that a 5 percent or less negative satisfaction rating is a reasonable goal. You also determine that it

DISCUSSION QUESTIONS

- What are the two most important areas of analysis when designing a course?

- In your analysis of a population, you learn that there are many learners who are unable to read at the required level of proficiency in the language used in the course. They are, however, able to read proficiently in another language. How does this impact the design of the course? What options might you suggest to address the problem?

- Do you think an NOP analysis provides sufficient information to design a course in most situations?

- KPIs, or key performance indicators, are being used by an organization for the expected outcomes for a sales course. As you gather more data, you determine that the KPIs are not directly applicable to the content of the course. How do you proceed with analysis and

is reasonable to allow six months after the conclusion of the training to expect to see any tangible decrease in the negatives.

From the design perspective, the KPIs are not traditional design process workflow elements. However, when you are performing analysis for course designs, you will be accessing and using much, if not all, of the same data that you would be using in the design process for the course. It is also important to remember that already established KPIs will provide key information on what content to focus on and how to design evaluation tasks that will most authentically reflect the real world that the learners will experience after the course.

In instructional design, a KPI has to be measurable and reliable before it offers any value, just as an objective has to be observable and measurable. This will ensure that the indicators are indeed more than just opinion or casual observations.

The reason we talk about this in analysis is that this information needs to be determined before any training actually takes place to ensure a reliable point of reference for later measuring results. This is another example of how all the ADDIE elements work together and are not as linear as some people suggest. Gathering benchmark data in analysis is a fundamental workflow component. This is true no matter the content or expected outcomes. There is no reliable form of measuring these types of results without this pre-implementation data.

Some might consider KPIs as benchmarking elements and others will use them as goals; it all depends on the context in which they are placed. Within the world of the instructional designer, KPIs are often discussed, and it is important that a designer and others reach consensus on what each KPI measures and how it will be used. Without this level of specificity, the use of KPIs is less than reliable.

Summary

Analysis is an indispensable element of the instructional design process. Without performing analysis, an instructional designer has no basis for any decisions that are made in the design process. There are different types of analysis used in ISD, the most common being task analysis and population analysis.

CASE STUDY 1

A small community-based nonprofit organization has recently hired a new executive director. The new director has initiated a number of new accounting policies, and there is growing tension and discord with the 20 staff members concerning the changes, including time sheets, per diem requirements, and mileage charges. The new executive director tells the general manager that all of the pushback can be addressed with a four-hour training course for all employees concerning the new policies and forms. The general manager investigates and finds out that there is no operational need for any of the changes and that the new executive director is not really familiar with how nonprofits function since he came from the corporate environment, where requirements were different.

- From the perspective of an instructional designer, what are your suggestions for addressing the perceived training need?
- Are there any course ideas that come to mind that might meet the needs of the executive director and the general manager?

discussing this with the organization sponsoring the course?

- In your analysis of a large population for a safety course, you find that there are more than five languages being used on job sites by different work groups. How do you address this challenge?

CASE STUDY 2

A 500-employee manufacturing company is seeing a sudden decline in the quality and quantity of its support staff's work. The human resources director investigates and learns that the office manager recently changed the office software to a cloud-based system that is completely different than the system that was in place. The new version is designed specifically for a mobile workforce; it uses smartphone apps as well as desktop software and requires the staff to learn two new systems. The office manager chose not to offer the training from the software developer, which was offered at a reduced rate at the time of purchase. It was felt that because the software had a tutorial built in, that was enough to get employees up to speed.

- Given the specifics of this situation, what recommendations can you offer to address the problems in quality and quantity of work now being observed?
- Is it possible that the problems observed in staff are not completely training related?
- Would you rather use the software developer's training or design your own?

CASE STUDY 3

A large solar panel reseller with most of its sales derived from online and direct marketing is seeing a decline in business due to decreased sales from its online division. Several employees have complained informally of the supervisor telling jokes that were inappropriate due to unappreciated sexual or ethnic content. When asked about the decline in sales, the supervisor blamed poor training and the training department's lack of good instructors and courses to use for improving sales. After an investigation by the department director, the supervisor was terminated. Sales have still not regained previous levels after more than three months with a new supervisor.

- What is the first analysis you would conduct to determine the cause of the decline in sales?
- Based on your analysis of the situation, is there a legitimate training need that can be corrected with a new course?
- Is it possible that there is more than one issue at play for the decline in sales and that a training approach might yield some results?

CASE STUDY 4

A small family-owned business operates three doughnut shops in a medium-sized rural community. Year-to-year sales are off by more than 30 percent at one location and the owners are concerned they will start to see declines at the other two locations. Anecdotal information indicates that customers are being treated poorly at the one location with the poor sales. This location has the most stable employee pool and has had the same manager for more than 10 years. How will you determine the reliability of the information and determine a solution if it's true?

- In performing analysis of the situation, what would you want to do and whom would you want to talk with about the issues?
- Is it possible that other factors, such as changing demographics in the location, could be at play in the sales decline?

CHAPTER 6
Design

KEY CONCEPTS

- Design is the controlling element of ISD
- Design plan elements and format in ISD projects
- Course mission statement or rationale as ISD elements
- Defining target populations
- A course description details the tangible elements of a course
- Objectives are a required element in course design
- Evaluation strategy as a process to define mastery
- Participant prerequisites and minimum learner requirements
- Facilitator prerequisites and minimum required teacher skill set
- Deliverables in a design project
- Cognitive loading is used in course design
- The nine events of instruction
- Lesson plan best practices for course design
- Alternative lesson plan sequencing approaches

CHAPTER OBJECTIVES

At the end of this chapter, the learner should be able to:

- Describe the process of design in ISD.
- List the key elements of a design plan.
- Write a design plan rationale.
- Write a design plan population profile.
- Write a course description for a design plan.
- Write terminal and enabling objectives for a design plan.
- Write an evaluation plan for a course.
- Write participant prerequisites for a course.
- Write facilitator prerequisites for a course.
- Prepare a list of deliverables for a design plan.
- Define cognitive loading in the context of course design.
- List each element in the nine events of instruction.
- List best practices for lesson plans.
- List alternatives for lesson plan sequencing.

In the practice of ISD, design is the guiding and controlling function; it is the touchpoint for every aspect of instructional design. Design both provides direction to the design process and contributes the two most important design deliverables—the design plan and the lesson plan. It is in this phase that all the analysis data is reviewed and operationalized for use in the course design. Design also provides the platform for the evaluation process. If ISD were allowed only one element, it would without question be the design element.

As an instructional designer, the majority of your time is spent in one aspect or another of the design element of ISD. From implementing analysis data for use as key design components like objectives, to the writing of design plans and lesson plans, design is the heart and soul of ISD. It is no coincidence that almost every term for the work in this field contains some form of the word *design*. Instructional designers do in fact design instruction, thus the importance and focus on this aspect of ISD. In this chapter we explore why design is so important to curriculum development.

A Systems Approach to ISD

As you review and compare ISD models, you quickly realize that a linear interpretation of the design element would suggest that you start working in design after exiting another element like analysis. You would then appear to move to development, leaving design behind. Nothing could be further from the reality of how instructional design takes place in practice. The design function is the touchstone element that is always engaged and guiding the entire process. From first analysis to final evaluation, design is always present. If ISD were a computer, design would be the central processing unit. Nothing else in instructional design really functions well, or at all, without design.

This is best illustrated using a systems approach view. A diagram of the process looks like Figure 6-1.

The ISD process is design centered, and each element of the system is managed by the design function. Each project will have a somewhat different process and product, which will impact the work done in each element. However, what never changes is the importance of the design function to the other elements in the process.

Figure 6-1. A Systems Approach to ISD

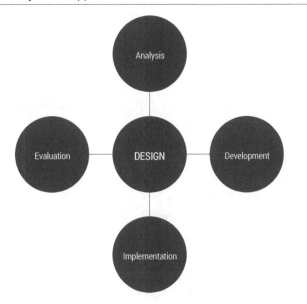

This centralization of the instructional design process evolved from the coordinating and managing role of the instructional designer in the process of curriculum development. This becomes obvious if you attempt to allow analysis, development, implementation, or evaluation to have the controlling interest in the process. All are important, but a single function needs to have ultimate authority and responsibility. This places the design function and the instructional designer in the central coordinating role.

Design Element Functions

With the design functions in the ADDIE model as the center of the process, it is obvious that everything must flow through design at one point or another. Sometimes it is important to visualize the design functions in a project management context to the degree that design requires coordination and staging of assets. Without at least a conceptual foundation of coordination and timing, design loses its value as the nucleus of ISD. This is true if a designer works alone on a project or works with a team of many designers and SMEs; it all requires the same processes.

These are some general functions within the design element:
· Coordinating analysis, development, implementation, and evaluation processes

- Centralizing control and staging assets, including design staff, development staff, and subject matter experts
- Writing design plans
- Writing lesson plans
- Writing objectives
- Writing evaluation tasks
- Coordinating among affiliate design project interests, including clients, sponsors, and other controlling interests
- Quality control of all processes and products
- Pilot testing coordination
- Designing and implementing analysis and evaluation instruments

Another critical aspect of the design phase is the somewhat subtle art of providing leadership throughout the process. An analogy that might fit for this key design role is a traffic cop at a busy intersection. From every direction arrive challenges and decisions that must be addressed, sometimes with very little time for reflection. The designer-leader role shows itself most prominently when the fog is thickest; the depth of a great instructional design is often tested at these moments. This is where a systems approach pays off handily as the emotion of key decisions is banished to the periphery and the logic of the choices sets in and becomes obvious.

> The most obvious analogy is a traffic cop at a busy intersection.

There are very few designers who are not leaders, too, and this is the real strength of the design process. In this phase the decisions are those relating to choices within a range of possibilities. In course delivery it might be a choice between online and blended, and choosing content is aided by criticality and other ISD tools. The seasoned designer in this environment facilitates decisions and designs within the boundaries of the data and choices.

In this chapter we will focus on the two most often used aspects of instructional design—the design plan and the lesson plan. We will look at every aspect of these and provide a completed example of each for you to use as a template. Additional design plan components, including objectives and evaluation tasks, will be covered in the chapters later in this section.

The Design Plan

As you think about the design process and how you are going to capture and share all planning and specifics of a course or project, the best way to reduce all the work to writing is by the use of a design plan. You will find this called many different things, including "executive summary" or "project overview." Regardless of what it is called, this is the working document that outlines every important aspect of a course design. Design plans are the blueprint for everything that takes place in the practice of ISD, from a single simple module to a yearlong design project. Decisions that will impact every aspect of your design and eventual course product are based on this document.

Communicating with internal and external clients, decision makers, boards of directors, and other stakeholders who are funding or managing your project requires a design plan, and it is often the first formal document that they will see. A design plan is the one document that is almost always the main component of a project presentation. Often, it will have a shelf life that is much longer than the project itself. It will also be valuable as the template for future projects and often saves designers many hours of work on future projects if they simply reuse the format and then modify specific elements to fit variables in new courses and projects.

It is often the case that designers are evaluated by their ability to produce a design plan, which is considered a basic skill requirement for hiring a professional instructional designer. Knowing these specific elements of a project and being able to define each in detail is as basic and necessary as a blueprint for an architect. To further expand the comparison, no construction project of any size or detail is attempted without a blueprint. Therefore, no instructional design project or course of any size or complexity should be attempted without a design plan.

As you know, the reality of designing an instructional program goes well beyond just implementing the training, although most outside observers consider implementation the only element that matters. This is because most others outside the design process see only the facilitator, learners, materials, and the tangibles and deliverables of a course or project. They are seldom aware of the hours, days, or months that went into the project from the design perspective. This is another area where a design plan becomes so important. Before, during, and after the observable aspects of the training are implemented, the designer's work is documented in a package of design elements that outlines the basics of the project from the ISD perspective.

A design plan is also the instrument that creates discussion, generates questions, provides options for design and implementation, and allows professional instructional designers to explore as many options as possible in order to provide

> There are very few designers who are not leaders, too, and this is the real strength of the design process.

> Design plans are the blueprint for everything that takes place in the practice of ISD.

REFLECTION

The design element of ISD is considered the nucleus of all the activity that takes place in the process of course design. There is always a design process in ISD even if the other elements are not as extensively engaged.

Do you think it is possible to design quality courses if an instructional designer uses only the design element as they prepare courses?

the best-reasoned and deliberated course and project. Designers must be able to answer all the questions raised by the elements discussed in a design plan and may need to spend more time reviewing specific elements to ensure that they have a well-designed project as viewed by every stakeholder.

Design Plan Elements

These are the minimum suggested elements to include in a design plan (Figure 6-2):

- Rationale
- Population profile
- Description
- Objectives
- Evaluation strategy
- Participant prerequisites
- Facilitator prerequisites
- Deliverables

A detailed description of each of these elements follows. Designers may add other items that are important for their project, and they should modify sections as their projects demand. Nevertheless, it is best to include at least these elements as a minimum to ensure a complete design plan that covers all the bases. For example, designers in the training or education department of an organization may feel that facilitator prerequisites are unnecessary because the facilitators are known, and so they may leave them out of the design plan. There is no right or wrong when it comes to what is included. The important point is that designers have a design plan and that it covers any elements necessary to explain their project fully. Outside of the professional practice of ISD, when some form of design plan exists at all, they are almost always too brief and generic. This is not the place to take shortcuts or to try and to save time.

Figure 6-2. Design Plan Elements

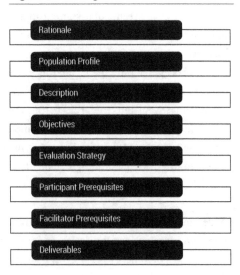

As we work through the design plan elements, we will use a course called Onboarding New Team Members as our content area, and each element of a design plan will be written for this course.

Rationale

A rationale is the mission statement for the project. A designer who can capsulize their project into a short, tightly written narrative has several important pieces of information about the effort and can communicate them to others. First, the designer knows where the project is going. Second, the designer knows how to get there. Third, the designer knows why it is important to go there in the first place. The rationale is comparable to a lawyer's opening statement.

In some design environments this may be called an executive overview, project goals, or executive summary. While specifics may change to some degree from organization to organization, the intent is the same with a rationale: Set the tone for your project and make a case for supporting and implementing it.

While a rationale can range from a paragraph to 30 or more pages, a typical rationale is several paragraphs to several pages long. It should not be a word longer than it needs to be or a word shorter than is necessary to make the case for the project. Let the scope of the project and details be your judge on length and complexity.

Don't be afraid to add research findings, survey results, public opinion polls, historical data, or other forms of information that add credibility to your argument. The more you make the case for the need for a project, the more likely you are to gather support. In many ways, the rationale is a research study related directly to your project. Make the most of this initial design plan element to set the groundwork and tone for your project. Let your academic side come to the surface as you compose a rationale for your project.

The rationale needs to answer several central questions:
- What are the reasons for having the course?
- What population or populations does it serve?
- Who is sponsoring the course?
- What is unique about it?
- Why should anyone participate as a learner or sponsor?

> The rationale is comparable to a lawyer's opening statement.

Rationale for the Onboarding New Team Members Course

Every year our organization hires more than 1,000 new team members; each new employee deserves to be welcomed and brought up to speed on their new employer and necessary work requirements. This onboarding process has previously been organized and administered by our human resources department staff in an unofficial capacity. However, the recent churn in the workforce requires that we find new ways to involve all levels of employees and managers in the process. We will now be offering a 90-minute course that will be required of all new hires within one week of their start date.

Research has shown that onboarding is a key decision point in new hire retention; in our organization alone, more than 65 percent of team members say that their first impression of the organization played a role in their staying for more than three years. It is also true that more than 20 percent of new hire turnover happens within the first 45 days and that more than 90 percent of first-year team members are retained when an organization has an effective onboarding process, including a first week training approach.

Under the direction of the training department, this course offers a unique approach to both welcoming and informing each new team member about key organizational operations; there will eventually be a synchronous online version for remote locations. Facilitators will be drawn from training staff and all departments and managerial levels of the organization.

The design approach for the course ensures that learners will be actively engaged in the course implementation rather than simply listening to a lecture or viewing a video. Participants will be partners in the course process and will also be asked to participate in designing their individual plan for onboarding, which includes milestones and timelines. Since each new team member's situation and location will be different, the dynamics of the course and outcomes will ensure personalization and ownership of the process.

Mastery of the course objectives will be determined by the evaluation of in-class assignments by the facilitation staff. Any participants failing to reach mastery will be mentored and reevaluated as necessary in real time, but failure to reach mastery is not anticipated to be a problem.

Certificates will be provided for all attendees who reach mastery.

This course is implemented in 90 minutes, with actual course time set at 75 minutes. The additional 15 minutes are for housekeeping items, such as sign-up, registration, and a brief welcome from a manager or officer prior to starting. To allow participant interaction and discussion, the anticipated class size is 15 or fewer for each in-person offering.

Cloud-based materials, including handouts, videos, and slides, will be provided for each facilitator via a tablet and either Bluetooth, cellular, or Wi-Fi-based interfaces. A USB flash drive containing these materials will also be distributed as a backup. A one-day train-the-trainer session will be mandatory for each facilitator being certified to implement the course.

Population Profile

The population or end user of a course or program is the moving target in instructional design. It takes analysis, and lots of effort, to make sure you have completely captured the pulse of this group, or everything in your design that follows is resting on an unstable foundation. There is no place in professional instructional design for anything less than a complete read of your populations since it is impossible to write objectives, create evaluation tasks, decide implementation choices, or even create the basic parameters of your course environment, such as language, reading level, and motivation, without this data.

The description of your learners should be all-inclusive; any shortcuts in this aspect of your design plan will be both noticeable and damaging to your design. These population profiles may be as short as several paragraphs, but are often in-depth, months-long analyses that net 50 or more pages of population information for major international programs. It is impossible to have too much data in this element of your work as a designer.

Although everyone involved in a project should be aware of its target population, people still make surprising assumptions about who will attend their courses. Some of these assumptions may be so irrelevant for the true population of the course that, if not corrected, they could ruin any chance that a design could work. For example, for a course in a technical area, designers assumed that their audience would include newly hired, entry-level personnel as well as seasoned veteran technicians or supervisors. However, unless these designers refined the target population early in the process, they would have wasted valuable time and money either by implementing the course to the wrong population or redesigning it at a point that required making major revisions of content and techniques. To avoid that lose-lose proposition, it is important to focus on the target population section of the design plan.

The target population statement must include those aspects of the population that can cause problems from a design perspective. Too much detail is clutter that should be avoided. It is not necessary to hinge design decisions on population elements such as gender and age if they will not affect course content. Designers should stick to the facts that illustrate the population and have the potential to cause them problems.

As designers begin to write the target population section of the design plan, they should close their eyes and picture the audience waiting for the course to begin. If they cannot give a detailed description of that group, they have either a design problem to solve or an open-enrollment situation. Designers should picture a group of people slowly emerging from a dense fog and, as they get closer, begin to add details to what they are viewing. Then, they should write down what they see and add as much detail as the situation demands. In some instructional designs, the population overview can become complex.

Population Profile for the Onboarding New Team Members Course

The population for this course consists entirely of new hires within the organization. This will include a range of occupational titles, from entry-level custodial staff to senior executives. Educational achievement will range from GED to PhD Age mean will be close to 35 and range from 18 to the early 60s; however, it is likely that older employees may join the organization.

English proficiency will range from L1 language capabilities (above eighth-grade reading) and writing skills to L2 (with some reading challenges in English at the eighth-grade level). There are no indications that reading ability or literacy issues will be present in this population to the extent that learner participation or mastery would be affected.

This population will be self-motivated to attend this course, and there are no expected issues of concern with attitude or unwillingness to engage and participate in exercises and discussions. While it is a mandated training course for all new hires, there is no sense that participants will resent having to attend.

> The target population statement must include those aspects that can cause problems from a design perspective.

Description

The description section of the design plan describes the structure of the training. It is here that designers include the basic attributes of the course and the items that will provide detail to the implementation and organizational elements of the course. Depending on the length and detail involved in a project, this may be either several paragraphs or many pages. This element needs to be very specific and detailed since it is the blueprint for later design decisions.

Common elements to consider for the course description are:
- Total course length
- Module length (if appropriate)
- Instructional method
- Materials

Course Description for the Onboarding New Team Members Course

The Onboarding New Team Members course is a 90-minute, in-person, facilitator-led course. Instructional methodologies employed include lecture, small-group activities, learner presentations, and discussions. The room must be compliant with the Americans With Disabilities Act (ADA) and have the capacity to provide computer projection and Wi-Fi. Recommended class size is 15 or fewer participants. Room setup is optional, but it is recommended that each participant have seating with no obstructions to projected media. Materials include documents from the HR department, forms to be completed, numerous handouts, copies of slides, and other materials as deemed necessary.

Objectives

The foundation and direction of the design plan are set under objectives, and everything else builds from them. All the terminal objectives go in this section. At times, the number of objectives may be so large that a designer must list them in an appendix or elsewhere for easy reference. Large projects can easily have hundreds of objectives.

The Terminal Objective for the Onboarding New Team Members Course

Given a presentation, slides, handouts, job aids, and class discussion, the Onboarding New Team Members course participant should be able to complete the process of onboarding, including reviewing and retaining of the organization's mission, values, standard operating procedures, and organizational chart; understanding key facility functions; completing required HR paperwork; determining if any training is required; and establishing organizational accounts without error.

The Enabling Objectives for the Onboarding New Team Members Course
After a presentation with slides, handouts, job aids, and class discussion, the Onboarding New Team Members course participant should be able to:
· Describe the mission and values of the organization.
· List organization and departmental standard operating procedures.
· Establish user account identity, including username and password.
· Complete required HR paperwork.
· List direct supervisor name and contact information.
· List necessary training required for new team members.
· Describe the location of key facility functions, including health and first aid, the cafeteria, and security.

Evaluation Strategy

In the evaluation strategy part of the design plan, designers detail their thoughts behind the evaluation plan; sometimes it helps to give examples of evaluation tasks. It is also important that designers address both the evaluation of learner mastery and the process of designing a course. Here is another area that finds pro-level instructional designers addressing with sufficient detail the rather complex processes that are generally unseen by anyone except another designer.

When addressing the process of evaluating learner mastery in a course, the key is matching the objectives to the evaluation process. The ways to do this are numerous, but the key is making sure that the objective domains are the same for both the objectives and the evaluation tasks. It is also imperative that each evaluation task is observable and measurable, again matching the objective's intent.

The Evaluation Strategy for the Onboarding New Team Members Course

Evaluation of Mastery
This course will use a multimodal Level 2 facilitator observation and peer-to-peer evaluation strategy. With this content mix, it is not necessary to implement a more traditional, quiz-based formal evaluation strategy. Mastery will be determined by several facilitator-led and evaluated exercises and peer interactions.

This will provide both direct and indirect evaluations. It is anticipated that participants should easily be able to meet the course objectives with this strategy since they are not designed to be overly rigorous.

Participants will also complete a Level 1 evaluation to measure their reactions to the course and the training room environment that will later be used to improve any related and required elements of the learner experience.

Evaluation of Design Process
The course design process will be evaluated at every key milestone in the development cycle, including but not limited to the analysis, design, development, implementation, and evaluation elements. Evaluations will be requested and reviewed by all stakeholders, including the design team, subject matter experts, and support professionals. Specific evaluations of implementation will be developed and distributed to facilitators so that they can review the course from their perspective.

Participant Prerequisites

There is no substitute for determining all prerequisites required of a learner in any course being designed. This gatekeeper process describes entry-level competencies that are necessary to prevent learners from being unable to participate on a level playing field in any designed course. Prerequisites may include items like language ability, reading level, previous course, or program completion.

Population-Ranging Technique

When a population changes or if it is a really wide-open learner group, designers can use a tool known as ranging to widen the gate for a course without throwing the prerequisites away. When a designer applies a ranging technique, they are setting the highest and lowest points of entry for participation in the course. A designer then uses these specific data points in the design.

Imagine that you are a designer working on a new word-processing program. The organization is standardizing its software and upgrading it at the same time. There are several objectives for the 90-minute course, and most require prior knowledge of the software's previous version. The dilemma is that many people in the target population have no experience with the software because they have been using a different program in their department.

The designer realizes that the new software is not that much different from the software other departments have been using. For the training course, the designer decides to remove some of the more advanced features of the software and provide a general overview of the new software.

Ranging allows a designer to establish reasonable prerequisites for participants and still provide a path for the learners who cannot meet them. This example shows how ranging would accommodate low-prerequisite learners. Ranging also accommodates overqualified learners.

In the software training example, a small group within the target population has learned the new software on its own. This group does not need the training but does need the certificate to qualify for an upgrade. Ranging can accommodate that population by adding the following paragraph to the prerequisite description:

Participants must have at least six months of experience with any word-processing software that includes mail-merge and label-making applications. Participants with less experience will be required to complete the Basic Features tutorial for the new software before attending the course. Participants with prior experience on the software have the option of completing a short evaluation to receive the course certificate.

Ranging works well in most situations, although it should not be applied in projects that require a very high level of entrance competency or prior certification. In these cases, the level of skills necessary at entry are fixed by the demands of the course.

The Onboarding New Team Members course will have a different type of participant prerequisite description than the software class. Since it includes every new employee, there needs to be a certain amount of ranging to include all variations on the group.

The reality that designers have to accept is that prerequisites are not always honored when implementing courses. It is not unusual to see a facilitator having to lower expectations or to provide training at a lower level based on an attending course population that doesn't meet prerequisites. In these cases, if you have listed your prerequisites and they are not enforced, any associated course mastery or related learner deficiencies can't be blamed on the course design. That's not a small point in expensive design projects that don't meet expectations.

Participant Prerequisites for the Onboarding New Team Members Course
Participants must have demonstrated English language skills at a minimum of a sixth-grade level in both reading and writing. They must also be approved for employment and must have been assigned to a specific department.

Facilitator Prerequisites

Anyone who has ever attended a course that was facilitated by someone who did not have any substantial knowledge of the subject matter knows how important it is to ensure that facilitators meet certain requirements. These prerequisites allow designers to prepare lesson plans and other materials knowing that facilitators meet a necessary skill level. Designers who add this information to their design plan move their work up a notch.

Always be as thorough as possible when listing your facilitator requirements. Even the smallest deficit in required skills can mean that your course implementation takes a hit. Don't be afraid to be honest about expectations of an instructional designer. There are times when these prerequisites are taken personally by those not meeting them, so everything you list in this element must be based on sound principles. As with participant prerequisites, don't expect these guidelines to be followed to the letter for every course or implementation. Just be prepared to gently point out they exist and if implementation fails in any regard based on your suggestions not being followed.

Facilitator Prerequisites for the Onboarding New Team Members Course
At a minimum, the course facilitator must meet or exceed the following criteria:
- A full-time employee of the organization
- A minimum of two years of continuous employment at a level of manager or above
- Documented ability to read and write English at a sixth-grade level or above
- Demonstrated computer skills at the minimum level required to open and navigate slide software
- Completion, with certification, of the eight-hour train-the-trainer program
- Consent of supervisor

Deliverables

In the last section of the design plan, designers specify all the tangible items that will be delivered as part of the project. Deliverables are almost always something that is either in a physical form, like printed reports, or in an electronic form, like files. They can include analytical reports, draft materials, texts, slides, videos, evaluation forms, and even the design plan itself.

The reason that so many designers include deliverables in a design plan is that they represent something that can be reviewed and used for comparison as the course or project moves through design and implementation. Even color choices in slides or materials can be misinterpreted if there is no sample of a color to review. There are times that deliverables will save you lots of time and money that might otherwise be spent in changing course or project elements that were not consistent with the understanding that a client or sponsor had about specific design elements. They also serve as documentation of project milestones and product.

> Deliverables can be used for comparison as a course moves through design and implementation. They can save you lots of time and money.

Deliverables for the Onboarding New Team Members Course
- Analysis report
- Design plan
- Draft and final versions of the lesson plan
- Draft and final versions of participant handouts and information sheets
- Draft and final versions of the evaluation instruments
- Final camera-ready copies of all materials
- Project evaluation reports
- Other reports or materials as requested and agreed

Complete Design Plan for the Onboarding New Team Members Course

Rationale for the Onboarding New Team Members Course

Every year our organization hires more than 1,000 new team members; each new employee deserves to be welcomed and brought up to speed on their new employer and necessary work requirements. This onboarding process has previously been organized and administered by our human resources department staff in an unofficial capacity. However, the recent churn in the workforce requires we find new ways to involve all levels of employees and managers in the process. We will now be offering a 90-minute course that will be required of all new hires within one week of their start date.

Research has shown that onboarding is a key decision point in new hire retention; in our organization alone, more than 65 percent of team members say that their first impression of the organization played a role in their staying for more than three years. It is also true that more than 20 percent of new hire turnover happens within the first 45 days and that more than 90 percent of first-year team members are retained when an organization has an effective onboarding process, including a first week training approach.

Under the direction of the training department, this course offers a unique approach to both welcoming and informing each new team member about key organizational operations; there will eventually be a synchronous online version for remote locations. Facilitators will be drawn from training staff and all departments and managerial levels of the organization.

The design approach for the course ensures that learners will be actively engaged in the course implementation rather than simply listening to a lecture or viewing a video. Participants will be partners in the course process and will also be asked to participate in designing their individual plan for onboarding that includes milestones and timelines. Since each new team member's situation and location will be different, the dynamics of the course and outcomes will ensure personalization and ownership of the process.

Mastery of the course objectives will be determined by the evaluation of in-class assignments by the facilitation staff. Any participants failing to reach mastery will be mentored and reevaluated as necessary in real time, but failure to reach mastery is not anticipated to be a problem.

Certificates will be provided for all attendees who reach mastery.

This course is implemented in 90 minutes, with actual course time set at 75 minutes. The additional 15 minutes are for housekeeping items, such as sign-up, registration, and a brief welcome from a manager or officer prior to starting. To allow participant interaction and discussion, the anticipated class size is 15 or fewer for each in-person offering.

Cloud-based materials, including handouts, videos, and slides, will be provided for each facilitator via a tablet and either Bluetooth, cellular, or Wi-Fi-based interfaces. A USB flash drive containing these materials will also be distributed as a backup. A one-day train-the-trainer session will be mandatory for each facilitator being certified to implement the course.

Population Profile for the Onboarding
New Team Members Course

The population for this course consists entirely of new hires within the organization. This will include a range of occupational titles, from entry-level custodial staff to senior executives. Educational achievement will range from GED to PhD. Age mean will be close to 35 and range from 18 to the early 60s; however, it is likely that older employees may join the organization.

English proficiency will range from L1 language capabilities above eighth-grade reading and writing skills to L2 with some reading challenges in English at the eighth-grade level. There are no indications that reading ability or literacy issues will be present in this population to the extent that learner participation or mastery would be affected.

This population will be self-motivated to attend this course, and there are no expected issues of concern with attitude or unwillingness to engage and participate in exercises and discussions. While it is a mandated training course and required of all new hires, there is no sense that participants will resent having to attend.

Course Description for the Onboarding
New Team Members Course

The Onboarding New Team Members course is a 90-minute, in-person, facilitator-led course. Instructional methodologies employed include lecture, small-group activities, learner presentations, and discussions. The room must be compliant with the Americans With Disabilities Act (ADA) and have the capacity to provide computer projection and Wi-Fi. Recommended class size is 15 or fewer participants. Room setup is optional, but it is recommended that each participant have seating with no obstructions to projected media. Materials include documents from the HR department, forms to be completed, numerous handouts, copies of slides, and other materials as deemed necessary.

Objectives

The Terminal Objective for the Onboarding
New Team Members Course

Given a presentation, slides, handouts, job aids, and class discussion, the Onboarding New Team Members course participant should be able to complete the process of onboarding, including review and retention of the organization mission, values, standard operating procedures and organizational chart; understanding key facility functions; completing required HR paperwork; determining if any training is required; and establishing organizational accounts without error.

The Enabling Objectives for the Onboarding New Team Members Course

After a presentation with slides, handouts, job aids, and class discussion, the "Onboarding New Team Members" course participant should be able to:

- Describe the mission and values of the organization.
- List organization and departmental standard operating procedures.
- Establish user account identity, including username and password.
- Complete required HR paperwork.
- List direct supervisor name and contact information.
- List necessary training required for new team members.
- Describe the location of key facility functions, including health and first aid, cafeteria, and security.

The Evaluation Strategy for the Onboarding New Team Members Course

Evaluation of Mastery

This course will use a multimodal Level 2 facilitator observation and peer-to-peer evaluation strategy. With this content mix, it is not necessary to implement a more traditional, quiz-based formal evaluation strategy. Mastery will be determined by several facilitator-led and evaluated exercises and peer interactions. This will provide both direct and indirect evaluations. It is anticipated that participants should easily be able to meet the course objectives with this strategy since they are not designed to be overly rigorous.

Participants will also complete a Level 1 evaluation to measure their reactions to the course and the training room environment that will later be used to improve any related and required elements of the learner experience.

Evaluation of Design Process

The course design process will be evaluated at every key milestone in the development cycle, including but not limited to the analysis, design, development, implementation, and evaluation elements. Evaluations will be requested and reviewed from all stakeholders, including the design team, subject matter experts, and support professionals. Specific evaluations of implementation will be developed and distributed to facilitators so that they can review the course from their perspective.

Participant Prerequisites for the Onboarding New Team Members Course

Participants must have demonstrated English language skills at a minimum of a sixth-grade level in both reading and writing. They must also be approved for employment and must have been assigned to a specific department.

Facilitator Prerequisites for the Onboarding New Team Members Course

At a minimum, the course facilitator must meet or exceed the following criteria:
- A full-time employee of the organization
- A minimum of two years continuous employment at a level of manager or above
- Documented ability to read and write English at a sixth-grade level or above
- Demonstrated computer skills at the minimum level required to open and navigate slide software
- Completion, with certification, of the eight-hour train-the-trainer program
- Consent of supervisor

Deliverables for the Onboarding New Team Members Course
- Analysis report
- Design plan
- Draft and final versions of the lesson plan
- Draft and final versions of participant handouts and information sheets
- Draft and final versions of the evaluation instruments
- Final camera-ready copies of all materials
- Project evaluation reports
- Other reports or materials as requested and agreed

The Lesson Plan

A lesson plan is a detailed guide to facilitating a course. It is created by an instructional designer for implementation by a qualified facilitator. It is directly linked to a design plan and is considered mandatory by most if not all organizations that employ ISD and instructional designers in preparing courses. They are based on a number of very well-respected and time-tested theoretical schools of learning, and while they are initially complicated to learn, seasoned instructional designers can easily build a lesson plan from a design plan's blueprint.

You may have heard it called an instructor's guide, teaching guide, course plan, or one of dozens of other terms. However, most instructional designers, especially those not formally trained in the field, have spent very little time thinking about how lesson plans should be designed. There is a great deal of theory and design experience just below the surface when lesson plans are developed using the Nine Events of Instruction format, which we will explore in depth in a later chapter.

Most instructional designers would agree that the single most important aspect of any course design is to see that each learner achieves mastery. It is equally important that learners are able to migrate a skill or concept from the classroom or desktop to application in their lives. To optimize the transfer of knowledge, learners must be able to input, apply, and receive feedback on content in a way that provides a cognitive path to storage in long-term memory. Without this transfer to long-term memory, mastery is short-lived. This is where lesson plan design becomes important.

From the back of a napkin to an outline penciled on a sheet of graph paper, numerous designs for lesson plans have evolved over the last 50 years. Sometimes facilitators and designers claim that their lesson plans have roots in a theoretical base, yet they don't reflect even the basics of cognitive theory or a foundation like the Nine Events of Instruction. In reality, most non-ISD lesson plans are the product of honest efforts that unfortunately fall well short of reaching professional standards for course delivery.

Learning Approaches and Differences

If you want to start a spirited debate in the world of instructional design, ask which learning theorist bests reflects the real world of training and education. Malcolm Knowles, Elwood Holton, Richard Swanson, Donald Norman, William Bechtel, and Dedre Gentner, among hundreds of others, will find support in the way they view and appraise the process of learning and its social, economic, and environmental factors.

If you want to further fan the flames of opinion with a toss-up question on which learning approach works best with adults, add the terms *behaviorist* and *constructivist* to the mix. This is sure to get things going, especially if you add the additional aspect of online versus classroom-based learning environments. To ensure complete chaos, suggest that social media will soon clear the trail for new and more immediate and personal forms of learning.

These conversations are enjoyable, and someone will often point out the limitations and fine points of each aspect of the topic. However, in the end, the work of an instructional designer centers on what actually works in a particular population and other implementation variables, and not what a theorist says should work. This opens the door for the work of Robert Gagné and the events of instruction approach to designing lesson plans.

Cognitive Loading

To best appreciate the work of Gagné, it is necessary to put the Nine Events of Instruction into a process-based schema that relates directly to how humans remember information and skills (everything, in fact) and how this supports mastery and the ability to learn and retain content. Unless a learner can later repeat a skill or remember content, there is no real value to teaching. The process for creating long-term memory events is based on a very simple system of input, processing, and storage. Rehearsal is key to moving content from working memory to long-term memory; this is one of the major building blocks of the nine events, which follow this process step-by-step:

- You present content.
- Learners practice content and receive feedback, and this aids encoding to long-term memory for use later.

A similar physiological function is muscle memory, which also includes processing through learning, practicing, and encoding (Figure 6-3).

The Nine Events of Instruction

All theories and intellectual discussion aside, the work of Gagné, Briggs, and Wager (1988) is the best source for background information on lesson plan design that works. This approach supports the notion that learners are more likely to retain the concepts, skills, and procedures taught to them if they are presented in a way that enhances and supports memory functions and moves

Figure 6-3. Memory Formation

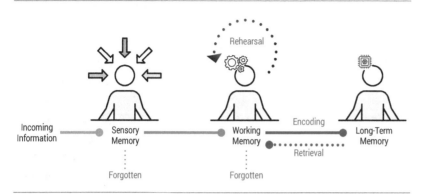

Adapted from Atkinson, R.C., and R.M. Shiffrin. 1968. "Human Memory: A Proposed System and Its Control Processes." In Spence, K.W., and J.T. Spence, *The Psychology of Learning and Motivation*, Volume 2. New York: Academic Press.

information from immediate experience and short-term memory to long-term memory in a way that allows for easy retrieval as needed.

Researchers have been studying human cognition and memory storage function for years. For instructional designers, the process of operationalizing this process is the important concern. The very essence of the designer's role is making sure learners leave with demonstrated mastery of objectives. The Nine Events of Instruction join theory and practice in a way that can be used in most design situations.

The nine steps in this process and each so-called event have a critical instructional design component. The nine events have application in lesson plans beyond lecture and other traditional delivery modalities. Every training program must be based on the way the learner processes information, or it just will not work. The nine events are universal in their importance to instructional design.

There are as many variations on the nine events as there are instructional designers. Gagné was said to have considered differing numbers of events in his years of work at Florida State, as reflected in conversations with his colleagues. The important part of this approach is that there is a process for moving content from short-term to long-term memory; the specifics are up to the designer. Certainly, online and distance learning environments challenge the nine events for no other reason than feedback is different without an ever-present and engaged facilitator. For the purposes of this text and the learning process, we will use all nine events with the understanding that designers will find a balance that works for their specific design environment.

Sometimes it is useful for a designer to think about the nine events as nine separate and distinct boxes of information and process that build to support the final goal of learner mastery of content. Each of the nine events must be viewed as a separate entity for the design to have validity. Each builds on the preceding events, and to change the order or to eliminate one of the events makes the design unbalanced and incomplete. This is true for every variation in course design, from classroom to online learning. The nine events mimic how a learner inputs information and then moves it first to short-term memory and then long-term memory. There is no valid way to redesign learning, which is why it is so important to be comfortable with these elements and the order in which they are used in design.

Figure 6-4 depicts the Nine Events of Instruction, also listed with my terminology to make them more descriptive of their current usage, and Gagné's original title in parentheses. (Gagné approved these wording changes, at my request.)

The Nine Events of Instruction:
- Gaining Attention
- Direction (stating objectives)
- Recall (recall of prerequisite information)
- Content (presentation of new material)
- Application Feedback Level 1 (guided learning)
- Application Feedback Level 2 (eliciting performance)
- Application Feedback Level 3 (feedback)
- Evaluation (assessment)
- Closure (retention and transfer)

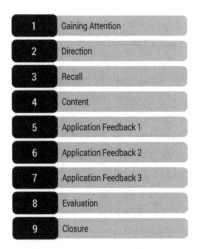

Figure 6-4. The Nine Events of Instruction

1	Gaining Attention
2	Direction
3	Recall
4	Content
5	Application Feedback 1
6	Application Feedback 2
7	Application Feedback 3
8	Evaluation
9	Closure

Nine Events Repackaged

It is also possible to take a more traditional approach to lesson design and arrange the nine events into three categories (Figure 6-5), which most people would view as a viable way to assemble a course.

Figure 6-5. The Nine Events Repackaged

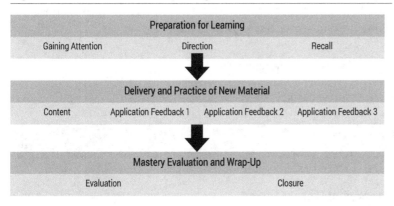

In that approach, the categories would follow this format:

A. Preparation for Learning
    1. Gaining Attention
    2. Direction
    3. Recall
B. Delivery and Practice of New Material
    4. Content
    5. Application Feedback Level 1
    6. Application Feedback Level 2
    7. Application Feedback Level 3
C. Mastery Evaluation and Wrap-Up
    8. Evaluation
    9. Closure (enhancing transfer)

A Detailed Examination of the Nine Events

A more detailed description of each of the nine events demonstrates how each element works with the others to move a learner to mastery of content. This deeper dive into the connection of the elements and the part each plays in creating learning events creates a foundation for how this seemingly complex nine-part learning framework is actually very logical and efficient.

Think of the nine events as an assembly line for learning. Each of these nine elements relies on the rest to build a complete learning package that moves each learner to mastery. This incredibly efficient method for designing courses is a perfect example of the systems theory axiom that the end result is always greater than the sum of each element. It is the connection and sequencing of these elements that make the magic happen. Let's see how this works by looking at the nine events as a system for learning.

Figure 6-6 shows how the nine events look.

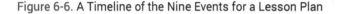

Figure 6-6. A Timeline of the Nine Events for a Lesson Plan

Preparation for Learning

The first three events prepare students to begin the process of learning new content and also provide them with a review of prerequisite information before any new content is delivered. These three steps alone separate the nine events lesson plan approach from other delivery designs.

Gaining Attention

In the beginning of a course, it is necessary to help learners focus on the course. Sometimes gaining attention means setting a tone for the course, whereas other times it means turning off outside interference that is rumbling through a learner's mind. In all cases, the attention-gathering process needs to relate to the topic. A funny story or a joke is not a good attention-getting method as a rule because it can prove distracting, unless a facilitator is certain that it refers to the topic and presents it in a way that is not offensive to the learners.

Here are some methods for gaining attention that have proven effective:
- Playing video or audiotapes of one minute or less on the topic
- Having a demonstration, such as modeling the task participants will learn in the course
- Role playing, particularly for addressing affective and interpersonal domain objectives, such as sexual harassment and workplace violence

Designers should not attempt to start a training program without knowing how facilitators will gain participant attention. Designers should let their imaginations go as they search for a way that will start their course with an attention-getting bang. For example, consider how designers might use a video to gain participant attention during a safety course that focuses on the increased risks of injury if proper safety procedures are not followed.

The facilitator says, "We are going to open our course with a short video highlighting the risks of injury that workers face in certain situations. The workers shown in the video are undoubtedly hard workers like all of us, but safety takes no holidays, and this is a good example of what might happen."

Show the video: a one-minute depiction of an accident that injures several workers during routine work.

Ask participants what they observed. The facilitator reiterates the video's point about using proper equipment and procedures.

Close by saying, "I think we can all agree that following safety procedures are necessary for every worker's well-being. None of us wants to be injured or killed on the job."

Direction

The presentation of objectives is a crucial factor in setting the framework for meeting the course objectives. Objectives set the destination so that learners will have a map that shows them where they're going.

Sometimes facilitators or designers say that they want learners to surmise the objectives or that the objectives should be a surprise. Some facilitators or designers ask learners what they would like to learn in a course. If there are any examples of instances in which these methods are successful, they are rare indeed! Objectives are the nucleus of all other aspects of instructional design.

Designers should state their objectives in a way that works for their audience. At this stage, they have already completed the audience analysis, which provides the direction for designing the objectives.

For the worker safety lesson example, the designer needs to set the direction for the participants early in the course. Stating the objectives in the second event acts as a stabilizing force in the lesson plan. The designer would take the time to think through what they want the learners to be able to do and what they should be able to do at the end of that particular session. Here is one approach to the presentation of objectives the designer might take:

"The risks of injury on the job are a matter of life and death. They involve every one of us. Before you leave, you should be able to identify the potential risks of injury you face on the job. You should be able to demonstrate how to conduct checks for unsafe conditions. You should be able to describe how to report unsafe working conditions to a supervisor or union representative."

Recall

To set the context for the objectives, a facilitator must prime learners for the new material by following the three warm-up elements—that is, gaining attention, direction, and recall. It often takes a little bit of information to get learners thinking about the course content and objectives.

In some cases, the recall session may end up being technical, to assure the facilitator that participants are ready to move to the new material. Other times, it may be no more than a simple question or discussion that builds the foundation for the information that follows.

This element levels the playing field for the facilitator. Depending on content and course design, participants who lack the necessary competencies need assistance. A simple solution that works with some designs is to provide a handout or give a brief review. A more thorough review may be necessary if there is a large gap in knowledge or enough of the participants are having problems with the prerequisites.

Designers need to think through this aspect of their design. Effective designs build in options for the facilitator that allow adding information as necessary once a group's level of competency is determined. For example, a designer could prepare to give participants handouts with prerequisite content as well as hold a group discussion that covers the content. The discussion would work well in affective and interpersonal domain objectives.

A facilitator who finds that one or more of the participants appears to be struggling with the prerequisite information could distribute a basic handout to provide them with a reference for the rest of the module. However, a facilitator should be aware that such handouts, although they enlighten some, may bore others who are somewhat familiar with the subject matter and find prerequisite information as stimulating as reading yesterday's paper for the second time.

If a facilitator determines that one or more of the participants is competent enough to assist them with the class, they should sign them up for that role. Those participants could circulate through the room, answering questions as necessary.

A pretest for review is a sound design practice. Instructional designers who are unsure of their population's entry competencies should screen potential participants before they attend a course, not after they arrive and expect to participate.

Delivery and Practice of New Material

It is now time to cover the course content and allow students to practice and receive feedback in a safe learning environment. These four elements are the core mechanism for supporting the transfer and storage of the new content into long-term memory.

Content

How content is presented has more impact on learners than any other facet of the design. Implementation is about presenting new material in a way that ensures that learners meet objectives. Designers can be as creative as they wish just as long as they balance this creativity with what their analysis has told them about the learners.

Designers who are presenting highly technical training that resides predominantly in the cognitive domain need to strike a balance between mandated content and its numbing effect on the learners. They must find a way to make everything interesting. Their projects will be different when it comes to content. They must use their imagination to its full advantage and choose presentation modalities that interest the learner and make the most of the resources available. Following is one example of how to do it:

The instructor may say, "You know your job like the back of your hand, right? So, tell me where the danger is in this picture. All of the pictures you're about to see show areas where there were unsafe working conditions. Some of the problems are more obvious than others. All the accidents were preventable. These pictures are also in your handouts."

Application Feedback Level 1

Instructional designers like to use interactivity when building a course. It is almost as if they have an overwhelming need to allow and encourage participation by learners. To be effective, interactivity should not be a question tossed out into the room and batted around until something emerges. Designers need to shape and build momentum to keep learners engaged. Application feedback is the point at which designers can give the facilitator and learner an opportunity to begin practicing skills or discussing concepts critical to meeting lesson objectives.

In this first level of application feedback, it is essential that the facilitator and learners share equally in the process. One excellent way to do this is to have a large group discussion that involves working through a problem or discussing a concept. It is important that the facilitator involve as many participants as possible in the discussion and draw in those who are holding back. Learners need to have a comfortable environment in which to ask questions. They also need to feel safe enough to experiment and ask a question that, in another environment, they may not ask for fear it would seem ridiculous.

Application Feedback Level 2

Individual performance and practice in a safe environment are the main benefits of this event. Learners should now be able to test the waters of the new material. Generally, this portion of the training is built around small-group activities. It is important that learners have an opportunity both to offer and to receive information at this point.

> Learners need to have a comfortable environment in which to ask questions.

Designers who want interactivity can make it happen during this stage. They should find ways to invite learners into the subject matter and offer a low-level evaluation by both the facilitator and other learners. At this stage, learners are largely on their own and receiving feedback from other learners and the facilitator.

By working in pairs or small groups, learners may ask questions of each other that they might not ask of a facilitator. Designers must provide an easy path from the small group to the facilitator so that learners who are unable to find an acceptable answer among themselves can go to the facilitator for answers and clarification as necessary.

Application Feedback Level 3

It is impossible for learners to reach mastery if they don't receive any feedback about how they are doing. This element serves as a learner's friend and partner in training. Avoiding this element produces weak training in both stand-up and technology-driven areas. No substitute exists for midcourse corrections in the learning process. A learner should never be allowed to get to the end of a training event without being given any information related to whether they reached mastery.

Designers must make sure, through the objectives, that each learner will get enough feedback about progress to allow correction of any uncertainty or error. A facilitator, another learner, or even a computer could deliver this information.

There are many ways to provide this feedback, and each design's specific objective domains, time limitations, level of difficulty of content, learner variables, and other factors influence each designer's approach. One of the true tests of a good designer is how they determine the best feedback scheme for a given project.

In the safety example, course participants can review diagrams of their work areas to identify danger spots. A course like this demonstrates how important it is that learners meet objectives. An uncorrected mistake at this point may never get corrected and could eventually have life-threatening repercussions for the learner if an accident occurred.

When thinking about the application feedback elements, it sometimes helps to establish a learner-ownership ratio for the process (Figure 6-7). In other words, what percentage of the ownership or responsibility for the learning should a learner have in each of these elements? An ideal ratio in application feedback level 1 is 70 percent instructor and 30 percent learner. This requires the instructor to have the responsibility for the process but requires a learner to also participate. This often manifests itself in large group discussions or working through exercises as a group with the facilitator in the lead.

Application feedback level 2 is usually a 50-50 ratio, with the instructor and the learner equally engaged in the process and the learner now taking more responsibility. Many times, you will see small group discussions, case studies, or role plays in this element because the instructor and learner share the responsibility for the process.

The application feedback level 3 element now shifts responsibility to the learner, with the facilitator on the sidelines observing and answering questions or correcting errors in content as necessary, but not leading the process. This is where you see presentations by groups or individual learners with the facilitator offering comments or suggestions as feedback. A ratio of 90 percent learner and 10 percent facilitator activity is ideal.

Figure 6-7. Learner to Facilitator Ratio

This portion of the training is built around small-group activities.

The application feedback level 3 element shifts responsibility to the learner.

Wrap-Up

It is now time to close the learning event by evaluating mastery at a more formal level and bringing closure to the experience while also preparing learners for what may follow.

Evaluation

At this point in a lesson plan it is necessary to measure mastery in learners. This must be accomplished using a Kirkpatrick Level 2 evaluation. This is different than the application-feedback elements in that it is the final opportunity for the learner to demonstrate mastery after having participated in the three informal practice and mentoring elements.

No learner should leave a training course without passing through an evaluation. This event doesn't always entail a test or other formal event; it may just require a check-off ensuring that the learner has met the objectives. But every objective has to have a Level 2 evaluation or it isn't worth having as an objective. This is the basis of the performance agreement principle. Objectives have to match evaluation tasks, and it is impossible to match these two if one is missing.

Evaluation needs to be a step above just providing feedback to the learner. It is easy to deliver the evaluation in designs that include a formal evaluation, such as a final test or certification exam. Designers need to find other ways of providing this feedback if they do not plan on offering an exam. For example, for a training program for a sales staff, designers might have a learner simulate closing a sale with a client. They can determine any remaining rough spots and provide the learner with any additional assistance needed to meet the project objectives.

There are several ways that designers could create the final evaluation for the safety class. One way would be for learners to describe to all members of the class the risks in their jobs and present a safety plan to reduce them. This provides one learner with an evaluation and the other learners with ideas that had not been presented before. Most important, the facilitator has the opportunity to comment on the learner's progress and correct any problems that remain.

Closure

During closure, instructional designers need to review the objectives and provide a recap for learners. It is important that learners appreciate the progress they have made and realize that they have met the objectives presented to them at the beginning of the course. The satisfaction of charting progress cannot be overstated. To accomplish these ends, designers have to provide the following information during closure:

Information about any course elements that follow: Those elements might be the next course in a series or an optional add-on that is being offered. It is vital that the design provide a path to anything that follows. This path is not only for continuity, although it does provide that assistance, but also for prerequisite information so learners know what to expect next. If they need to prepare any materials or read anything before attending the next course, they have the necessary information to do that.

Generalizing information about the knowledge, skills, or abilities provided in the course: If the content deals with learning to use a two-quart pot for boiling potatoes, the facilitator might generalize by pointing out that the pot also works for making soup or by explaining two different ways to cook using the same pan. To take another example, in designing a course for attorneys about the communication skills for presenting opening arguments, a designer might generalize by showing that attorneys can also use that skill in closing arguments. At a communications level, only the words change, not the process of presenting.

Synthesizing or finding ways to change the context of the learner's knowledge, skills, and abilities (KSAs): This skill is to help learners find application of the objectives in a different frame of reference. In the pot example, synthesizing would mean using the pot for catching rainwater. In the attorney communication example, it might mean using that communication skill to argue for a refund at a department store. Synthesizing is important for expanding the dimensions of the objectives. Once designers have moved the learner to the target objectives, they can really expand the value of the course.

In the safety example, learners might generalize by encouraging other staff members to look at photographs for dangers in their work areas and at home. The skill has not changed, but it is being generalized to include other areas where workers might confront safety issues. Changing the context of the objectives in this course might mean using a map of the learner's house and expanding it to include other danger zones. This is really using ISD to maximize the impact of the course.

> Synthesizing is important for expanding the dimensions of the objectives.

Offering Options for Nine Events Sequencing

There are content areas and design demands that are better met by offering options for the way the nine events are presented. This is often the case when a designer wants to break up the content into small segments and have a period of application and feedback before moving on to more content. There are several ways to address this, and both of the following options are perfectly acceptable.

Option one is to have content followed by an application feedback 1 element. This is repeated until all content is covered, and then the application feedback 2 and application feedback 3 elements are presented for all the content. Figure 6-8 is how the option looks.

Figure 6-8. Feedback Sandwiched Between Content

In this approach, the application feedback element 1 is only for the content area directly in front of it. The application feedback 2 and application feedback 3 elements cover all the content for the course.

The other option is to present a content element followed by both application feedback 1 and application feedback 2 until all that content is offered, then have a final application feedback 3 that covers all content. It would look like Figure 6-9.

Figure 6-9. Content Followed by Feedback

In this approach, the application feedback elements 1 and 2 following the content are only for those specific content areas. Application feedback 3 will cover all content in your course. The important design element in either of these variations is that you have to have all three application feedback elements for all content or the value of the design approach and the nine events is eroded.

Lesson Plan Mistakes

Designing a lesson plan for use by a facilitator is one of the most important design challenges you will encounter because it is such an obvious deliverable for any course development project. While most non-designers never see the usual design products, like a design plan, facilitators and learners are directly impacted by the quality of your lesson plan design, and a facilitator's ability to teach a course is tied directly to your choices.

Common mistakes made in lesson plan design are easy enough to avoid or correct; you just need to know what they are and how to address them. Here are the top mistakes for each of the nine events:

Things to Avoid in Gaining Attention
- Do not include introductions of learners or guests. Complete these before starting this element.
- Do not take attendance. Complete this before starting this element.
- Do not perform housekeeping. Complete this before starting this element.
- Do not include unrelated events or activities.

Things to Avoid in Direction
- Do not provide information or have any activities that are not directly related to presenting the course objectives.
- Do not present any course content, new or old.

Things to Avoid in Recall
- Do not present any information that is not directly related to the recall of prerequisite content.
- Do not present any new content since you are preparing the foundation for the new content, which starts in the next element.

Things to Avoid in Content
- Do not include any recall or other unrelated information here.

Things to Avoid in Application Feedback 1
- Do not present any new information except for content that is just additional detail to already presented content.
- Do not include any lectures or facilitator-only activities.

Things to Avoid in Application Feedback 2

- Do not present any new content except for content that is just additional detail to already presented content.
- Do not include any lectures or facilitator-only activities.
- Do not just continue with application feedback 1. This is a new application feedback cycle.

Things to Avoid in Application Feedback 3

- Do not present any new content except for content that is just additional detail to already presented content.
- Do not include any lectures or facilitator-only activities.
- Do not just continue with application feedback 1 or 2. This is a new application feedback cycle.

Things to Avoid in Evaluation

- Do not have any activity that is not related to a Kirkpatrick Level 2 evaluation of the course content for mastery.
- Do not leave this element until the learners each know if they reached mastery.
- Do not distribute Kirkpatrick Level 1 evaluations. Hold these until after the course is closed.

Things to Avoid in Closure

- Do not present any new content.
- Do not present any evaluations. Kirkpatrick Level 1 evaluations should be distributed after the course ends.
- Do not present awards, certificates, or other non-course-related activities until the end of this element.

Designing Lesson Plans for Facilitators

Facilitators are the key variable in any instructional design project. A facilitator may also be called a teacher, lecturer, discussion leader, professor, or any of a hundred different titles for the same function depending on the environment and practice within a learning environment. Facilitation also exists in distance learning and other distributed learning systems. The key factor to remember as an instructional designer when designing lesson plans is that facilitators must be given the right tools to make your design come to life and be successfully implemented. The more information you provide a facilitator in your lesson plan, the more likely they are to be successful.

For example, no one likes to get lost while driving. For many people, getting lost evokes feelings of aggravation and stress, and those feelings are only intensified if they are also late. Designers should keep this in mind when they are working on a training project. If they fail to offer facilitators all the information they need to implement the project, they will get lost. The stress associated with facilitating a misdirected training course can have disastrous effects on both the facilitator and the participants.

It is sometimes worse to get skimpy directions than none at all. Right now, a distressed trainer is sitting over coffee somewhere wondering how to deliver an eight-hour course from a two-page outline.

The facilitator is as vital to the success of a design project as any other element. The more information designers can provide facilitators, the more likely they are to succeed. Lesson plans must be complete enough to allow anyone with the necessary subject matter experience to lead the course.

One of the first things designers need to consider as they approach the lesson plan stage of their design work is who their facilitators are. They should consider the following:

- Can a range of experience within the pool of potential facilitators be identified?
- Are there any special issues to address, such as language or culture concerns? Will the facilitators require materials in a second language?
- Does the lesson plan allow facilitators to lead the course in a culturally appropriate way?

The information about the facilitators should appear in the design plan because it aids in the development of the lesson plan.

The Format of the Lesson Plan

Every lesson plan needs to have a format that lends itself to making the implementation of the course as simple as possible. Designers need to use a consistent format if there will be a series of courses. Some stylistic elements that allow for an easy transition from one course to the next include the ideas presented in the following sections.

Each of the nine events is covered in a separate section of the plan, and the title of each usually gets distinctive visual treatment.

In the final plan, the name of each event appears in a box along with the suggested time needed for implementing that event. Designers may choose different labels for the sections, but whatever name they use, they should let facilitators know how long each one should take to implement.

Level of Detail

One of the most crucial aspects of writing a lesson plan is making sure you have enough detail in both your wording and direction to a facilitator. The rookie mistake in this process is being too brief and not including crucial instructions and suggested wording. There is a belief among some less experienced instructional designers that facilitators don't need a lot of detail and that just setting a general direction is good enough. Lesson plans written with that philosophy are useless. You might as well hand a facilitator a napkin with an outline. Detail is king in instructional design, and there is no process or product for which this is more true than a lesson plan.

There are numerous reasons for this, so let's review several of the most important.

First, you want to make sure that your instructional intent is implemented the way you designed a course. If you leave anything to doubt or to the whim of a facilitator, you are asking for trouble. This isn't because they will intentionally sabotage your work, but if they have to interpret your instructions, they will fill in the gaps with their own ideas, and this may or may not bear any resemblance to your intent. As an example, in a lesson plan you simply say:

"The facilitator should describe the process for (insert process)"

Now you are asking both for an interpretation and a judgment on what the facilitator should do at this point. Wouldn't it be better to say:

"In your own words, describe the process for . . . as follows:
1. *The speed is selected on the L800 milling machine.*
2. *The safety switch is moved to the 'off' position.*
3. *The operation switch is moved to the 'on' position.*
4. *Once the item is milled completely, move the operation switch to the 'off' position.*
5. *The safety switch is moved to the 'on', position rendering the machine unusable."*

The first option allowed the facilitator to decided how many, if any, steps to describe and in what order. The second leaves nothing to interpretation and leaves out no details provided by a subject matter expert. The difference is obvious. Imagine this same scenario on every course you design. You must have this level of detail to ensure complete coverage of the content.

Second, being detailed in your lesson plan supports your facilitator; failing to do so leaves your facilitator hanging in midair when they need detailed instruction from you. Imagine that you have placed a number of questions in your lesson plan that a facilitator is supposed to ask learners, yet you provide no answers or guidelines about what to do while asking the questions and gathering answers from learners. For example, in your lesson plan you say:

"Ask the learners if they have ever been in a situation where they were unable to reach a supervisor when an emergency was occuring in the workplace."

With no follow-up instructions to the facilitator, this question and its answers have no context in your course except for the occasional on-topic response that goes nowhere toward mastery of your content. Now imagine adding this direction to your facilitator:

"The range of answers you need to hear should include references to the feeling of hope-lessness, anger, panic, and other emotions. If these do not come from the learners, inter-ject them yourself to make the point that everyone feels these emotions and that this course is designed to provide answers to what should be done in these situations."

Again, see the difference? One has no follow-up or direction; the second has detailed direction that builds toward mastery of the content in the course. This principle in writing lesson plans continues throughout the process. Always ask yourself, "Have I provided enough detail to the facilitator so that nothing is left to chance?"

A lesson plan must provide information about what facilitators need to communicate, but you may decide to specify that a facilitator should put the information in their own words. The plan might say, for example:

In your own words . . .

"In the next hour that we have together, we will learn about working in teams."

The suggested language should be styled so that it is easy for the facilitator to spot it on the page.

REFLECTION

A lesson plan is based on Gagné's nine events and involves a rather complex series of design features that start with gaining attention and work through to closure. This process is aligned very closely with the way learners receive, internalize, and store information.

Do you think that this detailed of a lesson plan design is required for all course design projects?

Action Items

Action items may be set in boldface type to allow facilitators to see what they are expected to do next, as the following examples show:

- *Show slide #78.*
- *Slide Content: This Is What Happens*
- *Start the video.*

Choosing to Eliminate Events

Occasionally, designers choose to eliminate events. Sometimes there just isn't enough time for them to go through all of them. Other times, nine events may be too complex for a particular project. When designing CBT or multi-media, it can be difficult to design the necessary feedback and interaction steps. Designers may then decide that they can reduce the nine events to seven or fewer events. Usually guided learning, eliciting performance, and feedback suffer the most in this environment.

Designers should be sure at least to consider all nine events when designing their course. Without this kind of guide for designing their lessons, they are likely to have an outline of the content and an instructional design with no structure, which is the cardinal sin of instructional design.

Technology and the Nine Events

The nine events become even more important if designers are working on a project that is not a traditional facilitator-led course. Designers who use the nine events as the framework for this type of delivery system can be sure they will at least consider the ramifications of all these elements in their design.

It is important to remember that the nine-events approach to lesson plans is not always appropriate. The technology involved may not permit its use. It takes a great deal of work to build lesson plans this way. After designers use this approach for a while, though, they find that the thought process it stimulates becomes instinctive and that it helps them become better designers even if they never again build a lesson plan this way.

Pre-Course Information Section

Professional lesson plans always include a pre-course section containing any information that a facilitator will need to set up a course. While most often designed for in-class courses, instructions for online courses are also useful.

Items to include in your pre-course section include:
- Implementation time
- Room setup
- Materials
- Evaluation forms
- Attendance list
- Handouts
- Computer/Wi-Fi username and password
- Laptop setup and test
- A/V equipment setup and test
- Internet access if required
- Name tents and name tags

It is also very useful to include timelines for certain elements of your pre-course setup to take place. Many designers group elements into:
- One week before class
- One day before class
- One hour before class

You may also want to include contact information for support staff and others who might be able to assist if there is a problem that needs to be addressed. No matter how you design this element of your lesson plan, be sure to be thorough and provide all the information and support that is necessary for your course to be implemented without a hitch.

How It Looks

Now let's see what a lesson plan looks like in practice. This is a very basic design; lesson plans can range in size from what we have here to hundreds of pages in length, with visuals and embedded instructional aids. Experienced designers may have much more complex lesson plans, but it is important to see the way these are formatted and the sequencing and content of each of the nine events.

Onboarding New Team Members Course Lesson Plan

Implementation Time: 90 minutes

Materials: HR forms, organizational chart, instructions for creating new email account, flipcharts and pens, sign-in sheets, and evaluation forms. All materials for learners should be in lots of at least 10 percent more than the anticipated attendance.

Equipment: Laptop computer with the presentation software, computer projector and screen or smartboard, extension cord, and surge protector.

Slides are available on a separate file and are only referenced in this lesson plan for purposes of advancing slides at the correct point in implementation.

Room arrangement: Classroom style with tables and chairs facing the front of the room with each chair having unobstructed views of the facilitator and projected media.

24-Hour Checklist

- **Day before:** Confirm room assignment, confirm equipment list, test internet, test computer equipment and software, check operation of the projector, check operation of the whiteboard, and confirm all materials are ready.

- **Just before the course starts:** Be sure the video is able to be accessed. Be sure the computer and projector are operating and that the software is operating.

- **Start of the course:** The instructions to the facilitator can take many forms. This lesson plan uses the nine events as a guide. The first event is gaining attention, for which we are going to show a short video. Following is how the lesson plan will look in the facilitator's guide.

Lesson Plan Nine Events

Show frame #1
Slide Content: "Welcome to the Family!"

Prestart: Call the group together and start the course. Introduce yourself and formally welcome the learners.

Advance to frame #2
Slide Content: "Starting Off Right"

In your own words . . .

"The first week at any new job is always a mix of anxiety, excitement, and some fear of the unknown. We are all here to make your first week something special and to provide you a strong foundation for your work ahead."

Advance to frame #3, video teaser
Slide Content: Start screen for "Intro From CEO"

In your own words . . .

"Our CEO has a few welcoming words for you, and you will be meeting with the board later in the day."

Show video (3 minutes). At the conclusion of the video:

In your own words . . .

"We are all excited you are now part of our family, so let's get going with our course."

Turn computer projector on.

Advance to frame #4
Slide Content:

Given a presentation, slides, handouts, job aids, and class discussion, the Onboarding New Team Members participant should be able to:

• Describe the mission and values of the organization.

• List organization and departmental standard operating procedures.

• Establish user account identity, including username and password.

• Complete required HR paperwork.

• List direct supervisor name and contact information.

• List necessary training required for new team members.

• Describe the location of key facility functions, including health and first aid, the cafeteria, and security.

In your own words . . .

"Let's review the objectives for today so that we all know what we are going to be able to accomplish."

"Any questions about the course before we begin?"

Advance to frame #5
Slide Content: "Your Journey to Our Team"

In your own words . . .

"Prior to today, there were a number of steps that provided the path to joining our team. Your application, interview, and contract offer were just some of the elements of coming on board, and we couldn't be happier that you are with us."

Advance to frame #6

Slide Content: Now that you are here . . .

In your own words . . .

"With the hiring process behind us, it is now time to get started and make sure you feel welcome and that we provide the best possible first week. Not only are we going to complete some of the formal aspects of joining the team, like getting on the network and completing some of the required paperwork, we also want you to know about your important role in our future."

Advance to frame #7

Slide Content: Building for your future . . .

In your own words . . .

"As we get started, please remember that we want to hear from you about your experience getting started. We want to hear and answer all your questions and we want you to feel comfortable letting us know when we can do something better."

Advance to frame #8

Slide Content: Let's get going!

In your own words . . .

"Now let's get started and build the foundation for your career as part of our team."

Advance to frame #9

Slide Content: That darn paperwork!

In your own words . . .

"As we get started, we have some paperwork to complete to get you on the network. We need to assign you a username and you will be asked to enter a password. We require password refreshes every month and a two-part authentication for access from outside our intranet."

Advance to frame #10

Slide Content: Online Access

In your own words . . .

"Using the username and temporary password shown on the form I am handing out, log on to the system using the screen displayed on your laptop or tablet. You will immediately be asked to enter a new password or to use the suggested password. The software will let you know if it thinks the password is strong enough for network requirements. Be sure to write down your password for future reference."

Advance to frame #11

Slide Content: HR Paperwork

In your own words . . .

"We are now going to take a minute and complete the last few documents that are needed for you to receive health coverage. Please complete these online using this link: hr.forms.hc.com."

Advance to frame #12

Slide Content: Standard Operating Procedures

In your own words . . .

"Every organization has a list of SOPs, or standard operating procedures, relating to expected behaviors and how to communicate within your department and directly with your supervisor. Please take a minute to review this handout and let us know if you have any questions."

Advance to frame #13

Slide Content: Mission Statement

In your own words . . .

"Now that we have the formal paperwork portion of the course out of the way, let's start to look at your new home and what the organization is trying to accomplish. Our mission statement is a very specific overview of our direction and goals. As a team member, these are your guiding principles in everything you do within the organization."

Advance to frame #14

Slide Content: My Immediate Family

In your own words . . .

"Since we have new team members from different departments with us, we have given each of you a list of the team members in your department. We have also included an organizational chart that shows the entire organization and how your department links to other departments."

Advance to frame #15

Slide Content: Site Map

In your own words . . .

"No one wants to have to wander around the facility looking for key areas you will need to visit. We are now distributing a map and contact information for services like security, health services, food services, and the HR department offices."

Advance to frame #16
Slide Content: Training Requirements

In your own words . . .

"Our last handout is a personalized list of training that you are required to attend in your first month as a team member. This includes organization-wide required training like first-aid and CPR as well as any specific training you may require for software and other related systems you will be using."

Advance to frame #17
Slide Content: Becoming Part of the Team

In your own words . . .

"Now that we have worked through the required paperwork to get you going with the organization, we are now going to spend some time sharing with each other about our roles as a member of the team. Let's review our mission statement, and I would like each of you to share one aspect of our mission that resonates with you."

Facilitator Notes
At this stage of the training, work with the group and call on each new team member to talk about their thoughts on the mission and how they can play a part.

Answer any questions that my come up and be sure to include everyone in the discussions.

Advance to frame #18
Slide Content: Your Role in Supporting Our Success

In your own words . . .

"I am going to ask you to pair with another new team member or two and discuss the following question:

Where do you see yourself fitting into the mission of our organization?"

Facilitator Notes
Circulate around the room and make sure everyone is teamed up and starting the discussion. Assist those needing any help.

Advance to frame #19
Slide Content: Our Ideas

In your own words . . .

"Now that you have had time to discuss your role in the mission, I want you to prepare a flip chart with your thoughts, which you will share with the group."

Facilitator Notes
Distribute the flip charts and markers and support the process of each group writing up their thoughts.

Advance to frame #20
Slide content: Sharing With the Group

In your own words . . .

"Who would like to go first?"

Facilitator Notes
Work through each group and make sure that the each member of the group reads the prepared thoughts and discusses their ideas. Encourage questions and discussions.

In your own words . . .

"That was incredible, and I hope all of you are as excited about our future as I am."

Advance to frame #21
Slide Content: Short Review

In your own words . . .

"We are now going to review our time together and I am going to ask each of you to write down the following information on a sheet of paper.

- What is the mission of this organization?

- Who is the head of your department?

- Where will you find the security office?

- Where is the cafeteria?

"Now let's review each question."

Facilitator Notes
Review the answers with each participant and correct any confusion or wrong answers.

In your own words . . .

"I am now going to distribute a short evaluation of the course so you can give us your thoughts on how it went. Don't be afraid to tell us how we can do better."

Advance to frame #22
Slide Content: Now It's Time to Get Going

In your own words . . .

"I want to thank all of you for being part of our welcoming program and training. As you start your first several weeks, we will be checking in with you to follow up and see how you are doing."

Facilitator Notes
Close the training and be sure to turn off all of the equipment before leaving the training area.

DISCUSSION QUESTIONS

- Why is the design element of ISD considered the most important aspect of instructional design?

- When looking at the elements of a design plan, which do you think are the most important? Which would you consider as optional?

- What additional elements would you add to a design plan for your work as an instructional designer?

- Some designers find the structure of a lesson plan using the Nine Events of Instruction too rigid for most course designs. What are your thoughts on the complexity of the approach?

- In your opinion, is there any type of course or implementation option where you would not use a lesson plan for a teacher or facilitator to use in implementing a course?

Summary

Design is the heart and soul of ISD, and the majority of the work performed by an instructional designer takes place in this element. The major deliverables of this phase are a design plan, a lesson plan, and many other required materials, including evaluation instruments. Design also serves as the central point for the workflow of any course design project. All elements of the design process pass through and are controlled by the design phase.

CASE STUDY 1

Your design team has been assigned a project to produce a series of 10 courses for a manufacturing client. The client wants to provide training in the use of an app-based solution for inventory control. It is anticipated that each course will contain enough content for approximately 45 minutes of learner participation.

The client has not decided whether to make the courses a series of tutorials that are based within the app or whether to have in-person courses for some or all of the content.

As your team works through the design plan, what are the considerations you will need to discuss and present to the client?

How will you design the course if it is a combination of tutorial and in-person courses?

Will you use the nine events as a model for the implementation of the courses?

CASE STUDY 2

The agricultural extension program for a large state university has been awarded a grant to train new farm owners on the economics of farm management. It is anticipated that the initial cohort will include up to 50 participants. As the lead instructional designer for the university, you have been asked to work with the program to make sure they are planning the courses to meet minimal expectations for quality and the ability to accurately evaluate learner mastery, as required by the grant.

The extension program director has always taught courses that were essentially slide decks with outlines of the course as handouts. There have never been any formal evaluations of mastery. The only evaluations were smile sheets to determine student satisfaction and these were seldom reviewed.

The director has voiced frustration that the courses have to be designed in such a way as to ensure quality and mastery evaluation and insists the old way worked just fine for the last 30 years.

As the designer in charge of making this project meet grant requirements, how are you going to convince the program director that this process is manageable and will produce a high-quality and measurable product?

How will you explain the design plan and lesson plan elements of the process?

What other aspects of the ISD process will you share and explain?

CASE STUDY 3

A community-based organization dedicated to providing shelter and support for the homeless is interested in teaching some of its clients the basics of interviewing for a job. They believe that some of their clients would benefit from this knowledge and be able to gain employment and move into more permanent, independent housing arrangements.

You are a volunteer for the organization, and with your interest in ISD and course design, you have offered to design the course for the group. They would like to have it available in two months. They are thinking that a course that lasts more than several hours is too long for this population. The population has at least a third-grade reading level and has a mix of English and Spanish as their primary language.

- Given what you know about the design process in ISD, how will you go about planning and designing this course?
- Will you work with formal design and lesson plans?
- How will you determine mastery of the content?
- What special design considerations do you think exist given this specific population?

CHAPTER 7
Development

KEY CONCEPTS

- Defining development in the ISD process
- Managing subject matter experts within the course design process
- Five types of subject matter experts:
  - Technical SMEs as content experts
  - Hybrid SMEs
  - Instructional SMEs and facilitating course design
  - Functional SMEs—programmers, artists, and other nondesigner resources
  - Sentinel SMEs and the design process from a managerial perspective
- Selecting SMEs as a design function
- Working with SMEs as a skill
- Pilot testing to ensure a design meets expectations
- Train-the-trainer courses to practice before wide-scale implementation
- See one, do one training

CHAPTER OBJECTIVES

At the end of this chapter, the learner should be able to:

- Describe the main operational elements of the development function in ISD.
- Describe the purpose of subject matter experts in the ISD process.
- List the five types of subject matter experts.
- Describe the process of selecting subject matter experts.
- List at least three ways to work productively with subject matter experts.
- Describe the reasons for pilot testing new courses.
- Provide at least three reasons for conducting train-the-trainer sessions for new courses.
- Describe the process used for see one, do one training courses.

The development phase of ISD is the link that connects the design process with the implementation of a project. Plans and prototypes move to realization as the designer moves materials to a final draft stage. As the buffer between design and implementation, development necessitates that the instructional designer carefully monitor the process elements. One of the most rewarding aspects of the development phase for instructional designers is seeing design plans coming to life. Manuals, videos, webpages, and a hundred different tangible deliverables finally take shape. There is usually a collective sigh of relief once this happens, and it is easy to see why.

It can be exciting for instructional designers to work with a variety of different professionals, but it can also be hectic. Careful communication at this point pays dividends later. One of the most important elements of the development process is working with subject matter experts (SMEs). In this chapter, we explore in great depth the different types of subject matter experts, the roles they play in instructional design, and how best to work with this group.

The development phase of ISD is typically the departure point for the designers and design team since the next phase, implementation, focuses on course delivery and the facilitation of the course design. While some designers may actually teach courses, many will have little if any role in what happens after this phase unless there are changes or updates to be completed after implementation starts. This point of departure requires considerable design skill because it is much more difficult to impact a course once it leaves the development process. This chapter also covers pilot testing before a project goes into implementation as well as developing train-the-trainer courses.

Look and Feel

Development presents many opportunities to make mistakes in training design and production. Everyone has opinions about the way materials should appear, and it can sometimes be hard to get general agreement about even the simplest things. Designers play an important role in finding consensus and working with all elements of a project.

The process of moving from draft materials to a nearly final product is crucial to a project's success. Designers need to address any number of issues in order to ensure that the materials are satisfactory. Generally, they need to consider the following aspects of development when working on materials production:

- **Cost:** Designers must be sure they know what products are going to cost and that they stay on budget.
- **Deadlines:** They must set firm deadlines for production of materials and require that vendors stick to the deadlines.
- **Written agreements:** They must have everything in writing concerning paper, color, size, quantity, fonts, and other variables in their materials.
- **Samples:** They must always check a sample of the materials before the production begins.
- **Final approval:** They must be sure to approve final copy of materials, not taking anyone's word for anything.
- **Pilot test:** Before producing the final materials, they must conduct pilot tests or have a review by stakeholders in the process, or do both. A pilot test evaluates the entire design, not just materials.

Working With Nondesign Subject Matter Experts

What is a subject matter expert? The term, sometimes shortened to simply SME, is the universal designation for an individual who is considered an expert in one or more areas of endeavor. This expertise can be in content areas such as math or science, or a professional field such as law or accounting; or as we will see shortly, a SME can also be a key noncontent member of a training or instructional design team.

In this context, the term accurately describes a building-trades craftsworker with 40 years of experience hanging iron atop the world's highest buildings and a village elder with no formal education sharing centuries-old herbal treatments for common ailments. The 14-year-old next door is a SME in the latest musical genre, and a 92-year-old World War II veteran could serve as an expert in the Battle of Stalingrad, which began in 1942. In all cases, the subject matter expert provides specific, detailed information that is not considered common knowledge. No two SMEs look the same or sound alike, and there may be no other defining element besides their related subject matter knowledge.

Subject matter experts earn this standing in countless ways, depending on the circumstances surrounding their knowledge. Some have years of experience in a field and have written articles or books and may offer seminars in a specific field. Others may be recognized by their peers as the "best of the best" and earn the SME title by virtue of their reputation. A very small minority are self-proclaimed subject matter experts and offer little in the way of credentialing to substantiate their standing. All of that being said, there is also sometimes a subjective art to labeling someone, or in some cases oneself, as a subject matter expert. There is no group called the International Order of Subject Matter Experts that crowns the worthy few with this credential.

For our purposes in training, becoming a subject matter expert generally requires that someone has passed the associated litmus tests within the field. This is often based on academic achievement, licensure, and certification; publishing in the field; or some other formal credentialing process. There should always be an experience component to ensure that even the best educational credentialing is supported by years of actual practice in a field. In some professions the yearly in-service training required to continue licensure or credentialing supports SME status.

The title of subject matter expert should not be given without credentials that match the practice among professionals in a specific area. Many times, these are also the generally accepted entry points for professional practice. In academic circles, this is generally a terminal degree like a PhD or EdD. In law, it is being licensed to practice law and perhaps holding a JD degree. In medicine, it is having a terminal degree like an MD or a DO and board certification. In the building trades, this can be having journeyperson status and many years' experience as an apprenticeship instructor. The examples go on and on and really have no limit. What is important is that there is some tangible, reliable, and documented evidence to support expert standing.

There are also notable exceptions to all these common standards. There are without question uniquely gifted individuals who represent the outliers in this labeling process. Musical prodigies like Mozart or Chopin join Enrico Fermi in physics, Bill Gates in software design, and Steve Jobs at Apple, who unquestionably defied accepted definitions of *expert* at some point in their careers. To apply a strict, credential-based standard to any of these geniuses would be laughable, and yet there are still the unenlightened few who argue that the line in the sand standard must always be supported.

The irony in all of this for trainers and instructional designers is that we are also subject matter experts. We are SMEs in our chosen profession in the same way that our colleagues in other fields are content experts. It is the context that changes when we work with other content experts.

Why Subject Matter Experts Are Important to ISD

Often the term *SME* is tossed into a conversation as if it is just one single entity or function. It isn't, and the more you know about subject matter experts, the more important they become to your success. Best practice in ISD demands that subject matter experts take their rightful place as part of the design family with equal expectations and responsibilities as every other facet of the process.

The rapid maturation of instructional design over the last decade has curiously allowed a vacuum in the appreciation and integration of subject matter experts in the design team. This may be linked to a heightened focus on the key process elements of training and instructional design, whether represented by the ADDIE model elements of analysis, design, development, implementation, and evaluation or other priorities like online learning and social media.

This unenlightened view of SMEs is not intentional, but nonetheless detrimental since it minimizes the potential benefits of incorporating this asset where most useful. In a professional practice predicated on thoroughness and attention to detail, SMEs often languish as a disassociated element in the practice of ISD. In truth, they are often as essential to success as any other factor in our work.

Subject Matter Experts in Training Occupations

It is difficult to find anyone associated with training and curriculum design who was not first involved in a non-training field, and by default a subject matter expert in something other than training and curriculum design. The same can be said for almost everyone holding the title of trainer, teacher, facilitator, professor, or various other coaching and mentoring roles. From the earliest oral traditions, education, training skills, and knowledge were passed from the most proficient to those with less experience following them.

Almost all academic programs in instructional design and learning performance are offered in the context of someone who has experience in something other than training and education and is now advancing their career by learning more about the finer points of designing and implementing training. The ATD Certified Professional in Talent Development (CPTD) is a perfect example of the transitory nature of skills in training from subject matter expert in a variety of professions to learning and performance subject matter expert. The

University of Maryland Baltimore County master's degree and graduate certifi-cates in instructional systems development do not have any prior experience or specific undergraduate degree as a requirement for participation.

It is this path from subject matter expertise to training roles that has the poten-tial to create uncertainty since there exists an implied truth that someone who is good in one area of endeavor is also good in another. This questionable nexus between individual expertise specifically to a more general expertise invites con-flicted role perceptions and opens the door to dysfunctional committees, groups, and projects.

Subject matter experts generally work and fit best in the role of subject mat-ter expert. To expect more of them is to invite a variety of potentially nega-tive consequences. At the same time, for a SME to expand their participation to a level that interferes with established non-SME roles within the project development process may create equally negative results. It is the balance of role and expectation that creates the best and most productive fit in this environment. It is for this, and a variety of other reasons, that going beyond the simplistic notion of a one-size-fits-all definition for subject matter expert is now imperative.

Different Types of SMEs

Until recently, SMEs were rarely, if ever, thought of as having differing roles in the design process. A one-size-fits-all mentality had amalgamated these experts into a single content expert stereotype, which isn't remotely accurate in most design environments. The designers who limit their operational perspective of SMEs are destined to underuse and therefore waste the talents available to them. They are also predisposed to a marginal definition of *SMEs*, preventing designers from expanding their network of influence and resources. The mat-uration of our work with SMEs is in many ways similar to the jump from pre-ISD course design to today's complex world of instructional design.

SMEs working within present-day ISD are categorized as technical, hybrid, instructional, functional, or sentinel (Hodell 2012). As we work through these categories, you will see that the SMEs of today are a dynamic group of profes-sionals tasked with many different design roles, some of which were not consid-ered within the ranks of SMEs previously (Figure 7-1).

Figure 7-1. Types of Subject Matter Experts

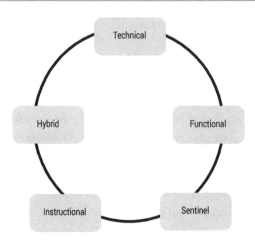

Technical Subject Matter Expert

Technical SME	
• Content Expert	• Demonstrated Expertise
• Professional Standing	• Design Support Only

Before the recent evolution of our thinking on SMEs, almost every instructional designer would have described a generic SME as what we now call a technical subject matter expert (TSME). As the name implies, a TSME provides the technical component in training. Many times this individual or team is the seasoned professional content expert that shares knowledge of a particular area of specialty, which becomes the core of the content in a course.

TSMEs are the cream of the crop. They have worked their way up in careers as diverse as master craftpersons, engineers, scientists, lawyers, physicians, biologists, electricians, human resource professionals, and thousands of other content areas. Not only are they the go-to person in their field; they are seasoned veterans of the academic, corporate, and professional battlefields that often influence a designer's work.

A TSME's history with instructional design will vary. Some may have little experience with the training design process and are appointed to these positions with or without their knowledge or approval. It is often true that any assignments related to their role as a TSME is in addition to their regular job responsibilities, and this may become a point of contention.

In other cases, TSMEs are consultants who work on a number of these projects and are very familiar with their role and function. They are sometimes thought of as hired guns since they work on so many different projects, but that experience will often work to your advantage.

Hybrid Subject Matter Expert

Hybrid SME	
• Content Expert	• Demonstrated Expertise
• Professional Standing	• Design and Implementation

A very valuable SME is the one who first assists in the design of a course and then also participates in the implementation. This hybrid subject matter expert (HSME) provides technical assistance within the design process based on their knowledge of both the content and the end user population. This unique set of skills has its own set of challenges that must be recognized and addressed. There are times when content knowledge and facilitation skills are not equally beneficial to the project. In these situations it is necessary to set reasonable expectations for the HSME in order to be realistic about what is of value and what may not be as useful. As we will discuss later, strong content knowledge does not always equate to strong facilitation skills.

In academia, the HSME is the rule rather than the exception and this classification of SME is generally stronger in content knowledge and weaker in designing courses. This becomes especially noticeable when courses move online, either in a blended mix of online and classroom or in a full online course. It is a very difficult transition to move from designing courses based primarily on lecture and systematic evaluations to designing courses using ISD.

The HSME is also a standard category when working with apprenticeship and other technical content areas. It is common for the best skilled-trades person to be brought in to teach others, and through this work we gather most of our HSMEs for designing skills training.

Instructional Subject Matter Expert

Instructional SME
• Trainer/Teacher/Facilitator
• Implements Design Products
• Content Knowledge Supports Implementation

The assistance of a very skilled facilitator often provides valuable insight when designing courses that are either in non-traditional implementation areas or working with populations that are unique in their needs and expectations from those of the instructional designers. Examples are foreign languages and cultures different than that of the design team.

The role of facilitator, mentor, coach, and teacher are all included in the instructional subject matter expert (ISME) category. While this group possesses vast subject matter expertise, its primary role is to enhance the instructional aspects of the training during implementation. It is not unusual for a technical course to be taught by an ISME who does not participate in the design, development, or management of the training and serves as the instructional leader in implementation. Still, their technical expertise is key to their ability to facilitate or enhance the learning experience.

Functional Subject Matter Expert

Functional SME
• Support Function Professional
• Graphic Artist, Writer, Software Specialist
• No Content Knowledge

One of the categories of SMEs that may be unfamiliar to many is the functional subject matter expert. In many training environments there are any number of subject matter experts that have little to do with building the content in a course but contribute in ways that build and enhance the final product. While they are seldom involved in forming the content itself, their skills are unique to training and should be recognized as such.

A functional subject matter expert (FSME) might be a graphic artist, programmer, web designer, technical writer, photographer, or any other associated professional. The recognition of an individual's expertise goes a long way in defining and building this role in the training function. We seldom think of these skills in the context of subject matter expertise, but they possess all the qualities we seek in a SME, and to bring them into this discussion enhances our ability to build a winning training function.

Almost no one considers these professionals to be SMEs in an instructional design context, and taking the time to consider the importance of the designation works to your favor. This group is proud of its work and seldom gets any recognition beyond the usual in-team appreciation. However, once you think of them as subject matter experts, you begin to change the way you work with them in some very important ways.

As a group of people, they deserve the same respect and treatment as the content-related SME categories, and all of the ideas presented here apply equally to them in the context of their work and role in your project. Making them part of your team and not just an adjunct participating on the margins will bring tangible results over time. Don't ignore this group and take them for granted. They can negate any advantage you have gained with your other SME groups if they are left unappreciated and unrecognized as subject matter experts.

Sentinel Subject Matter Expert

Sentinel SME
• Oversees Course Design From a Distance
• Limited or Dated Content Knowledge
• Ensures Quality and Related Organizational Concerns

One challenging aspect of working on a large design project is the role managers, committees, C-staff, and other non-designers play in the project. In the world of training, the sentinel subject matter expert (SSME) is the individual who serves as the overseer or guardian of the content in the process of designing and implementing courseware. While this individual may possess limited and often dated technical expertise, they serve the managerial role of reviewing and approving content and other course particulars related to design and implementation of the final training product.

They are considered subject matter experts because their role in the process is to ensure that both the content and the product meet, and hopefully exceed, expected professional and organizational standards. And, while their content-specific knowledge might be limited, they still have the organizational responsibility to act as the sentinel for both content and process. In training and instructional design, the SSME must be treated differently than any other participant. Their knowledge of the content places them in a unique organizational situation that may see them experiencing pressure from several directions when trying to make important decisions.

This group can be especially challenging because their first priority is not necessarily the content. In most cases they are more concerned with budget and deliverables than specific content issues above general discussions of what is being designed. They will endlessly churn the most minuscule budget item and they want answers when a deadline is missed. While they are genuinely concerned about the content, they have higher authorities to make happy, and that group has limited knowledge of the details of the process and project. When working with this group, make sure you have all your facts in order and that you have answers for even the smallest details relating to budget and deadlines.

SSMEs appreciate and respond to having tangible items to review and share with those higher in the organizational food chain. As professionals, they have grown weary and suspicious of anything they can't see or hold in their hands, and trying to float something by this group is impossible. Have copies of every deliverable ready for them to review. Make sure they have timelines and budgets in ad nauseam detail and always appear to have much more information for them than they will ever have time to review.

Another helpful approach in working with this group is to have other technical SMEs talk about their work and share their insights on how the project is going (assuming it is going well). SSMEs really pay attention to the SMEs that they have assigned to work on a project talking about their role and success. This allows the SSMEs to take away a feeling of accomplishment, and they can then float this success higher in the organization.

Of all the subject matter experts you work with, this group above all others has to feel comfortable with your leadership and the investment they are making in a project. If they are happy, most other levels of the process will respond positively to your facilitation, if for no other reason than knowing that the sentinels are satisfied with the way things are progressing.

Matching SMEs to Your Needs

Categorizing subject matter expertise provides several advantages in training, not the least of which is the ability to find the best and most efficient way to incorporate these valuable assets in each individual training environment. It's really a matter of respect and appreciation for the time and effort that these professionals invest in making our training successful.

To best utilize our valuable SMEs, we need to be able to first identify what we need and when we need it. Using the ADDIE model of ISD as our guide, there are certain elements of the process that best suit themselves to the different types of SMEs.

We can see that each element of ADDIE has a specific need for SMEs (Table 7-1). Each different classification of SME will likely fit best within particular ADDIE elements. While each project is different, it is reasonable to assume that generally these are appropriate associations.

Table 7-1. SME Types and the ADDIE Process

	Analysis	Design	Development	Implementation	Evaluation
Technical	x	x	x		X
Hybrid	x	x	x	x	X
Instructional				x	X
Functional			x		
Sentinel	x	x	x	x	X

As we review this chart we can see that technical SMEs are generally used in analysis and evaluation since these require the most content-specific resources. Functional SMEs are most likely only used in the development within a course and instructional SMEs are going to be used in the implementation and evaluation phases. Hybrid and sentinel SMEs are likely to be useful in all the ADDIE elements.

Being able to determine when we will need different types of subject matter experts will allow us to accomplish several things at once. First, we will be able to quantify the amount of time each of these experts will need to be plugged into the process. A resource may become overwhelmed if they think that their time and effort is necessary for the entire design process. This allows us to better define what we are asking an individual to contribute and it furthermore allows each individual to gauge the scope of their participation.

REFLECTION

The choice of subject matter experts for an instructional design process is an important decision that must be made with the same attention to detail as any other design element.

Each SME candidate comes with different credentials, experience, and the ability to communicate and work with a design team.

As a designer, what are the most important aspects of a SME's skills that you will be considering when it comes to choosing someone to work on your design projects?

Second, we are able to plan our project with a more realistic timeline and resource and cost model that reflects real-world asset allocation. A department head considering allowing a SME to work on a project at a 5–10 percent time allocation may be much more likely to participate if he thinks that this is not an open-ended commitment with undefined limits that he must then cover with other employees.

Choosing Content Subject Matter Experts

The majority of instructional designers work with subject matter experts who are project-related content experts. Whether you have any choices about whom you work with is as variable as the projects you work on. SMEs for a project are usually either chosen by a client based on political or organizational issues, or found by an instructional designer. In either case, it is to the benefit of the designer to see that certain criteria for selection of the SMEs are established. Consider these factors in your selection process:

- **Determine if the prospective subject matter experts have recent experience in the content area.** On the surface this may seem a rather odd selection criteria, but it is based on the fact that many times the selection of SMEs for a project is not based on recent experience in the content. Their assignments are sometimes seen as rewards, and it is not uncommon for selections to be made without any detailed analysis. This may leave a designer with someone who is at least one generation away from current experience. Any SME with more than a year or more between actual time on task and participation as a content expert is likely to be less than reliable.
- **Make sure that any subject matter expert has relevant experience in the content.** In today's complex world of rapid changes in technology and process, data ages very quickly and a process or skill that was current a year ago may already be considered legacy knowledge and not relevant to your content. Recent experience does not always mean relevant experience. Five years of recent experience within a field of skills does not mean that someone was working with the specific skills you are looking for in your project. A physician who is a family doctor may have years of general experience, but if your course is directly related to trauma center care of accident victims, you are not going to be well served. Most choices are not that obvious, but they are all equally important decisions about content subject matter expertise.
- **Try to have a mix of novice, experienced, and expert SMEs if at all possible.** This allows you to gather data from the entire range of experience levels. This is useful because experienced content experts often leave steps out of processes since they perform them almost without thinking about the

steps. Experienced SMEs are more likely to be detailed, and many have more recent experience. A novice (or potential member of the course's population of learners) will almost always ask excellent questions about a process since they are less likely to have detailed knowledge, but they do know what they don't know and that is vital for a designer who is collecting data for a course. If you have to leave any of these groups unrepresented, it is probably best to work with the experienced and expert groups and leave out the novice.

· **When working with a national, mult-geographical, or multi-organizational groups, look for as much variety as possible in subject matter experts.** In many areas, regional variations are critical factors in the success of your work. Sometimes it is the simple variations in jargon and the way different regions refer to tools or processes. At other times it is the fact that different areas may or may not do the same things in terms of process. For example, groups on the West Coast perform only skills a, b, and c, while groups in Canada have to have experience in cold weather skills d, e, and f. Never assume that regional variations are not present or important.

Developing a Working Relationship

The best way to be successful with non-designer professionals in an instructional design setting is to build a solid working relationship. This is true for everyone who becomes part of your extended design team but is usually most critical with content SMEs.

There can be a certain tension between subject matter experts and designers, and this is true almost universally, regardless of the content area or the designer. There are several reasons for this, and all must be considered in the equation for building a working relationship.

Pilot Testing

Pilot testing is a chance to evaluate a project before it goes into full implementation, and is a key component of the development stage. The theory for instructional design is the same as that for a play: Both need rehearsals. It takes time to get all the bugs out of the implementation materials and lesson plans.

It is logical to pilot test before designers start producing final materials and begin the process of delivering their course. Some designers include pilot testing in the

7 TIPS FOR WORKING SUCCESSFULLY WITH SMES

1. Subject matter experts must be respected for their knowledge and experience. Like most elements of the design process, working with SMEs requires designers to take a neutral stance on personalities, working styles, and other environmental variables. The goal is to get the best product from the process.

2. Recognize that most SMEs have also taught, and many have designed training themselves. It is natural for them to feel that their input on the design process is important based on their experience. Designers may see this as competitive, or in some way challenging their subject matter expertise. Don't fall into that trap. Listen and make decisions based on your instincts, but there are occasions when a SME has valuable insights on certain design areas.

3. Initiate and negotiate as necessary the ground rules for the relationship. You will find that 15 minutes spent at the beginning of the relationship will save endless hours and sometimes days of stress and misunderstanding later in the design process. If there are clear lines of authority, it is sometimes best to review them for clarification and make any modifications that might be necessary early. Also make sure that the role of the instructional designer is clear to everyone.

4. Make sure that the design process, deliverables, and deadlines are clearly explained and that any points of contention are ironed out early. If there are likely to be negotiations concerning any of these, now is the time to initiate that discussion and resolve the conflict before it develops a life of its own that works against the success of the project.

5. Work as an instructional designer—never a subject matter expert—while designing. In the same way that a designer doesn't want to be challenged on their design expertise, a designer should never challenge a SME on their subject matter expertise. Fair is fair. It is often best to just say early and often that your role is to be the designer and any questioning of the content is meant for clarification. If there is a problem with the reliability, value, or usefulness of the information you are receiving from a SME, make this a discussion with the client or sponsor. This is true in both internal and external design relationships.

6. Make it easy for a SME to be a subject matter expert. The more a designer can put SMEs in a comfort zone with the process, the more valuable the relationship will become. Always make it easy for them to concentrate on their knowledge and experience and not on the design process. Most SMEs really enjoy the process if their participation is seen as appreciated and non-competitive.

7. Communicate constantly with your SMEs. This includes both the times when you are working in direct contact with them, such as during meetings, and when you are working independently of them on other design issues. No one likes to feel out of the loop, and it is often extremely useful to keep in contact with the SMEs even if there is nothing you actually need from them. A little time spent communicating may ease the way for future requests and consensus.

implementation phase, rather than in development, and that is fine. It is more important to test a project before finalizing deliverables than it is to worry about whether testing happens in the development or implementation phases.

Organizations often view a pilot test, or a pre-implementation practice session, as a luxury. Even if it is a luxury, that doesn't mean designers cannot expose their project to some scrutiny before moving it into implementation. At the very least, it can be useful to do a dry run with a colleague or a friend. Here are some things that designers should look for in a pilot test. If they detect any problems, they should correct them before finalizing that aspect of the program:

- Does the lesson plan work as designed?
- Are the directions to the facilitator clear and concise?
- Are the facilitator's materials appropriate and thorough enough?
- Are the learner's materials appropriate and thorough enough?
- Are the support materials (slides, overheads, handouts) what you expected?
- Does the timing of each segment match your estimates?
- Are the technology components (audio, video, computers) appropriate?
- Do the instructional methods work as planned?
- What does not work the way you thought it should?
- What needs to be changed?

During the review, designers should look for anything that doesn't seem to fit. Sometimes a designer's instinct brings to their attention problems that may not be obvious to the subject matter experts or the client. It is this sixth sense about design that makes the role of the instructional designer so important.

Train-the-Trainer Courses

Another way to discover any problems is with a train-the-trainer (TTT) program, an often-neglected aspect of instructional design. Like analysis, the process of providing this level of support for facilitators involves work and requires resources; in the end, however, the extra effort can make the difference between success and failure.

This critically important aspect of course implementation is often ignored for a variety of seemingly logical reasons. You've probably heard that TTT courses are not necessary because professional facilitators can take any course and implement it with a little practice. Another excuse is that there isn't any time or resources available to bring everyone together for the TTT process. Others

REFLECTION

Train-the-trainer courses are one of the most common methods for making sure that a course design is implemented by facilitators in the way it is intended. There are several options for types of train-the-trainer courses, including the "see one, do one" approach. In this scenario, facilitators watch one offering of the course, usually given by the design team, and then teach the course on their own, after which they are given feedback and suggestions for improvement.

- Do you think it is necessary to train teachers the correct way to implement a course, or do you think that a well-designed lesson plan or teacher's guide should be enough to make sure the course is implemented to the design expectations?

- Do you think that different types of courses will have different requirements for instructor training?

- What other options for this process do you think might work?

might suggest that any well-designed course should not require any additional support for facilitators to implement.

As with every aspect of instructional design, the decision to require a TTT course is related to the rest of your course elements. If your system demands it, then you have to consider the ramifications of ignoring the warning. Here's a list of reasons for including a TTT element in instructional design:

- New or unfamiliar content
- New or unfamiliar delivery system
- Facilitator population with little or no previous facilitator experience
- Changes in content specifics that must be first taught to facilitators
- New or unfamiliar technology demands on facilitators
- Online course management systems training specific to content
- Requirement that content be rigidly and uniformly implemented
- Licensure or certification required for facilitators

A TTT course also provides the opportunity for pilot testing, with the caution that the target population may not be in perfect sync with the design plan population profile. In some ways it may be a preferred method of piloting if the content must also be delivered to the facilitators. This is sometimes the case with mandated training or organization-wide rollouts. In this option, the training is often presented by the instructional design team, SMEs, or some combination of the two.

Train-the-Trainer Course Design

Several styles of TTT courses have evolved over the years, with most being some variation of the "see one, teach one" model. With this approach, facilitators first observe or participate as learners for one implementation cycle of the course. They then facilitate all or some of the course content while being coached by both the design team and other facilitators. This approach works for both online and in-class settings.

There are many advantages to incorporating a complete observation cycle of the course in this model targeted toward future facilitators, including the fact that any questions facilitators have about the content can be addressed at the same time as issues associated with their implementation of the content.

The disadvantage of this approach is the time it takes to work through the process. In most cases it takes at least twice as long to implement the TTT course as the course takes in implementation with the intended population profile. That is why variations on this theme are becoming more focused on the unique aspects of a course and less on the actual art of facilitation, except in populations of novice facilitators.

Things to Consider in TTT Designs

As you work through the design of your TTT course, consider the following issues:
- To what degree does the population of facilitators require a facilitation skills upgrade or refresher?
- To what degree is the content new to the facilitators?
- Do you have any doubts about the ability of the facilitators to implement the course in areas that you can address in a TTT session?
- Are there any unique aspects of your course design or implementation that require facilitator participation in the content preparation (for example, having a facilitator gather data in real time that must then be interpreted for inclusion in the course)?

No matter what you decide concerning offering a TTT option, at least work through the advantages and disadvantages of your choice. As with most things in ISD, there is no one right or wrong answer.

Summary

The development function in ISD is the composition and proof testing phase of instructional design. From working with subject matter experts to pilot testing course designs, this element of ISD produces most of the tangible materials and products that learners see as end users of instructional design. The role that subject matter experts play in course design is almost exclusively focused on the development function.

CASE STUDY 1

Your ISD group has been assigned a project designing detailed and sophisticated training for the operators of a large university-based radio telescope project spanning from Australia to Chile to the United States. Each of the sites will require certified equipment operators, and the population includes many nationalities and several different primary languages.

DISCUSSION QUESTIONS

- Why do you think the development phase of the instructional design process is not typically recognized as part of ISD by non-designers?

- What percentage of the work involved in instructional design is considered part of the development phase of ISD?

- How many of the five types of SMEs do you think you would typically work with during an instructional design project?

- How is pilot testing critical to course design?

- Are train-the-trainer courses necessary in most course design scenarios?

You have access to a limited pool of subject matter experts who can assist with the technical side of designing the courses. However, they are primarily native speakers in English, Spanish, and Portuguese.

As a design team, what is your approach to the following design challenges:
- In what language will the courses be offered?
- How will you work with the various subject matter experts given the language variables?
- Do you think it is necessary to have all the SMEs in one place when working with them? Why or why not?

CASE STUDY 2

A small marketing company has hired your ISD firm to produce a series of video courses on how to work with them to ensure a better relationship and higher-quality marketing approaches. The president of the company insists on being involved in every aspect of the design process and would fall under the category of a sentinel SME.

How will you try to work with the president to allow for both a smooth design process and meeting the expressed expectation of day-to-day involvement?

Is it possible that the president could also be considered one or more of the other classifications of SME and provide additional value to the project?

CASE STUDY 3

A midsize community college is starting a new applied science program in hospitality management with a focus on front-of-house careers like manager and shift lead. The department's new dean is an academic from the accounting program and has never worked in the hospitality industry. The project requires at least several SMEs from the industry to assist in course design. The dean is insisting that students be used in that role to save money.

How will you address the problem of being expected to use students as SMEs when it is likely they do not have the experience to act in that role?

How will you explain to the dean the role SMEs are expected to play in the project and why students may not be the best choice?

CHAPTER 8

Implementation

KEY CONCEPTS

- Implementation is the most widely recognized element of ISD
- The flowchart approach of three elements: pre-course, delivery, and evaluation
- Level 1 evaluations in implementation
- Level 2 evaluations in implementation
- The performance agreement principle
- Quality rating rubrics for objectives, design plans, and lesson plans

CHAPTER OBJECTIVES

At the end of this chapter, the learner should be able to:

- Define *implementation* in the instructional design process.
- List the three elements in a standard implementation flowchart.
- List at least two reasons for implementing Level 1 evaluations.
- List at least two reasons for implementing Level 2 evaluations.
- Explain the three elements of performance agreement.
- Define the purpose of the three quality ratings used in the evaluation of the implementation ISD element.

Implementation is the most easily recognizable element of the instructional design process, since everyone has been a student at some point in their life. From the ISD perspective, it is during this time that the facilitation process is implemented and evaluation of the course content takes place beyond the view of learners. While an instructional designer may not be part of the facilitation process directly, pilots, and early implementations require rigorous instructional design overview to determine course design efficiency and to allow for changes as required before more course implementation takes place.

Even knowing when a course is ready for implementation is a design decision that isn't as easy as it may seem at first glance. It is time to move on to implementation when a designer has completed a process of due diligence and determined that there is little to be gained by waiting. Project management professionals say you are never more than 90 percent complete on any project you are working on. It is the same with instructional design and implementation decisions. Holding things up for that next 10 percent improvement in a course might take longer than the total time allocated for the project.

The traditional approach to evaluation during implementation is the use of smile sheets, which show the reaction or response of the learner to the experience. Although these are an important part of a great evaluation strategy, they are only one small part of what a designer needs to do. Evaluation in this phase needs to cover every aspect of the interaction between the product and the end user. In this chapter, we examine the three phases of the implementation process—pre-course, delivery, and evaluation—before discussing performance agreement and quality ratings.

The Designer's Role in Implementation

Full-time instructional designers seldom if ever implement the curricula they design; their role is more observation than participation. In some situations, a designer may have some evaluative role in early implementations just to make sure the course is going as planned and as designed. This is because it is not generally considered cost effective to have designers also be facilitators. However, there are many times when a designer also teaches a course or when a teacher also designs their courses. Regardless of the role a designer plays in implementation, there are numerous responsibilities on the design side of the equation that need to be addressed.

Not having the designer facilitating each new course design is a good idea for several reasons. Designers who are also facilitators tend to believe that they can improvise or fix missing or faulty design elements on the spot during implementation, and the changes seldom make it to the course design for future implementations. This creates a vacuum in information that makes lesson plans and other deliverables less detailed and therefore less useful to someone who may later facilitate the course. While these are not considered fatal flaws, they are something to think about if you are a one-person design and facilitation shop. Seek an independent set of eyes when evaluating implementation of a course.

The other truth in implementation from a design and scheduling perspective is that almost everything must be completed before the start of the actual implementation process. Designers must display a very high level of preparation for all the variables and intangibles that can happen in implementation since these have to be addressed ahead of time. This requires a designer to envision and design for every possible variable in each implementation scenario. The most difficult part for an instructional designer is the fact that the designer is almost never present for the actual implementation and can't save a faulty course design until after the first implementation.

The Implementation Process in Design

The usual flowchart for implementation contains the following elements:
- Pre-course
- Delivery
- Evaluation

This flow assumes a professionally designed course and materials.

Since we have covered design and development in earlier chapters, we can now focus on the course implementation process specifically as it relates to the design function.

Pre-Course

It is an understatement to say that each course implementation is different. Online, blended, and in-person deliveries all have unique qualities and necessary preparations. The same course may be implemented in different ways when variables like location, population, and software are taken into consideration. From the view of an instructional designer, planning and preparing a pre-course element for a lesson plan or facilitator's guide is required for each course. Without a plan, the preparation for implementation may or may not be performed by a facilitator.

Elements of a pre-course lesson plan may include:
- Implementation time
- Room setup
- Materials
- Evaluation forms
- Attendance list
- Handouts
- Computer and Wi-Fi username and password
- A/V equipment setup and test
- Internet access if required
- Name tents and name tags

It is also very useful to include timelines for certain elements of your pre-course setup to take place. Many designers group elements into:
- One week before class
- One day before class
- One hour before class

Here is an example of the pre-course section of an actual lesson plan prepared by UMBC graduate student Tina Butcher.

Pre-Course Preparations

At Least Two Weeks Prior to Class
- Contact the host jurisdiction and identify four participants to serve as leaders for the small group activities. These individuals need not be subject matter experts. Their role is to lead the group through the activity and keep the participants focused on completing the activity.

- Provide the sample activities and the following list of responsibilities to each group leader.
  - Review the group activity with the participants in the group.
  - Keep the discussions moving and focused on the activity.
  - Encourage all participants to contribute to the group discussion and ensure each person has an opportunity to provide input.
  - Identify and appoint a scribe and a spokesperson, if needed, for the activity. Arrange a follow-up call with each to review these responsibilities.

- Provide your contact information for questions prior to the training class.

- Obtain a copy of the building diagram where the class is located, identifying the emergency exits, and insert this into the Introductory Session slides.

Day Before

- **Equipment confirmation.** Check for the availability and functionality of your laptop computer, presentation software, presentation slide shows, and interface with the projector. Verify availability, positioning, and functionality of the projection screen and extension cords.

- **Materials shipment.** Verify shipment of materials have arrived and are complete and intact. If materials are missing, follow up with shipper tracking number. Presentation and handout materials are provided in electronic form on both the laptop and a memory stick provided by the organization. If needed, arrange with the host or a local printing service to reprint materials prior to the class.

- **Classroom confirmation and setup—general.** Confirm classroom availability the day before the training. Classroom setup must be complete at least one hour prior to student arrival in the classroom. If logistics permit and you are able to access the classroom, the organization recommends you complete the bulk of the setup the day or evening before the course. Using the checklist below, verify the following are in place.

- **Instructor materials.** In addition to a copy of all materials listed below for the participants, verify each instructor has the following materials:
  - Flash drive with electronic copy of all course materials to answer key for Activity 1
  - Answer key for Activity 2 for each facilitator
  - Answer key for Activity 3 for each facilitator
  - Copy of final exam
  - Copy of final exam answer key

No Later Than One Hour Prior to Class

- **Participant seating.** Ensure tables and chairs are positioned according to the diagram included and that there is sufficient space for each participant to fully open their binders and other reference materials and take notes. Make adjustments to the layout as needed, procuring additional tables and chairs if necessary.

- **Facilitator seating.** Ensure a table is reserved for facilitators when not actively teaching. Designate this seating with a sign or tip the chairs inward to avoid students sitting in this spot. This space is to allow the facilitator who is not teaching to take notes during the course, provide additional technical and logistical support to the primary facilitator, and scan the room for issues that may arise with students. Ideally this table should be positioned closest to the room entrance so the second facilitator can assist students who may arrive late or need to make an unplanned departure with minimal class disruption.

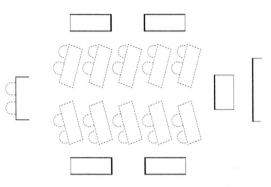

- **After-action review notes.** Place a notepad on the facilitator table labeled "Items for Improvement and Items That Went Well" to allow facilitators to make notes of areas for improvement and questions or problems that arose during the class. This will be used during the after-action review following the end of the class.

- **Acoustics.** Have each facilitator speak from the front of the classroom and ensure you can hear the facilitator from the seat farthest back in the room. This will allow you to become accustomed to the acoustics of the room and make necessary adjustments.

- **Projection screen.** Locate the projection screen and set it up.

- **A/v equipment.** Set up your projector, laptop, and speakers and verify they are working properly. Run through a few slides in each presentation to ensure clarity and proper lighting.

- **Flipchart or whiteboard—front of room.** Place one flipchart or whiteboard at the front of the room. Ensure it is readily visible to students and convenient for the facilitator, but does not obscure the views of any students. Reposition the flipchart or whiteboard as needed. Some whiteboards are permanently mounted, which may require the facilitator to adjust how it is used. Verify appropriate markers and erasers are available.

- **Welcome note.** Write the following on the flipchart or whiteboard:
  - Welcome to "Conducting Witness Testing on Commercial Weighing and Measuring Devices."

- **Flipchart or whiteboard—entrance.** Position one flipchart or whiteboard just outside the entrance to the class, writing the name of the course on the flipchart.

- **Power strips and extension cords.** Verify power strips and extension cords are secure and taped to avoid them being tripping hazards.

- **Internet access.** Verify internet access is working. Verify password access for students and write this information on the flipchart or whiteboard at the front of the room.

- **Participant materials.** Place one of each of the following items at each participant seat:
  - Course-specific materials
  - Two-inch notebook for each participant
  - Handouts of all slide presentations
  - Checklist for preparing for and conducting witness testing
  - Handout for activity 1
  - Handout for activity 2
  - Handout for activity 3
  - Copy of level 1 assessments—participant survey
  - Facilitators' biographies and contact information
  - Reference Materials
  - Copy of the current edition of "NIST Handbook 44, Specifications, Tolerances and Other Technical Requirements for Weighing and Measuring Devices"
  - Copy of the current edition of "NIST Handbook 130, Uniform Laws and Regulations in the Areas of Legal Metrology and Fuel Quality"
  - Copy of "NIST105-1, Specifications and Tolerances for Field Standard Weights"
  - Copy of "NIST105-7, Specifications and Tolerances for Dynamic Small Volume Provers"
  - Copy of "NIST 105-8, Specifications and Tolerances for Field Standard Weight Carts"
  - Copy of "NIST Handbook 112, Examination Procedure Outlines for Commercial Weighing and Measuring Devices: A Manual for Weights and Measures Officials"
  - Presentation—"The Essential Elements of Traceability, Georgia Harris, NIST OWM"

- **Entrance table.** Place the following on a table by the entrance to the classroom:
  - Sign-in sheets (2)
  - Name badges
  - Tent cards

As you can see, it's not possible to supply too much information to the facilitator prior to the course starting. The same approach should be followed for online and blended courses; only the information will differ from this example.

Delivery

While it is rare for a designer to be directly involved in course delivery except as an observer, creating a pilot course element works well since everyone involved knows the course is still being designed and improved. While larger projects are more likely to have the budget for pilot testing, most courses are simply offered for the first time to learners without a pilot implementation.

Evaluation in Implementation

The key role an instructional designer plays in implementation is the evaluation of the implementation product. With most sophisticated designs and courses, instructional designers gather complex data on mastery and the implementation process and then prepare reports based on the data collected. In the case where a course does not evaluate for mastery, it is as simple as a smile sheet evaluation to judge learner reaction to a course. In either case, the designer is in the background during implementation.

While we will cover the evaluation process in great detail in the next chapter, we will briefly look at the evaluation process that is typically part of course implementation. The reasons we talk about several different types of evaluation like the quality rating process and instruments is because a designer can observe and keep notes and data while observing implementation. There are times when the best designs have problems in implementation and a designer will need to have the information necessary to make corrections for future offerings.

We will first be looking at two of the four levels in Kirkpatrick's evaluation model. Then we will look at the performance agreement principle and how it relates to implementation. Finally, we will review the three quality rating rubrics of quality rating for objectives (QRO), quality rating for design plans (QRDP), and quality rating for lesson plans (QRLP).

Kirkpatrick's Levels of Evaluation in Implementation

Donald Kirkpatrick (1994) divided evaluation into four levels, which have become the benchmark for evaluation. While they are usually referred to as levels, these are operationally separate evaluative elements that can be used together or separately. Each of these has specific qualities and fits distinctive needs. Although these levels are linear, designers do not have to use them in any specific order to achieve their evaluation objectives. The four levels of evaluation are:

- Level 1: Reaction
- Level 2: Learning
- Level 3: Behavior
- Level 4: Results

In this chapter we will be looking at Level 1 and Level 2 evaluations; all the levels will be covered in much more detail in the next chapter.

Level 1: Reaction

Anyone who has ever completed an evaluation that asked for a reaction to a training course probably was responding to a Level 1 evaluation. The most common evaluations at this level are smile sheets, which ask about likes and dislikes. Smile sheets are so common that some people use the term to refer to all evaluations at this level. Other Level 1 evaluations are focus groups, which are held after training, and selective interviews, in which people ask a sample of learners their opinions of training as they leave a program.

The aim of each of these Level 1 evaluations is to discover learners' reactions to the process. More than anything, Level 1 evaluation provides instant quality control data. ATD (2019) reports that "about eight in 10 organizations" use Level 1 evaluations.

A good strategy for Level 1 evaluation is to determine learners' initial responses to the experience as they exit the training. Every minute that elapses from the end of the training to the reaction from a participant adds to the risk that inaccurate data will be collected.

Typical questions include:
- Was your time well spent in this training?
- Would you recommend this course to a co-worker?
- What did you like best?
- What did you like least?
- Were the objectives made clear to you?
- Do you feel you were able to meet the objectives?
- Did you like the way the course was presented?
- Was the room comfortable?
- Is there anything you would like to tell us about the experience?

It is important that you realize the limitations associated with a Level 1 reaction evaluation. First, it has little if any relationship to whether a learner reached mastery on the content of the course, which is the single most important evaluation. Second, working toward a high positive on a Level 1 may not be a sound course design criterion. There are some courses that are never going to be enjoyable for learners or content that is not going to be fun to learn no matter what you do in the design of the course. The real shame with Level 1 evaluations is that some organizations evaluate facilitators and hire and fire based on Level 1 results. There are better ways to evaluate facilitators than expecting a reaction evaluation from a learner to be valid enough for this purpose. Use these as they are intended to be used: to determine learner reaction and nothing else. These are not intended to be a peripheral facilitator quality control vehicle.

Level 2: Learning

For instructional designers, evaluations at the learning level are tied directly to objectives. These are the evaluation tasks that designers develop to match their objectives. Most industry studies show that fewer than 35 percent of training includes a reliable form of Level 2 evaluation.

Level 2 evaluations include everything from quizzes to tests to final exams. These are covered in greater detail in the next chapter. For the purposes of implementation, Level 2 evaluations are already part of the lesson plan and a designer will observe how well each evaluation works when delivered by using one or more of the following techniques.

Performance Agreement and Implementation

Performance agreement, which we look at in depth in chapter 15, goes a long way toward ensuring that objectives are correctly evaluated as they are observed in implementation. If the designer or a member of the design team can perform an evaluation of the performance agreement principles, there is a high probability that objectives and evaluation of mastery are well matched and objectives are in fact being evaluated as required by design standards.

Let's review the following objective:

Given a realistic role-play situation with Sales for the Beginner, the learner playing the part of the salesperson should be able to present three reasons the client should purchase a specific product.

With the objective in mind, the designer then generates an evaluation task:

You have just entered the office of a major client. You have to make a case for buying your top-line product. It is important that you present at least three reasons the client should purchase your product.

The next step has the designer matching the key elements of behavior, condition, and degree in the objective and the evaluation task. The key elements in performance agreement are shown in Figure 8-1.

Figure 8-1. The Key Elements in Performance Agreement

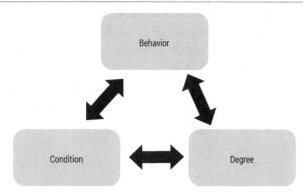

Designers who follow the performance agreement principle of comparing the behavior and condition elements of both an objective and an evaluation task will be accomplished Level 2 designers.

Other Elements of Evaluation

During implementation, other elements of evaluation that must be present are:
- Evaluation from the perspective of the facilitator
- Evaluation of the materials or technology
- Evaluation of the environment (room size, arrangement)
- Continuity and conformity of implementation with the design plan

These elements are independent of the level process and have the potential for providing data that suggest that changes are necessary. Every aspect of the design is subject to further alteration once implemented. As noted earlier, designers should never consider a project more than 90 percent complete. This means they have a work in progress, not a project that has no hope of redemption. Careful evaluation will provide ample opportunities for tweaks during and after implementation.

Even perfectionists can relax, knowing that everything is a work in progress, including content and materials. They may get paid for their work or be assigned to another project, but the designs they have worked on are still maturing.

REFLECTION

- The performance agreement principle was designed to ensure that evaluation of mastery was credible and based on the quality of the relationship between objectives, learning conditions, and evaluation tasks. If these three elements are not in sync, it's impossible to establish credible or reliable mastery.

- In your past experiences as a learner, have you ever taken a course where the evaluation of the course content delivered, as either a quiz or a test, was inconsistent with the course content or the course objectives? How did you feel as a learner in this situation?

Quality Control During Implementation

One of the missing pieces in the practice of professional ISD has been the lack of any formal quality control process beyond some very basic subjective overviews or having a supervisor or team review design work like objectives, design plans, and lesson plans. It is important to establish a system of quality control that allows an unbiased and objective evaluation of ISD projects. It is no longer good enough to assure a client or others that your work meets generally accepted design standards based on your subjective opinion. There is now a way to reach well beyond an opinion and enter the world of objective review.

The work you review may be your own, something you have been asked to review for someone else, or the work of your department or employees. Regardless of the source of the work, you need a benchmark for each of your design elements that allows you to gauge quality.

The quality rating evaluation instruments presented here are just some examples of how you can accomplish this task. Whether you choose to use these as they are or modify them to fit your work environment and process, it is important that you elevate your professional skill standards as your experience allows. The very fact that you have a quality review process says much about your approach to ISD and your commitment to professional standards.

Quality Rating Rubrics

For designers and teams that want to go beyond the normal evaluation during implementation, the use of one or more of the quality rating rubrics is an option. All are intended to make the process of reviewing any ISD project more organized and standardized. The three matrices are:
- Quality rating for objectives
- Quality rating for design plans
- Quality rating for lesson plans

Each of these quality rating tools is based on the standard instructional design formats appearing in this book. As you review the quality rating for objectives, you'll see that it is based on the A-B-C-D format for objectives. The quality rating for design plan format is based on the basic elements most designers use, which are featured in this book. The quality rating for lesson plans is based on the nine-events format.

While these three quality ratings are based on the specific elements and formats of objectives, design plans, and lesson plans as they are presented, you may find yourself modifying these to fit your specific needs. You should also use the concept of quality review and develop rubrics and methodologies that fit your unique work environment.

Quality Rating for Objectives (QRO)

Writing objectives is both art and science. As such, it retains the best and worst qualities of subjective and objective thinking on the part of instructional designers. To make the process of reviewing the quality of formal ISD objectives more, well, objective, it helps to have a standard tool for evaluating them. The quality rating for objectives (QRO) is just such a tool.

The use of the QRO requires a standard from which to benchmark the quality of each individual objective, whether terminal or enabling. The standard described in this chapter has its genesis in the key elements of an objective as presented. It can be modified for individual settings, but it gives you a basis for establishing your own standards either for an organization or as a personal standard for quality.

All the elements of an A-B-C-D objective (audience, behavior, condition, degree) are based on standards that conform to sound practice in ISD. Each of these elements is then assigned a numerical value; when summed, the values should total 100 percent for each objective.

Audience

Although the audience statement of an objective is simple in theory, writing a great audience statement is not always easy. The use of the words *student, learner,* or *participant* is not always the best choice for your objective. Great ISD practice requires that you be much more specific and name the course or population as clearly as possible.

For the QRO, consider the three elements of the audience statement:
- **Clarity:** Who is the intended audience? (*Learner* or another generic term is not sufficiently clear.)

- **Format:** How well is the audience statement written? Does it make sense?
- **Perspective:** Is it written from the perspective of a single learner, rather than from that of a group, a facilitator, an organization, and so forth?

The rubric shown is used to rate the audience element (Table 8-1). The maximum score for an audience statement is 20 percent of the 100 percent total for each objective.

Table 8-1. QRO Rubric for the Audience Element

	Maximum Value (%)	Rating (%)
Clarity	10	
Format	5	
Perspective	5	

Behavior

The behavior statement is the most important element in any objective, and that importance is reflected in the QRO. The elements of importance to use in the QRO are:

- **Observable:** Is this a behavior that is tangible, or is it ambiguous?
- **Measurable:** Is it possible to measure learner mastery?
- **Format:** How well is it written? Does the behavior statement make sense?

A rubric for rating the behavior element is shown in Table 8-2. The total for this element is 40 percent of the quality rating, a significant part of the total.

Table 8-2. QRO Rubric for the Behavior Element

	Maximum Value (%)	Rating (%)
Observable	15	
Measurable	20	
Format	5	

Condition

When measuring condition elements, it is important to make sure that each objective has a clear foundation of what will be provided within the learner-objective relationship. An objective lacking in conditions is instructionally unstable.

The QRO should address three areas of condition statements:

- **Clarity:** Are all the conditions clearly defined in the objective?
- **Comprehensiveness:** Are all the conditions mentioned?
- **Format:** How well is the condition statement written? Does it make sense?

The QRO rubric for the condition statement is shown in Table 8-3. You can have a maximum of 20 percent for your condition element.

Table 8-3. QRO Rubric for the Condition Statement

	Maximum Value (%)	Rating (%)
Clarity	10	
Comprehensiveness	5	
Format	5	

Degree

The value of a degree statement in an objective can never be overstated; however, it is one of the most neglected elements in most objectives written. Consider these three important elements of degree statements in the QRO:

- **Clarity:** Is there any doubt about what is expected? Does the objective use any ambiguous and unquantifiable language, including "-ly" words such as *safely*, *carefully*, or *honestly*?
- **Measurable:** Is the degree statement in a format that is measurable?
- **Format:** How well is it written? Does it make sense?

The QRO rubric for the degree statement will look something like Table 8-4. The degree element has a maximum total of 20 percent.

Table 8-4. QRO Rubric for the Degree Statement

	Maximum Value (%)	Rating (%)
Clarity	10	
Measurable	5	
Format	5	

Format for a QRO

Table 8-5 shows what a complete QRO rubric looks like before entering the values.

Table 8-5. Complete QRO Rubric

	Maximum Value (%)	Rating (%)
Audience		
Clarity	10	
Format	5	
Perspective	5	
Behavior		
Observable	15	
Measurable	20	
Format	5	
Condition		
Clarity	10	
Comprehensiveness	5	
Format	5	
Degree		
Clarity	10	
Measurable	5	
Format	5	
Total	100	

Variations

You might decide to add or subtract elements or to change the rating criteria or ratios on your version of the QRO. You should feel empowered to change anything to match your needs. You will probably want to keep as close to a 100-point scale as possible to make your results consistent and to use numerical values that have a common meaning.

Quality Rating for Design Plans: The QRDP

The design plan in ISD is the standard document of the profession. Whether you use the format illustrated in this book or a variation, the standard elements of a design plan are the equivalent of the blueprint in architecture.

The quality rating for design plans (QRDP) provides a common format to review your design plans and make some objective judgments relating to the quality of each design plan document. As with all quality rating strategies used here, the specifics of your design elements will vary with the specifics of your approach and will not diminish the usefulness of this instructional design tool.

Most design plans consist of eight elements:
- Rationale
- Target population
- Course description
- Objectives
- Evaluation strategy
- Participant prerequisites
- Facilitator prerequisites
- Deliverables

Each element is reviewed and assigned a numerical rating; the total for each design plan should be 100 percent.

Rationale

In reviewing a rationale, consider whether it has met the basic requirements of presenting your project in a way that allows the reader, usually a non-designer, to catch the important elements of your plan. Is your rationale truly a short, concise mission statement that delivers the message you want to convey?

The QRDP rates the following elements of a rationale:
- **Mission:** Is it clear why this course exists?
- **Detail:** Does the rationale provide the details of the course, including audience and sponsors?
- **Format:** Is it well written and as brief as possible? Does it make sense?

This rubric can help you rate the rationale element (Table 8-6). With a total value of 13 percent, the rationale is an important foundation for your design plan and is weighted to reflect that.

Table 8-6. QRDP for the Rationale Element

	Maximum Value (%)	Rating (%)
Mission	5	
Detail	5	
Format	3	

Target Population

Defining a population within your design plan is key when getting started. Most of your decisions, including media, methods, and objectives, will flow from this element. Several important elements of your target population are reviewed in the QRDP:

- **Clarity:** Is it clear whom the population includes?
- **Detail:** How much do you know about the population? Is this enough?
- **Challenges:** Does this element of the design plan identify specifics—both positive and negative—about this population?

Table 8-7 provides a strategy for rating the target population element. Your maximum for the population element is 12 percent of the rating.

Table 8-7. QRDP for Target Population

	Maximum Value (%)	Rating (%)
Clarity	5	
Detail	5	
Challenges	2	

Course Description

The course description comprises the logistics and methods of your design plan. Make sure that all the detail you need for your project is here. At a minimum, have at least these elements in your ratings:

- **Course length:** Is it clear how this course is timed (how long, when, and so forth)?

- **Instructional method:** How is this course implemented?
- **Materials:** What does the facilitator need in terms of handouts, texts, video, audiovisual equipment, and so forth?

The ratings for the description element within the design plan are shown in Table 8-8. The course description represents a maximum of 15 percent of your total.

Table 8-8. QRDP for the Course Description

	Maximum Value (%)	Rating (%)
Course Length	5	
Instructional Methods	5	
Materials	5	

Objectives

Because objectives are the heart of your design plan, you want to make sure they are up to your quality standards. At this point in the quality rating process, you can use the existing QRO rubric, or you can just use the QRDP for more operational elements of the objectives in your plan. For this example, we are going to use the latter approach.

- **Number:** Have you included all the objectives that are needed for this content?
- **Format:** Are the objectives in the A-B-C-D format?
- **Detail:** Do you have both terminal and enabling objectives?

The quality rating system for objectives is shown in Table 8-9. Your objectives have a maximum rating of 12 percent of your total.

Table 8-9. QRDP for Objectives

	Maximum Value (%)	Rating (%)
Number	5	
Format	5	
Detail	2	

Evaluation Strategy

This quality element involves all the other elements in your design plan, because you want to make sure that you have evaluated both the project and the process involved in finalizing your design plan. Possible elements for this matrix include:

- **Detail:** Have you listed and explained your choices for evaluation (type, forms, and so forth)?
- **Process:** How will you implement your evaluation?
- **Thoroughness:** Have you been thorough in your evaluation process? Does it reflect the most likely real-world application of the objective?

The quality rating rubric for evaluation in your design plan is shown in Table 8-10. Evaluations are a maximum of 15 percent of your total rating.

Table 8-10. QRDP for Evaluation

	Maximum Value (%)	Rating (%)
Detail	5	
Process	5	
Thoroughness	5	

Participant Prerequisites

Prerequisites are important to your design plan, so make sure you have covered all the bases. Evaluate your participant prerequisites according to these criteria:

- **Clarity:** Is it clear which prerequisites each participant is required to meet?
- **Ranging:** Have you listed the highest and lowest recommended prerequisites?

The rubric to rate your participant prerequisites in the design plan is shown in Table 8-11. Eight percent of the total score for the design plan represents the participant prerequisites.

Table 8-11. QRDP for Participant Prerequisites

	Maximum Value (%)	Rating (%)
Clarity	10	
Ranging	5	

Facilitator Prerequisites

Setting the standards for those who facilitate your course is an important aspect of instructional design. At a minimum you should list the qualifications you expect from a facilitator. Be sure not to use vague wording or ambiguous standards. For example:

· **Minimum standards:** Have you listed your expectations?
· **Clarity:** Are your standards clear and unambiguous?

The rubric for rating your facilitator prerequisites in the design plan is shown in Table 8-12. Facilitator prerequisites comprise a maximum of 10 percent of your total.

Table 8-12. QRDP for Facilitator Prerequisites

	Maximum Value (%)	Rating (%)
Minimum Standards	5	
Clarity	5	

Deliverables

Knowing what is required for a project is a great communication tool for designers working with both a design team and clients. Make sure you have considered the following:

· **Thoroughness:** Have you included everything?
· **Clarity:** Is it clear what each deliverable really is?
· **Responsibility:** Is it clear who is responsible for each deliverable?

The rubric for evaluating the deliverables portion of your design plan is shown in Table 8-13. The importance of deliverables is reflected in the maximum of 15 percent of your total rating.

Table 8-13. QRDP for Deliverables

	Maximum Value (%)	Rating (%)
Thoroughness	5	
Clarity	5	
Responsibility	5	

Quality Rating for Lesson Plans: The QRLP

The lesson plan in ISD is a standard document for learning professionals spanning the gamut from kindergarten teachers to corporate coaches. Whether you use the exact format used in this book or some variation, the standard nine elements of a lesson plan are included in this quality rating system. Each of the first eight elements also includes a rating for transition. This rating measures how well one element flows into the following element. Stated otherwise, do all the elements fit together to create a comprehensive whole? This is important because a lesson plan should appear seamless to the learner.

Each of the nine elements of a lesson plan are reviewed and assigned a numerical rating; totaling the individual ratings should yield a maximum of 100 percent for each lesson plan.

Gaining Attention

In this first element, make sure you have started the process of focusing a learner on the task at hand. Is it short but powerful, and does it relate to the formal objectives in your design plan? Consider these criteria as you evaluate this element:

- **Gains attention:** How well does it begin focusing a learner's attention on the content?
- **Brevity:** Does it last less than five minutes?
- **Relates to content:** Is there a direct correlation?
- **Transition:** How well does this element flow to the next?

The criteria for evaluating the strength of your lesson plan in terms of gaining the attention of participants are shown in Table 8-14. Gaining attention accounts for 12 percent of your total in the QRLP.

Table 8-14. QRLP for Gaining Attention

	Maximum Value (%)	Rating (%)
Gains Attention	5	
Brevity	2	
Relates to Content	3	
Transition	2	

Direction

This section of your lesson plan is where you present your objectives; you want to be both clear and complete in the way you do this aspect of your lesson plan.

- **Objectives present:** Are the program objectives clearly identified?
- **Clarity:** Is it clear what you are asking learners to do?
- **Transition:** How well does this element flow to the next?

Evaluate the direction element of your lesson plan using the criteria shown, accounting for 12 percent of your QRLP (Table 8-15).

Table 8-15. QRLP for Direction

	Maximum Value (%)	Rating (%)
Objectives Present	5	
Clarity	5	
Transition	2	

Recall

This key lesson plan element serves as a safety net for learners, so make sure that key prerequisites are reviewed and any deficits in knowledge or performance are addressed before you start with the new content. Ask yourself these questions:

- **Key prerequisite content covered:** Have you covered all of the necessary prerequisites?
- **Strategies for over- and underqualified learners:** Have you prepared a plan and any necessary materials for both over- and underqualified learners?
- **Transition:** How well does this element flow to the next?

Recall constitutes 9 percent of your QRLP total. Use this rubric for evaluating the recall element (Table 8-16).

Table 8-16. QRLP for Recall

	Maximum Value (%)	Rating (%)
Key Prerequisite Content Covered	5	
Strategies for Over- and Underqualified Learners	2	
Transition	2	

Content

This is the heart of your lesson plan. Be sure to present the content in an ordered and dynamic format; make it real for your learners.
- **Lively:** Is it more than just boring regurgitation of content?
- **Clarity:** Is the content detailed and clear in the way it is presented?
- **Transition:** How well does this element lead to the next?

Content accounts for 11 percent of your QRLP total. Use this scoring system for evaluating this element (Table 8-17).

Table 8-17. QRLP for Content

	Maximum Value (%)	Rating (%)
Lively	5	
Clarity	4	
Transition	2	

Application Feedback Level 1

Now you are ready to reinforce your content, and at this first level, you need to have your facilitation at an balanced keel with your learners—a joint engagement of content-related interaction with focused and precise feedback. Consider the following:
- **50:50 facilitator-learner ratio:** Is this an even engagement?
- **Application feedback opportunity:** Is there feedback provided?
- **Clarity:** Is the feedback clear from a learner's perspective?
- **Transition:** How well does this element flow to the next?

The method for evaluating application feedback level 1, which accounts for 13 percent of your QRLP total, is shown in Table 8-18.

Table 8-18. QRLP for Application Feedback Level 1

	Maximum Value (%)	Rating (%)
50:50 Facilitator-Learner Ratio	4	
Application Feedback Opportunity	4	
Clarity	2	
Transition	3	

Application Feedback Level 2

At this point you want to start handing off the ownership of the content to the learner. Small group work is an example of an implementation modality.

- **30:70 facilitator-learner ratio:** Are you handing off ownership to the learner at this point in the lesson plan?
- **Application feedback opportunity:** Is there feedback provided?
- **Clarity:** Is it clear?
- **Transition:** How well does this element flow to the next?

Application feedback level 2 accounts for 13 percent of your QRLP total. Break down the scoring of this element as shown in Table 8-19.

Table 8-19. QRLP for Application Feedback Level 2

	Maximum Value (%)	Rating (%)
30:70 Facilitator-Learner Ratio	4	
Application Feedback Opportunity	4	
Clarity	2	
Transition	3	

Application Feedback Level 3

Now is the time to provide the learners with almost all the ownership of the content. Think of this as the pre-evaluation phase of your lesson plan.

- **10:90 facilitator-learner ratio:** Are learners really in control of the content?
- **Application feedback opportunity:** Is there feedback provided?
- **Clarity:** Is the feedback clear from a learner's perspective?
- **Transition:** How well does this element flow to the next?

Application feedback level 3 accounts for 13 percent of your QRLP total, as shown in Table 8-20.

Table 8-20. QRLP for Application Feedback Level 3

	Maximum Value (%)	Rating (%)
10:90 Facilitator-Learner Ratio	4	
Application Feedback Opportunity	4	
Clarity	2	
Transition	3	

Evaluation

Now that learners have had three opportunities to practice the objectives, they are ready for the formal evaluation—if it exists. If not, have you designed a process for facilitators to double-check previous informal evaluations from application feedback elements at levels 1, 2, and 3?

- **Evaluation present:** Does an evaluation take place in this element?
- **Clarity:** Is the evaluation component clear?
- **Transition:** How well does this element flow to the next?

Evaluation accounts for 9 percent of your QRLP total. Table 8-21 represents a systematic way of assessing the evaluation element of your lesson plan.

Table 8-21. QRLP for Evaluation

	Maximum Value (%)	Rating (%)
Level 2 Evaluation Present	5	
Clarity	2	
Transition	2	

Closure

Closure—the final element of your lesson plan—is your last chance to perform a quality check. Make sure you also recap the lesson and apply any opportunities to generalize and synthesize the content from the lesson.

- **Recap of content:** Have you reviewed the objectives?
- **Generalization:** Have you generalized the content?
- **Synthesis:** Have you synthesized the content?

Table 8-22 shows how to evaluate your closure element. Closure accounts for 8 percent of your QRLP total.

Table 8-22. QRLP for Closure

	Maximum Value (%)	Rating (%)
Recap of Content	4	
Generalization	2	
Synthesis	2	

Summary

The role of an instructional designer is not diminished when a course and project go to the implementation phase. There is considerable work that must be done to ensure that the course is well designed and delivers the content and evaluation of mastery required. While usually not the instructor at this point in the process, the designer must use a variety of evaluative tools to make certain that the course quality exists at the desired level.

CASE STUDY 1

A professor at a large state university teaches in the physics undergrad program, and most of the classes are 101-level courses with up to 200 students. The professor has asked that the school's instructional designers observe both the online and in-class sections of the entry-level course and offer suggestions on how to make the course better for the learners. In recent terms, the average grade for the courses has been a low B, or 82 out of 100 points. More than 10 percent of each section is not passing the course.

Details:
- Physics 101 course
- Average class section is 150 students with up to 200 during some terms
- Two online sections and one in-classroom section held in an amphitheater-type lecture hall
- Two grad students assigned to the professor to assist with grading and attendance

You are the instructional designer assigned to the project. The first course sections will be offered next term, which starts in three weeks. What is your plan for observing the implementation of this course and offering suggestions for both online and in-classroom sections?

CASE STUDY 2

You are the lead instructional designer at an association that provides courses and licensing in the field of electrical engineering. Because of the recent forced move from classroom to online courses, the organization feels that the online courses are not as effective as the in-classroom courses. While participation is down, there is some feeling that it is more about the forced change to online rather than any problems with the course or instructors.

REFLECTION

Quality control is a term and process that is part of most organizations in one form or another. In the instructional design world, there is generally not a lot of discussion concerning QC in the design process. Some think it is assumed that this takes place; others feel the design project speaks for itself. In a world of ISO and numerous other standards, the lack of a visible quality control process in ISD seems to create a void in the profession. While the formal quality rating rubrics that appear in the text are available, they do not yet see wide implementation.

As a designer, what would you use as your quality control process for the design process? Would you use the QRLP, QRDP, or QRO as a part of a formal ISD quality control process in your work?

DISCUSSION QUESTIONS

- What are the most important tasks for a designer to perform during course implementation?

- Is it possible to not require or perform any evaluation in implementation? Why do you think so many courses are never evaluated?

- How would you modify the QRO, QRDP, or QRLP to fit your specific design needs?

- Are there any other quality control measures that you use as an instructional designer?

- Which do you think is most important to an instructional designer, the evaluation of learners or the evaluation of the instructional design process itself?

Details

- 10 courses now online
- Five full-time instructors
- Average class size is 20 learners
- Course length is two weeks or 40 hours
- Implementation using a popular LMS product

You are requested to offer suggestions to the organization on how well the courses are working and the efficiency of the evaluations of mastery in this technical content area. What is your strategy and what evaluation tools will you use to review the courses as they are implemented?

CASE STUDY 3

A local nonprofit serving the community with a food bank and daily meals sees the need to offer a course in how to prepare healthy meals for children for caregivers on a tight budget. One of the association's board members is a retired K–12 teacher who thinks the course can easily be one of the volunteers talking off-the-cuff about how to prepare the meals. The board member is opposed to designing a formal course because it is "a waste of time" and anyone should be able to do this.

You are a food bank volunteer; another board member has discovered you are an instructional designer and wants you to take on this project. There is a feeling that this needs to be more than talking heads in front of a group, that it could possibly be something offered at a number of locations besides at the organization's offices and warehouse.

How will you address the issue of one board member thinking this is only about implementation of the content and that anything more complicated is unnecessary?

Is it possible that the board member who is a retired teacher could be brought into the design process in a productive way to clear the path for this to be completed without any additional problems?

CHAPTER 9
Evaluation

KEY CONCEPTS

- Evaluation is the ISD phase where all the design and implementation processes and products are evaluated
- Conducting evaluation for the analysis, design, development, implementation, and evaluation phases of ISD
- Conducting evaluation of objectives to ensure quality and for mastery determination
- Degree of difficulty as a necessary aspect of evaluating content rigor
- Performance agreement and the fit between objectives and evaluation tasks

CHAPTER OBJECTIVES

At the end of this chapter, the learner should be able to:

- Describe at least two uses for evaluation in the:
  - Analysis stage of ISD
  - Design stage of ISD
  - Development stage of ISD
  - Implementation stage of ISD
  - Evaluation of a course or project
- Provide at least three reasons for evaluating the design of behavioral objectives.
- Explain why designers should care about the degree of difficulty in objectives.
- List the elements of the performance agreement principle.
- Provide at least two examples of the use of psychometrics in the evaluation process.

In the past, evaluation was sometimes an afterthought and sometimes completely ignored in courses that didn't require examinations for academic or licensure reasons. There was a commonly held feeling that simply sitting through a course was enough. Designers always knew this wasn't true, but now almost every course has to have a rigorous evaluation process in place, and it has to be more sophisticated than asking a learner if they liked participating.

This demand for precise and reliable evaluative documentation requires designers to engage in a much more detailed look at every facet of the design process and product. Designers must be concerned about three different but related areas that are monitored to design and deliver quality courses and projects. Specifically, we work with learner-centered, facilitator-centered, and design process evaluations. This is the evaluation trilogy in instructional design (Figure 9-1).

Figure 9-1. Aspects of Evaluation

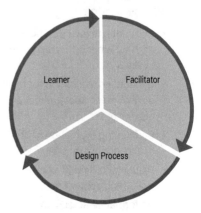

Learner-centered evaluation is the more traditional role of evaluation in learner mastery, with the influence of Donald Kirkpatrick's work and his evaluation levels. Facilitator-centered evaluation looks at the facilitator's role in moving learners to mastery. In design process evaluation, we are focused on the actual process and deliverables related to course development. All of these are evaluation, but they require different skills and different tools to be effective.

As an example of how evaluation works in this environment, let's look at the development of a single course. First, you have the design and other ISD elements that go into developing the final course, which is then implemented. Once the course is implemented, the second part of evaluation comes into play during the course as you determine mastery of each learner. Both are evaluations, but the information you are evaluating is completely different.

This chapter will examine how evaluation has become more than learner related; it is now about evaluating the design process and even the evaluation process itself.

Kirkpatrick's Four Levels of Evaluation

One of the most important contributions to the work of instructional designers as it relates to evaluation was made by Donald Kirkpatrick (Figure 9-2). Starting with his PhD dissertation in 1954, Kirkpatrick was one of the first wave of instructional designers, including Robert Gagné and Robert Mager, to establish science-based theory and practice in ISD. This former president of the American Society for Training and Development (now the Association for Talent Development) gave the field the most logical and enduring model of evaluation.

While most refer to Kirkpatrick's model as the four levels of evaluation, in reality they are four areas of evaluation. Just like ADDIE and other models, the seemingly linear appearance of Kirkpatrick's evaluation model, based on using the terminology of levels in his work, is not consistent with how a designer works with evaluation in practice. Kirkpatrick's four levels of evaluation (1994) are:

- Level 1: Reaction
- Level 2: Learning
- Level 3: Behavior
- Level 4: Results

Figure 9-2. Kirkpatrick's Levels of Evaluation

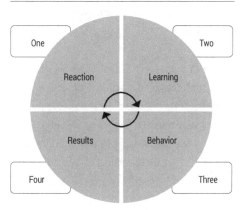

Kirkpatrick, D.L., and J.D. Kirkpatrick. 1994. *Evaluating Training Programs.* Oakland, CA: Berrett-Koehler.

Level 1: Reaction

When we look at the first level of evaluation as instructional designers, we are trying to determine how a learner reacted to a specific course or program. Did they enjoy it? Do they feel they learned something? Did they like the facilitator and would they recommend it to a friend? These are the typical types of data being sought with this evaluation. These evaluations in their distribution mode are often called smile sheets, and it is easy to see why. Was there a collective learner smile at the end of the course?

Instructional
designers have
always held a
rather mixed
view of the
usefulness
of Level 1
evaluations.

Instructional designers have always held a rather mixed view of the usefulness of these types of evaluations. One view is that any information is valuable as a designer and that even this type of affective feedback has some usefulness in evaluation and future adjustments of course properties. The other view is that these evaluations have little if anything to do with mastery and therefore have little durable value in design. Both points of view have merit.

The smile sheet–supportive designer will argue that having data on environmental issues like learner perception of facilitators, learning environments, and depth of commitment to their feelings, with questions, like "Would you recommend this to a friend?" is valuable. Many facilitators feel that these evaluations unfairly and certainly unscientifically evaluate their effectiveness based on arbitrary post-implementation emotional reactions. Some organizations rely entirely on this type of evaluation when it comes to hiring, retaining, and promoting facilitators.

As with any aspect of instructional design, it is important to place the information and data in the context of what it offers in terms of evaluation. Universal adoration or dislike of an instructor tells us something, but what? It is possible that a very talented facilitator was given a horribly designed course to implement and no learner is going to feel good about the experiences. Always evaluate data across the entire spectrum of available information and don't just make a judgement based on one very vertical data point.

Level 2: Learning

The heart and soul of instructional design rest in learner mastery, and the evaluation of mastery is critical in the practice of professional-level ISD. Learning evaluations can take many forms; we looked at this extensively in the chapter on objectives since it is impossible to measure learning accurately without objectives. The instructional designer is responsible for making sure that mastery is measured based on the expected outcomes for a course or project. This type of evaluation must be objective, without any subjectivity in either the process or the provider.

While most instructional designers consider it mandatory to implement and review evaluations of learning, the majority of organizations still don't require this type of evaluation. Academia, applied sciences, apprenticeships, and other credentialed and certified programs are almost universally required to have documented evaluations for learners to retain their institutional licensing and authority.

Level 3: Behavior

The most important question Level 3 seeks to answer is, "Did the training stick?" How much of the training transferred from delivery to the workplace? In many organizations and course design projects, this evaluation is never actually implemented to determine behavioral change. The most recent study showed that between 11 and 12 percent of training is evaluated for behavioral change (Bassi and Van Buren 1999). This is not surprising given the focus on the immediacy of course implementation and results. However, there are many times when Level 3 evaluations should be part of a design approach, and the more a designer can make the case for performing this evaluation, the more likely it is to be actually used in practice.

There are several ways to conduct Level 3 evaluations that any designer can add to a toolkit. Surveys and observation are two powerful ways to evaluate at this level. The thing to remember about this level of evaluation is the behavior. Did the behavior move to the workplace? If a designer's objectives are written well, they contain half of what they need to be used in the design of a course. The other half is to select a way to measure where participants start and where they are when designers measure long-term results.

Other Evaluation Questions

Designers who are interested in seeing if participants can meet the training objectives will evaluate learning, whereas those who are interested in seeing if performance has improved will measure behavior. Both of these can be satisfied with evaluation.

For example, evaluations would differ for a course on the use of new software for entering orders in a retail sales environment. A designer is interested in finding out if the course had any impact. Accurate data is available on how long it took to complete a transaction before the training with both the new and old software. At regular intervals, the designer accumulates new data on how long it takes to complete a transaction and compares the numbers. The designer can easily see any difference in time to see if the training had any impact and how much.

Designers who want to find out how much of the training objectives learners can still meet can sample a representative number of participants with the formal evaluation task used during the course. They then compare the scores on

> Surveys and observation are two powerful ways to evaluate at Level 3.

an individual or group basis and do the math. This method will go a long way toward evaluating if the content, as well as the instructional and delivery methods, were the best choices for the project.

In situations in which the evaluation is not so simple (with soft skills or affective domain courses, for example), designers can interview or survey participants and gauge the participants' opinion of their ability to meet the objectives. If possible, designers can also retest a sampling of the participants.

There are three basic reasons participants may lose the ability to meet objectives after the course, each of which tells the designer something important about the course. The reasons are covered in detail here.

Participants Never Learned the Skill or Concept

On those occasions when learners fail to achieve mastery of course content, the designer will see this in the Level 3 evaluation of the course objectives. It is typically the case that a large percentage of learners in this category points to errors in implementation or design. The first place for the designer to revisit is the course design and make sure that the population truly fits the content level and course design choices.

It is possible that the facilitators who carried out the implementation may have done a poor job or didn't follow the lesson plan as provided. It might be that the participants ignored the prerequisites for the program. It is also possible that the evaluation tasks were either ignored or compromised to the point that participants were never evaluated at all. The lack of an evaluation sets up a scenario in which neither participant nor facilitator can really tell if the objectives are being met.

It can be as simple as poor performance agreement or a sloppy lesson plan structure supporting acquisition of content. It is also prudent to review motivation and attitude if objectives are not being met across the cohort population.

The Skill or Concept Was Never Retained

Problems with retention may come from any number of issues. The most common problems are too much content in too short a time or a lack of any supportive materials or methods after the conclusion of the course. It is also possible that the content had no meaning or importance to the participants. Ownership of the content is important if participants are to retain information for any length of time. Ownership necessarily implies content and course design that allow that to happen.

The Skill or Concept Was Never Used After the Course

Designers who determine that participants had no opportunity to use the skills or concepts sometimes face issues beyond their control. They may train 300 learners to be motorcycle mechanics, but if nearly all of them end up in sales, the training will not stick. These kinds of issues are especially important in psychomotor and cognitive objective domains. Yes, people may be able to ride a bike after many years of no practice, but how many years of practice have they had to support those skills?

Level 4: Results

A Level 4 evaluation is about bottom-line results. What was accomplished? Did the training pay off? Were the expected or promised results accomplished? This level of evaluation has also drawn more than a few skeptics because inflated claims of return on investment (ROI) have sometimes entered into the process and driven many to question any claimed results.

Probably less than 3 percent of training is evaluated for results (Bassi and Van Buren 1999). Make no mistake about it: Figuring out results can be a tricky and sometimes expensive undertaking. One reason for this is that the value of results can be both monetary and societal. Although the impact on an organization can be calculated with some degree of certainty, the impact on a community is tough to measure and is largely subjective.

However, no one should discount the power that training can have for change in a community. A poison prevention course, for example, is community based, and the impact could be literally lifesaving, a true Level 4 result.

Learner Evaluation

If learners are able to reach Level 2 mastery of the content in significant numbers, you should probably feel confident that the course design itself is reasonably solid. A low percentage of content mastery would indicate an issue somewhere in the course design, and it would then be prudent to review the course design for obvious problems. The second immediate concern relating to learners and evaluation is a review of the Level 1 results to see if there are any issues with the way the course was perceived by the learners. Both levels of results are important to a designer, as well as sponsors, facilitators, and others, since these are the most easily recognized evaluative tools in ISD.

> In the practice of professional ISD it is important to go deeper into the relationship between the facilitator and learner mastery.

After a course or program has been implemented, and the immediate evaluations of mastery and reaction have been administered and reviewed, a designer should consider the use of an evaluation of learning effectiveness after a period of time has elapsed. These are sometimes considered a Level 3 or behavior evaluation since they are used to see if any changes in learner behavior related to the course objectives were still present after course completion. Organizations that are looking for specific improvements like fewer accidents or increased productivity will find these evaluations extremely valuable.

Facilitator Evaluation

One of the most important elements of learning is the role that the facilitator plays in moving learners to mastery. This is typically measured indirectly by looking at learner mastery or how a population in a course feels about the experience. In the practice of professional ISD it is important to go deeper into the relationship between facilitator and learner mastery; we can look at it through several different measures. It is possible that learners can be successful with even the worst facilitator, and without an objective way to look at this aspect of the learning equation, designers miss an opportunity for evaluation that does not exist in any other environment. For our purposes, we will look at facilitator evaluation from these four areas:

- Credentials
- Teaching style
- Course structure
- Effectiveness

Credentials are the demonstrated ability of a facilitator to teach a specific subject area. This might include educational credentials like a degree or certification. This area also includes prior demonstrated experience in the content area. This is important in apprenticeship and other teaching areas that are not reliant on formal educational credentials.

Teaching style relates to the ability of a facilitator to connect with a population of learners in a course. This might include the ability of a facilitator to create an encouraging learning environment or an online community to support learning. Other elements would be ethical treatment of all students and professional behavior within the learning environment.

Course structure is one area that relates directly to a facilitator's ability to deliver a course that is well designed and focused on ISD principles and practices. The facilitator must demonstrate behavioral objectives and observable and measurable evaluation of mastery.

Effectiveness is tied directly to the measurement of mastery within the learning population. If a course doesn't deliver on the expected level of mastery across the population, this would be revealed in a facilitator effectiveness evaluation.

Design Process Evaluation

Evaluation of the design process, separate from the learners' mastery, informs the designer about a host of other issues. Evaluations and feedback should be solicited from everyone who is not an instructional designer but was involved in the course design itself, which at a minimum includes facilitators, subject matter experts, graphic artists, programmers, photographers, and even the clients themselves. While the course may have gone well relative to learner mastery and reaction, this level of evaluation may reveal an entire list of other issues that in some ways are more important to future work. This might include a perception of less than acceptable communications, lack of involvement in decision making, and even late payment on invoices. Facilitators will also offer incredibly important information concerning the implementation and learner interaction issues. They are also experts on the materials and flow of the course design who provide data you just can't get anywhere else.

Evaluation during all project elements provides the quality control mechanism that ensures an honest and meaningful snapshot of both process and product. It is almost impossible for a project to be considered valid without a comprehensive evaluation strategy that goes beyond looking at the issues associated with learners and facilitators; the process itself must be examined. Analysis, design, development, and implementation all have evaluation needs that designers should include in their projects. Let's look at some other evaluation concerns in ISD.

Evaluations and feedback should be solicited from everyone who is not an instructional designer but was involved in the course design itself.

Evaluation During Analysis

During the analysis phase of course design, it is important to make sure a designer has covered all the necessary analytic areas required for a project. This may be a checklist of areas in which data must be gathered and reviewed. In other projects, evaluation at this stage ensures that when assets are available for gathering data, everything is covered and there isn't a need for a second trip to the analytic well, which always costs money and time that can be better spent elsewhere.

This is an example of an informal checklist of questions that designers need to find answers for in the analysis process. In actual practice, a list might be many times more detailed or even somewhat simpler, depending on the project.

Checklist for Evaluation of Analysis Process
- ❑ Is this an issue or a problem that can be completely fixed by training alone?
- ❑ Is this an issue or a problem that can be improved by a training program?
- ❑ Have you gathered all the data (enough data) concerning:
  - ○ Population
  - ○ Subject matter
  - ○ Organizational goals
  - ○ Learner goals and needs
  - ○ Logistics
  - ○ Resources
  - ○ Constraints
- ❑ Have you reviewed your analysis results with:
  - ○ Stakeholders
  - ○ Subject matter experts
  - ○ Target population sample
  - ○ Other designers
- ❑ Have you compared your findings against other internal or external benchmarks?
- ❑ Have you double-checked all of the above?

Evaluation During Design

Design-phase evaluation is critical to the success of a project. Designers have little chance for success if they allow a flawed instructional design to move forward to development and implementation. Objectives, evaluation tasks, and all the critical elements of course design take shape in the design phase, and they need to pass some level of evaluation. Evaluations here address problems early and save time and money as a result.

The value of design phase evaluations is that they enable coordination of information among all those working on a project. For designers working on their own, it is important to have someone review their design phase work because it is easy for designers to lose focus when they become glued to the process. A quick evaluation of both product and process is an absolute necessity.

Information from even the best analysis can go astray in the hands of a technical writer or designer. A SME is the best resource to use to check that the content is correct and clear. A SME's review can prevent embarrassing errors from occurring when the course is rolled out.

Designers need to ensure that the following evaluations take place:
- Review of all the design plan elements by the SMEs and at least one other designer
- Review of all objectives and evaluation tasks by the SMEs and at least one other designer
- Review of evaluation strategy and materials
- Review of all draft participant materials
- Review of all draft facilitator materials
- Review of all draft media
- Review of everything by the decision makers
- Sign-off on everything

Evaluation of Design Elements

The designer must incorporate evaluation components to assess the validity of the objectives and the extent to which the objectives correlate with the desired behavior and the process employed for learning-level (Kirkpatrick Level 2) evaluation, that is, performance agreement.

Evaluation of Objectives

The first step in the process is to identify each component in the objective. Following the recommendations made in other chapters, designers should scrutinize

> The value of design phase evaluations is that they enable coordination of information among all those working on a project.

the four elements of a learning objective—audience, behavior, condition, and degree—and rate each element from one to 10 on the basis of how well it is written.

Two examples follow. The first objective is not written well, and the evaluation of it shows where the problems exist. The second objective is much better and reflects good instructional design practice.

The first objective says:

At the end of this course, the learner will know about radar.

The components of the objective are as follows:
- Audience: the learner
- Behavior: will know about radar
- Condition: at the end of this course
- Degree: not available

Here is a suggested rating:
- 5 for the audience statement
- 5 for behavior
- 3 for condition
- 0 for degree

The designer would then calculate the quality of the objective. First, the ratings would be added for a total of 13, then divided by four to result in a number between 1 and 10. For this objective, the score is 3.25 out of a possible 10. It is not very good, but it gives an idea of what the course is about.

The next objective uses language more successfully:

Given four hours in the classroom and two hands-on exercises, the Weather Radar Repair participant should be able to describe without error the five basic operational modes for a model WSR 88-D radar unit.
- Audience: the Weather Radar Repair participant
- Behavior: should be able to describe the five basic operational modes for a model WSR 88-D radar unit
- Condition: given four hours in the classroom and two hands-on exercises
- Degree: without error

The audience rates a 10 because it is not possible to have more information unless you name the students individually. The behaviors are a 10 because the objective states clearly what the participant is expected to do. The condition is a little weak because it could include materials, so give it an 8. The degree is clear enough to deserve a 10. The score on this objective is 9.5, much better than the first objective's score of 3.25.

This use of a 1–10 rating system may appear subjective, but a system can be developed that will apply to different designs and provide great value to the evaluation process.

Degree of Difficulty of Objectives

The term *degree of difficulty* does not refer to how difficult objectives are to write, but to how difficult they are for the learner to meet. An evaluation is important regardless of the complexity or age group a designer is working with. There are several reasons designers are concerned about difficulty. First, the level of difficulty in a series of objectives ensures placement from easy to hard in the design. The level may not be obvious unless the designer rates the objectives. Second, designers need to be aware of difficulty to assure themselves that they are challenging their learners at the level at which their analysis shows the learners can both absorb and synthesize. Third, if they are evaluating another project, they need to make sure that the level and sequencing of objectives are consistent with the project's goals.

Designers use the verb in each behavior for rating the difficulty because it is the heart of the objective. The verb shows that the designer is asking a participant to do "something" and that something is associated with a particular level of difficulty. Designers should rate the difficulty the same as they do the objectives, using a scale from one to 10. Consider, for example, ratings for these action verbs:
- "List" is not very difficult, so it will be a 3.
- "Apply" is more difficult and deserves a 5.
- "Critique" is a 10 because it is more difficult than the first two.

These ratings are just an example because there are contexts in which a designer may classify "apply" or "critique" as less difficult than "list." Subtle differences between items, for example, may make it hard to list them in certain orders; a lesson may be so clear that it is easy to apply it; or the merits and demerits of certain items may be so obvious that criticism comes easily.

> Designers use the verb in each behavior for rating the difficulty because it is the heart of the objective.

If these three behavior verbs were in one module, a designer would want to order them from easy to hard. There are exceptions, such as when a designer wants to start with a more difficult concept or skill and then move to easier objectives. But use your design skills to write and sequence your objectives according to their level of difficulty.

Performance Agreement

Performance agreement is the relationship between behavior and condition elements in objectives and evaluation tasks. The link between the two is critical to ensuring that the performance stated in the objective is in agreement with the performance in the evaluation task.

Performance agreement is comparable to motion pictures in that one of the most important jobs on a movie set is known as continuity. The person who handles continuity makes sure the filming and the sequence of the final product matches the script.

Similarly, the designer must make sure that objectives are written correctly and that the evaluation task supports the objective in behavior and degree. The designer facilitates this process by checking performance agreement.

Here is an example of an objective and its evaluation task:
- Objective: Given a car and a filling station, the Fueling the Car participant will fill the car without spilling any gas.
- Evaluation task: You have just stopped at a filling station. Fill the car completely without spilling any gas.

This example has performance agreement since the behaviors, conditions, and evaluation task match one another in objective domain and other issues (Table 9-1).

Table 9-1. Performance Agreement Example

	Objective 1
Behavior	Match
Conditions	Match
Evaluation task	Match
Objective domain	Psychomotor

Following is an example without performance agreement:

- Objective: Given a defibrillator and a stethoscope, an intern working with a doctor at the hospital in the Internal Medicine Rounds program should be able to perform cardiopulmonary resuscitation (CPR) on a patient during a "code blue" emergency without error.
- Evaluation task: You are performing rounds with your assigned doctor when a "code blue" is called in the next room. The nurse calls out that it appears to be a heart attack. You and the lead physician hurry to the room and determine that it is, in fact, a patient with no pulse. The lead physician orders you to perform CPR while she finds the defibrillator. In 500 words, describe how you would perform CPR.

Here the behavior in the objective and the evaluation task do not agree, as shown in Table 9-2.

Table 9-2. Example of Missing Agreement

	Objective 1
Behavior	No Match
Conditions	No Match
Evaluation task	No Match
Objective domain	Psychomotor/Cognitive

The conditions somewhat match. The behaviors do not match since performing and describing are two vastly different behaviors and two different objective domains. In this case the mismatch could prove life threatening.

To fix this missing agreement, the designer could either rewrite the objective so that the behavior says "should be able to describe" or change the evaluation task to say "perform CPR on the patient."

It is a good idea to check performance agreement for all your objectives, even if the consequences are not life threatening.

Evaluation in the Development Phase

Evaluation is also important in this phase, when many critical decisions are made that can greatly affect the success of your project. Designers must make sure their evaluation plan is ready for the pilot testing of the project. Issues that typically come up as they pilot test are segment timing, deficiencies in materials, lack of clarity in the course structure, and failure to design for the target population. A dozen other minor things may arise as well.

Segment timing is sometimes the hardest task for a designer. Differences in facilitators, equipment, and materials affect timing. A designer should allow for the possibility that any variable may affect timing. It is usually a good design strategy to add extra time. It is also valuable to time several run-throughs of a segment and average the time for the design. It is common to find deficiencies in materials during pilot testing. These problems can range from typographic errors in the copy to offensive graphics or wording. Sometimes simple issues, such as having the materials in the right language, come into play. Just when a designer thinks everything is under control, someone will notice a problem in the materials, perhaps an error in the chief executive officer's name. Designers should fix all errors.

Clarity in the structure of a course is essential if the course is to be effective. Designers do not devote weeks and months to preparing a course just to watch facilitators struggle with the flow of the course or the participants roll their eyes skyward. Pilot tests often reveal holes in the population analysis, indicating that it undershot or overshot the average learner. It is the designer's responsibility to adjust the population information and content to match the pilot test's findings.

> Segment timing is sometimes the hardest task for a designer.

Evaluation During Implementation

The process of evaluation in implementation was covered in great detail in the preceding chapter. Elements of this evaluation process include pre-course, delivery, and learner evaluations at Levels 1 and 2. Other important aspects of this evaluation are the use of the quality rating rubrics for objectives, design plans, and lesson plans.

Evaluation of Your Evaluations

Designers who have evaluated everything in the other four phases will probably find that the evaluation phase is the easiest part of the evaluations. Evaluation products that designers complete during the evaluation phase may include project-end reviews and program evaluations for grants. Each of these is important and requires designers to do some thoughtful retrospection of both process and product for the project.

Project-end reviews have two purposes. First, they look at how well the process worked for delivering the project. Designers should conduct these reviews whether they are working alone or have 30 staff members. To arrive at some objective data, it is important that each person involved reflect on what happened and share those observations with the other people involved.

If the training was contentious, it is best for the initial feedback to be gathered anonymously because participants may not want to give honest evaluations if they fear reprisals for their answers. Later, the designer can bring everyone together and work through the problems. If the problems are not fixed at the evaluation stage, they will be repeated.

Grants usually require program evaluations because the groups that give money want to know what they got for it. These evaluations give designers an opportunity to highlight the best parts of the project.

Evaluation data, when presented with graphs or other visual elements, make the case for success. Designers should review the objectives and course rationale and then ensure that the evaluation underscores the results that support those goals.

Psychometrics

One of the interesting aspects of evaluation, or assessment, as some call it, is the field of psychometrics, which is generally related to psychological measurement of skills and knowledge. One branch of this field is related to the construction and validity of analytical and evaluative measures such as tests, quizzes, and other Level 2 measures. There is also another facet of the field that studies the theoretical aspects of testing.

There is a fair amount of controversy relating to some aspects of this work since some of the evaluations are related to IQ, going back to the Stanford-Binet IQ Test. Later offshoots of this are the Myers-Briggs Type Indicator evaluations and the Minnesota Multiphasic Personality Inventory. While you may or may not run into these or similar evaluative instruments, if you do, make sure you do the necessary research to determine the validity and usefulness of these for your specific situation. You may also find it interesting to review some of the literature and theoretical papers offered from the field.

REFLECTION

Psychometrics in the field of ISD is beginning to be discussed among designers and others involved in course development. This uptick in discussion of statistical analysis of ISD joins just about every other professional endeavor as they try to capture accurate and unbiased data on every aspect of life.

As a practitioner in the field of ISD, what kinds of psychometric data do you think are important to gather and review?

Do you ever feel that going to this level of evaluation is unnecessary for the work that you perform in the field?

DISCUSSION QUESTIONS

- As a designer, what do you think is the single most important element of evaluation?

- Is it ever reasonable to not measure mastery in learners?

- Are there ever times when a learner's apprehension of the mastery of content will impact results?

- What are the most important aspects of evaluating the design process itself?

- Does the degree of difficulty evaluation provide data that assists in choosing content for a specific population?

Summary

Evaluation in the field of instructional design is a multifaceted process that involves different approaches and instruments to measure every aspect of the design process and product. A designer must be certain and be able to show objectively that every facet of the design process meets or exceeds expected standards of performance. Additionally, learner evaluation must be the keystone of any course design to ensure and be able to measure content mastery.

CASE STUDY 1

A local community organization that you have as a client doesn't see the benefit of having a rigorous evaluation process for mastery in learners in all of its courses. It is more concerned with learners enjoying taking the courses and recommending them to friends and associates. It also says that several learners have complained that the tests were too hard and didn't prove anything. The organization has asked you to present to it your reasons for continuing to offer evaluations of mastery as part of their courses.

Facts:
- Organization offers courses in gardening
- Presently 25 courses
- Average of 20 learners in each course
- Courses are offered at community centers, public gardens, arboretums, and similar facilities
- Facilitators are mostly community volunteers with no training in facilitation of the courses
- Learners are awarded certificates for participation

What is your report to the organization?

CASE STUDY 2

An international maritime training center has asked you to review several of its courses in the training of merchant marines to be able to defend their ships against attacks by pirates. The courses are well received by the participants, but they do not have any formal review or approval by any external maritime organization. The outside groups are requesting detailed information concerning the courses, their design approach, and any data relating to reliability of the courses to teach proven methods for defending the ships.

What is your first step in addressing the requirements for documentation and proof of conformity to the expressed objectives of the courses?

There is a list of well-written course objectives. How will you show that the objectives are taught and mastery is achieved by the learners?

CASE STUDY 3

A motorcycle maintenance company is getting a lot of complaints that its courses are not meeting the needs of the dealerships it is serving. Technicians are saying that the information they received in the courses is dated by the time they have to use it. They are also saying that the materials—like checklists—that they are given in the courses are no longer current or accurate.

You have agreed to take the company as a client and you are meeting with the board of directors and training manager in several days to begin the process of reviewing the problems. You know as a designer that the longer course content is not used after implementation, the less likely it is to be useful or remembered accurately by learners.

How will you address the problem and where will you begin?

CHAPTER 10

Behavioral Objectives

KEY CONCEPTS

- Behavioral objectives are a foundational element of instructional design
- Behavioral objectives are both observable and measurable
- Short-form objectives
- Long-form objectives
- Four parts of long-form objectives:
  - Audience element
  - Behavior element
  - Conditions
  - Degree
- Terminal objectives
- Enabling objectives
- Objective domains
- Performance agreement principle
- Content mastery continuum

CHAPTER OBJECTIVES

At the end of this chapter, the learner should be able to:

- Describe the role objectives play in the instructional design process.
- Illustrate why objectives need to be both observable and measurable.
- List the two types of objectives.
- Describe the key features of short-form objectives.
- Describe the four elements of long-form objectives.
- Describe the difference between terminal and enabling objectives.
- List at least two reasons objectives are different than goals or procedures.
- List the four objective domains with key features of each.
- Explain the importance of performance agreement.
- Describe at least two uses for the content mastery continuum in writing objectives.

The importance of behavioral objectives in the instructional design process cannot be overstated. They are both the blueprint and the road map for every ISD project. While deceptively simple in appearance, they contain every important detail and data point necessary to design and implement courses.

One of the most visible milestones in the practice of instructional design came when outcomes were formalized to be more than simply having learners participate in a course. Bloom, Mager, Gagné, and others provided the foundation and format for modern behavioral objectives that include as a minimum four elements—audience, behavior, condition, and degree. This ABCD format for objectives has evolved to be the cornerstone of professional design since it provides observable and measurable milestones for learners as well as the basis for evaluation of mastery.

The ability to write objectives is now seen as one of the most reliable performance indicators for hiring and advancing instructional designers within the field of ISD. This is true from the perspective of displaying the skills necessary for writing objectives and for the skills necessary to group and sequence objectives to match how learning best takes place in a learner. One of the most common requests made in interviews for instructional designers is to write or provide samples of objectives.

This chapter examines objective formats, two types of objectives, objective domains, and other professional-level elements necessary to write and interpret objectives.

Behavioral Objectives and the Practice of Professional ISD

If you are going to be a professional-level instructional designer, you have to know how to write behavioral objectives. To be more precise, you have to master every aspect of this process and feel comfortable working with objective domains, evaluation tasks, and the concept of performance agreement. While all aspects of this profession are important, there is something about this process that distinguishes the great designer from the rest of the pack. The reason for this is actually pretty simple; properly written four-part objectives contain the major building blocks of ISD, and from this seemingly simple foundation a designer builds a course, series of courses, academic majors, and even programs that lead to licensure in anything from being a paramedic to a board-certified surgeon or oncologist. Look anywhere in the professional world and you find objectives in some manner.

There is also a precision to objectives that escapes the untrained eye. Even one word or phrase that is off in an objective will flag the writer as inexperienced or ignorant of the subtle demands of making these work in a design. This is because writing sound objectives requires detailed knowledge of the ISD process and considerable practice to master; it carries a lot of weight in defining the maturity and experience level of a designer.

One example of this precision is an objective that contains subjective language like *successfully* or *learn*. This sets off an immediate flag in an experienced designer. Stop for a second and consider the fact that there is no way possible to evaluate a learner for mastery if you are using these terms as a degree element. You have to go deeper, be more concise, and define what *successfully* and *learn* actually mean in terms of observable results.

Imagine also an objective that is written only from the perspective of a teacher or facilitator and uses language such as *the teacher will provide knowledge in the field of adding fractions*. When a designer reads something like this, it is pretty difficult to take any element of a course seriously. The work of the teacher is prescribed in a lesson plan and not in the objectives—pretty basic ISD once you know the difference.

Even seasoned pros in ISD sometime struggle to write objectives. It is almost impossible to write an objective if there is something amiss in the relationship between the four elements of audience, behavior, conditions, and degree within an objective. There are some very important reasons for this relationship, the most common being that objectives have a rhythm to them when written to this standard. The four elements fit well together. When one or more of the elements signals a design issue, the fit is off and it is obvious to the designer writing the objectives and those reading them.

Objectives Basics

There are different approaches to writing objectives, and each has its own validity based on your design environment. You will find different titles for the elements of an objective within varying approaches, although this is generally semantics; the core elements remain the same. There are also approaches that use three, four, and even five different behavioral elements.

As we get deeper into this topic and discuss subtle variations within behavioral domains, you will see that some schools of thought use Bloom's Taxonomy (Bloom 1956) and its classifications of knowledge, comprehension, application, analysis, synthesis, and evaluation as the basis for different behavioral scenarios. I prefer the four more specific objective domains of cognitive, psychomotor, affective, and interpersonal, the last of which I have added to the three classic domains from the work of Dr. Romizowski (1981). It's your choice of which you use, but both will get you to the same place instructionally.

One unwavering principle you need to keep in mind when writing objectives is that every objective you write must be both observable and measurable. You must be able to read an objective and visualize what a learner must be able to do to reach mastery. Any subjective wording that isn't specific enough to describe this process is invalid and, for all essential purposes, useless in a design capacity. When you start to build your evaluation process for an instructional unit, you need to be very specific about how a learner demonstrates mastery.

As mentioned earlier, novice designers often write objectives using words like *understand, learn, successfully, safely, quickly,* and other descriptors that are not observable and measurable. Ask yourself, if you are a facilitator and a lesson plan requires you to determine if someone understood the content, how would you observe that in the absence of any other criteria? You can't. If the required degree for level of mastery is listed as *quickly,* how do you measure that? *Quickly* to a novice learner might be perceived as a glacial pace to an experienced facilitator. Again, make sure you are specific and detailed in writing objectives. If your intent for the criteria of *quickly* is five minutes or less, then write your objective with the degree of five minutes or less.

> Every objective you write must be both observable and measurable.

Two Types of Objectives in Instructional Design

Depending on the level of design complexity and the needs of a designer at specific points in the workflow of a course design project, it may be useful to think of objectives from two different levels of complexity. Most designers will find each of these useful at different points in the design process. The two types of objectives are:
- Short-form objectives (SFO)
- Long-form objectives (LFO)

Early in a project, when more general direction is useful for objectives, the short-form objectives are most useful. In the later stages of design, when more formal objectives are necessary, the long-form objectives will work best. Let's review each in more detail and explore the role they play in an instructional design project.

Short-Form Objectives

Short-form objectives have a very useful role to play in a design project. They represent the quick and easy way to capture important thoughts on learner exit competencies without the rigor of writing detailed four-part objectives. SFOs are meant to be the bridge between initially identifying concepts and skills within a design and later writing formal objectives. They are an excellent way of working with SMEs and others using nontechnical terms or processes, and allow a designer to gather the data necessary to drill down to the more technical detail necessary for a design plan.

In comparison to long-form, four-part objectives, there are two main differences in the way short-form objectives are written. SFOs do not contain audience, condition, or degree statements, or even well-defined behaviors. Additionally, these are not usually grouped or subdivided into terminal and enabling categories, which are the hallmark of formal objectives seen in most design and lesson plan applications.

Since SFOs are written to reflect individual learning episodes, they may or may not be initially grouped with other objectives to build more traditional terminal and enabling statuses. The process of grouping and categorizing comes after the process of writing draft objectives. Examples of short-form objectives for a course might be:

- Define the term *system.*
- List the elements of the ADDIE ISD model.
- Give an example of designer activities in each element of the ADDIE model.
- List the four parts of an objective.
- Define the term *terminal objective.*
- Define the term *enabling objective.*
- Write terminal objectives.
- Write enabling objectives.
- List the elements in a design plan.
- Prepare a draft rationale for a course or program.
- Define the term *prerequisite.*

- Define the term *facilitator prerequisite.*
- List examples of facilitator prerequisites.
- Define the term *participant prerequisite.*
- List examples of participant prerequisites.

SFOs can also be more general expressions of direction or outcome that do not necessarily reflect specific learner performance or behavior, yet are important considerations for the designer to keep in mind during the design process. Although these objectives may seem like more traditional goals, they provide clear direction to the design process. Goals are general statements, whereas these are considered more concrete; yet they do not contain the level of detail that long-form objectives do. These allow for a more efficient connection with non-designers participating in the design process.

Examples of short-form objectives for this application might be:
- Building learner identity with the sponsor is important.
- Case study examples must be written using content derived from actual cases.
- Excellent facilitation skills are required for this content.
- Learner motivation issues must be addressed early in this course.

Short-form objectives can not only become one of the building blocks of instructional design work; they also serve as the foundation for building a solid working relationship with clients and other professionals in the design process. In some ways they are the Rosetta stone of this process; they allow an avenue for translation for the many participants in the process. Everyone's ideas and suggestions have a common language that is used easily by all involved, and the language and operating environment of each participant is translated readily into tangible discussion and action points.

Imagine having a design team that consists of one instructional designer, one client representative, one writer, and one media designer. Depending on the experience of each of these individuals with the design process, you might encounter a range of communications and project style challenges. By starting with a common set of short-form objectives, a designer will be able to communicate an informal set of guidelines to work with. Because this preliminary step involves reducing these ideas to writing, you not only have a paper trail, but also have tangible points for discussion if everyone isn't on the same page. This element of the process can save a project, as well as many hours or days of frustration and misunderstanding among participants.

Long-Form Objectives

During ISD's long history, there have been different ways to approach long-form objectives, but almost all have contained the four basic elements of audience, behavior, condition, and degree (Figure 10-1). When writing long-form objectives, the most common protocol is what is termed the ABCD format.

Figure 10-1. A-B-C-D Format

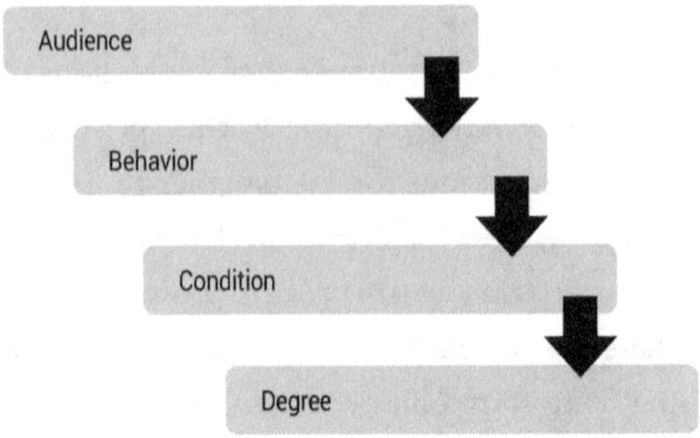

Format for Writing Objectives

There is a generally accepted format for four-part objectives, and a designer's job of writing objectives is easier if you can use this format, because it allows you to focus on each element of an objective and how you write one. While there are always variations on this theme, you will most often see this format:

Conditions.........Audience.............Behavior...........Degree

Here's an example of what this looks like:

Given two graham crackers, a piece of chocolate, and a roasted marshmallow, the Basic Scouting student should be able to assemble a s'more in a minute or less without error.

So where is each element in our example?
- **Condition:** Given two graham crackers, a piece of chocolate, and a roasted marshmallow
- **Audience:** the Basic Scouting student
- **Behavior:** should be able to assemble a s'more
- **Degree:** in a minute or less without error

Now written as you would see in practice:

Given two graham crackers, a piece of chocolate, and a roasted marshmallow, the Basic Scouting student should be able to assemble a s'more in a minute or less without error.

You will see that his format holds true for both terminal and enabling objectives, which we discuss later in this chapter. There are several variations for the enabling objectives that allow for some more efficient formatting if the conditions are the same for all the enabling objectives.

The A, B, C, and D of Long-Form Objectives

Let's take a more in-depth look at each element and, as we do, remember that writing objectives is more than just making sure you have written something for each element. Writing objectives creates the framework for everything else you do in a project. It requires thoughtfulness, investigation, and consideration of all variables before committing to an objective. The journey to writing an objective is in many ways much more important to the design process than the final product that appears in writing.

Audience

When you think about the end user of a design project, you are thinking about your audience. These are also called students, learners, and participants, and in the case of courses for a very specific population, you may see the audience element written as *employee, apprentice, associate, barista,* or a countless number of other occupational classifications.

At a minimum, designers must make sure that the audience statement is specific to the course and intended population. The crucial element in defining the audience in an objective is the knowledge a designer gathers from such diverse sources as population profiles, subject matter experts, program and course titles, and project decision makers.

You must be able to capture in a few words a very specific design icon for this population. This is much more than using terms like *learner* and *student,* which could easily represent millions of individuals. For pro-level instructional design you need to be as specific as possible when writing audience statements for your objectives.

A professionally written audience element usually contains the course or program title, the educational level of the course if it is an academic project, and the sponsoring organization if appropriate. Here are some examples:
· The Dayton Manufacturing Corporation Onboarding learner
· The Better Grades in Graduate School Without Studying participant
· The UMBC LAPT 602 student

> Writing objectives creates the framework for everything else you do in a project.

- The Selling in Your Sleep learner
- The IMTEF Instructor Certification Program participant
- The Using Social Media to Attract a Future Partner student

Each of these is more detailed than the common fallback audience statement of *student* or *learner,* and this reflects both good design practice and an attention to process. As an instructional designer, always spend the time necessary to ensure that your audience statements are based in reality and convey an accurate design interpretation of your audience within your objectives.

The question often arises concerning why the audience element of an objective is even needed. Isn't this so obvious as to be practically meaningless? The answer is simply "no." Many experienced instructional designers and training department VPs will tell you of the time when ignoring the audience in the objectives for a course or program cost them dearly.

For example, an organization had a series of more than 10 courses that were not performing as well as expected. After redefining the audience and rewriting the objectives for the courses, the new target populations were clearly defined and the courses were implemented within the new, now clearly defined audiences, leading to a significant increase in Level 1 and 2 evaluation scores.

Always take the time to review and investigate your audience and write objectives that match your specific population. If you find that you can't narrow down your audience element beyond a generic student or learner wording, you don't have enough information to realistically design a course with any promise of success.

Behavior

The most easily recognized element in an objective is the behavior. Even poorly written objectives usually contain some form of a behavior statement. Behaviors are the key focus in the process of designing a course. Audience, condition, and degree elements generally flow naturally from well-written behaviors in an objective. A close examination of the behavior statement must present a vivid description of an anticipated outcome.

Formatting a behavior statement is important for reasons of clarity, legality, and consistency. Your choice of wording will have an impact on the design intent of an objective. Most behavior statements are worded in the format "should be able to _____" or "will be able to _____." Designers must be careful about which of these formats they choose for writing their objectives. "Will" and "should" have two distinctly different meanings, and the selection is more than just stylistic.

In some cases where eventual licensure or formal examination is an integral part of a course design, it is not unusual for the wording to read "must be able to" or "is required to," because the standard applies beyond the course; anything less and the standard will not meet the requirements licensure. This is especially true with medical professionals such as paramedics and EMTs, who are required to renew their credentials on a regular basis, and anything less than 100 percent mastery is usually unacceptable.

Promising that a learner "will" be able to do something has its own set of concerns. It is much different than stating one "should" be able to do something when writing objectives. The argument against "will" is based on the concept of promising absolute results. For example, if an objective states that the "The Golfing for Beginners participant will be able to score in the low 60s for 18 holes of golf," the designer had better have one great golf program developed! Designers should not make promises they cannot keep.

The behavior statement must not use verbs such as *learn* and *understand* because there is no way to measure or observe them. Just because a learner's frequent nods and thoughtful looks give the facilitator reason to believe that they are learning and understanding does not make it true. Behavior needs to be observable and measurable. Verbs such as *create, write, list, construct,* and *repair* are observable, measurable, and suitable for statements of behavior in written objectives.

Make sure that the behavior matches both the objective domain (described later in the chapter) and the expected mastery. This is where performance agreement issues can arise; being able to avoid them with excellent objectives is the best way to avoid any problems with the relationship between objectives and evaluation tasks.

Acceptable Behavioral Verbs

Here is an exhaustive list of verbs that can be used for your objective's behavior element. While there are other verbs that might work, don't fall into using unacceptably subjective wording like *understand, learn,* and *know.* There are two

> Audience, condition, and degree elements generally flow naturally from well-written behaviors in an objective.

lists of these verbs, the first an alphabetized list based on my experience writing objectives (Table 10-1). The second is from Bloom and represents a more historical perspective on the use of verbs (Table 10-2).

Table 10-1. Modern Objective Verbs

Apply	Design	Interpolate	Repeat
Argue	Diagram	Interpret	Rephrase
Assess	Differentiate	Inventory	Report
Calculate	Discuss	Judge	Restate
Change	Dramatize	Manage	Schedule
Choose	Draw Up	Measure	Score
Cite	Employ	Name	Sketch
Classify	Estimate	Operate	Solve
Combine	Examine	Organize	Specify
Compare	Express	Prescribe	Standardize
Conclude	Extrapolate	Question	Tell
Contrast	Formulate	Rank	Translate
Criticize	Identify	Rearrange	Transmit
Decide	Illustrate	Recognize	Underline
Define	Infer	Record	Use
Derive	Integrate	Relate	Validate

Table 10-2. Verb List Based on the Work of Benjamin Bloom

Knowledge		Comprehension		Application	
Cite	Recite	Associate	Extrapolate	Apply	Order
Count	Record	Classify	Interpret	Calculate	Predict
Define	Relate	Compare	Interpolate	Complete	Practice
Draw	Repeat	Compute	Locate	Demonstrate	Relate
Identify	Select	Contrast	Predict	Dramatize	Report
Indicate	State	Describe	Report	Employ	Restate
List	Tabulate	Differentiate	Restate	Examine	Review
Name	Tell	Distinguish	Review	Illustrate	Schedule
Point	Trace	Explain	Translate	Interpret	Solve
Quote	Write	Estimate	Sketch	Interpolate	Translate
Read		Express		Locate	Use
				Operate	Utilize

Analysis		Synthesis		Evaluation	
Analyze	Distinguish	Arrange	Integrate	Appraise	Measure
Appraise	Experiment	Assemble	Manage	Assess	Rank
Contrast	Infer	Collect	Organize	Choose	Rate
Criticize	Inspect	Compose	Plan	Critique	Recommend
Debate	Inventory	Construct	Prepare	Determine	Revise
Detect	Question	Create	Prescribe	Estimate	Score
Diagram	Separate	Design	Produce	Evaluate	Select
Differentiate	Summarize	Detect	Propose	Grade	Test
		Formulate	Specify	Judge	
		Generalize			

There are many variations of Bloom's Taxonomy that have appeared over the years from different sources. Each has its strengths and weaknesses and should be judged by its selection of verbs that are observable, measurable, and objective. Bloom's original work has stood the test of time and is still the gold standard in this regard.

Condition

The condition element in a behavioral objective is the foundation for creating an environment for learning. At this point in our objectives we are looking to express those items, both tangible and procedural, that are used as the conditions for implementation and evaluation for the objective. This information is key to evaluating mastery since the conditions in an objective must match exactly how an evaluation is given. A simple example is using a textbook as a condition in an objective. If you don't actually use the textbook or you use a different textbook than the one named when you evaluate the learner for mastery, you can't say your evaluation is valid.

Generally, you write a condition statement starting with the word *given* and followed by the elements that relate to the objective. For example:
- Given classroom discussion, handouts, and a short presentation
- Given a working computer, access to the internet, browser software, and a study guide
- Given a chapter reading in the text, participation in a role play, and facilitation
- Given a real-life scenario, a resuscitation dummy, and a portable defibrillator
- Given a model 19t54x digital multimeter and a malfunctioning 15-amp breaker

Conditions may include tangible things, like tools, books, equipment, or hardware; they may also have their basis in an instructional method. For example, a condition might read, "given a screwdriver and 10 screws" or "provided with a 1329A test set." Other less tangible conditions are "following participation in a role play" or "after having read chapter 4 of the text."

Although it may appear at times that condition statements are either too obvious to be useful or overly complicated, subtle differences in context can sink an otherwise great course. Some facilitators omit books or other reading material, or instructional methods intended for the course are replaced or eliminated based on a facilitator's whim. Failing to mention a specific book, other reading material, or an instructional method might seem insignificant, but it could result in a facilitator taking a different approach to teaching. General condition statements, such as "having completed this course," are inadequate because they do not provide any foundation from which to work. Try to be as thorough as possible in setting the context.

For a course in poison prevention, the conditions might be:
- Given a planning sheet and sketch of a home or office
- Given a practice session with another participant in the course
- Given several real-life scenarios of potential poisoning hazards

Never write conditions that are not tangible or procedural. Also don't write conditions that are so obvious as to be expected conditions in any situation. For example, don't ever write conditions like:
- Given participation in the course
- Given time to attend class
- Given a facilitator/teacher/professor
- Given a motivated student
- Given a lack of anger

Degree

The degree element in an objective is the finishing line of mastery. In colloquial terms, an objective's behavior element says "jump" and the degree element tells the learner how high. Degrees are the real anchor for evaluation, and once a standard for mastery is established it is very easy to design a course based on these standards. You may also hear this called *criteria* or similar terms.

As you consider an objective's degree element, you may want to use the mastery continuum principle to make decisions on a level of difficulty based on your population and relative content experience. Populations with little previous content experience or learners who should be able to meet mastery with more than one attempt might best be served with degree statements like these:

- At least once without error within three attempts
- Until completed without error
- Three or more times
- At least five times during a practice session

For populations that are near the expert level with specific content, degree statements like this might be more appropriate:

- Without error
- On three different models of the equipment
- Within 5 minutes
- A grade of 90 percent or better on a qualifying exam

If your objective is in the affective domain, a different perspective on degree statements is sometimes necessary since binary evaluations are less important than measures of participation, for example:

- By offering an opinion
- Citing an example
- Participating in a discussion
- Completing a personal skill's inventory

All these degree statements meet the criterion of being a good objective element because they are observable and measurable. No doubt should exist in anyone's mind about what needs to be done to meet the objective.

It is extremely important that instructional designers not write degree statements that include ambiguous words. Do not use *safely, carefully, honestly,* and similar adverbs; they only create confusion in evaluation, because every learner could have a differenwt interpretation of the meaning for any of these terms. If you insist on using them, they require additional clarifying information if they are put in an objective. The word *safely,* for example, could not be evaluated for mastery in the phrase "use the machine safely," but could be evaluated if written this way: "will be performed safely, as documented in the Occupational Safety and Health Administration (OSHA) 500 standards." Other degree statements that are generally not acceptable include:

- At the discretion of the instructor
- After participating
- Until finished
- At the end of the course
- Until tired

Be very careful using percentages in degree statements. First make sure that they make sense for your objective and that you can actually evaluate mastery using a percentage as your criterion. If you find yourself being tempted to have a degree element worded like this, think twice about alternatives:

"Given a presentation, a block of wood, nails, and a hammer, the Beginning Carpentry student should be able to hammer a nail into a block of wood, sinking it no more than 4 percent below the surface of the wood."

Yeah, that might be a bit tough to measure. How about this instead?

"Given a presentation, a block of wood, nails, and a hammer, the Beginning Carpentry student should be able to hammer a nail into a block of wood, nailing the head flush with the surface of the wood at least twice in three attempts."

Better, and it is easily evaluated for mastery.

A passing grade of 85 percent or better on a final exam is fine as a degree. However, a cardiopulmonary resuscitation (CPR) class that says students should be able to perform CPR correctly 85 percent of the time would not be an acceptable threshold. For certain skill sets, anything less than 100 percent proficiency is of dubious value or wholly unacceptable.

Percentages must be reasonable. It is better to have an employee of a coffee shop meet an objective of making three perfect lattes in five attempts, rather than one of operating the latte machine correctly at least 70 percent of the time, which would require 10 tries at the process with at least seven being correct. Always do the math before deciding on a percentage.

Examples of Acceptable and Unacceptable Objectives

Now that we have had a chance to review the basics of writing objectives, let's review a range of objectives and see if they are acceptable for our use in professional instructional design.

Example 1

The graduates of the dental assistant course will be able to secure an entry-level position in a dental office as a dental assistant upon graduation.

Not acceptable. This objective, often seen in academia, has several problems. First, it uses a plural noun in the audience statement (*graduates*). Second, it promises a job, which we know isn't something anyone can guarantee in a behavioral objective. Third, the timeframe for the degree element is after the course is completed, which we can never have in an objective because all evaluations of mastery must take place during the course. Such a timeframe might work as a goal statement in a rationale, but it won't work as an objective.

Example 2

The course's objective is to develop an understanding of international trade law, the obligations of the parties in an international contract for the sale of goods, and the remedies available in the event of a breach of contract.

Not acceptable. First, there is no audience statement. Second, the use of any wording like "understanding" renders this unable to be evaluated since you can't objectively determine if someone understands something in the absence of any other evaluation of mastery.

Example 3

Given a personal computer and software, the Accounting 101 student should be able to create a spreadsheet that incorporates a minimum of three basic math formulas without error.

Acceptable. It has all four objective elements in the correct format and uses the correct wording.

Terminal and Enabling Objectives Classifications

There are two classifications of behavioral objectives that must be part of any objectives list written for a learning event (Figure 10-2). Terminal objectives should be viewed as the final or exit competency expected of a learner. This objective is a statement of all of the enabling objectives in a learning event. It is written as if you are describing the sum of all enabling objectives and must always precede enabling objectives when written.

Enabling objectives enable a terminal objective by providing a detailed set of objectives that break down a terminal objective to its most basic learning elements. These are the building blocks that create your final terminal objective. There can be any number of enabling objectives for one terminal objective.

For some reason, learning the relationship between these two classifications of objectives is somewhat difficult. It is not unusual to see instructional designers who can write incredible terminal objectives struggle with enabling objectives. You will also see just the opposite—a designer who can write really great enabling objectives but who can't seem to find the words to capture the totality of the many enabling objectives into a single terminal objective.

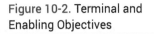
Figure 10-2. Terminal and Enabling Objectives

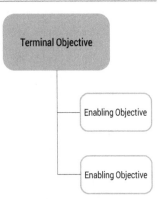

Terminal Objectives

As the name suggests, terminal objectives define terminal or exit competencies expected of a learner at the end of a course, module, or program. These are meant to express the sum of the objectives written for a course (Figure 10-3). If you are designing a course with the content area of learning to ride a bike, a terminal objective for this course might read like this:

Given a functioning, two-wheeled bike, the Learning to Bike Basics student should be able to ride a bike for 100 or more feet without assistance.

A more detailed terminal objective is shown in this example for a course on the safe handling of asbestos on a job site:

Given a realistic scenario depicting the handling and disposal of asbestos at a work site, the participant in the asbestos supervisor's course should be able to supervise the work of at least two asbestos removal technicians. The participant must comply with all OSHA standards that relate to the specific situation depicted in the scenario. No deficiency will be allowed, and the participant must repeat the process until able to comply with the zero-deficiency standard.

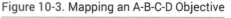

Figure 10-3. Mapping an A-B-C-D Objective

Audience	Learning to Bike student
Behavior	should be able to ride a bike
Condition	given a functioning, two-wheeled bike
Degree	100 feet or more without assistance

This description clearly states the skill the participant should have at the end of the course. There can be as many terminal objectives as needed, whether one or 1,000. In large projects, instructional designers can end up with design plans that fit in a series of three-ring binders, but it is also possible to have just one. The number varies with the design needs.

Enabling Objectives

On the other hand, enabling objectives are the supporting behaviors that, when grouped together, build the path to a terminal objective. Using our bicycling example, we might see several enabling objectives that read like this:

- *Given a functioning, two-wheeled bike with training wheels, the Learning to Bike Basics student should be able to adjust the handlebars to the correct height in two attempts.*
- *Given a functioning, two-wheeled bike with training wheels, the Learning to Bike Basics student should be able to adjust the seat height so that each leg is almost fully extended during the down stroke on the pedals.*

But as you can see, each enabling objective supports and adds detail to the terminal objective's outcome of being able to ride the bike without assistance. There could easily be 10 or more enabling objectives in our example that support our one terminal objective.

In our asbestos training course example, the learner will have to display mastery of all the tasks that will be taught. Following are two possible enabling objectives for the asbestos course:

REFLECTION

Long-form behavioral objectives are always either a terminal objective or an enabling objective. Terminal objectives define the final outcomes or terminal behaviors expected from a learner in a course. Enabling objectives are the building blocks of a terminal objective.

Do you think that it is necessary to classify objectives as either terminal or enabling in the practice of instructional design? Is it possible for an enabling objective to also be a terminal objective at the same time, and if yes, when?

- *Given a bag of asbestos materials collected on the work site and in a sealed container, the technician should be able to dispose of the material in the removal containers without any leakage of material.*
- *Given a presentation, a hammer, a chisel, and the asbestos-abatement-approved protective suit and associated respirator, the technician should be able to remove asbestos without violating established safety protocol.*

When formatting your enabling objectives, here is the recommended way to write them:

Given a valid Metro farecard, a $5 bill, and a functioning farecard machine, the Traveling for Adventure learner should be able to add $5 to the farecard without error in three or fewer attempts.

You must have conditions and degrees as well as a behavior for all enabling objectives.

If your conditions are the same for all your enabling objectives, you can use this format:

Given a valid Metro farecard, a $5 bill, and a functioning farecard machine, the Traveling for Adventure learner should be able to:
- *Add $5 to the farecard without error in three or fewer attempts.*
- *Remove the farecard from the farecard machine in two or fewer attempts without error.*
- *Check the farecard for total fair available in two or fewer attempts without error.*

Enabling objectives are always sequenced to allow for a gradual building of skills from simple to complex; you will learn more about this in chapter 15, in the discussion of the mastery continuum.

Common Problems When Writing Objectives

When an instructional designer first starts writing objectives, there are several specific reasons they might struggle. While not an exhaustive list, these are the most common problems when writing objectives.

Using Subjective Language

A designer can never use subjective language in an objective since it eliminates any possibility of the behavior being evaluated for mastery. Words like *understand* and *successfully* are so generic that in practice they can't provide any clarity for expectations for what is actually required for mastery in an objective. For example, an objective written like this is completely useless for evaluation:

The learner will be able to understand the operation of a plasma cutter.

If you are tasked with evaluation of this objective, there is nothing you can use to determine a learner's mastery of the behavior. To be more specific, what does *understand* really mean in this context? It is very possible that each learner and teacher could have a different interpretation of what *understand* means in this context. Does it mean the learner stayed awake for the course or that the learner now has a complete and total mastery of the tool?

Now let's look at an objective with un-subjective language:

The learner will be able to demonstrate the operation of a plasma cutter by cutting a 6" circumference circle in 2mm steel within a tolerance of .5mm in three or fewer attempts.

Now the subjective *understand* is defined to mean cutting a circle to a specific tolerance within a defined number of attempts. The difference is obvious between these two objectives; every long-form objective needs to be written to this level of specificity.

Never use subjective words like:
- *Learn*
- *Understand*
- *Knowledge of*
- *Successfully*

No Requirement for Mastery

It is impossible to write objectives when the design project isn't really training or education as defined as a course that requires evaluation for mastery as opposed to simply expecting a participant to just be listening. It is also difficult to write objectives for a seminar or presentation that doesn't include any meaningful student participation or evaluation of mastery. Review your experiences with conference breakout sessions for examples of this issue. No one can say with a straight face that attending a session where the participants simply listen to the sage on the stage or view a video presentation is anything approaching a legitimate learning experience. The truth of this lies in the fact that you can't write a valid long-form objective for this type of experience.

No Evaluation

In academic settings, if there is no evaluation of the mastery of the content by the student, there is no way to write an objective that works within the framework of ISD. Having students sit through a lecture or presentation for the entire implementation time in a classroom or lecture hall and then evaluating them at the end of the term does not rise to the level of acceptable instructional design, and there are no legitimate objectives that fit this scenario. Call this what it is: broadcasting.

Population Not Well Defined

Attempting to write objectives for a population that is not well defined or is too diverse for the specific content is a nightmare and signals that a designer needs to return to the analysis and perhaps redefine the population to more closely fit the content. This often happens when a project attempts to combine populations with very diverse levels of content knowledge or interests. Open enrollment courses, where anyone walking in is a participant, can be a designer's nightmare because prerequisites that serve as the starting point for the content's level of difficulty can't be defined. These prerequisites can be as simple as reading level and language skills.

Defining Units of Instruction

One of the more difficult concepts to master early on as an instructional designer is the ability to determine how to logically divide up content. We are going to call them units of instruction in this text, but you may have heard these discrete groupings of content called a module, lesson, unit, or chapter. For design purposes you must be able to determine what is contained in a unit of instruction, which by definition contains one discrete grouping of content.

With so much content and so little organization of this data, it can be very confusing and time consuming to make sense of everything. The easiest way to determine a unit of instruction is to apply the chunking process, separating your content into chunks of similar information or skills. This requires you to look at the content objectively and see what elements logically fit under one terminal objective. This also allows you to have a preliminary idea of how many modules you are going to have in a larger project.

Let's say you're designing an orientation course for a large organization. You have been given a box full of materials and a list of departments that want to have some part in the orientation. Specifically, you have content or requests from the following departments:

- Accounting
- Security
- Human Resources
- Catering
- C-suite officers
- Housekeeping

Since you have been given a time limit of one day (eight hours) to deliver the course, you begin by deciding that you will have at least two modules running four hours each with the option to break either of them into smaller units. You begin to look at which of the six distinct content areas can be combined logically into one module. After reviewing the content, you determine that three of the departments—security, catering, and housekeeping—all have a similar scope, which is facilities information for new employees, so you will combine these into one module with a single terminal objective.

Further review of the content shows that the remaining departments' content cannot be easily combined under one terminal objective, so each will have a separate module; your final modules will be:

- Security, Catering, and Housekeeping
- Human Resources
- Accounting
- C-suite

You can now start writing terminal objectives for each of the four modules and begin designing each module based on your terminal and enabling objectives, which are based on the supplied content.

Don't Confuse Objectives With Procedures

Many times, novice designers will confuse objectives with procedures when beginning to learn to write objectives. While objectives and procedures incorporate some of the same language and wording, they are worlds apart in terms of instructional design use. Objectives define instructional intent from an ISD perspective; procedures are a step-by-step guide to completing a task.

A procedure might include wording like:

"Next you install integrated circuit U21555 in socket U7."

The same content written as an objective would be:

"Given an integrated circuit U21555, a circuit board, and instruction, the Basic Digital Circuits student should be able to place the integrated circuit into the socket U7 on the circuit board in two or fewer attempts without error."

You can see they contain the same general information, but a procedure doesn't contain the necessary detailed information needed to set the conditions or perform evaluation to determine mastery of the learner. This may seem like a very subtle difference, but to a seasoned instructional designer these are nowhere near the same.

Objectives Dos and Don'ts

Long-form objectives should always be written in the ABCD format. The one exception to this rule is for enabling objectives, which don't always require an audience statement. In all cases, terminal and enabling objectives must provide a formal, well-written framework that allows design projects to grow and mature.

Designers frame objectives from the perspective of the end user of the training, not the facilitator. They do not say what a facilitator is supposed to do, but what the learner should be able to do at the end of the course. It would not be correct to say, "The facilitator will teach the students how to use the fax machine," or "At the end of this course, the facilitator will have presented all of the course materials in a friendly and persuasive manner." Learners are the focus of objectives because they are the reason for the course. Although directions to a facilitator are important to instructional design, they say nothing about what the learner is supposed to be able to do at the end of the course.

Objectives are always written for the individual learner. Writing an objective that describes more than one learner presents several design issues, the least of which is how designers can provide meaningful evaluation. It is also problematic for a designer to think of an entire subset of learners as if they were a single learner. To do so challenges clarity. An objective for a group project can be written at the level of the single learner.

Following is an objective for a group:

Given paint, brushes, and a bare wall, the apprentices in the Painting for Pleasure course will create a mural with the dimensions of at least 4 feet by 4 feet.

Better is this group objective:

Given paint, brushes, and a bare wall, an apprentice in the Painting for Pleasure course will create a mural element with other apprentices, each of whom contributes at least one section of the completed work.

The second objective makes it possible for each learner to be evaluated on their individual accomplishment, without relying on other learners. Following is a learner-centered version of an objective on use of a fax machine:

Given a working fax machine, the Office Technology participant should be able to send a two-page fax to another location without error.

Objectives are necessary for each learning activity. Every concept, skill, or objective-worthy behavior needs to be identified and honored with an objective. If an activity is important enough to be included in a design plan, then it is important enough to have a written objective. An objective is the best way to guarantee that the designer will be able to evaluate whether course participants have mastered each skill or concept for which there is instruction. Designers tend to write either too many or too few objectives. They can decide if they need to write an objective by answering the question, "Does it stand on its own?"

Objectives Are Not the Same as Goals

Goals and objectives are not the same things. Goals are general statements of desired outcomes, whereas objectives are detailed statements of planned outcomes. Draft and process objectives are a much closer fit for expressing these interests. For example, a process objective might be to improve communications within an organization, whereas an enabling or terminal objective for that design need might be:

Given several role-play situations and class discussions, the Better Communications participant should be able to develop at least three specific ways to improve interoffice communications.

Designers should write objectives so that they can be met within the implementation time of the course. This is a nice way of saying, "Don't promise something you have no control over." Writing an objective that is so subjective that it can't be evaluated for mastery, such as stating that a learner "should be able to construct an effective marketing plan" is much different than an objective that unequivocally states that the expectation is for "increased sales in six months." Designers only have control over the process of training a learner to assemble a marketing plan; they cannot influence sales volume.

How Objectives Are Written

Objectives should be measurable and observable. An objective that cannot be measured or observed is probably not going to have much chance for evaluation. That shortcoming significantly diminishes the usefulness of the objective.

How instructional designers write and format their objectives is up to them. Sometimes it is a good practice to combine elements of a terminal objective with those of an enabling objective to provide a much more readable format, as in the following example:
- *Given all required tools and safety equipment, the participant in the asbestos supervisor's course should be able to:*
  - *Remove asbestos, without exposure, wearing proper safety equipment*
  - *Remove debris from the work site using the proper containers without any leakage of material*

It is important to be certain to have all the objectives in the proper order. In the previous example, the participant must wear the proper equipment before removing debris, so that objective comes first.

Objective Domains

Objective domains are categories or classifications of objectives that assist instructional designers in determining important design elements. The four objective domains are cognitive, affective, psychomotor, and interpersonal. Primarily, they assist instructional designers in determining how to structure objectives, evaluations, and delivery systems. Designers seldom mix objectives and evaluation tasks from different objective domains because they may then lack validity.

Here's an example that demonstrates the importance of objective domains to designers without going into the science behind domains. An instructional designer who was working on a training program for technicians to repair a certain type of computer might use all four domains in the following way in the design process:

- **Cognitive domain:** A learner should know how to repair the equipment set.
- **Psychomotor domain:** A learner should be able to physically remove cases and insert boards.
- **Affective domain:** Learners should be able to offer strategies to overcome negative feelings about repairing certain models.
- **Interpersonal domain:** Learners should be able to provide excellent customer service.

Figure 10-4. Objective Domains

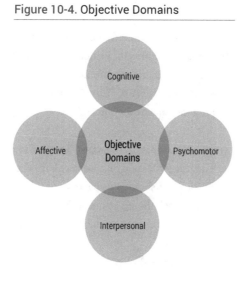

Following are descriptions of each domain in detail.

Cognitive Domain

The cognitive domain usually accounts for most of an instructional designer's objectives. Generally, the definition of *cognitive domain* in training is the processing actions of the brain that result from the brain interpreting and codifying information. The cognitive domain can be viewed as the output from this process. One could argue successfully that every objective has some component of the cognitive domain. The distinctions among domains become important because of overlaps like this. The output of the behavior is the point at which instructional designers can judge the predominant domain. For example, if the output from a behavior is mostly the processing of data, then the domain would be cognitive.

Following are examples of objectives in the cognitive domain:
- The learner should be able to distinguish between circuit boards 14R and 17Y.
- The learner should be able to add and subtract fractions.
- The learner should be able to identify risk factors associated with hepatitis.
- The learner should be able to recite the organizational oath.

Psychomotor Domain

The psychomotor domain is undoubtedly the easiest one to identify. If an objective mainly requires movement, it is probably psychomotor. Learning to operate a machine or using a computer mouse are two examples of skills that are in the psychomotor domain. Although they both have some cognitive influence, they require movement for successful completion of the objective.

Here are examples of objectives for psychomotor behaviors:
- The learner should be able to change the toner cartridge in the copy machine.
- The learner should be able to assemble circuit pack 2349.
- The learner should be able to repair a broken antenna on a field radio.
- The learner should be able to attach option 7T to the main assembly.

Interpersonal Domain

Alex Romiszowski (1981) established the premise for the interpersonal domain in his publication "The How and Why of Performance Objectives." Although most instructional design literature pays far too little attention to this concept, it is a vital dimension to the objective domain concept and, in practice, offers the missing element that defines key objective sets that exist in the real world.

Many of the soft-skill training programs in large organizations are related to the interaction of two or more individuals. This is why interpersonal behaviors are important. Designers are often forced into serving as mediators in organizational disputes involving individuals or departments. Dealing with such interpersonal problems requires a separate objective set.

Examples of objectives involving interpersonal behaviors include the following:
- The learner should be able to identify an area of disagreement between the two departments.
- The learner should be able to answer the phone and take a message without displaying obvious anger or impatience.
- The learner should be able to participate in a role-play situation reflecting the key areas of conflict in the office.
- The learner should be able to answer a question without resorting to name-calling.

Affective Domain

Objectives in this domain are soft skills that are difficult to observe and measure. Constructing evaluation tasks for affective domains is difficult and may be the reason that some designers shy away from writing this objective.

Many instructional designers think it is nearly impossible to write a behavior statement for some affective domain objectives. Others argue that you cannot change the way someone feels about a subject. It is not easy, but it is usually possible to work effectively as a designer in these behaviors. The designer cannot work to change a learner's attitude, just the learner's behavior. For example, a training program on customer service for new clerks in a retail environment would have affective domain objectives. If the goal of the training is to influence behavior, and not the interpersonal aspects of the issue (that is, how a clerk tells a customer that 32-inch jeans do not fit a 48-inch waist comfortably), an instructional designer would write objectives for affective domain behaviors.

An affective domain objective for this situation might be stated like this:

The learner in the New Clerks Training will describe at least two anger-displacement strategies in a case study situation involving a customer being aggressive about a return with no receipt.

The intent of this behavior statement is to get the new clerk to process the anger and maintain composure in this difficult situation, which the clerk will likely face on the job. It certainly is not the intent of the objective to keep the clerk from wanting to confront the customer.

Affective domain objectives and the issues associated with trying to operationalize the process will always be difficult. It can be very hard to separate behavior from the trigger that brings the response, and that is a challenge designers constantly face. Workplace violence is a good example of an affective domain issue.

A strategy for the training is to address an individual worker's violent tendencies, and that involves the affective domain. Helping supervisors deal with potentially violent workers before violence erupts addresses the interpersonal domain. Clearly, there are elements of all four domains at work in these examples. However, the focus is on one domain, while the others play an enabling role.

Following is how an objective might be written for the affective domain in the workplace violence example:

Given a stop-action role-play situation in which the Workplace Violence Prevention participant assumes the role of a worker who feels anger at another worker on the job, the participant should be able to successfully articulate at least two strategies to keep their anger under control when the role play stops for discussion.

Following is how an objective might be written for the interpersonal domain in the workplace violence example:

Given a role-play situation in which the Workplace Violence Prevention for Supervisors participant assumes the role of a supervisor who is facilitating a potentially violent workplace confrontation, the learner should be able to enact a strategy that prevents the situation from moving from confrontation to violence.

The difference in these two objectives is their focus. One approach intends to work within the emotional framework of the individual, whereas the other relies on interpersonal skills to defuse a violent situation. Both have the same long-term goal of stopping violence, but they approach it in very different ways.

Determining the Dominant Objective Domain

It is important that you determine not only which domains an objective contains, but also which is the most important domain (if several are represented), because this is the one you will use for evaluation and performance agreement purposes.

Let's say you have an objective like this:

Given a smartphone, the Twitter app, and access to either Wi-Fi or cell data service, the Trolling Social Media student should be able to create and post a minimum of three tweets responding to a tweet from another user that either agrees or disagrees with the original message of the tweet.

Looking at this from a design perspective, you see that you have elements of psychomotor, cognitive, and interpersonal domains at work here. Most designers would probably say that the cognitive domain is dominant since it could reasonably be assumed that a learner knows how to use the phone (psychomotor) and also knows how to word a message using the app

Figure 10-5. Objective Domain Agreement

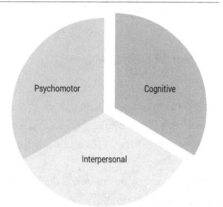

(interpersonal). It is predominately cognitive since the overriding behavior of the objective is the creative aspect of writing a post, not the actual use of the device or the act of communicating. You can of course disagree with this labeling, but for now let's just say you agree. Given that information, your evaluation has to be in the cognitive domain or you have a serious performance agreement issue (Figure 10-5).

In our example, the cognitive domain is dominant and would be used for evaluation. Instructional designers should think about the following once they establish their primary objective domain:

· **Consistency throughout the design in domain-related areas:** These areas include performance agreement, materials, instructional methods, evaluation techniques, and any design elements that are influenced by domain. Crossing domains will disrupt the design and confuse or negate the objectives. For example, objectives written for a training program that instructs paramedics in the use of a defibrillator are probably going to be psychomotor. The designer's objectives and course design should stay largely in that domain. If the course ends up focusing on the emotional trauma associated with being a first responder, the designer has switched domains and endangered the original goal of the course, the use of a defibrillator.

· **Consistency with analysis data:** Designers should not cross domains when moving from analysis to design. They must not ignore analysis data by misreading the predominant domain. For example, in a course for paramedics, if the analysis data show that learners are worried about learning when and if to use the siren and lights on the ambulance, the topic of the final course should not focus on how to use specific brands and models of sirens and lights. Rather, the topic should be when-and-if concerns about the use of sirens and lights.

Degree of Difficulty

Several taxonomies suggest that certain behaviors are more difficult to learn than others. For example, predicting is more difficult than defining, and distinguishing is less difficult than synthesizing.

A designer needs to know the degrees of difficulty to ensure that an objective follows a continuum from simple to complex or from easy to hard. Most learning theories suggest that moving a learner slowly up the slope of difficulty allows a gradual accumulation of information. People who are learning to play an instrument start with simple exercises to help them learn the basics. As they acquire more skill, they move to playing sequences of notes and then to playing short melodies.

As designers develop their objectives and evaluation tasks, they must keep in mind the degree of difficulty of single objectives and then the sequencing of all the objectives in a project. A good practice is to assign a numerical value for difficulty from one to 10, and then to rate each objective. The objectives should begin with the lower numbers and proceed to the higher. By following that sequence, it would be easy for designers to see if they have a problem in their sequencing.

In a course about running a marathon, for example, designers would sequence objectives so that the less difficult skills or concepts are given in the beginning and the more difficult are offered at the end. For example, an early objective might be for a participant to take one-mile runs every other day for a week. This objective is relatively easy compared with a terminal objective of running a 26-mile race and would probably rate a one or two, whereas a series of five-mile runs would rate a four or five. The terminal objective of running 26 miles would rate the maximum (10) in this series because it is the most difficult objective in the course.

Content Mastery Continuum

The work of Benjamin Bloom and others on evolving taxonomies to assist in describing learning competencies across a scale of different complexities and domains was a turning point in the modern practice of instructional design. These added levels of classification of behaviors allowed designers to fine-tune objectives to match the learning environment in which they are being implemented. This is crucial in writing evaluation tasks and making sure there is performance agreement within a learning module, course, and project.

Even with Bloom's incredible work, we were still missing an overarching principle to draw these concepts together. When performing the activities of an instructional designer you often find that you are defining where a learner should be placed within the seemingly endless range of possible content entry points for a course or program of instruction. Many one-size-fits-all approachs have learners either taking courses with content they have already mastered, or trying to bridge knowledge of content that was assumed by an instructional designer to be a prerequisite. Often, you will struggle with placement of learners within content areas when you are designing only one course. You will find that learners on both ends of prerequisite content mastery are either bored or unable to reach mastery.

With surprisingly little additional analysis work, a designer can determine across a population or for an individual learner where they appear on a continuum from complete novice to expert in a specific content area. Making this determination and charting this data, even informally, will quickly tell a designer both the range of content mastery and whether there needs to be some scaling of an entrance point or prerequisite across an intended population.

It is sometimes extremely difficult to accurately write objectives, sequence content, and determine appropriate evaluation strategies without this data. When used in conjunction with other instructional design elements, a precise map of learner mastery is available to guide critical design decisions.

The principle behind the CMC is that all learner mastery can be charted along a line or continuum that extends from a theoretical entry point of no mastery or novice to an exit point of demonstrated mastery of a content area that is usually considered expert. This relates to the progressive nature of learning and the fact that complete mastery of a skill or concept never happens instantly.

The best way to conceptualize the CMC is to start by reviewing Figure 10-6. First look at the point in the lower left corner of the chart labeled novice. This point represents a learner or population with no demonstrated mastery of a content area. It starts at the 0 percent level of mastery. Now look at the point in the upper right hand corner of the graph labeled mastery and corresponding to the 100 percent mastery level. This point represents a learner or population with demonstrated mastery of a content area. The line connecting these two points is the content mastery continuum.

Figure 10-6. The Content Mastery Continuum

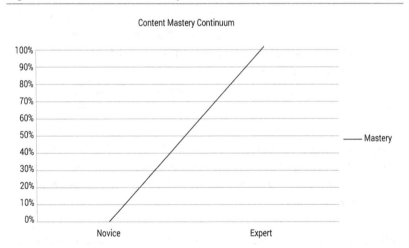

Inherent in the design of the CMC is that learners may have some content knowledge before being involved in a learning activity. The CMC is designed to recognize any relevant content knowledge by allowing a designer to place a learner or a population at fixed points on the continuum based on analysis of the learners. As you will see, this placement provides data for making key decisions concerning prerequisites and content starting points for each content area.

The CMC in application is contextual in that it can represent different design scenarios, from charting the mastery of a single objective of a single learner to charting an entire population to all of objectives within a program. In practice, the continuum will be divided into as many points as necessary to define your population.

The use of the CMC is usually considered an element in the analysis process and requires some level of data to produce CMC charts. It is possible to use observation and review of readily available evaluation data for this purpose. In some cases it may be necessary to gather data by a more formal analysis process such as pre-testing or skills analysis. The strength of the process begins with accurate data, and the reliability of the results and value in the design process rests on this foundation.

Let's start with a very basic course titled How to Ride a Bike that is going to be offered at a local community center. The design team starts by looking at the basic outcomes likely to be associated with this course, namely the ability to ride a bike without any assistance for a specific period of time, perhaps 10 seconds.

When thinking about terminal objectives for this course, the design team sees three important points of mastery:
1. Mastery of basic safety rules
2. Mastery of preparation and adjustment before riding the bike
3. Mastery of riding for 10 seconds

In the context of the CMC, the team sees three very important points of mastery along the continuum from novice to mastery:
1. Safety rules are in the cognitive objective domain and require no prerequisites
2. Preparation and adjustment are in both the cognitive and psychomotor objective domains and require some prerequisites
3. Riding is predominately in the psychomotor domain and requires both elements one and two as prerequisites

A quick population analysis by the design team shows that none of the students are expected to have any significant skills in these three areas, so when we chart the CMC for this course we see the following in terms of content mastery:

> When the CMC is used in conjunction with other instructional design elements, a precise map of learner mastery is available to guide critical design decisions.

REFLECTION

The content mastery continuum defines the content space between the beginning basic concepts to complete content mastery, also explained as the difference between a novice and an expert as a learner. This continuum extends through the various learning levels for each content element.

As a designer, why is it important to define the entry point for learners with the content as you design a course? Does it matter if you start with the most difficult content and then teach the easier and less complex content last?

Mastery Level	Skill 1	Skill 2	Skill 3
Mastery			
Functional			
Novice	x	x	X

As one would suspect, all students enter the course as novices, so the design team must plan on covering all the material in each of the three skill levels.

When the team charts the CMC in relation to the objective domains, they find the following:

Domain	Skill 1	Skill 2	Skill 3
Cognitive	x	x	
Psychomotor		x	X
Affective			
Interpersonal			

This tells the team that skill one can be evaluated with a written or verbal evaluation. Skill two must contain both written/verbal and observational evaluation, since we have both cognitive and psychomotor objectives. Skill three is psychomotor and is evaluated by an observational approach.

Because this is a very elementary course, the results are obvious. But when the CMC is applied over a series of skills in more complex design environments, the value of the process becomes clear.

Evaluation Tasks and the Performance Agreement Principle

The usefulness of objectives is severely jeopardized without evaluation tasks. In fact, it makes little sense to bother with objectives if there is no intention to evaluate a learner's progress toward meeting them. Designers must develop the ability to construct evaluation tasks. The tasks must not be a hurdle in themselves; they must be achievable and based on real life.

Examples of simple evaluation tasks are:

- *Using the circuit pack labeled B-75, replace the defective processor board on the server and confirm that the server is operating without error.*
- *You have until 4 p.m. to correctly solve all 25 math problems.*

Evaluation tasks are created during the design phase to ensure that every objective has a corresponding learner-level evaluation as part of the course. Every objective needs to have this evaluation to ensure performance agreement.

Performance Agreement Principle

Performance agreement is a design term that describes the process of matching objectives and evaluation tasks together in a curriculum. This is a key concept in ISD because it mandates that objectives always have an evaluation and that evaluations always have an objective.

One of the reasons that ISD is so useful is that it sticks to a process. The correct use of ISD makes it almost impossible to leave out major chunks of curriculum design. Performance agreement insists that instructional designers pay careful attention to balance in their design work by insisting on an evaluation of every objective.

As an example, here is an objective written for a segment of a course called Sales for the Beginner:

Given a realistic role-play situation with Sales for the Beginner, the learner playing the part of the salesperson should be able to present three reasons why the client should purchase a specific product.

With the objective written, the instructional designer will have to construct an evaluation task. Here is a suggested approach:

You have just entered the office of a major client. You have to make a case for buying your top-line product. It is important that you present at least three reasons why the client should purchase your product.

The designer would then have to measure the performance agreement. The behavior, condition, and degree statements are the key elements the designer would have to match in the objective and the evaluation task. The first step in determining performance agreement is to identify these three elements in each. The table shows each element in the objective and the evaluation task. When all the behaviors, conditions, and degree statements agree, the designer has created a performance agreement.

A good test of objectives is whether instructional designers are able to come up with an evaluation task. If it is not possible, the objective may be flawed in one or all three elements.

Correcting Performance Agreement Problems

The best way to fix problems with performance agreements is to change either the objective or the evaluation task to ensure the two are in agreement. Designers should base their decision about which to change on their analysis and the context of their course. Consider the following objective:

Figure 10-7. Performance Agreement

Performance Agreement
All of these match between an objective and an evaluation task.

| Behavior | Condition | Degree |

Provided with a stethoscope and blood pressure measuring equipment, the Nursing 304 student should be able to determine the blood pressure of five patients, as verified by the instructor.

If the evaluation task and objective do not agree, the designer could change the evaluation task to have the student take the blood pressure of all the patients. Another possibility would be to change the objective to include determining need and then measuring the blood pressure of only those patients who need to have it done.

Take a look at the following example:

Given participation in a role-play situation, the Effective Intercultural Communications student should be able to say hello and good-bye in at least two languages other than English.

If the evaluation task and objective do not agree, the designer could change the objective from the requirement for hello and good-bye fluency to something else, or the designer could rewrite the evaluation task to have the student say hello in a large hotel lobby where numerous languages are being spoken.

Summary

This chapter began the exploration of design. It covered the process of writing four-part objectives and explained how instructional designers use terminal and enabling objectives and the objective domains to make certain the objectives make sense. It explained how instructional designers adhere to the performance agreement principle to ensure they can assess the objectives.

The next chapter addresses the design of lesson plans, a crucial aspect of any instructional design project.

CASE STUDY 1

Your design team is working on a project that includes at least ten courses for the healthcare industry on the topic of the process of disinfecting equipment, surgical suites, hospital rooms, and common areas. Each course will be 60 minutes and include an evaluation that will be required by employees before they will be authorized to work in each area of a facility.

It is the desire of the client to be able to offer immediate certificates of successful completion for learners when exiting the training. They consider this a just-in-time evaluation and authorization process that is required given the number of learners they are anticipating will need to be certified.

Given the professional ISD requirements of having objectives that meet performance agreement requirements and the need for long-form objectives in this content area, how will you approach the following issues?

- In writing objectives, how detailed will the conditions and degree statements need to be for each objective?
- How will you ensure that each objective will have behaviors, conditions, and degree elements that match the required evaluations of mastery for certification?
- What will you recommend if you find that 60 minutes is not enough time to both implement the course and the required evaluations for mastery?

DISCUSSION QUESTIONS

- When reviewing the differences between short-form and long-form objectives, when do you see yourself using each as an instructional designer?

- Since long-form objectives are more complex, do you think as a designer writing them is an important part of the ISD process?

- Do you believe that differentiating between terminal and enabling objectives when writing long-form objectives is important, and why?

- Why is recognizing objective domains an important consideration in writing objectives?

- Is performance agreement in instructional design a critical design issue, and why or why not?

CASE STUDY 2

A small liberal arts college has recently been through a 10-year regional accreditation review and the final report required that all for-credit courses must have a formal evaluation plan and documented evaluation of mastery. Prior to this time, a small number of courses were graded as pass or fail and didn't contain any form of evaluation of mastery except participation requirements and some written assignments.

The university president wants this requirement met immediately. However, some faculty are upset that they have to start meeting this requirement with their courses.

You are the director of the team assigned the task of making sure all university courses meet the regional accreditor's requirement.
- What plan will you follow for determining which courses must be modified to meet this requirement?
- How will you work with disgruntled faculty who do not want to change their courses?

CASE STUDY 3

A local community organization that sponsors local arts festivals and concerts has approached you to help them design a course in the art history of their city. They are convinced that the more the community appreciates the rich history of art and artists who lived and worked in the area, the more they can use the course for fundraising and other outreach projects.

The group has told you they do not want a formal course, but more of an overview or survey course approach with no evaluation elements at all. They feel this will seem less formal and more desirable for most potential participants.

As an instructional designer, you realize that any course that doesn't involve some element of evaluation is really just broadcasting information and hoping that participants take something from the experience.
- What will you suggest to the group that allows for some form of evaluation while still addressing their expectation of informality?
- Is it possible to meet their concerns and still design a course that meets at least minimal ISD standards and expectations?

Digital Learning

CHAPTER 11
Distance Learning

KEY CONCEPTS

- Learning at a distance is not new to ISD
- Four generations of distance learning
- Massive open online courses (MOOCs)
- Social media in distance learning
- Learning packets

CHAPTER OBJECTIVES

At the end of this chapter, the learner should be able to:

- Define *distance learning.*
- Describe the key distinguishing features of each of the four generations of distance learning.
- Define a MOOC and its key components.
- Describe at least one challenge for each of the ADDIE elements when designing distance learning.
- Explain the concept of packet learning with at least two examples.

Distance education is the practice of moving learning from a traditional setting, such as a classroom, to a distance from the instructor either through distributed learning or online learning. The recent growth of social media and the need to provide safe learning environments for students for health and safety reasons has made distance education a necessity in some situations. While often seen as a modern development, distance learning has been in place for hundreds of years in one form or another. Even before the unexpected move online forced by the COVID-19 pandemic, designers were seeing an increased interest in and investment by organizations in distance or blended learning. What we now experience is simply a transition to offerings using the most recent technology. World events have pushed the practice of remote learning to new extremes and shown that formal classroom learning environments may never be the same. This doesn't represent a new normal; this is the latest positioning of technology as it increasingly becomes a self-evolving way of life in teaching and learning. The legacy era of traditional classroom education, with a lecturer and attentive, face-to-face students, has now evolved into a more immediate and technology-linked medium.

In the practice of instructional design, distance learning presents both challenges and unlimited opportunities. Many design challenges are technology based as designers try to match available hardware and software with the instructional needs of particular content or populations. As the products and processes mature, these are often addressed successfully and are no more problematic than issues associated with traditional classroom environments.

With entirely new methodologies and options available and growing every day, the ability to reach previously underserved populations and learners living and working in remote locations provides designers new and powerful ways to evolve the learning landscape. This process is always changing, and each new generation of thought brings with it new ways to make learning more efficient and tied to the needs of individual learners.

In this chapter, we look exclusively at distance learning that involves some level of technological integration. Earlier forms of distance learning are rarely the focus of a designer's work and are easily addressed with traditional design skills and approaches. Our focus is the latest iteration of distance learning and how instructional designers approach these courses.

When we discussed the generations of learning transfer in chapter 1, it was clear that even though learning transfer is driven by advances in technology, it is still, at its roots, the same combination of delivery and reception of content that takes place in each learning experience. The real differences are based on the medium, whether it is guttural utterances in the earliest learning or smartphones and social media in contemporary learning environments. As we have evolved, the mediums have become less intrusive and have become almost second nature to the learner—an extension of one's everyday life and communications process.

This chapter offers some history of distance learning, outlines the four generations of distance learning, and describes some essentials as well as challenges in designing for distance education, including using social media and a learning management system, both of which are covered fully in the next two chapters.

Generations of Distance Learning

Just as we discovered that learning transfer has easily identified generations of advancement, so does distance learning. While there are several existing generational models for distance education, including Anderson and Dron (2011), the instructional design community has seen four generations of distance learning as it relates to how learning episodes are designed.

The generations of distance learning as they relate to the practice of ISD are:
- **Generation one:** Materials and courseware are designed to be distributed manually by mail or other analog means.
- **Generation two:** Materials and courseware are designed to be distributed mono-directionally by radio, email, DVD, or similar technology.
- **Generation three:** Materials and courseware are designed to be accessed by the internet or other bi-directional technology.
- **Generation four:** Materials and courseware are designed to be distributed by social media and other forms of instantaneous technology as brief packets of data.

Now let's look at how each of these generations of distance learning impacts instructional design.

Generation One

In its first generation, distance learning was derived from content that already existed for classroom use, and that was distributed to students with a set of instructions and any supplemental books or other materials. A student would take the contents of the box and follow the instructions on what to read and do. If any evaluation was involved, it was usually a quiz or test that was returned to the seller to be scored. A certificate of completion was then sent back to the learner.

An early example of distance learning was a shorthand course advertised in 1728 in *The Boston Gazette* (Figure 11-1).

Figure 11-1. Distance Learning Ad

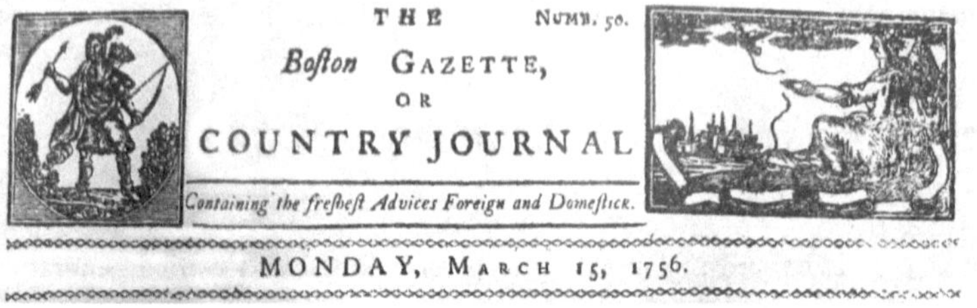
THE NUMB. 50.
Boston GAZETTE,
OR
COUNTRY JOURNAL
Containing the freshest Advices Foreign and Domestick.
MONDAY, MARCH 15, 1756.

1728 Boston Gazette

The instructional design concept was simply the idea that any materials that worked in a classroom setting could be sent to the learner and evaluations returned for grading. The role of the instructor was removed and replaced by a set of instructions and assignments. There was no immediate feedback, and if a learner didn't master the content, it could be weeks before they knew. This means much of the content being learned was stored in long-term memory whether it was correct or not. There were obviously some attempts at evaluations with answers, which might have worked at some level; however, questions and confusion were weeks in the waiting for this generation of distance education learners.

The real value of this first generation of distance learning was that it allowed for underserved populations to participate in some form of formal learning. One of the best examples of distance education serving otherwise underserved populations was the group of South Africans, including Nelson Mandela, who could study only via distance education because of apartheid. He studied at the University of Fort Hare and obtained a bachelor's degree from the University of South Africa. He later obtained a law degree from the University of Witwatersrand. Many of the leaders of the anti-apartheid movement received their law degrees while in prison via distance learning.

Generation Two

The second generation of distance learning was marked by the use of radio in 1922, with Penn State offering a series of courses followed quickly by the University of Iowa in 1925. The new medium was a massive success, and extending this to education made perfect sense. Instructional designers of the day were as much radio producers as they were course designers. It was incumbent on the broadcasters to provide entertainment as well as education, since radio was largely a commercial enterprise. If nobody tuned in, it didn't matter how much learning content was broadcast.

Two examples are Sunrise Semester, on television from 1957 to 1982, and Video Professor, which offered VHS-tape-based tutorials starting in 1987. This all opened the door for the introduction of DVD-based training, usually called multimedia training, beginning in 1993. All were groundbreaking at the time and eventually claimed some portion of the training landscape.

This mass broadcasting and distribution now made access to these learning opportunities almost limitless. Everyone with a radio, VHS player, or DVD player could participate and learn something at their own pace. The number of learners who took advantage of the follow-up evaluations when offered was probably a very small fraction of the audience. But it did allow for learning to be part of everyday life. However, these new distribution methods inherently contained the same problems as the previous generation of distance learning, with substantial time lags in learner participation.

In 1981, the next iteration of this medium saw the Western School of Management start offering courses online. This was before the personal computer and readily available internet. Courses were still being broadcast, but now with email. At least this upgrade allowed for somewhat quicker communications concerning questions between the learner and the facilitator. Evaluations could be emailed and, depending on the time lag on the provider end of the process, responses could be substantially quicker. However, using email eliminated the mass distribution aspect of distance learning and severely limited participation to those with email access and some form of registration. The other limiting factor was that there were no synchronous communications possible between learner and facilitator with email; it was still a one-way-at-a-time broadcast medium.

One of the best examples of distance education in action was those South Africans, including Nelson Mandela, who could study only via distance education because of apartheid.

Generation Three

Synchronous distance learning got its start in generation three with the use of newly evolving online systems, including early versions of learning management systems (LMS) and bi-directional communications apps. The virtual world of learning now had a reliable and authentic medium for closely mimicking the classroom and learner-facilitator environment. An LMS is the software interface that allows learners and facilitators to meet in a virtual world. Content and other course materials are joined together with access provided by the internet, an intranet, or other technology-based platform. Even conferencing, journaling, and other social media can be incorporated into these systems. There are presently more than 500 of these learning platforms available in the marketplace, including Blackboard, Moodle, Canvas, Docebo, Talent LMS, Schoology, and ANGEL.

Early adopters of this software-based distance learning had a rather sharp learning curve, both on the teaching and learning sides of the equation. Providers were required to either have the systems hosted by the software vendor or a third party or host the systems on their own servers. Either of these approaches exponentially increased the cost and sophistication of the process. It was no longer a simple email exchange between teacher and learners. Recent popularity of cloud-based systems has incrementally increased the flexibility and availability of these systems.

Generation Four

Social media is the signature feature of the fourth generation of distance learning. Learning is now being distributed as packets of learning and not necessarily as an entire module of content. There is no need for a computer, classroom, specific meeting time, or any other traditional limitations to learning. Learners can be taking a walk, sitting in a restaurant, or riding on the subway and participate in a course using a smartphone. Social media was the genesis of this generation of distance learning and created an entirely new way of thinking about learning and learners.

This fourth generation of distance learning demands that the instructional designer break up content into packets, or short, condensed bits of information. This is an entirely new way of thinking about instructional design since it challenges the existing design philosophy of learning units that are module length and focused on terminal objectives with supporting enabling objectives. Now, the enabling objectives stand on their own and group to support

> An LMS is the software interface that allows learners and facilitators to meet in a virtual world.

one or more terminal objectives. There will be more detailed information on packet learning later in this chapter.

One important aspect of this fourth generation is that it can support courses from several different approaches:
- Supplement available course materials
- Supplement interaction between teachers and learners
- Access to learning materials and texts unavailable in the classroom
- Access to research and other supplemental data
- Real-time access to information
- Replace classroom requirement for homeschooling
- 24/7/365 access to course, materials, and other resources
- Unlimited and instantaneous interaction between learners

The generational growth of distance learning is a dynamic process, and there will undoubtedly be many more generations of growth and change in what we now know as distance learning. From the perspective of an instructional designer, we should expect and embrace these advances as they come along.

Nine Interfaces for Distance Learning

The increased use of technology in education and instructional design has opened the door for considerable new research into information and communication technologies (ICT) and how these are used in learning. Researchers assembled this list of nine tools that are routinely used in implementing online learning (Martinez-Cerda et al. 2018):
- Media
- Wikis
- OER (Open Education Resources)
- Games
- Mixed reality
- Personal webpage
- Social media
- Personal cloud
- Sharing files

While the usability and implementation of any or all of these tools depends on the specific design requirements, these and additional tools should always be part of the discussion when designing distance learning courses.

REFLECTION

The experience of an international pandemic has forced many organizations to migrate in-person classes to online learning. While there has been much discussion of the impact on K–12 and college-level courses, there is less conversation about other organizations that have had to change their offerings or face serious financial losses due to not being able to offer courses in person.

As a designer, what kinds of issues will you be concerned about as you assist non-academic partners as they think about how to migrate learning to the internet?

MOOCs

MOOCs were first seen around 2008 as a result of the MIT OpenCourseWare project and an open educational resources movement. They became so popular that the *New York Times* deemed 2012 the "year of the MOOC." Many organizations, including major universities like Harvard, MIT, and Stanford, have participated and have created Udacity, Coursera, Stanford eCorner, and MIT OpenCourseware platforms for the purpose of hosting these courses (Vorbach et al. 2019).

Results have been mixed with this approach; after the initial rush to try these courses, two important issues arose for instructional designers to consider. First, there is a general lack of will by participants to complete the courses. Second, the lack of interaction with others, both instructors and students, led many to simply start and never complete a course.

From the design perspective, MOOCs, as originally offered, were broadcasting moved to the internet. Thousands watched the courses online and then could optionally complete the course for credit or a certificate. This is no different than what took place in the second generation of distance learning when local community colleges would offer courses early in the morning on the local TV channels. Listening to the information was often good enough for these learning audiences, and there was little in the way of incentive to complete a course. This feeds directly into the issue of interaction for learners. While this could be mitigated by allowing a chat function for participants and perhaps evolving other forms of online community building, the problem still exists. It will be interesting to see if MOOCs can overcome these early challenges to move to a useful learning tool at scale.

Instructional Design Differences in Distance Learning

Idealizing distance learning, that is, describing it as something more than it is—an implementation method—increases the likelihood that the technology will be selected solely for the iconic value of the technology itself. Distance learning can be very seductive, and falling blindly for a vendor's promises could leave even an accomplished designer with major, unexpected challenges. Just because a learner has access to the internet or an organization has a network server, and a webpage, and tweets out messages through social media does not mean that distance learning is the best design choice for their courses. The seasoned instructional designer considers all aspects of the population, budget, resources, content, objective domains, and performance agreement when deciding how to implement a learning program.

ADDIE Elements in Distance Learning

As a designer works through any distance learning project, they should ask these questions directly related to each of the ADDIE elements:

Analysis

- Is distance learning appropriate for this population?
- If technology is going to be used, is the technology easily and economically available to the population?
- Is the population likely to be able to use any required technology at the level of proficiency necessary for participating in the training?
- Is the population motivated enough to participate at a distance?
- Are facilitators with the necessary technological skills available if required?
- Is the content reasonably suited for distance learning?

Design

- Is the course interface conducive to participation by learners?
- Are objectives sufficient for the determination of mastery if using a technology for participation?

Development

- Is there access to any required application engineers if necessary?
- How will courses be pilot tested before being implemented?
- Are materials aligned with the requirements of the intended technology?

Implementation

- Does the target population have reliable access to the necessary software and applications, and the internet?
- What happens if the technology is down or unavailable at key times during implementation?
- How will instructors be trained to teach the courses?

Evaluation

- How will you implement the evaluation of mastery for a course?
- Does evaluation require in-person testing?
- Does evaluation require on-site proctoring?
- How will you conduct reaction surveys of course participants?

Distance Learning Design Challenges

Here are some important considerations when designing in distance learning environments:

- The population must be suited to online learning.
- Additional apps and software design skill are required.
- Evaluation of mastery is more complicated.
- Budget impacts can be enormous.

Population Must Be Suited to Online Learning

Any distance learning discussion needs to start with the population it is meant to serve. You must determine if your target population is suited for online learning and has a reasonable chance for success in that environment. All other decisions rest on this decision. Keep these factors in mind when evaluating the target population:

- **Technological savvy:** Some aspects of the digital divide still exist and remain an issue as each new generation of hardware and software arrives on the scene. Smartphones are not universally available or even universally accepted, and internet access speed differences can be huge in some populations and locations. Although you can be creative with how you package online content and supplement with social media and other technologies, there are limits on how much of this a population can absorb and use effectively in a training setting. While learners are generally able to use the technology to the degree required for successful participation, that is not always the key issue. When thinking about social media, for example, you have to consider privacy issues and the fact that every learner may not want to get a Twitter or Facebook account; forcing them to do so opens up an entirely new area of legality and concern on several different levels.
- **Learning modality options:** There are learners who prefer online to classroom instruction, and others who prefer classroom to online. Older

populations generally prefer face-to-face training, but that is no longer a universal preference for any demographic.

- **Implementation timing:** If you are going to require synchronous activities (everyone online at the same time), can your population meet at the assigned times? Ten in the evening in New York City is noon in Seoul, South Korea.

Research suggests that older learners are more likely to engage in online learning than younger, college-age students. The American Enterprise Institute (2019) says that 15.4 percent of students older than 25 take online higher-education courses, while 8.5 percent of college-age students participate online. This is somewhat surprising given the stereotype of older learners not feeling comfortable with technology. This has of course been changed in the short term by the requirements of distance learning in light of the COVID-19 pandemic. We may find that preferences involving online courses are not based on age at all, but on necessity regardless of age group.

For an instructional designer, this is a wealth of variables to mingle with the expectations of learners who aren't tweeting and posting every several hours. The good news is this is nothing new from a design perspective. New is good when designed with the system.

Apps and Software Require Additional Design Skills

Designing for distance learning requires a more advanced and complex set of skills than for traditional classroom courses. It is sometimes useful to think of it in terms of going from a one-dimensional design to a multidimensional design approach. Learners and content are now connected by technology that has its own set of requirements and challenges. Everyone has had difficulty at some point using a software package on their laptop or app on their smartphone. As a designer, you have to find a way to design courses that use these technologies in a way that is supportive of learning transfer and mastery of content. The courses have to involve more than just using an app or logging into a learning management system. Designs must allow for the interface and the inevitable challenges for usefulness before they can begin transferring knowledge.

This complexity often means that a single designer has to be current on all of the required software and applications they are going to design with, or else they will need to find SMEs to assist in making the interface work for the desired design purposes. It isn't impossible to be a one-person show when it comes to designing in this environment, but it is becoming much more difficult to be at the necessary level of technological proficiency to go much past basic design interfaces.

Evaluation of Mastery Is More Complicated

One critical area of design in distance learning is how to provide a reliable and accurate evaluation process for determining mastery of content. When designs involve mastery checks for certification, licensure, or academic credit, among other critical learning environments, the responsibility to get this correct is enormous. As much as we would like to believe that every learner is honest, the reality belies our hopes.

There are several different ways to approach this issue, ranging from no formal evaluation to in-person proctored evaluations. The choices are often based on the criticality of final mastery determination. An online noncredit course in repairing drywall or making a household budget provides little in the way of responsibility on the sponsoring organization other than the wish that the course addresses an identified need. At the other end of the spectrum, an online academic program in law will require many evaluations of mastery with its student populations to meet state and regional requirements for licensure and accreditation. Simple participation is not going to meet any meaningful requirements in most academic programs.

Evaluation also includes various aspects that might not seem as important as the more well-known evaluations of mastery and other content-based criteria. Nonetheless, these are required features of most programs and take on a new significance in distance learning. Here are several of these elements of online evaluation of learners.

Attendance

Online and distance learning have attendance requirements in many scenarios. In for-credit environments, many regional and state accreditation organizations require that online students attend (check in online) on a regular basis. This stems from the days of classroom attendance and students being required to physically be in class for a minimum number of class sessions.

Participation

Not only do many courses require some sort of attendance policy; they also require participation in course sessions that may be synchronous or asynchronous like chats or discussion boards. A facilitator may provide a video or teach in real time, and participating in either delivery may be required of the learner. Presenters and guests might also provide videos or real-time offerings. Other participation requirements include discussion board posts, assignment posts, and direct collaboration with other learners. Chat sessions through Zoom or other software are not unusual either with the instructor, groups of learners, or all class participants.

Assignments

This is often the most difficult aspect of designing for distance learning. How does a designer provide the most efficient, yet most reliable form of formal evaluation of learners? Some options include required in-person testing, online observation of learners while testing, and proctored testing at independent testing sites staffed by paid professional proctors. There are also many times when students submit work through third-party software such as Turnitin, which manages the process ensuring independent integrity of evaluations.

When designing for distance learning, keep these issues in mind:

- **Formal evaluation:** If you are required to have formal evaluations for a course, will you be able to provide an accepted environment for that process? Many for-credit requirements demand that you provide a proctored test environment for online courses. Make sure you know what is required in your content and accreditation environment early in the design process so that you do not have any surprises later. Finding proctors for a national program is not a small logistical or budgetary issue. There are also online proctoring programs and services, which take control of a learner's computer and don't allow the computer to be used for anything except the formal evaluation. It even requires a camera that is monitored by a proctor to ensure that the student isn't using any resources not permitted for the exam.
- **Performance agreement:** Can you evaluate your objectives in the same domain in which they are written? For example, if your objectives are in the psychomotor domain, will you be able to evaluate in that domain?

Budget Impacts Can Be Enormous

The cost of distance learning in today's design environment can range from negligible to enormous, depending on the requirements of a design. A college or university hosting a learning management system for distance learning can quickly get to seven digits ($1 million) just to get it up and running. On the other hand, there are low-cost solutions if you want to dig around and find a product that meets your design requirements.

You must also budget for any additional staff necessary for work associated with integration of applications and software. This may include materials development and modification for use electronically. It is also possible that instructors will need to be trained on using any new implementation systems, like an LMS.

Additional Challenges in Online Learning Design

Be aware of the following potential challenges to your design time, technology investment, customer experience, content presentation, and implementation setup.

Increased Design Time

The added design element of technology has the potential to make the design process lengthier. This is because many technology comments require some interface design for any applications. It may also be necessary to add time for pilot testing, because there are often issues that come up as a design is put into implementation with subtle application elements that are not perfect fits for the course approach. It is also possible that application features won't work as intended when tested as part of the course design.

Technology Changes Constantly and Is Never Future Proof

No matter what technology is chosen as part of a design, there will eventually be updates or complete changes in application features that don't work as originally intended in a design. Fit and purpose can change on a whim on both applications and software. Even the most reliable LMS platforms will go through routine upgrades and changes in features.

Clients Expect a Different Level of Support After Design

When traditional course designs are complete and learners are engaged in courses, it is typically the end of the design process as it relates to the instructional design team. With technology-based designs, there may be an expectation from clients that the design team continues to work on projects when there is a change in the technology, ranging from a routine update to new features and operability.

In these scenarios it is critical that there is an understanding, and probably some written provisions, relating to how much a design team is going to continue to support courses. Without some formal agreement—at least in principle—about these future fixes, there could be an unexpected problem down the road.

Utilizing the Latest Technology Too Soon

As with any technology, and certainly in social media course design, there is the temptation to implement the latest popular application. This is problematic at best and should be avoided. First, the useful shelf life of some applications is measured in months. Making a choice to include one of these applications may require a complete redesign later in the process when it is found to be buggy or obsolete.

Second, in the world of application design and public availability, it is not unusual for there to be legal or patent challenges to some aspect of an application or its features. In this case, there is no option but to change choices and rebuild the interface as required to fit the new choice in software.

Concerns About Online Content Presentation

Certain content areas drive a decision concerning online learning suitability. Here are a couple of things to consider:

- **Objective domains:** Is your content in a domain that requires hands-on or first-person demonstration, for either presentation or evaluation? If so, can you meet this design need using distance learning?
- **Migration of content:** Will you need to transpose content from one format to another—for example, migrating handouts and other materials to online accessibility? Can this transposition be accomplished easily and inexpensively?

How Will Online Implementation Occur?

When implementing your lesson plan, view these aspects of the design:

- **Facilitator workload:** It generally takes more time to facilitate an online course than a similar classroom-based course. While this can be mitigated by design choices, it is still something to keep in mind.
- **Synchronous, asynchronous, or blended:** If you are going to incorporate synchronous activities, make sure your technology is learner friendly. Many chatroom environments in course-management software leave much to be desired, and these have a way of diverging into off-topic chats unless they are closely facilitated.
- **User satisfaction:** Does the implementation mode match the needs of the learner? Is it the best choice?

The Differences Between Synchronous, Asynchronous, and Blended Learning

Three terms you will hear constantly when designers discuss distance learning are *synchronous, asynchronous,* and *blended,* and each refers to the way that courses are implemented. Synchronous learning takes place in real time; examples include chats, videoconferencing, social media, and other instant implementation scenarios.

Asynchronous learning takes place on demand and includes discussion boards, assignment posts, email, and other non-real-time communications that can be designed for courses. Most online learning is designed to be delivered predominately by this method because it doesn't require a learner to be online at a specific time or day and allows almost unlimited flexibility for participation in online courses.

Blended learning has become a popular learning option, usually consisting of some percentage of course content offered in person and the rest online. This format allows a lot of versatility and offers designers the choice to offer prerequisite or non-interactive content online and the more interactive content elements in person. It also provides an opportunity to offer savings to learners in terms of travel costs to a course location.

For example, a college course in a 15-week term could easily be offered in a format that requires classroom visits only during half the weeks in the term. This immediately allows for seven or fewer trips. For a student living an hour or more from a campus location, this amounts to at least 14 hours less time in commuting. These opportunity costs are not insignificant, and when similar formats are applied to organizational courses, they can amount to more than the course design costs.

One possible misconception that designers must be aware of is that blended learning is directly tied to the same location-based issues as a face-to-face course. If a learner can't reasonably visit a specific course site, then blended learning is also out of their reach since even one trip to a location might prevent participation. There are other ways to address the distance and travel problems, but organizations with worldwide learner populations have to think very carefully about blended learning as an option for most learners.

Social Media in Course Design

Social media includes apps like Facebook, Twitter, Instagram, Skype, Snapchat, Pinterest, LinkedIn, and WhatsApp. Each has a unique twist to its approach to communications and how it packages data. For our purposes it is probably best to look at social media as a subset of communications before even thinking about it as an instructional design tool. At their heart, social media goes back to a very basic telecommunications model in which data is clustered into small discrete units called a packet. The internet is largely a packet network that moves these small units from one location to another. Each of these packets contains source and destination identification. The next chapter in this section covers social media and design.

Social Learning

Social learning and the subset of training using social media is yet another variation of informal learning and is actually as old as learning itself. From the first learning moments sitting around a campfire strategizing how to gather food for winter to millennials using social media, the learning is exactly the same; informal yet effective passing of knowledge from one person to another.

The reality is that most of the tools in social media products essentially mimic what is already available in the present generation of learning management systems, albeit at a different level of sophistication. There is nothing new about posting comments and pictures or chatting online; the real challenge is making all these elements work flawlessly together in a course to the point where the technology is invisible to the learner.

Packet Learning

Packets originated within a telecommunications framework because of the necessity for efficiency in using limited bandwidth for new technologies like cell phones and for military communications using satellites. Engineers found that rather than assign a complete conversation or file to a single channel, breaking these conversations into small units allowed these to be combined on the same channel as other conversations, and this process allowed exponentially more data to be shared across a network. That is why long-distance calls used to sound a little different from one moment to the next—because the conversations were being switched from one cable pair to another continually to allow greater efficiency. This is now what happens on almost every online or smartphone-based transmission of data. As you can see in this simple diagram, seven conversations are taking place on three pairs of cable with increased levels of capacity (Figure 11-2).

Figure 11-2. Seven Conversations on Three Cables Illustrated

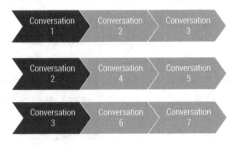

At some point, the concept of creating digital packets of a short length and using them for sending data between two or more smartphones was born. This led to social media apps that generally limit data to a very small packet or unit of data. The advantage in the beginning was that data networks for smartphones were originally very small and slow, and digital packets allowed quicker and more reliable communications between users.

This quick tutorial in data and creating packets on the internet illustrates a valuable instructional design concept. When we design courses and programs, we are breaking up large quantities of content into discrete instructional elements. This is parallel to the same conceptional framework used with the internet to pass data. We break up content into discrete elements, and we then write behavioral objectives to represent each of these units of instruction. Networks and other digital communications do exactly the same thing, and this opens the door for the integration of social media and other digital products into our instructional designs.

With all of this in mind, if we were to create a working definition of instructional social media in the context of ISD, it might read like this:

Instructional social media shares discrete packets of content for use with learning management systems, smartphone applications, websites, or other software, enabling learners and facilitators to share content and to communicate nearly instantaneously within a course implementation setting.

Now that we have some background and a working definition, how does social media work with training? Just like any variable in our system's approach to designing curriculum, we have to see how social media aligns with our target population for a course. Let's look at the potential for using social media as a mobile link to a course with the population using a smartphone application.

> When we design courses and programs, we are breaking up large quantities of content into discrete instructional elements.

Let's take this a step further and see if we have something in this and other data that shows where we might find social media useful. While millions dabble in social media in one way or another, it is a giant leap of faith to think that anyone wants to participate in a course using social media, unless the course itself is about learning or using social media. In fact, my research and that of others in the field seem to agree that if you take the "social" out of social media, you might as well call it training media. On the other hand, the very populations that you think might embrace social media for implementation will likely tell you they don't want to use a communications tool like Facebook for formal learning. It would be the same as using the telephone for a course back in the 1950s or 1960s.

While some might think that social media is a new phenomenon in instructional design, it has been part of the design playbook for a while. The seasoned designer has seen this happen many times in the past with new technologies and realizes that each new generation of technology may have potential, but it probably isn't automatically a game changer in how we design and implement courses. Some degree of design hysteria has happened at every stage of technology build-out since 1984, and this has included the personal computer, VHS tapes, cassettes, CDs, iPods, DVDs, multimedia, laptop computers, tablets, smartphones, and now the world of apps.

SCORM and Section 508

In recent years, the online ISD landscape has become much more complicated than just setting up a website or hosting an online course. Designers now have to consider the ramifications of online products as it relates to conforming to the law and requirements of certain clients in terms of these edicts. For example, the Sharable Content Object Reference Model—usually referred to as SCORM—and Section 508 are two such evolving legal or regulatory requirements. Evolving from an executive order in 1999 given to the Department of Defense, SCORM standardizes e-learning across all platforms, both private and federal. The latest learning protocol is Experience API (xAPI). Section 508 refers to a requirement that federal agencies ensure that their online information is accessible by everyone, including those with disabilities.

Both of these topics are well beyond the scope of this book, but a designer needs to know they exist and be ready when a contract or client is bound to meet one or both of these requirements. There will undoubtedly be more compliance law and directives in the future, and keeping up with the latest in these areas is not

REFLECTION

Packet learning modules are a direct descendant of the discrete packets of data in technologies like cell phones and fiber-optic cables. The technology transmits many short packets of data instead of one continuous stream. This enables efficiency by allowing many independent data streams to share the same path. In learning, packets are considered single objectives or segments of learning that are then sequenced in a way to provide a learning unit. This is the basis of social media apps like Twitter, Messenger, and hundreds of others.

As an instructional designer, how do you see packet thinking used to its best advantage in the course design process?

DISCUSSION QUESTIONS

1. How does distance learning bring learners to mastery? How does it compare with classroom learning in effectiveness?

2. Would you be tempted to incorporate a new smartphone app into a distance learning course just because it is popular with your target population?

3. Do you believe there will be a fifth generation of distance learning? If yes, what will it be?

4. As an instructional designer, what value do you see in MOOCs for course design?

5. In your opinion, what is the most valuable ADDIE element when designing distance learning courses?

6. Are learning management systems necessary for the average distance learning course design? Why or why not?

7. Are packet learning events more efficient learning tools than standard, analog design approaches?

optional. In certain design environments—including federal, military, and just about any projects receiving grants, technical assistance contracts—any project involving technology and an online presence including e-learning will be required to be in compliance with these mandates.

Summary

Distance education has provided training and educational opportunities to millions for more than 100 years. The latest generation of distance learning involves the use of the newest technology and software systems—like learning management systems—and applications like Twitter and Facebook. Instructional designers are finding incredibly creative ways to design distance education courses to maximize the technology and to provide learners with new and exciting ways to engage in learning.

CASE STUDY 1

A small private university has traditionally offered only in-person courses for undergraduate students. The recent pandemic has forced it to move to distance learning courses using online meeting software and apps since it has no LMS or other way to deliver online courses. Early feedback from faculty and students is that the system is working to some degree, but that it doesn't seem to have the same quality or rigor of their traditional classroom courses. There was also a feeling that the normally strong faculty-student relationship is now more polite than enduring.

Background Information:
- Four-year liberal arts college
- 1,000 students
- 100 faculty
- Single campus
- Presently only have online email and simple student support systems in place

As the designer responsible for suggesting solutions for the present situation, what are your suggestions and approaches that will allow the university to offer state-of-the-industry distance learning courses and programs?

CASE STUDY 2

A statewide training organization that offers courses and certifications in the field of firefighting, emergency medical services, and emergency management has decided to move away from a reliance on brick-and-mortar facilities and focus on a centralized distance learning approach. This decision means that more than 100 courses will need to be reviewed for the possibility of being migrated to online offerings.

The organization has an instructional design department with four designers, and you are the director. The group has designed only classroom courses in the past, and everyone is more than a little concerned about how this will all work.

- What kinds of issues will you have to think about as you contemplate this process?
- Do you think it will be possible to use existing staff for the new requirements of online learning as it relates to course design?

CASE STUDY 3

A consortium of nonprofits from around the country are concerned that its online course offerings, though technically state-of-the art, are missing out by not integrating social media into the design. It feels that adding it will make them more appealing to certain key demographics it is trying to reach with its programs.

A small, but vocal group has been opposed to this idea and says that many potential learners will not participate if they are required to use social media as part of a course. It is hearing from some learners that social media can be an invasion of one's privacy and they do not want to have their name, location, or any other identifying information in public view.

As the consultant hired to address the issue of social media and distance learning courses, how will you address the concerns voiced by the group that is opposed to its use?

Is there a way to include social media without having learners feel like they are giving up their privacy?

CHAPTER 12
Learning Management Systems

A learning management system (LMS) has become increasingly common in academic and large-organization learning markets. Even small organizations with limited budgets and little experience with online learning can use an LMS if they are willing to work with an open-source software product.

The first commercial LMS that can be considered commercially successful was WebCT in 1996, and it was developed in Canada. It was quickly followed by Blackboard in 1999, and the first open-source LMS, called Moodle, followed in 2002. Canvas followed in 2010. There are now well over 500 of these learning platforms available in the marketplace, with several having considerable market share over the rest. There has also been a lot of reshuffling within the industry as former players like WebCT have been absorbed by larger companies.

With the advent of sophisticated online learning programs, the learning management system has come into popular use. You may also hear it called an LCMS (learning content management system), which for our design purposes is the same thing. An LMS is the software interface that allows learners and facilitators to meet in a virtual world. In a very real way, it is the foundation and structure that coordinates and facilitates every aspect of online learning for an organization. An LMS is part software and part hardware and most often also integrates with an organization's other elements, such as human resources, and in the case of an academic institution, will include the registrar functions and other departmental elements as required. For an instructional designer, the basics of the LMS is required knowledge.

This chapter describes how an instructional designer uses LMS tools and elements, the challenges to LMS course design, and what to look for in open-source and commercial LMS software.

Adaptive User Interface

One of the most important concepts behind the growth of the LMS is the concept of adaptive user interface (AUI). An AUI is key to sustaining student engagement (Bagustari and Santoso 2018). You may also hear about self-adaptive user interfaces, too, which are a variation on the original and which may provide more flexibility in design.

Essentially, AUIs change the user experience based on the needs of the learner within an established set of guidelines. Regarding e-learning, adaptive e-learning systems (AESs) have "the aim of providing customized resources and interfaces" (Kolekar et al. 2019).

Design Elements of an LMS

As an instructional designer, it is necessary to look at any LMS as a tool to reach your goal of mastery for learners. Course design elements within an LMS are each available to enhance the learner experience and assist in efficient and effective course design. Some elements aid in building learning communities online, while other elements are largely logistical and aid in usability. Designers can choose to have very sophisticated course shells or just use the basic components available.

The LMS contained in most popular online learning systems contains some mix of these basic components:

- Student management systems—names and attendance information, for example
- Discussion boards—where students post assignments and questions
- Announcements section—for facilitator and organizational announcements
- Chatrooms for synchronous discussions with the instructor
- Chatrooms for synchronous activities with students and the instructor
- Wikis
- Journals
- Syllabi
- Materials
- Blogs and vlogs for students and instructors
- Group activities section for projects
- Resources—links to web content and embedded files and materials
- Course shells—discrete homes for courses that are usually designated by course name and section numbers
- Course tools—blogs, email, research links, spell check
- Course support—wikis, glossaries, access to library resources and other help functions
- Course grading systems—online gradebook function usually available to students for instant access to progress reports, interim, and final grades

Course Shells

Course shells are the individual course locations within an LMS. Each course will have a shell, and they usually are identified by the organization's specific method of labeling courses. In large organizations that offer courses by specific terms—usually but not limited to academic users—a course shell might be identified as, for example:

LAPT602 ISD (09.7336) Fall2024

In this case, the course designation is LAPT602, which stands for Learning and Performance Technology course number 602. The (09.7336) designation is the specific course number within the registrar's system. The term for this course shell is fall 2024. Of course, there are variations of these identifications for a course shell, and this will be different for each organization, but it is vitally important that these exist. This will become obvious when multiple sections of one course are offered at different times, and each section will have its own student rosters, instructor, and other possible variables.

These elements of an LMS are easily divided into three distinct groups:
- Student learning tools
- Course operational elements
- Course management tools

Each of these is reviewed in detail to provide designers a good foundation for what is available as course design elements.

LMS Student Learning Tools

When you design within the framework of an LMS, you have an incredibly diverse group of tools available to accomplish different tasks. Some of these tools are content-mastery related, some are informational, and others are meant to promote and support online communities of learners within a course. Let's start with the basics and some terminology to become familiar with as you navigate these systems.

Announcements Area

Announcements in online courses are one of the most valuable tools that exist in creating community and communicating information that changes often. Some designers establish systems that require instructors to add or change announcements at regular intervals to keep learners engaged and to show that a course is being monitored and that an instructor is participating actively.

Depending on the design approach, it is possible to post deadlines, highlights of assignment requirements, notes of encouragement, highlights of learner accomplishments, or even photos of conferences or other content-related events. It is generally possible for a designer to choose the opening or landing screen a learner sees when first logging in to a course section, and making that opening screen the announcements area makes a lot of sense in many design approaches.

Syllabus

Every LMS will have a specific area that is labeled "syllabus" or uses similar language. This makes it easy for learners to click and visit the syllabus for a course at any time while they are in the course shell. Like any syllabus, it will contain all the required elements, including objectives, deadlines, assignment specifics, attendance and grading policies, and contact information.

In the academic world, a syllabus is considered the contact between a learner and the instructor and is required for almost any academic credit course. In some cases, this is also considered a legal contract between learners and the instructor or organization. The instructor promises to deliver a course with specific requirements to a learner who is then awarded credit for meeting or exceeding those listed requirements. The nice part of having these within an LMS is that learners can access the information at any time during the course, which is much easier than the traditional printed syllabus, which often gets lost or never reviewed. One thing to remember is that once a course opens, you can't change elements of the syllabus that might impact a student's grade. With this in mind, make sure your syllabus is what you want it to be, at least for the remainder of the specific course section in which it appears.

Course Materials

This is the LMS equivalent of distributing handouts, and may contain documents, copies of slides, articles, research, and textbooks. The challenge with online courses is converting everything to electronic formats. This is not as easy as it may appear on the surface. A 30-page handout distributed in a classroom setting must now be migrated to a PDF or similar format for use by learners and designed in a way that makes the content effective in the new presentation.

A very common practice is to use only e-books or texts that have electronic distribution. Why require a student to purchase physical copies of textbooks if they don't want or need to? There will always be students who prefer hard copy texts, but limitations on time and distribution of texts can hinder the ability of a student to start when the term opens. If possible, having everything available electronically is really a much more efficient online learning model.

One very common problem with online materials and specifically online texts or e-books is the fact that page numbering can be different or nonexistent when using e-books and some materials. This may not seem like a major concern until you think about designing reading assignments in a textbook that is accessed electronically in an LMS when there are no page numbers in a publication that could be several hundred pages in length. Page numbers are a problem because not all books that are migrated to electronic versions are able to retain the numbering systems used in a printed book.

There are several design considerations for course materials. First, make sure that document size is not too large to prevent viewing or downloading by students. There are any number of ways to reduce file size of pictures, slides, audio, videos, and other files. It is important to make sure that all files are reviewed and placed in a format that can both be read within the LMS and still sized according to the most efficient format available. A SME in video or audio production could be helpful.

Second, be consistent on types of files you use and make the ability to view these files part of your syllabus and course requirements for learners. If your files are software-specific files, you might be better off using PDF format files instead of requiring a student to open a file in a specific program, like PowerPoint.

Third, arrange materials and documents in a manner that allows for easy and reliable access by students. In courses that run for multiple weeks and have more than one module, consider grouping materials by module, week, or other distinguishing factor. This allows for minimal problems for students as they work on assignments.

Discussion Boards

In an LMS design, discussion boards are often where 90 percent or more of the work in a course takes place. Everything, from self-introductions to final project postings, can take place in this part of the LMS. Since these are bi-directional and asynchronous, students can read and post in discussion boards at a time of their choosing. Many LMSs allow an instructor or administrator to view the logs for when students access different parts of a course, and patterns will emerge for when students access these boards. With working adults, evenings, overnight, and weekends are the most active times.

Chatrooms

In the world of LMS design, one of the most versatile aspects of such a system is the ability to design synchronous and asynchronous chatrooms for learners and instructors to use during the course. These can also be used by guest presenters and other outside participants. Chats can usually be designed to be continuous or one-shot events. They are different than a discussion board since participants can jump in or out with comments; discussions continue in one place in the course for all to participate in. Discussion boards require posts each time a student wants to participate.

Blogs and Vlogs

The use of blogs is common in course creation. They can be used for informal comments on content, but they can also be used as a community-building tool by allowing students to comment on their lives, frustrations, or challenges in general and as they relate to a course. This can be a double-edged sword in some populations, since opening up a forum for comments leaves the instructor open to whatever a student might be dealing with, course related or not. It is also possible that politics and other off-topic commentary might be posted.

Vlogs are video blogs that may or may not be recorded and edited and then placed in the course. These differ from an instructor making a presentation and recording it, in that the nature of the content is seen to be informal and not meant for anything other than expressing a view or an opinion. As with blogs, these can be the course equivalent to open mic or speaker's corner material and might not really resonate with the course or participants. So, caution is necessary with these elements.

Journals

Personal journals are one way for students to document their journey through a course or program. When designing using an LMS, the journaling function can provide an outlet for a learner's thoughts as they participate in a course. Depending on the settings, these can be private to the student or shared with an instructor and other course participants. For online courses, a student could reflect on assignments, course requirements, and usability factors from their perspective. This is much more valuable than a post-course reaction evaluation since it is in nearly real time and allows for modification of a course if required.

For designers, having the ability to review the thoughts of learners about a course can be invaluable. In implementation, the ability of an instructor to see where students are struggling or where a course could be potentially designed better is extremely useful. Not all journals will contain useful information, and it can be expected that journal entries that are not guided by specific content boundaries could wander off the path of usefulness quickly. Again, it falls back to the designer to see that a journal is designed to be a benefit to the learners and instructor.

Wikis

Ward Cunningham programmed and posted the first wiki in 1994. The concept behind a wiki is that information can be placed and edited by anyone who has access to the portal. The word *wiki* is Hawaiian for quick and is perfect for some course designs online. Wikis have been the subject of some discussion relating to their usefulness and the reliability of information contained in them since there is often no governing body or responsible party to verify posts and edits. That discussion aside, a wiki used in an LMS can have considerable value when used either to create an online course on participants' common beliefs or information, or to provide basic course operation information that can easily be updated and changed by all members of the course, both instructor and students.

This notion of giving everyone a voice has a lot of value in some courses and populations, and wikis are often a core function in LMS-implemented courses. Creating opinions and placing them in a wiki often allows for building definitions, projects, or other group activities. For example, a course could require that each learner contributes to a definition of a specific concept in a course. There are many creative ways to use wikis as offered in an LMS.

LMS Operational Elements

As instructional designers, we focus on the design functions related to content on the learning side of the equation. However, when we are working with online interfaces, and specifically an LMS, there are numerous operational or functional elements that we must pay attention to in the design process. These include basic navigation tools for the interface, such as Getting Started, and the always necessary Help function. Let's consider some of the common operational elements in an LMS.

REFLECTION

While an LMS course design and implementation approach is now commonplace in the world of academic learning, there are still learners who are hesitant to take any online course because they don't have experience with online systems much past social media and email, or they are intimidated by other learners.

As an instructional designer, how will you create an online LMS learning environment that is welcoming to all students and creates community among all learners and the instructor?

Getting Started Function

In any LMS course design, there must be a road map for getting started with both using an LMS and for each specific course. LMS basics and navigation are often part of a core package of links in an LMS course. If not, this will have to be provided by the designer, who should include step-by-step instructions on how to navigate the basic functions like discussion boards as well as other course design features like journals, blogs, and wikis.

Help Function

One element that is not optional is the help function. Most LMS designs include both operational help and course help links. Operational help is for learners who are having problems with the LMS itself—such as not being able to access different elements or not being able to make or view posts.

Course-specific help functions might include a panic button for students who are feeling lost and don't know what to do for an assignment or a post. Other course help functions include access to the instructor through email or chat.

LMS Course Management Tools

Designing for LMS courses includes the aspects of course management that are almost entirely unseen by learners. These are tools that are used by instructional designers and later instructors to manage and monitor the course as it is in implementation. Tools here include course settings, grading, evaluation of learner participation, and other necessary course functions. Here are some of the more common tools you will need to be familiar with as you design.

Grading

Once the course is designed and placed into implementation, the most frequently used course management tool is the grading function. It can be as sophisticated or binary as the designer chooses to make it. Some courses require grading of every post and assignment, and others don't require any grading.

In most systems the designer assigns grading values to each assignment, then the instructor evaluates and posts the grades, which are then available to the specific student to view. There is also generally an ability for the instructor to comment on an assignment as well as just assign a numeric value for the grade. Grades are only viewable by the student and the instructor, making it safe for academic situations that require complete confidentiality as dictated by the Family Educational Rights and Privacy Act (FERPA).

Look and Feel

Each LMS has specific menus that allow for customization of how the course appears to learners. Options will include fonts; button color, shading, and style; and the opening screen banner.

Enrollment

Almost every LMS will have functions that allow an instructor to control who sees and uses the course. There will be options to enter and delete students, guests, grad assistants, and instructors, and whether to allow outsiders to view any portion of the course without specific permission.

Course Term Length

This function allows the instructor or administrator to set the open and closing dates on a course. In the academic world this is usually the terms, like spring and fall. In organizational settings this might be a window of a day, week, or other predetermined period. There are core courses like onboarding that may be continuously open for learners.

Course Tools Availability

Designers and instructors have the option to pick and choose which of the LMS tools are available to learners. Options might include chat, journals, wikis, or emails to the group. A designer will want to think carefully about these options because allowing access to unused or counterproductive tools for a specific course can end up being a logistical nightmare for an instructor. For example, imagine an unhappy student sending a group email concerning their feelings about the course or instructor.

Course Archive and Copy

Designers will want to make ample use of these functions to keep from having to make changes to each course shell every time it is placed in a system. With this function, a designer can use a course development shell to design the course and then distribute to the specific course shells used for individual implementations. A designer would simply use the copy feature in the developmental course shell and then place it into each new section shell.

The archive feature can be a lifesaver for a designer and an instructor. Imagine being halfway through an implementation and the system drops a course section. If an instructor has archived their course at regular intervals, it is simply a matter of placing the archived copy of the course shell back into the course.

Course Document and Materials Management

An LMS will almost always have an instructor-accessed feature that will allow for the management of texts, videos, slides, and other course materials. In most cases, an instructor can view which files are available, the date they were placed or last edited, and their size. While this area is of some use to an instructor, designers will also pay attention to it since management of course supplemental materials is an essential part of course design. Course shell size will be an important consideration when archiving and copying course shells and with designs containing large video files or other stored materials.

Evaluation

The evaluation function on the operations side of an LMS is not directly related to grading assignments, but more of a look at participation and the timeliness of posts. For courses with specific deadlines this function will usually tell you when a post is made or edited. Other useful features may include the number of days since a student last entered the course and specific discussion boards.

Other features include activity in blogs, journals, and groups. The group activity logs can prove to be significant if part of a student's grade is tied to active and measurable participation in a group activity. If one or more group members are not meeting minimum participation requirements, it will show up in this section of the course management functions.

Of course, an LMS will contain hundreds of features, and each of these will vary by version. Make sure your choice of LMS meets your needs and provides the necessary structure, tools, and support required for your program. Also be sure of what is coming down the road in later versions and how stable each of the existing features is likely to be so you can design with some confidence that you won't have to make unnecessary changes later.

Design Challenges With LMS Courses

Designing using an LMS as the delivery vehicle is incredibly useful and will provide a designer with almost unlimited options. There are, however, several common problem areas that designers need to think about in the process of getting courses through to implementation.

Cluttered Learner Interface

The look and feel of an LMS course is critical to the success of your learner engagement and course community goals in design. A cluttered learner interface is not only going to result in poor learner participation, but it will also likely result in frustration and perhaps even cause a learner to drop a course because they are simply lost in the maze of interface errors.

Having too many visual elements like competing fonts, rarely used links, and other distracting features is a temptation that designers must avoid. There are times when designers feel that being online leaves a learner alone in the online community and try to offer every possible support function available to modern science. This is a fatal mistake. While interface design is a world unto itself, the designer needs to know when something is too crowded or confusing, or ask for the help of a SME in interface design to assist. Most LMS packages have basic interfaces for designers to start with.

Smartphone Limitations

While an LMS is a powerful interface and design tool when working with computers and tablets as the target learning interfaces, their use with a typical smartphone is less than perfect. There are several reasons for this, including limited phone static memory and storage availability. The biggest issue is almost always the fact that trying to use a small screen for accessing an LMS is a daunting experience even for smartphone addicts.

For myriad technical reasons, most smartphones are not capable of displaying the images within a course in the same way that a learner would see them on a computer screen. This means that compromises limit what is seen and how it is navigated. The simple act of gaining access to discussion boards and other LMS core features and functions can be a real chore on the smartphone version.

The learners will often miss key announcements or other required actions in the course because they simply don't see them or can't access them. It is not uncommon for learners to report missing course elements when in fact it is just the smartphone limiting access and accurate screen views.

Internet Access Limitations

LMSs from the user side can be massive internet burdens. While the stated requirements for an LMS program may be relatively low, the adjunct materials and links in a course challenge even broadband systems. Even a JPG on an opening screen can bring some internet access to a halt. The same can be true if a learner is trying to download a handout or access a link to a busy server.

In this age of anytime and anyplace LMS access and use, many learners are tempted to take advantage of this option at points of convenience like restaurants, coffee shops, libraries, airplanes, trains, buses, hotel lobbies, and even sitting in a car in front of a public internet access point. Setting aside the obvious security issues with this access, the very real problem for learners is that almost all these systems are incredibly slow and often severely limit access by download size or even the URL location.

It is not unusual for learners to be on vacation and innocently think they can wander down to the local tiki bar and use the internet to finish an assignment in their statistics class. This will almost always end in a panicked email to the instructor explaining why the assignment is late. Many designers actually list in course prerequisites access to a reliable and speedy internet connection. This at least acts as a warning that most remote access systems are not suitable for LMS access at a reliable level.

Unequal Learning Populations

LMSs are completely neutral providers of the design and content they are given. This is both a blessing and a problem at some levels. The notion of a neutral learning space as viewed from the learner's perspective is something that a designer must consider when working with these systems.

While most teachers will tell learners that there are no dumb questions, an LMS system thinks every learner is equal in skill, experience, or confidence and will never consider the individual learner shortcomings in these areas unless an instructional designer places support elements within the LMS shell.

This includes the usual navigational and access design considerations discussed elsewhere in this chapter. However, the deeper concern in some online learning populations is the question of skills and fit held by some learners. They might have trouble accessing, logging in, and even clicking around the course and come to the conclusion they are not a good fit for the online environment.

The other very real issue faced by some online learners is that they do not feel experienced or smart enough to be taking an online course. If students are asked to post a short biography, there will always be students who appear to other students online to be much smarter or more qualified to be in the course. At this point a learner might feel lost in accessibility and course navigation areas and then read a post that seems as though a Nobel winner in the content area is also a student.

This is why an instructional designer must equalize the expectation and prerequisite field for all students as part of the introductory course materials and assignments. It is not unusual for these courses to contain some boilerplate language that the online interface can misrepresent and sometimes distort the reality that might be present in an in-class course environment. Sometimes a simple statement that "all levels of experience and knowledge are welcome in this course" can also address any other issues that may be present.

Nonlinear Design Approach

It is easy when working with an LMS to think that course flow staging and sequencing of course design content and modules is somehow not important in these scenarios, since the learner is able to access everything anyway. Designers need to think about the timing and sequence of content in the same way as they would in designing a traditional classroom course.

Content sequencing should be by module and from entry to exit competencies—in other words, simple to complex within the content range for each specific course. Placing modules in numerical order from one to 10 or alphabetically from A to M really makes life easier for a learner. One important aspect of design within an LMS is that you can usually open and close online modules by date using the course management menu options; typically, this is available in each discussion board option or elsewhere in the Properties element.

Lack of Reporting Data

Organizations often complain that with all the great things about online courses using an LMS, they seldom get the data they need on student progress, participation, and grading. This is more complicated in stand-alone LMS

REFLECTION

The use of LMSs increased exponentially in 2020 with the forced move to online learning in all age groups, including K–12 students.

As an instructional designer, how will this more common and distributed utilization of LMSs play into design decisions when thinking about populations? Will the fact that many learners will already be able to navigate most of the LMS functions change your design approaches?

scenarios, in which the systems are not linked to student management and enrollment functions like PeopleSoft or similar data management software. In these cases, a designer needs to be sure to design these tracking functions into the design course shells before implementation.

Outside Software Integration

One of the most common complaints from designers and learners is that working with outside software is potentially complicated and time consuming. Even the seemingly simple process of cut and paste from an external word-processing program into an LMS discussion board can result in frustration. This is because formatting and codes in the software are removed or changed as they are placed in the discussion boards by students.

For designers, placing content, links, videos, and other supplemental files into the LMS may involve many hours of trying to figure out why one font on the imported file is showing up as another in the placed file. Each LMS has a list of supported external software products. There are also extensive lists of supported browsers with specific versions that have been tested and shown to be working. To a designer, this information is mandatory for placing materials; it is also key for making sure that students know what will work and what may not work so well when they start making posts and placing files in a course.

IT Requirements and Security

No one should be surprised that most IT departments are less than thrilled when they have to integrate an LMS or if their users are trying to access an external LMS for employees to take courses online external to the root IT system. There are employer IT systems that simply won't allow anyone to access an external LMSs, even when hosted by an accredited university or another reliable and reputable source.

There are also issues around security when it comes to login names and passwords. A system may not accept a username as simple as user1 or a password like mypassword. It is even possible that systems will not allow more than one username or password for employees, and that external systems simply can't be accessed. For a designer, this means that access issues have to be addressed in deadlines and other related course design decisions.

Boring In = Boring Out

Boring content is even more boring online and when using an LMS. If an organization is still presenting courses with slides filled to the brim with data, charts, overly clever graphics, or any other design elements that scream "nap time," you will need to work with them to move their content into chunks that are inviting to the learner. New technology and delivery options should be supported by new designs and interfaces. Even budget training can be made interesting with a little ingenuity on the design side.

Open-Source Versus Commercial LMS Offerings

When you start to investigate the world of LMS offerings, one important distinction is the open-source systems, which allow some degree of manipulation on the software side, as compared with more traditional systems, which are more expensive with largely fixed options. Another way to look at it is that open source allows you to tinker with the coding and other variables in the program and has a community of different programmers and users who coordinate at some level on the design of the software; best of all, it is offered at little if any cost. The more commercial offerings don't allow much modification without paying for it, and the costs to initiate and host a commercial LMS are sometimes staggering for small organizations.

You will find open-source LMS offerings such as Moodle, LearnUpon, Absorb, Docebo, Accord, Travitor, Canvas, and Open edX. More traditional LMS offerings are Blackboard, Desire2Learn, Brightspace, and Learning Studio. It is extremely important that a designer investigate all options when looking at a new LMS or when inheriting an older system as part of an acquisition or being involved in a new project. Things can change quickly in this part of the technology landscape.

Always get all the facts before making any decisions about which LMS best fits a specific set of needs. While open-source options may appear to be a great bargain, specific products may have implementation limitations or additional expenses just below the surface, such as paying for programmers, server hardware, robust internet access, or helpdesk support. If you are in higher education or have to keep detailed records on student participation, you are required to have your LMS talk to your student information system, and that can be a very expensive and complicated interface to design and maintain.

Instructional designers should invest whatever time is necessary in reviewing and investigating the numerous aspects of each LMS. Designers can also depend on the fact that each LMS will undergo regular versioning changes. This sometimes means features present in one version will be dropped or significantly changed in the newest version. For example, your current LMS may contain options—like a webpage, wiki, or chat function—that you have integrated into your course design. A new version of the LMS then eliminates or drastically changes some of these features and causes major redesign in courses relying on these LMS tools. These updates are very common and can be both expensive and frustrating for faculty and designers. In the academic world, version changes happen between terms, which means designers and faculty may only have several days or weeks to get courses back up to speed before the next term starts.

Summary

A learning management system is one of the most widely used learning interfaces an instructional designer will encounter when designing distance learning. There are a number of variables with each system and design that will have a significant impact on the design process and outcomes.

CASE STUDY 1

A small nonprofit is considering offering online, noncredit courses on fundraising since their population is so geographically diverse and recent health concerns have forced it to cancel almost all in-person training sessions. It has come to you for advice.

Here are the specifics:
- Worldwide membership of 5,000 volunteers
- Staff of 25
- Training staff of five
- Potential for five courses in first offering, each one hour in length when delivered in person
- Budget of less than $100,000 for the project initiation

What is your recommendation?

CASE STUDY 2

A small campus of a large state university has decided to begin using the same LMS that the rest of the university system is presently using. It is going to first try it with large enrollment courses like Biology 101 and other core general education requirements. This is based on the fact that access is severely limited due to enacted health and safety requirements now in place and that these large courses are the toughest to plan for on-site.

Each section of these courses generally has between 50 and 75 students, and there are sometimes two or more sections each term. Each section will have one faculty member teaching and at least two graduate assistants to assist with attendance and grading functions.

First-year students are required to take these courses, and they must receive a C or better to move on to taking more advanced general education credits.
- As the lead designer for the university, what are your concerns and considerations for migrating these courses to an LMS-based online platform?
- How will you divide up course responsibilities in the LMS environment using faculty and graduate assistants?

CASE STUDY 3

A midsize technical company that manufactures water restoration equipment like commercial dehumidifiers and fans has seen a 250 percent increase in its orders with climate change and the resulting increase in hurricanes and inland flooding events. Proper use of the equipment requires some training, and this is usually performed using YouTube videos that clients can access at their convenience. The firm now needs to provide more stable and controlled access and also wants to offer certifications in each piece of equipment, which will require attendance and evaluation elements that YouTube cannot provide.

Your ISD consulting firm has been hired to provide the courses on a newly purchased open-source LMS the company's IT department has secured.
- What are the most important design considerations as you start working on this project?
- How will you address the mastery issues since this is an online LMS and learners will never be actually observed to determine mastery?

CHAPTER 13
Social Media

KEY CONCEPTS

- Social media is a common element of instructional design
- Distinguishing between instructional and personal social media usage
- Integrating social media into course designs
- Designing social media into courses
- Designer considerations relating to populations during implementation

CHAPTER OBJECTIVES

At the end of this chapter, the learner should be able to:

- Describe social media use in instructional design.
- Define the concept of social media as it applies to instructional design.
- List at least three ways to include social media in course design.
- Describe at least three ways social media must be managed within a course.
- List at least three areas of concern for learners when using social media within courses.

Social media use has become second nature to billions of users around the world. From the very beginning of apps appearing on smartphones, the instructional design community has been finding ways to integrate social media into course designs. Almost every teacher using social media will share experiences where their learners were hesitant to participate enthusiastically, citing privacy and usability concerns. From the use of an app to supplement communications, to complete use of social media for course implementation, every instructional designer needs to understand effective use of social media for learner engagement. This chapter describes the history of social media, some of the ways to incorporate social media in course design, and the challenges to using social media in course design.

The Road to Today's Social Media

In a world saturated with social media platforms and with politicians, actors, musicians, and a billion other people sharing selfies of what they had for dinner, it is easy to be jaded by the medium. Before we dig into the role of social media in instructional design, let's take a look at how it evolved and the story of its growth to what it is today.

Most historians say that social media started with software applications like CompuServe, which allowed instantaneous communications among members via their computers using what were then labeled "forums." CompuServe was founded in 1969 as Compu-Serve Network for an insurance company in Columbus, Ohio, and was intended only for use by its customers. It originally had message boards, which were asynchronous and later evolved into the famous CompuServe synchronous forums. It doesn't take much imagination to see how those evolved into Twitter, Instagram, and Facebook.

Andre Gray, a Belizean who came to the United States in 1981, is most often mentioned as the one who brought social media into the digital age in 1995 with his electronic press kit, also called EPK. He also placed the first complete song on the internet in 1988, titled "Internet Killed the Video Star," which is a musical instrument digital interface (MIDI) creation. As we look back, we can see that most of the popular elements of social media are in some way associated with both CompuServe and Andre Gray.

In 2003, Harvard sophomore Mark Zuckerberg launched Facebook, and it soon overtook competitors like Friendster, Second Life, and Myspace as the most popular social media site. The instructional design community has been using social media almost since its inception, largely as an adjunct to traditional course designs. The early banning of cellphones in classrooms has now largely evolved to using smartphones as part of most courses, either as communications tools or for the value they bring in research and external materials access.

Defining Social Media

Before digging too deeply into social media in the process of instructional design, it is important to define it for our use as designers. Some define social media by listing apps or software platforms by name, like Facebook, Twitter, Instagram, and TikTok. Others have a much more diverse definition that includes all forms of electronic media, including smartphones and emails. Within the profession of instructional design, most consider the specific apps and software to be social media and the wider range of electronic communications, such as emails and smartphones, to be electronic media. This may seem like a distinction without a difference, but in the design of learning it is a crucial area that must be specifically defined for each learning event or program. There is a huge difference between distribution asynchronously by email and synchronously by Zoom, Twitter, or Facebook Messenger.

For the purposes of this text, *social media* is defined as:

Electronic applications and software programs that are utilized by learners to receive content, communicate with instructors and other students, share information, research topics, and enhance learner participation.

The Role of Social Media in Education and Training

To appreciate the design implications of social media, step back and look at the various transformations that have taken place as a result of the transition of education from analog to digital—in other words, from classroom to computer. These changes are fundamental, and as long as technology continues to advance and become more all-encompassing and readily available, instructional design will have to evolve to address the changes.

Scholars Christine Greenhow, Julia Sonnevend, and Colin Agur (2016) note that social media has changed education in several specific ways:

- Reduction of spatial and temporal limits on education
- Creation of digital and peer-to-peer education
- Challenges to scale and hybridity of designs
- Technology-based limitations

In other words, the increased instructional design opportunities with social media are also joined by a new set of challenges and limitations that are not present in legacy on-site delivery models. Specifically, while the limits of what is offered and to whom are diminished, the problem of access (the digital divide) and the ability to scale up distribution to match learning populations are both very real issues standing in the way of unlimited digital learning.

Designing With Social Media

There are countless ways in which social media is being designed into courses across the entire spectrum of content and populations. From having a course presence on Facebook to implementing all or most of a course on Twitter—all are within the span of social media integration. That said, safeguards must be put into place, or understood, that secure fair participation for all.

Distinguish Between Personal and Professional Social Media Use

Within the framework of instructional design and social media, there needs to be a clear definition of personal and professional social media participation by learners and facilitators. Every day there are examples of social media users being challenged and sometimes disciplined for expressing a viewpoint on a topic via social media. The moral and legal issues are beyond the scope of this text; however, the issue is real when a learning event involves social media.

Most organizations have no specific policy, or have left it purposely vague. Some argue that this is because organizations want to retain governance over both personal and professional social media participation (Mistry et al. 2018). This raises the question of whether any social media participation is considered protected speech. For the purposes of instructional design, it may be important to either state clearly the expected standards of participation or create unique accounts for each learning event that are tied only to that specific course.

Support Social Media Training

The use of social media by both learners and educators is almost always seen as an assumptive skill. Everyone is perceived as well versed in the best practices and even the basics of how to participate in social media. Teachers, learners, and administrators are universally expected to be proficient in the apps and software, and this can lead to some very sizable errors in population analysis.

Many organizations are now seeing value in supporting social media training, and it is also seen as a prerequisite skill in almost every professional endeavor. "Educators have moved past social media as a fad" (Vie 2017), and this makes it incumbent on instructional designers to see that learners are indeed ready for social media participation at the level required for a course or program.

Increase Learner Engagement With Visuals

One of the most engaging aspects of social media from the perspective of both the learner and the instructional designer is the ability to provide unlimited visuals to the learning product. Li and Xie (2020) found that "the mere presence of a directly viewable image" increased user "likes and retweets" in the Twitter environment; the implications of this for instructional design are exceedingly valuable. By comparison, they found that linked images were not nearly as well received, and this brings us to a key design point: Learners in the social media environment will not want to waste even several seconds to click a link to a visual; they'd rather view a visual that has been embedded in the social media directly.

From Fad to Fact

There is some thought in instructional design that social media is merely another fad and that it will soon join the stack of VHS training tapes in the dustbin of content distribution media. Sadly for them, social media has never been more popular and learning generations that have only known smartphones and social media in their lives will consider any learning product without it archaic. Even older X, Y, and boomer generations consider social media acceptable for professional development and communications. It is also seen as a responsibility to prepare learners for the world of professional social media that awaits them. Vie (2016) writes that "educators have moved past social media as a fad; now they have a responsibility to equip students for the kinds of communications they are likely to do post-graduation."

From this perspective as an instructional designer, it is not only necessary to use social media in course design; it is also imperative that we provide learning related to using social media in the larger context of professional development. The medium has grown from its novelty stage to the institutional status it enjoys today.

Examples of Social Media Integration in Course Design

There are almost limitless ways to use social media in course design, but it can be both challenging and a bit intimidating to find a design opening for social media when first getting started. Here are the most popular approaches for integrating social media into courses both in a classroom and at a distance.

Communication Tool

One of the most obvious and undoubtedly most often designed benefits of social media is its ability to instantly communicate information to students. At a practical level this can be as simple as a message board for reminders that assignments are due and room changes for in-person courses. Other common uses are updates on course information and alerts if something changes. This can be accomplished with Facebook or Twitter with equal effectiveness, although Twitter is a more instantaneous communication. There is almost no limit to how social media can be used for communications, with the caveat that the designer needs to have a plan for making sure that every student is using the app or software that is being used for the communications.

Visual Opportunities

Instagram and similar apps are perfect for posting pictures, videos, and memes that are used to support content and participation. A visual arts course could require students to post one picture each week to highlight a specific concept or artist. An apprenticeship program in masonry could require students to post photos of different types of architecture and product choices. There is almost no limit to what can be accomplished in a design sense with the visual opportunities within social media.

Blogs and Vlogs

Using social media to house student and instructor blogs and vlogs is a powerful way to create structure and content for a course you are designing while enabling learners to share information and their thoughts on any topic covered in a course. For affective domain programs like counseling, it allows students to talk about challenges and problems that they are facing as they learn the profession.

Live Content

If a designer wants to include live lectures, discussions, and presentations, social media has a way to accomplish this. YouTube Live, Facebook Live, and other applications and software offer real-time options for presenting any live content. These can be private or publicly available depending on the course design specifics. An organization may want to use some of these opportunities as marketing courses and training programs.

Group Pages

Facebook and other apps allow designers to establish private groups where only learners can view and participate. These are the perfect place to post links to articles, have group discussions, and provide a safe online space for students to share concerns and frustrations. These can be as formal or informal as you choose as a designer, and this latitude makes it much easier to find the right fit for each content area and population.

External Linkage

If you want to design a dynamic course experience for learners, consider using one of the hundreds of social media sites, which students can access as part of their participation in a course.

Things to Watch for in Social Media Learning Environments

While many aspects of social media are beneficial to learning communities, there are some aspects of social media that can't be ignored and must be part of the discussion when looking at implementing a social media design strategy. While some of these can be mitigated with the proper ground rules and oversight, they are nonetheless concerns.

Permanence of Participation

This is a nice way of saying that anything posted in social media has the potential to be a forever artifact within the system. Whether it is a Facebook post, a tweet, or an Instagram picture or comment, social media has a life of its own after a post is made. Some apps may allow deleting a post, but if someone copies or does a screen capture of any posted material, deleting may be immaterial to the damage done.

Privacy

One of the most-often-heard concerns raised by learners relating to social media is that it opens them up to privacy and other online security issues. Identity could be compromised or stolen; elements of a learner's private life could be revealed without their direct or implied consent. While a designer can use internal social media components in course design, there is always the chance that another student will compromise the sanctity of the course environment.

Reduction in Productivity

It is possible that a focus on the social media aspects of a course can lead to other elements of a course being neglected. Assignments, posts, and discussions might take a lesser priority for these learners. While not a common issue in most well-designed courses for organizations and academic institutions, it is something a designer should keep in mind. Don't over-engage in social media at the expense of other aspects of a course.

Bullying

There is the chance that one or more participants will try to intimidate and even bully other participants in an online environment, and social media sometimes makes it easier to attempt to do this. While professional and academic organizations are likely to see less of this than appears in society in general, it is not unheard of and it often takes on a more subtle tone when participation is monitored.

While ground rules and active oversight can prevent most of this, a designer still needs to have a strategy for instructors to use when it occurs. It is possible to review posts by instructors or moderators before making posts available in some apps and software. It is also possible to delete offensive posts. Part of the design of any social media aspect of a course must include guidelines and a process for making sure that bullying isn't part of the social media environment for courses.

Trolling

When a participant posts something outrageous or something that is sure to elicit a negative response from some or all the learners, it is deemed trolling. There are times when it appears to be an innocent misrepresentation of information, but there are times when it is well thought out and posted to generate a response.

Inappropriate Posts

This type of participation can range from personal, unrelated photos posted to a course site to blatantly inappropriate pictures, sayings, reposts, or anything else clearly unrelated to the course content. It might be a picture of a family pet or a meme that was reposted from a political or lifestyle site.

While many of these posts are simply a case of bad judgment, they can also be seen as a lack of respect for the course, the instructor, or other participants. Guidelines for posting will make it clear what is appropriate and what is not, but it can still be rather subjective. Examples will often help make the intent of the guidelines clear.

Overzealous Posting

This is an issue of one or more learners who post constantly. There are times when one, two, or three posts are never enough for a learner and they can become overwhelming to the point that other learners just stop looking. Sometimes it is innocent; sometimes it is somewhat intentional in that a learner wants to make sure that a participation grade minimum is met. The best way to deal with this problem is to limit posts to one or two per question or discussion. This is much easier to manage than a vague definition of too many posts.

Active to Passive Participation in Social Media

There exists a micro-population of learners who were once active on social media and have now stopped participating. They may have very strong reservations on participation for learning purposes. This includes individuals who have experienced bullying or other forms of online harassment. It also includes learners who may also be migrating to a new career or professional position that might be impacted by past social media posts or comments. Finally, there are some professional fields like law enforcement and counseling that demand that learners not participate in any way that compromises privacy of themselves or others. A designer must honor these feelings and find a way to allow participation that addresses their concerns. In some cases, it may not be possible to expect participation.

Fear of Missing Out (FOMO)

There are learners who will be focused on continuously checking social media and online course elements that are available without restriction and open to learners constantly posting. They will want to be the first to view and possibly comment on both the instructor and other learners' posts as quickly as they appear. This can be controlled by having windows of time for each assignment, post, or discussion and not allowing early or post-participation.

Social Media Addiction

While it seems that any activity is open to some form of addictive behavior, social media and internet addiction is on the rise. It is considered to be in the same category as other behavioral addictions like gambling or shopping. The Pew Research (2019) group says that 74 percent of Facebook users access the application daily and that 51 percent access it multiple times a day. While this isn't a design issue specifically, it does open the door to awareness when a design is excessively focused on social media and raises the opportunity for a small sample of a population to become overinvolved with the social media aspect of a course.

Don't Expect Robust Participation

As much as some would like to suggest, adding social media to courses may or may not increase meaningful participation by learners. As with any design consideration, knowing your population of learners will provide the most information on whether social media is the best choice for the design of supplemental activities. This might be influenced by age, but it is also possible that active social media users might consider course-related social media activity as just another requirement for grading and only participate at a minimal level.

REFLECTION

When Facebook launched in 2003 it was one of hundreds of similar social media platforms that competed for the same audience. Today it is used by billions of users, and it is often incorporated into the design of courses, both online and in person. From an ISD perspective, it is something that has to be considered when designing courses, if for no other reason than its massive user base.

As an instructional designer, what are your design considerations when using social media such as Facebook for new courses? Are there populations and content areas that you would not consider as receptive to social media incorporated into a design?

One recent study (Jenson 2019) found that using Twitter with a unique hashtag specifically as the interactivity and discussion element of a college course resulted in almost no participation and, as was noted in the report, "The activity flopped." During the term of the course, there were over 1,000 tweets from more than 100 students, and not once did a student reply to another student's tweet. That is pretty amazing given the volume of tweets sent in a single day, which is a staggering 350,000 per minute; 500 million each day; and 200 billion per year (Sayce 2020). This is a known and actively used social media app and it still generated almost no dialogue during this particular course offering. So, design to fit your population when it comes to social media.

Additional Cautions When Designing for Social Media

One aspect of design with social media that must be addressed is the issue of privacy of learner information. In the academic world, this is covered under the Family Educational Rights and Privacy Act (FERPA), which has specific regulations on how much student data can be made public—essentially none of it. This is of particular concern for designers when students participate using social media in one of their designs. At the very minimum, a designer must ensure that an instructor will not be able to:

- Mention in any way a student's level of performance
- Post grades
- Provide any personal information of any sort

There are other FERPA regulations that may be involved, and most academic institutions have guidelines to assist in this process. If a course design is for an academic environment, make it a rule that no personal information, grades, or other data that relates to a student is part of a public space viewable by anyone, even other students.

For other nonacademic design environments, designers must work with the human resources or legal departments to ensure that no privacy provisions are being violated or unwittingly infringed on within the design and implementation of the course. This is not optional for a designer.

Summary

Social media is an ever-expanding element of modern instructional design. In a few short years it has become one of the most promising aspects of course design for almost all learning populations. It is not without its challenges, both as it relates to designers' buy-in and learners' participation. Knowing the range of options and the design considerations for social media is a required skill for instructional designers.

CASE STUDY 1

A small, private four-year college is looking at ways to increase participation by students in courses since all on-campus offerings have been temporarily suspended due to an international health crisis. While they are using a popular LMS for hosting courses, they still feel like they are not incorporating all the options available to them in the course designs. Many instructors have suggested looking at ways to use social media, specifically Facebook and Twitter, to increase activity and interest in online courses.

- The college presently has 1,000 students in 34 majors, generally liberal arts.
- The student population ranges from 18 to 65-plus, with the majority under 30.
- 90 teaching faculty, most with limited or no online and social media experience in course environments.
- Budget is limited because of the uncertainty of tuition being reduced due to offering only online courses for the near future.

What would your advice be to the college?

CASE STUDY 2

An international software developer with an app that is used for financial transactions around the world has asked a local college professor to offer a half-day training program for customer service representatives on working with difficult customers in an online environment, like using the chat function in their software.

The professor wants to use Twitter as a communications tool and establish a unique hashtag specific to the course so learners can tweet questions or comments in real time to the professor. The questions and comments will be visible to everyone participating in the training by being placed on monitors in the training rooms. The professor does this for every similar course that is offered.

DISCUSSION QUESTIONS

1. Do you believe that social media is a viable course design option?

2. How can you help learners distinguish between personal social media use and course-related social media participation?

3. What do you see as the largest benefit to providing social media course activities?

4. What concerns do you have for social media in design projects?

5. Are some learning populations more likely than others to benefit from social media use in a course?

6. Is there any course design scenario in which you would not include social media?

7. How can a designer ensure that no student personal information is ever available as part of a social media course design approach?

The company says that they do not want learners to use their smartphones or tablets in the training rooms for security reasons since smartphones or any similar devices are not allowed to be turned on or used anywhere inside the company's facilities. They are stored in each worker's locker on arrival at a facility. Workers must go to designated areas to use their phones, usually only while on break.

The professor is dumbfounded by this rule and is trying to determine a way to convince the company that social media is now an important aspect of course design and that it is a key element of this course. It is especially confusing since this is a software company that uses social media as part of its applications.

You are the professor. What are you going to say or do to convince the company that this is something that needs to be allowed for this training?

CASE STUDY 3

A small start-up company that manufactures radon detection equipment for consumers wants to offer online courses through YouTube on the basic operation and calibration of its three primary products. It has an established marketing program that is almost entirely based on social media placement for ads.

Each course will need to be less than 30 minutes in length and the evaluation of mastery will be based on the learner working through a short installation and calibration process that results in a specific message that will appear on the device verifying correct installation and calibration.

You have taken this company as your client, and the instructional designer in you wants to take it one step further and incorporate social media for course design purposes. You are thinking that a function for questions or expressing frustration after viewing the course online might work well. There is also the possibility that some of the equipment might be defective or damaged in shipment, resulting in frustration expressed online when attempting to participate in the course.

What ideas are you going to suggest to the company to include social media and how will you explain the instructional design considerations and advantages of using this approach?

Advanced ISD

CHAPTER 14
ISD Workflow

KEY CONCEPTS

- Workflow in ISD is critical to design process efficiency
- Workflow elements: imagining, defining, planning, assigning, producing, reporting, implementing, evaluating, improving, and closing

CHAPTER OBJECTIVES

At the end of this chapter, the learner should be able to:

- Define the concept of workflow in the context of instructional design.
- Describe why workflow is different than a theoretical ISD model.
- List the 10 elements of workflow for an ISD project.
- List a key feature of each of the 10 workflow elements.

REFLECTION

The practice of ISD is not different than any other profession that requires a specific road map for accomplishing certain tasks. Physicians treat patients using a diagnostic schema. 911 operators follow a blueprint for answering calls and directing fire, EMS, or law enforcement to assist people. In instructional design, professionals always have a plan of action that follows a specific workflow. It will be modified for each different course or project, but there is always a plan for how to successfully complete the work required.

As an instructional designer, what do you think are the required elements of any workflow plan? What do you think could happen to require modification of a plan once a course design project begins?

The professional practice of instructional design is a complex, multifaceted process that requires an organized and efficient workflow. Designers often evolve their own specific workflow elements based on need for each project. Ten individual elements in the workflow process are presented in this chapter; each is dynamic and adaptive to any specific designer's needs. Every project, no matter the size and scale, should include a workflow approach.

Workflow in the Practice of ISD

When it comes to practicing professional instructional design, having an efficient and productive workflow strategy is one of the most important facets of the profession. Time spent learning the basics, reviewing the theory, and starting to gain practical knowledge of ISD will always serve as a strong foundation for working as an instructional designer. As all designers soon discover, the real challenge starts when beginning to design courses, programs, and other real-world instructional design projects. Each designer will evolve a specific, formal approach for how they are going to manage each project. There is no single approach or solution for every situation, but there exists a dynamic approach that provides a blueprint for getting started with the process of settling on a personal workflow design.

All projects, designers, and specifics are different. If you work with a team of designers on large projects, the elements presented here might be of value to you without too much modification. If you work by yourself or on small, isolated projects, these ideas may provide some depth to a project flow that is traditionally more casual and less dependent on interaction, but which nonetheless has the same basic elements that may be combined or omitted based on each unique project's specifics.

Workflow Is Not ADDIE

One of the counterintuitive aspects of learning ISD models like ADDIE is that novice designers are tempted to fall into the trap of thinking that the workflow for a project or course design is as linear as ADDIE or other models might suggest. Don't confuse workflow with an ISD model; workflow is about operational process elements and not the generic theoretical elements of ADDIE, SAM, or any other model. You can generally associate workflow elements with ISD model elements to build confidence that any specific workflow choice is based on a model, but don't expect them to line up or be in the same order.

As a designer evolves workflow for a project, there are elements that will determine sequence and timing for each element. ADDIE suggests that you need to have analysis, design, development, implementation, and evaluation in that specific order. This is the same for all ISD models to some degree. In the case of ADDIE, workflow might start with analysis, and it might not. For designs that rely on a predetermined population, stable content, and already obtained materials, it is realistic to start with design and use what you already have as the analysis element. To the same degree, evaluation is present from the beginning to the end of a project and is a continuous workflow process element.

Workflow Elements

The list of 10 primary elements in Figure 14-1 addresses the most common operations an instructional designer will have to face in an average course design project. As we all know, each project is unique, so consider this an approach that assumes a high level of sophistication and staffing that might run months or even years depending on the complexity involved. It is possible you won't use all of these in every project. But this list is dynamic enough that you can add or subtract elements to meet your specific process needs.

Because workflow is a process, the elements are designed to be used in a linear fashion. It is realistic to think that more than one element will be active at any one point in a project, especially when looking at evaluating and improving. It is also probable that assignments and reporting will be dynamic and may be more or less important at various phases of design.

Figure 14-1. The 10 Elements

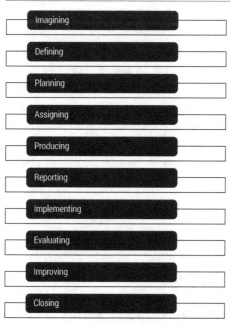

Imagining

Defining

Planning

Assigning

Producing

Reporting

Implementing

Evaluating

Improving

Closing

Each of these elements is rich with variables addressing each possible scenario in a project. You may decide you only need several of these, or you may add more. However, not having a plan for your projects will eventually catch up with you in unexpected ways; following this or another workflow model will put you on the path to creating your own personal approach to workflow command and control. Here is a description of each element in the workflow.

Imagining

This is the initial phase of workflow, where the project is first discussed and ideas begin to be vetted to see both what is possible and reasonable. Sometimes ideas are generated by a need that is recognized by someone in authority, and at other times there is a direct link between either mandated or results-oriented demands for training. At this stage, instructional designers may or may not be part of this element, but often they are the ones to actually suggest needed programs.

Imagining is included in the discussion of workflow because analysis will later include the question of why a specific program or course was seen to be needed, and while a designer or design team may not be initially involved, the information about this process can be helpful and sometimes critical in later workflow decisions.

Walt Disney established his Imagineering group in the early 1950s to focus on the construction of the original Disneyland in Anaheim, California. Over the years, the Imagineers have been the leaders of all creative activities within the chain of Disney parks and attractions. The idea that a group of employees would be tasked with imagining what is possible lends itself perfectly to our discussion of workflow and how to begin the process of course design. The more mental space we can allow for being creative and thinking about possibilities in the beginning of a project, the more likely we are to capture the possibilities available for any content and population. This may seem like a luxury and something that will never be budgeted, but the very idea that we can be creative as instructional designers carries as much value as any budget line might provide. Be an Imagineer as you design.

Defining

Many experienced designers will say you begin the traditional design project activities and initiate the process of creating the foundation for a project at this point in the workflow. You might consider this the "get to know you" phase; it brings the key players into the conversation. You will probably be starting the process of building consensus on goals; any remaining areas of disagreement are resolved.

It isn't necessary to dwell on content and related project specifics at this early point. Think of this as a view from a thousand feet and use it to bring every diverse aspect of the leadership, budget, and approval process together. Make sure that everyone agrees on the answer to the key question of "When will everyone call this a success?" All uncertainty about outcomes, process, finances, resources, timing, and other operational aspects of a project must now be addressed. From here forward, you want to concentrate on the project itself as opposed to allowing any uncertainty to remain and slow down your progress later in the project.

Ask questions like "What obstacles do we have that will slow us down or prevent us from reaching our goals on this project?" Another question that must be asked is "What are the things that might go wrong on this project as we move forward?" This is the same as the worst-case scenario exercise we talked about in chapter 5 on analysis. While some might argue that this is unnecessary, it is much better to plan for any contingencies than it is to try to deal with problems that appear seemingly out of nowhere that could have been predicted and perhaps prevented.

Planning

The planning phase is where the project really gets started. It is now time to operationalize the design process. The design team, subject matter experts, and other project specifics must be defined at an operations level. You will want to utilize project management tools to chart out the weekly, monthly, quarterly, and annual expectations on specific project milestones. Plan now on a reporting approach that ensures funding, grants, and other required reports are prepared on time and in the manner required. You will also need to provide detailed reports to organizational leadership, SMEs, associated groups, and any other groups or individuals not part of the formal reporting schema.

This is also a great time to consider how you might present information publicly, either by formal press release or through a social media reporting strategy for news and updates. If you are planning any "story of" video efforts to document and highlight the design process, this is also the time to put this process to paper and formalize approaches and responsibilities.

Always make sure to have a master calendar for team members and keep everyone in the loop when and if changes are made to the schedule. This is probably best managed online through a popular scheduling application. Scheduling will also be available in any project planning software if you decide to use one for your project.

Assigning

If you haven't done so already, it is now time to assign specific tasks to the design team. It is possible that most of the assignments up to this point have been more general in nature. From this point forward, it will be necessary to make specific assignments of a milestone to a specific person or team.

You will also want to start planning for the addition of SMEs, artists, programmers, photographers, and any other outside resources that will be used in your project. The earlier in the process you can confirm and schedule these, the easier it will be to meet your schedule.

Producing

When it is time to begin the actual production work on your project, you are in the producing workflow phase. You can argue that all elements of workflow include some degree of producing, and that is certainly true. The difference is that we are now in the project-specific production space, where behind-the-scenes tasks become tangible products for the courses.

You will likely be working on the production of the design plans, lesson plans, materials, videos, graphics, learning management system formatting, evaluation instruments, study guides, work aides, train-the-trainer guides, and any and all associated course products. All prototypes will be developed, and requirements and formats for all final materials will be reviewed and approved.

Pilot testing, if it is part of your project, is now put in motion with the draft courses. You will want to make sure that the obvious and more easily remedied problems are corrected before general implementation. This is also the time to offer any train-the-trainer courses for your facilitation team members.

Be sure to keep thorough records in this phase and have a plan for achieving each generation of materials and other tangible project items. Not only is this important for record-keeping purposes—such as billing if scope issues cause a budget to be impacted—it also allows you to retain important products that can be used later, either in this project or future projects. Never get rid of anything until it has passed its service life and an established archival date of release.

Reporting

While this should be a constant element in your workflow process, it is critical that you make a specific effort at reporting at this crucial state of the design process. You now have a tangible product to share, and this is the last stage before you go into implementation. Any remaining issues need to be addressed, and you will want to have buy-in and any necessary approvals at this point. While not the time for a full, final report, this is a turning point for the project, and any last-minute issues or uncertainty anywhere in the process has to be resolved.

Implementing

Finally, your project is ready for implementation. This is generally one of the easier workflow elements since it is usually carried out by the facilitation team. It is a good idea to have at least one of the design team present for the initial implementation to address immediate issues and to take notes and make recommendations for changes.

Evaluating

This element of workflow will sometimes be more of an attitude than a phase in the project. It should be taking place throughout the entire life of a project. At times, it is a more informal, simple 360-degree process of the project and staff giving an informal assessment of progress. At other times, it is a formal evaluation of procedures that is necessary to ensure quality control.

For the formal evaluation process there needs to be a multidimensional review, including at a minimum:
· Evaluations of the process and product by all team members
· Evaluations of the process and product by the leadership team
· Evaluations completed by learners in the program, both Level 1 and 2
· Evaluations completed by the facilitation and support staff for implementation

Never ignore or undervalue evaluation in your design philosophy or process. It always pays dividends for the time invested. It is also a major confidence and credibility element for the design team and associated organizations. A project team that can document the process, corrections, and final product can rest assured they have performed due diligence in their work.

Improving

Every project needs to have an element where lessons learned and other important process information are acted on for implementation in future projects. Any necessary changes to the product and work process need to be reviewed and implemented if possible. These are often a result of the data obtained from the evaluation and debrief process. This includes changes to the content and courses and any related process concerns. It is in this element that any plans for improvement are created and implemented.

Improvements can range from very simple areas, such as correcting wording, typos, and other tangible materials-based deliverables, to more complex and fundamental changes. Feedback, either in Level 1 or 2 evaluations or directly from designers, facilitators, learners, or others involved in implementation, should also be part of the improvement process.

Closing

When a project comes to an end, there is usually some combination of relief and satisfaction—and sometimes even a bit of regret. There are projects that have been productive and fun to work on, and that produce incredibly great courses and projects; these should be celebrated. Occasionally, there are projects that were far from perfect, and leaving them behind is a relief, but these should also be celebrated. You learn something from each project; even if the results are not perfect, take the time to reflect and catalog the things that could have been done better.

Always take the time to formally close a project. Final budget and related financial issues must be addressed and closed. There are reports to be finalized and submitted and people and organizations to be thanked and acknowledged. Never walk away from a project without closure.

Personalizing Workflow

When you think about workflow and the way a designer addresses the associated issues in a design project, keep in mind that ISD is a science that is based on any number of variables that are unique to each project. Sometimes there will be familiar patterns in your work. There may also be subtle but important differences that require some modification to an established and comfortable workflow from past projects.

Many designers create a template for their work, then add the variables specific to each project in order to make sure that each factor of staff, time, and materials is addressed. Don't be surprised to find that you don't need all 10 workflow elements. You may want to combine or even eliminate one or two, depending on your needs. On some occasions you may find that you need more elements in your workflow to meet unusual needs and circumstances.

It is probably obvious at this point that the most important element of workflow is actually having one. Take the time to think about what you need, the folks you need to manage, and the sundry other elements in your project that need a home and a plan. Once you have done this for a while, it will become second nature to you and will quickly become a common denominator in your professional practice of ISD.

Summary

Having a workflow process is considered essential for any design project, ranging from simple, one-course designs to multiyear projects containing hundreds or even thousands of courses. The efficiencies and productivity obtained by engaging in workflow-based operations are sometimes the difference between success and something less on many projects. Whether you use the model presented in this chapter or develop your own approach, make sure you have a workflow process that performs to your benefit as a designer.

CASE STUDY 1

You have been given an assignment to manage a large design project that will include both online and in-classroom courses. The content is technical and will require the participation of SMEs, software designers, and other team members.

The specifics are:
- 15 courses of approximately four hours in length for each
- Target population of nearly 500 learners

- Population is dispersed, with 50 percent able to attend in person; the rest will participate online
- Organization has access to an LMS for online implementation
- Six-month timeline to completion

You are the project manager and you have been assigned one senior instructional designer, two additional instructional designers, a support staff member, and the option for an intern. You will be required to use SMEs as necessary. You have the option to have the team work remotely.

What is your plan for workflow?

CASE STUDY 2

A community organization specializing in supporting cancer victims has need for a series of courses on how to help family members work through a myriad of issues, both emotional and physical, that are the result of a cancer diagnosis and subsequent treatments. One of the hallmarks of its approach to working with this population is to celebrate each victory no matter how small.

You have volunteered to design the courses for the group since you are both an instructional designer and a cancer survivor.

As you work through the course design, you are actively trying to adhere to the group's philosophy of celebrating each victory.

As you and another volunteer begin work on the courses, you establish a workflow and are trying to decide whether you should take the time to celebrate achieving each milestone as a victory.

What do you think you should do?

What advantages and disadvantages are there for building celebration into your workflow as a designer?

CASE STUDY 3

An instructional designer has been working independently for many years and works with a number of clients on the design of courses. The designer has never really established a replicable workflow process and typically "goes with the flow" on projects.

The designer has agreed to start working on a large project that includes several tight deadlines and penalties if course design milestones are not met.

If you were this designer, what approach would you take to establishing a workflow process that meets the demanding client expectations but also the desire to be less formal and more able to roll with the punches in a project?

Do you think there is a middle ground on workflow that can be found for most designers and projects?

CHAPTER 15

Criticality and the Content Mastery Continuum

KEY CONCEPTS

- Criticality approach to content selection
- Four levels of criticality:
  - Critical content
  - Required content
  - Prerequisite content
  - Unnecessary content
- The content mastery continuum and learner mastery from novice to expert levels
- The mastery tipping point and the point where mastery of a specific objective is met

CHAPTER OBJECTIVES

At the end of this chapter, the learner should be able to:

- Use criticality to select appropriate content.
- List the four levels of criticality in ISD.
- List the six frequency of application levels in criticality.
- Define *content mastery continuum.*
- Define *mastery tipping point.*

As a designer progresses through the profession and faces more difficult projects and challenges, there are more advanced design approaches and concepts that are available to them. In this chapter we explore two high-end aspects of instructional design. First, we look at criticality and how a designer determines what content should be included in a course or program. We then look at the relationship between content and learner and how to determine the correct fit for mastery based on a population and the specific content location on a continuum from simple to complex based on decisions made by the criticality process. Each of these areas is considered part of the practice of instructional design as project complexity increases.

Criticality Basics

Criticality is a well-known field of study in scientific fields. You may have heard the term as it relates to nuclear reactors; criticality is part of the process to create an ongoing series of reactions that then are used to produce electricity by heating water to turn turbines or one of many other methods. For our purposes in instructional design, criticality is defined as:

A purposeful process for content inclusion guided by criteria that contextually define objectives into four areas of criticality: critical, required, prerequisite, and unnecessary.

Designers can use criticality in a number of different ways; we are going to focus on the way that content and skills data gathered in analysis can be focused on a specific set of objectives, thereby eliminating any unnecessary content and objectives. This is useful because there are many times when a designer needs to reduce the quantity of content. This may also be necessary in order to trim content to fit a specific amount of implementation time available. Budget constraints may also drive the need to reduce content. This process is especially important when an instructional designer working with SMEs or in a content area that is unfamiliar to them wants to undertake the process of thinning the content.

Designers can use this approach for any variety of situations, and it can be easily expanded as the complexity of the content demands. This is based on the concept that all content can be rated in this process by two factors: frequency of use and importance, or as it has been named, criticality. This process works well since you rate each skill or objective based on these specific criteria. There are no favorites or biases at play in the process. This is critical when working with SMEs who have content they are less willing to surrender to the cutting block in this process.

To make this process effective, you need to create a series of rubrics that contains and ranks all content by both importance and frequency of use. You are then able to compare each individual objective against the others and through a process of simple addition of rankings determine the most critical objectives that must be included. This works so efficiently that it almost makes decisions for you if you let it, or you can simply take the data and utilize it with SMEs or a design group for discussion.

The steps for implementing the criticality rubric are as follows:
1. Create draft objectives for all content.
2. Assign a criticality value to each objective.
3. Assign a frequency value to each objective.
4. Enter the data for each value into a four-point scale on the rubric.
5. Rank the values for criticality and frequency for each objective.
6. Determine criticality by ordering the combined values for each objective.

Let's look and see how each rubric works and how you then work together to form the criticality rankings.

Step 1: Write Objectives

This is the easiest part of the process since a designer already knows how to write objectives. For the purposes of criticality, these can even be short-form objectives that contain only the behavior that will be used for ranking.

Step 2: Assign Level of Criticality

We will now create a criticality rubric for rating each objective or content element based on its level of criticality within the course in one of the following ranges (Figure 15-1).

Figure 15-1. Ranges of Criticality

Although you may eventually evolve your own definition of each of these classifications, it might help to look at the range of each of these classifications.

Critical

Critical objectives are those that cannot under any circumstances be omitted from your course. Among them are:

- Mandated critical: objectives involving required legal or technical content
- Performance critical: objectives that because of the severity of the consequences of omission or poor performance must be included
- Organizational critical: required for reasons other than mandate or performance, such as internal political issues, policy, or practice

Essential

Essential objectives are those objectives that are not critical but are required for a thorough course in the content area. Examples are:

- Skill steps: detailed content or procedures on a particular skill or concept
- Objective domain specific: objectives that match a required domain requirement, such as teaching learners specifics of a skill rather than just providing an overview

Prerequisite

Prerequisite objectives cover content that is sometimes marginal in terms of necessity for implementation but is useful as background information or for ensuring learner conformance with prerequisites. Examples include the following:

- Relevant policy, practice, or organizational procedures: setting the background
- Skills review: equations, safety rules
- Adjunct information: background readings, history, or added detail on a topic

Unnecessary

Unnecessary objectives are just about every other objective you may have, and are not always easy to eliminate. This classification can cause distress in group or team settings where decisions need to be made to shorten a course and issues other than content are involved. For example:

- Unrelated content: information that just isn't necessary, connected, or useful
- Loyalty content: the video of the organization's president adds nothing to the course
- Political content: objectives that are clearly meant to aid organizational presence but offer little or no tangible content

Each objective is ranked by level of criticality, which is assigned a numerical value. A scale of three to five is used for this rating (Table 15-1). You enter a value for each objective in the corresponding cell. This is how a typical rubric will look for rating the four objectives for level of criticality. You will see how these numbers in the ranking work together shortly.

Table 15-1. Ranking Objectives by Level of Criticality

Level of Criticality	Objective 1	Objective 2	Objective 3	Objective 4
Critical (5)		5		
Essential (4)				4
Prerequisite (3)	3		3	
Unnecessary (0)				

So for this set of four objectives, objective 2 is rated as critical, objective 4 is rated as essential, and objectives 1 and 3 are rated as prerequisite.

Step 3: Assign Frequency of Application

How frequently an objective is used in actual practice is determined by review by SMEs or others in a position to be able to make that determination. You can use any scale that works for your needs. The most generally used frequency classifications are daily, weekly, monthly, quarterly, yearly, and never (Figure 15-2).

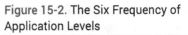

Figure 15-2. The Six Frequency of Application Levels

We now complete the rubric shown for each objective as you measure the relative value of specific objectives based on the frequency of application of the content by a learner. This value may be entered for each individual potential learner or averaged over a population, accepting that each individual learner may have somewhat different frequency of use requirements. Use a scale of zero to five for values in this rubric. Table 15-2 shows how four objectives might look in a typical frequency of use rubric.

Table 15-2. Frequency of Use Rubric

Frequency	Objective 1	Objective 2	Objective 3	Objective 4
Daily (5)				5
Weekly (4)				
Monthly (3)	3		3	
Quarterly (2)		2		
Yearly (1)				
Never (0)				

For this rubric, we have now rated our four objectives for frequency of use, with objective 4 rated as daily, objectives 1 and 3 rated as monthly, and objective 2 rated as quarterly.

Step 4: Combine Criticality and Frequency Data

It is now time to combine the criticality and frequency of application data into one rubric, providing you with another dimension for comparison of objectives. It is important to add this additional data rubric because critical objectives that are used most often by learners will trend toward the high range on this scale. Similarly, less important objectives that are seldom if ever used by learners trend toward the bottom of the scale.

Now you need to combine the data into one rubric for each objective (Table 15-3). You will combine the criticality and frequency ratings and place that number in the appropriate cell. This is what the rubric will look like before you enter the data from the previous rubrics.

Table 15-3. Combining Data for Objective 1

Objective 1	Critical	Essential	Prerequisite	Unnecessary
Daily				
Weekly				
Monthly			6	
Quarterly				
Yearly				
Never				

Step 5: Rank the Objectives

For ranking, you will use a rubric that takes the data from your combined criticality and frequency rubrics and places it in one ranking rubric (Table 15-4). This process provides you with clear and concise placement for each objective and makes the process of prioritizing objectives much easier.

Table 15-4. Rank the Objectives

Objective	Ranking
1	6
2	7
3	6
4	9

Now we have a clear picture of both how the criticality process works, but also how each of our four objectives ranked in our review. We have objective 4 as one that we can't delete and objective 2 as one that we should probably keep. Objectives 1 and 3 are the lowest rated and therefore give a designer some options.

Step 6: Make Final Decisions

Now is the time to make the final decisions about your objectives and chart them in this rubric, which will be the final worksheet you need for preparing your design plan. As you can see, there are different options for disposition listed. It is up to a designer to decide disposition options and what would be appropriate choices in this rubric (Table 15-5).

Table 15-5. Make Final Decisions

Disposition	Objective 1	Objective 2	Objective 3	Objective 4
Mandatory				
Recommended				
Optional				
Work/Job Aid				
Prerequisite				
Pre-course Reading				
Post-course Reading				
Unnecessary				

Putting Criticality to Work

Now let's work through the operation of the criticality rubric system using a real-world example. Let's say that you are going to make critical content decisions for a course entitled Safety in the Workplace for first-year apprentices in the building trades.

You need to make determinations concerning final disposition of the following terminal objectives in a four-hour course. For this exercise, short-form objective wording will be used because you are still in the early stages of the design process and would not yet have formalized the objectives into long-form four-part (A-B-C-D) ones:

- Objective 1: Should be able to state OSHA regulation(s) concerning hard hat use
- Objective 2: Should be able to demonstrate recommended hard hat use
- Objective 3: Should be able to list union or company policy on hard hat use
- Objective 4: Should be able to cite possible types of head injury resulting from failing to use a hard hat
- Objective 5: Should be able to list sources for purchasing hard hats

Now we will work through the level 1 rubric using our five objectives. Table 15-6 represents a possible scenario for these objectives.

Table 15-6. Level 1 Rubric: Rate Objectives

Rating	Objective 1	Objective 2	Objective 3	Objective 4	Objective 5
Critical		5			
Essential				4	
Prerequisite	3		3		3
Unnecessary					

Although you might not agree with these ratings for each of these objectives, it is clear that there is a pattern of criticality based on these choices. Objective 2 is considered critical, objective 4 is essential, and the remaining objectives (1, 3, and 5) are considered prerequisite. What this tells us as instructional designers is that we have a clear road map to use for gauging inclusion of objectives. If you have time for implementing all five objectives, you are fine. If there's time for implementing two objectives, you also have a clear guide to follow: objectives 2 and 4 will be included, and the remaining objectives would be prerequisites or pre- or post-course reading assignments.

The level 2 rubric allows you to dig deeper into objectives when the issues are not so clear cut as those in the first example. Assume that there is some disagreement about the outcome of the first rubric and you need to dig deeper to see which objectives should be included. Now, you will include the frequency of application data for review.

Table 15-7 depicts how we might rate these objectives in terms of the frequency of application.

Table 15-7. Level 2 Rubric: Rate Objective Frequency and Application

Frequency	Objective 1	Objective 2	Objective 3	Objective 4	Objective 5
Daily		5			
Weekly					
Monthly	3		3		
Quarterly				2	
Yearly					1
Never					

Now you can see a definite pattern starting to appear for our five objectives. Objective 2 is something that a learner will probably use every working day on the job. The other four objectives will probably find less frequent use, with one having only yearly value in terms of learner implementation. Again, you can argue with my rating, but those decisions can be made as a group and ironed out in the course of the conversation. We have now further refined our content criticality to the point where one objective, objective 2, is by far the most important for this course.

Now, let's make your head swim! We are going to further define each of our objectives using the level 3 rubric, which adds each objective's rating (from the level 1 rubric) and application (from the level 2 rubric), arriving at a final, multidimensional criticality. The level 3 rubric is completed for objective 1, which we rated as prerequisite (criticality) and monthly (frequency) (Table 15-8).

Table 15-8. Level 3 Rubric: Add Ratings for Objective 1

Objective 1	Critical	Essential	Prerequisite	Unnecessary
Daily				
Weekly				
Monthly			6	
Quarterly				
Yearly				
Never				

As you can see, we added the two values from the first two matrices and came up with a rating of six for this objective. Tables 15-9 to 15-12 show the level 3 criticality matrices for the remaining four objectives.

Table 15-9. Level 3 Rubric: Add Ratings for Objective 2

Objective 2	Critical	Essential	Prerequisite	Unnecessary
Daily	10			
Weekly				
Monthly				
Quarterly				
Yearly				
Never				

Table 15-10. Level 3 Rubric: Add Ratings for Objective 3

Objective 3	Critical	Essential	Prerequisite	Unnecessary
Daily				
Weekly				
Monthly			6	
Quarterly				
Yearly				
Never				

Table 15-11. Level 3 Rubric: Add Ratings for Objective 4

Objective 4	Critical	Essential	Prerequisite	Unnecessary
Daily				
Weekly				
Monthly				
Quarterly		6		
Yearly				
Never				

Table 15-12. Level 3 Rubric: Add Ratings for Objective 5

Objective 5	Critical	Essential	Prerequisite	Unnecessary
Daily				
Weekly				
Monthly				
Quarterly				
Yearly			4	
Never				

We now need to rank our five objectives based on the last rubric results (Table 15-13).

Table 15-13. Rank the Five Objectives

Objective	Ranking
1	6
2	10
3	6
4	6
5	4

This tells us that objective 2 has the highest ranking of 10, with objectives 1, 3, and 4 tied for the next highest ranking of six. Objective 5 is last with a four ranking.

Our final rubric provides the final disposition for each objective (Table 15-14).

Table 15-14. Final Disposition for Each Objective

Disposition	Objective 1	Objective 2	Objective 3	Objective 4	Objective 5
Mandatory		X			
Recommended	X		X	X	
Optional					
Work/Job Aid					X
Prerequisite					
Pre-course Reading					
Post-course Reading					
Unnecessary					

How Content Mastery Works at the Program Level

In chapter 10, we introduced the concepts of content mastery and the content mastery continuum (CMC) as a means to fine-tune objectives, a critical part of performance agreement. Let's look at an example at the program level in the knowledge content area of physics and the general requirements expected at different levels of education. In this case, we are looking at expected outcomes, so this is considered benchmarking for a general level of academic study. These figures are arbitrary; don't consider them anything more than an example.

Figure 15-3 represents a fictional general content mastery chart of the field of physics as an academic discipline in a university. What this shows us is that a high-school graduate entering the university has about a 10 percent content mastery of physics. A bachelor's degree in physics offers 60 percent content mastery. A graduate degree offers 72 percent mastery, and a

Figure 15-3. General Physics Content Mastery

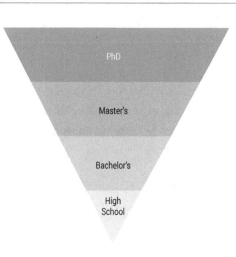

PhD

Master's

Bachelor's

High School

PhD indicates an 85 percent or greater mastery of physics. This, of course, does not relate to any specific subset of content areas, only physics as a general course of study.

Let's look more closely at this concept at the graduate school program level. We know that our entering graduate students will be starting with approximately 60 percent mastery, and they need to leave the program at 72 percent mastery in general physics. Our graduate program needs to meet that 12 percent expectation in order to meet our established standards.

The CMC in Skills Training

Imagine we are designing a course for first responders in a large county fire department. To be certified as a first responder, an individual must complete a 40-hour course and then complete two formal evaluations. The first evaluation is a 100-question exam that must be completed with a score of 90 percent or better. In the second evaluation, learners must demonstrate 10 key skills with no errors allowed. Both sections must be completed before a learner is certified and allowed to assume a first responder role in the fire department.

If we look at this on the individual learner level, we have a CMC chart that looks similar to Table 15-15.

Table 15-15. Individual Learner Level CMC—One Learner

Mastery Level	Skill 1	Skill 2	Skill 3	Skill 4	Skill 5
Mastery	x				
Functional		x			
Novice			X	x	x

This CMC chart tells us that this learner has mastery of one skill, functional mastery of one skill, and no mastery of three skills. This tells a designer that a course in this skill set might easily begin with skill 2 and perhaps skill 1 could be made a prerequisite skill.

Now let's look at a CMC chart for a population of 50 learners in the same content area (Table 15-16).

Table 15-16. Population of Learners CMC—50 Learners

Mastery Level	Skill 1	Skill 2	Skill 3	Skill 4	Skill 5
Mastery	36	8	2	1	2
Functional	10	29	15	10	5
Novice	4	13	33	39	43

This population-level CMC chart tells us that our population of 50 learners has 46 learners with at least functional mastery of skill 1. This may allow the designer to either make this skill a prerequisite or provide minimal coverage of the skill in a course. Skill 2 has 37 functional or above learners; however, 13 learners have no mastery of this skill. This probably means at least minimal coverage of this skill in a course. Skills 3, 4, and 5 contain enough novices that coverage of these skills is almost mandatory for the course.

The CMC in Analysis

Determining where a population falls in specific points of content mastery can be critical in the analysis process. Once a designer has determined the content required for a course or program, the CMC can easily be charted for that population and the data used to make crucial decisions concerning which content to include in the course and which content can either be required as a prerequisite or is unnecessary due to mastery already being met by the population.

This next example of a CMC chart for analysis illustrates five specific skills being considered for a particular course (Table 15-17). After gathering data, the designer is ready to chart and determine the population's mastery of the five skills. The designer is using the three variable mastery classifications: novice, functional, and proficient. Novice ranking represents a population having little or no mastery of a skill. Functional populations are able to reach mastery with assistance. And, proficient populations need no assistance to reach mastery. The skills are sequenced from left to right on a continuum from simple to complex within the content area as determined by subject matter experts.

Table 15-17. Mastery Analysis of Five Skills

Mastery Level	Skill 1	Skill 2	Skill 3	Skill 4	Skill 5
Mastery					
Functional	x	x			
Novice			x	x	x

This chart shows us that our population is functional in skills 1 and 2 and novice in the remaining three skill areas. They are not proficient in any of the skills. This information provides several design options for content inclusion in this course. On one end, skills 1 and 2 could be made prerequisites and the course could then focus on skills 3, 4, and 5. This would shorten implementation time and perhaps save money. Option two is to simply review skills 1 and 2 and focus most of the course time on the remaining three skills.

To go one step further, our designer has also determined the objective domain for each skill and has charted that data (Table 15-18).

Table 15-18. Skill Analysis of the Objective Domain

Domain	Skill 1	Skill 2	Skill 3	Skill 4	Skill 5
Cognitive	x	x	x		
Psychomotor				x	x
Affective					
Interpersonal					

This chart tells us that skills 1 through 3 are predominately cognitive and may lend themselves to online learning or a blended course delivery methodology. Skills 4 and 5 are predominately psychomotor and may require classroom or on-the-job learning implementation.

Each of these examples shows only five skills, but this process works for five or 500 (or more) skills; the larger the number, the more valuable the chart becomes since the skills that need designer attention will jump out.

The CMC in Evaluation

One use for the CMC is to determine the appropriate type of evaluation for a content area within a program or series of courses within a field of study. Imagine a training program on servicing sophisticated medical equipment for hospitals. It contains six courses of 35 hours each to obtain a certificate. Each course requires demonstrated mastery of specific installation and maintenance skills before a learner is allowed to pass to the next course in the series or be granted a certificate after the last course.

Since these courses contain complex technical knowledge, there is no expectation that a learner will be able to demonstrate mastery of a specific skill in the beginning of the course. It is likely that the early course content is predominately cognitive and requires learners to study information and memorize and contextualize theoretical data. This is necessary since learning the theory of how a specific piece of equipment works is required before any training on installation or maintenance is possible.

As the learner moves up the CMC, a base is being built for operationalizing the cognitive theoretical background and learning the more psychomotor aspects of the skill sets, such as installation, testing, and maintenance of the equipment. Evaluation necessarily mirrors the CMC since the closer we get to mastery, the more demonstrated evaluation is required. Simply being able to describe how to service the equipment is of little value unless a learner can demonstrate the required skills. This is the essence of the CMC in evaluation of course and program content. This is where the mastery tipping point comes into play.

We must also recognize that evaluation of content is usually more demanding at the mastery end of the CMC and less demanding at the novice entry point. This relates directly to objective domains and the performance agreement principle.

The Mastery Tipping Point

The mastery tipping point (MTP) is defined as the location on the CMC at which content shifts from one objective domain to another. This is important because of the way that objectives are evaluated, since cognitive and affective domain objectives are evaluated differently than psychomotor and interpersonal objectives. It is most valuable in working with cognitive and psychomotor objectives within a single course or a series of related courses that contain objectives in both domains.

While this may seem like a trivial point in the scheme of designing courses, one of the most costly mistakes made in the design of courses and programs is evaluating objectives in an incorrect domain. Doing this causes an immediate loss of credibility and can dramatically impact a program's reputation and viability.

Imagine that an applied program in nursing has 12 courses; six are theory-based cognitive courses and six are designed to be hands-on, hospital-based applied courses. The six theory courses are evaluated for mastery by a series of quizzes and tests designed to determine mastery of the basic concepts contained in the courses. The final six courses are evaluated by observation of learners applying specific job-related skills within the hospital in locations in which these skills would normally be implemented. But as a cost-saving effort, the program decided to evaluate the final six courses by quizzes and tests instead of mastery observed and measured on-site. As a result, program graduates are not prepared for the eventual work environment and the program loses most of its credibility.

Now let's look at an example using a rubric to determine if there are any evaluation issues. We will be looking for the point at which the content and evaluation of mastery move from predominately cognitive to predominately psychomotor and the evaluations move from a learner writing or talking about a process to the learner demonstrating skills related to the equipment.

This directly relates to the performance agreement principle: Evaluation must match the intent of the objective in behavior, condition, and degree. If we are evaluating a learner with written or oral tests and the content is specific to a demonstratable skill, we have a serious performance agreement mismatch.

Note that objectives 1 through 3 for our course are cognitive objectives and objectives 4 and 5 are psychomotor (Table 15-19). Our MTP is between objective 3 and objective 4. This tells us that our evaluations must shift, too, or we have a performance agreement problem.

Table 15-19. Analyzing Mastery Tipping Point

Obj Domain	Objective 1	Objective 2	Objective 3	Objective 4	Objective 5
Cognitive	X	x	x		
Psychomotor				x	x

Our evaluations should match our objectives as shown in Table 15-20.

Table 15-20. Matching Evaluations and Objectives

Eval Domain	Objective 1	Objective 2	Objective 3	Objective 4	Objective 5
Cognitive	X	x	x		
Psychomotor				x	X

If we chart our evaluations and they look like this, we have a problem that needs to be addressed (Table 15-21).

Table 15-21. Mismatched Evaluations and Objectives

Eval Domain	Objective 1	Objective 2	Objective 3	Objective 4	Objective 5
Cognitive	X	X		X	
Psychomotor			X		X

Summary

Criticality and the content mastery continuum are two advanced instructional design concepts and tools that can be implemented to address questions related to content inclusion and prerequisites for courses and learners.

CASE STUDY 1

A large manufacturing company has a series of courses that runs for more than 40 hours each. Depending on their job title, some employees are required to take at least one of these courses every year to retain competency.

There is a strong feeling among managers and employees alike that most of these courses are too long for the required learning to take place—and some are 10 to 20 hours too long. Both groups think there is an abundance of unnecessary content and some duplication between courses. The company manager is very technically oriented and will expect courses to cover all required information with associated evaluations of mastery.

Specifics:
- 25 courses in 14 content areas
- Each is 40 hours in length
- Average participation is 20 students

You are an independent ISD consultant who has been brought in to review the courses and make recommendations on their length and content. You have no specific content knowledge in any of the areas and will be working with company SMEs, employees, and managers.

Where do you start? How will you approach the process?

DISCUSSION QUESTIONS

1. When analysis shows a population displaying a range of mastery levels and you are trying to determine the entry point for the content, what do you do as a designer to solve this problem?

2. Using the mastery tipping point, how would you determine mastery points for a course design?

3. It is common for clients and a designer to have different views on course mastery requirements. How would you use the tools in this chapter to address this issue?

4. After performing a criticality study, you find that most of the content in a course is unnecessary and the 10-hour course could easily be implemented in three hours or less. How do you present this to the client?

5. When classifying objectives, do you think it is possible to have an objective rated as "critical" and yet never considered for inclusion in a course?

CASE STUDY 2

A large, nationwide governmental agency has a certification program, which presently takes six weeks in residence to complete. Recent budget cuts have mandated that this program be shortened to no more than two weeks in length. While some think it is impossible to cut enough content to meet this expectation, others have argued for years that the program was more focused on socializing this population to the agency and building loyalty than actually teaching the necessary content.

You have been hired as an outside consultant to provide the process and leadership to reshape the program to fit the two-week requirement. You have access to numerous SMEs, managers, and past participants in the program as needed.

What plan do you have for addressing the need to cut two-thirds of the present program and still make the case that it will be as robust as before and cover all the core requirements for the certification?

CASE STUDY 3

The local volunteer fire department has a course in home fire safety that has been offered to community schools and other organizations for many years. Over time, little has changed in the course and there is a feeling among the younger department members that the content is more dated than it needs to be. The older members think it is just fine and doesn't need to be touched.

You are a volunteer paramedic who is also a college student taking an ISD course as part of an education degree program. You have offered to take a look and see what the options might be for the course.

Given the obvious range of feelings about the course, how can you use the content mastery continuum process you just learned in school to address the course content issue without it appearing to be political or biased?

CHAPTER 16

Competency-Based Instructional Design

KEY CONCEPTS

- Competency-based education (CBE)
- Competency-based design
- Competency-based evaluation
- Designing CBE programs
- Financial aspects of implementing CBE

CHAPTER OBJECTIVES

At the end of this chapter, the learner should be able to:

- Define *competency-based education* in the context of ISD.
- Discuss the history of CBE and why it has become popular.
- List the steps in designing courses for CBE.
- Explain the process of designing competency-based evaluation programs.
- Explain the financial implications of replacing courses with competency-based evaluation programs.

Instructional design has entered a new level of efficiency with the advent of competency-based education (CBE). CBE is focused entirely on the competency of the learner in a specific skill set. While not all content areas and populations are a good fit for this approach, skilled trades, construction, maintenance, and other related content are uniquely appropriate for CBE. Instructional designers can easily focus on the outcomes in a program and provide focused training that is efficient and productive without the normal overhead of unnecessary content and expense. CBE is also a path for learners who have not received formal education in a content area to be evaluated for equivalent knowledge and skills in cases where these were obtained experientially. This chapter describes the history of CBE and the steps to designing courses for CBE.

A Short History of Competency-Based Evaluation

For the entire history of training—from the guilds of thousands of years ago that built the great castles and cathedrals to the latest in online and technical delivery systems that train apprentices in every imaginable skill—the predominate approach to mastery in skill-based learning has been "watch, learn, practice, feedback, mastery." The reason this approach has lasted so long is that it works for the purpose for which it was designed, the immersion and training of new skilled tradespersons in psychomotor or tactile-based skills like masonry, pottery, carving, milling, cooking, baking, and farming. Before World War II, it was not unusual for most workers to be cast in an occupation very early in life, from either family history or necessity, and stay in that occupation all their working lives. This meant that training happened as a natural evolution from apprentice to journeyperson, with a few even rising to the title of master craftsperson. During this time the worker was slowly immersed in the skills necessary for the trade and evaluated by the more senior members of the craft. There was little in the way of formal training because each craft was somewhat different in the way they approached teaching new workers.

As the trades became more technical and complicated, they also encompassed many new areas of expertise, including the medical, legal, and military occupations. Training also became more formal, and it was also a natural progression that mastery of these occupations was now accompanied by a formal evaluation process and the issuance of some form of licensure. In the building trades you worked from apprenticeship to licensed journeyperson with a credential issued by the trade or a governmental authority. This formalization of trades also eventually extended to titles like accountant, paramedic, firefighter, and police officer. The licensure was now the currency required to get and hold an occupation, and these were almost always limited to individuals who went step-by-step through a formal training period that combined traditional classroom and on-the-job training for a set period of time before any mastery would or could be documented.

The traditional foundation of academic credit was the first column to fall when experiential credit began to appear in community colleges after WWII. Veterans needed a fast track to a college degree and since many training courses and work experiences from the war were somewhat or even totally duplicated in a formal setting, students could document this learning for possible licensure or college credits. The same logic applied to the non-credit world of training, but would take a slightly different and longer road to utilization.

The first generation of this new system provided a way to fast-track college credits to some level, but never allowed for these experiential credits to apply toward a specific major, since that was deemed the province of the issuing college or university. Regional academic accreditation still requires that a student take all or most of their courses in a major with the issuing school. So, while students could shorten their time in college, they couldn't really take what they learned through previous informal learning and use it toward a credentialing for a particular skill set or profession without retaking courses that contained content they had already mastered. Enter competency-based evaluation.

Competency-based evaluation is essentially a system for allowing a formal and reliable way to evaluate previous learning from any source and turn that into some form of recognized currency with the same standing and level of acceptance as existing formal learning in specific skill and content areas. The early adapter to this new approach to learning and credentialing is the skilled trades system of apprenticeship, which normally requires years of classroom and field experience before being considered a credentialed journey level in a trade. Competency-based evaluation allows a path for informal or nondocumented learning to be evaluated for mastery toward a skilled-trades credential.

Competency-based education, training, and evaluation are each worth a book on its own. This is but a small subset of the competency-based suite of tools for an instructional designer. The most important element to remember is that there is an alternative to traditional approaches to earning licensure, certification, or a college degree. As the legacy world of "time in class" or "contact hours" starts to crumble, the new normal is finding credible, observable, and

REFLECTION

The guilds of ancient times, starting with the building of King Solomon's Temple and the pyramids, played a major role in the process of competency-based education and evaluation. The apprenticeship programs in thousands of applied fields are a modern-day, state-of-the-art example of this tradition.

As an instructional designer, how do you balance the fact that this approach is centuries old with the constant expectation that professional instructional design practice, courses, and programs are examples of the modern world of professional ISD?

measurable ways to move learners through the system to productive careers based on the principle of experiential learning.

How Competency-Based Evaluation Works

The premise of competency-based evaluation is that a learner's competency is not dependent on where or when it was obtained, and there are no requirements for a formal classroom training component. The only thing that matters, and is therefore evaluated, is mastery of a specific learning objective. With this in mind, competency-based evaluation starts at the exact same place for a designer as building a course from scratch: determining and writing behavioral objectives.

For example, in the world of apprenticeship, a course might consist of training in how to complete a specific skill, such as laying brick to the line in a masonry apprenticeship. If a student is in an apprenticeship course, they would be required to attend classroom lectures and demonstrations and then practice the skill under supervision of an instructor. In the world of CBE, someone would be required only to pass a written test on the content and then perform the skill while being evaluated by one or more instructors. Instead of several days or weeks in the traditional classroom-based process, someone might be able to show mastery with CBE in several hours. Imagine the time savings over a four- or five-year apprenticeship for someone with experiential skills but no formal credential, such as a journeyperson standing.

This approach works for any content area. First you determine the objectives, then you provide a consistent evaluation process that ensures that mastery can be determined to the degree required and in the domain that is equivalent for determining traditional mastery. For example, if a learner is required only to complete a written evaluation at a specific degree of performance, then a CBE would probably stipulate that a prospective learner complete the same written evaluation to the same degree of mastery.

In the case of a demonstrated skill like performing CPR, the CBE student would be required to perform CPR to the same standards expected of a course participant for credentialing while also passing the written portion of the credentialing process. The requirement is that CBE participants meet or exceed the original level of mastery in an objective domain consistent with the existing course.

CBE Course Design

When you design courses with CBE as the design approach, there are certain things that you need to think about from the beginning of the process. Rather than focus on the learners being able to cognitively memorize and recite, the course design must focus on moving a learner to mastery through the process of demonstration, application, feedback, and evaluation (Figure 16-1).

Figure 16-1. CBE Design Approach

This process directly relates to the nine events of instruction we discussed in chapter 8. The difference in CBE is that these are all applied elements that are observed and measured, which is not the case in all course designs. Any theory and other non-application learning are not part of this approach. It is very simple, to the point, and exceptionally efficient. Specific skills can be taught and learned without any busywork for learners to endure.

The designer will want to make sure that a CBE course stays within the limits of efficiency and focus, which is inherent in this approach. Designers should always eliminate redundant and unnecessary course elements that don't directly support the skills being taught. Among other things, this typically means long lectures and other traditional course elements that don't support direct application and feedback by a learner.

How to Design CBE Evaluations

The process of designing CBE evaluations can be rather simple or as time consuming as designing the basics of a course, including objectives and evaluation tasks. In an established course that already contains acceptable objectives and evaluation tasks, you will primarily need to migrate the existing evaluations into a format that allows for the necessary mastery checks. In the case of a written exam, a proctored exam process will suffice. Simply implement the test and score the results.

In skill-based evaluations that require observation and scoring of a task or skill process, you will be required to develop a rubric that scores each objective. The scoring is best accomplished by observations performed by two or more SMEs in the skill area. Each completes the rubric independently, and a score is determined by averaging the SMEs' scores (Table 16-1). In some situations, one SME entering a failing score for an individual stops the process and no average is necessary. Another option is to average in the failing score and see if the final score passes the mastery threshold. Each SME is required to score and initial their rubric for record-keeping purposes.

Table 16-1. Example of a Scoring Rubric

	Reviewer A	Reviewer B
Skill 1		
Skill 2		
Skill 3		
Skill 4		
Skill 5		
Skill 6		

Scoring in rubrics can be pass/fail; a score of A, B, C, and so forth; or even a numeric score from one to 100 or one to five, depending on the needs of each organization and course. You may design the process so that an individual can retake a section of an evaluation again after a set period of time, like a week or a month. There are also programs that simply don't allow second chances on the process since they are afraid an individual will keep taking the CBE exams and just get lucky and pass at some point.

Since many CBE programs are sponsored by an organization that also awards a credential, the standards and process of scoring each section of a CBE will be at their discretion and may ultimately be the result of a governing body's preferences to ensure consistency and rigor. Each of these situations is unique, so don't be surprised if determining the scoring method is more work than designing the test itself.

The role of most CBE programs is not to eliminate the requirement for any formal training; it is primarily to reduce the amount of time spent in a program for those with abundant life experience in a specific skill set. This rests on the premise that there is no justification for a learner taking courses in content areas that they have already mastered. CBE can cover an entire program's content, but it is usually only a percentage of the mastery required for credentialing, and other content would need to be taken and mastery proved in a more traditional course-based context. Of course, there will be exceptions to this for individuals with many years of undocumented mastery.

Financials

One aspect of using a CBE approach in many environments is financial. Schools and training programs cost a lot of money to initiate and maintain. This is especially true if there is licensure and detailed record-keeping associated with an occupation. Without some additional forms of significant monetary investment by associated groups or individuals, a program is going to have to find a way to supplement traditional tuition or fees to reach credentialing using CBE. There are several approaches to making CBE at least a break-even proposition.

One approach is to have a fee for each CBE mastery evaluation regardless of outcomes. Another is to charge administrative fees and application fees as well as a charge for implementing the evaluation. Other approaches include a blanket charge for the credential regardless of the combination of traditional coursework and CBE mastery events.

As you think about how this might work, you will need to include the financial elements of this process and outcomes to make sure you don't design a bottomless financial burden when trying to streamline the process of credentialing a learner. With some time and effort, you can advance a model that will make a program at least solvent, given the options for learners and the organization.

Summary

Competency-based learning and course design is a critical element in modern ISD. While the elements of the process are not unique to CBE, what is important is the focus on moving learners to being able to learn, practice, and receive feedback on skill sets in the most efficient and timely fashion possible.

DISCUSSION QUESTIONS

1. You are asked by the owner of a large electrical contractor to find out if several of their non-licensed electricians can test out of the training program for becoming licensed. Where do you start?

2. Do you think it is fair that learners with more experience can essentially test out of some or all of a credentialing process?

3. Is there any downside to using CBE?

4. What is your answer to a client who thinks the level of detail required for competency-based learning is unnecessary?

CASE STUDY 1

A union apprenticeship program has asked your team to design five courses in the use of a new precision survey technology and related equipment. The courses will include the initial setup, use, and maintenance of the equipment. It wants the courses to be CBE and focused on just this equipment and the related operations. It expects every learner to be able to use and maintain the equipment at the end of the courses. It will issue a certificate to each student who reaches mastery for all five courses, and this will be required for the worker to be placed on any work site needing this equipment. There is no need for theory or background on the design of the equipment or other superfluous training.

Specifics:
- Five courses, each four hours in length
- 500 students, including apprentices and journey workers
- Maximum class size is 30 students
- A team of five instructors
- Deadline for starting the courses is the first of the year since that is the time when most of the members are not working due to the weather
- Budget of $25,000 for the design and materials, including lesson plans, slide decks, handouts, and other necessary materials

What plan will you present to the program for the project?

CASE STUDY 2

A large community college is investigating the possibility of providing certifications in the field of dietary sciences with a focus on food-handling safety. Since it is located in an area that is economically tied to casinos, coffee shops, restaurants, and a group of high-end food trucks, its leaders think that many people will want to have this certificate to enable finding work. The focus will be on the local and state health department rules and regulations, and they are going to work with local health officials to make sure the course teaches all the required skills.

During a college board meeting where the plan was being discussed, several board members pointed out that there existed a large population of food industry workers who would probably not benefit much from the program but would like to have the certification. It was then suggested that the university also provide a process for others to test for mastery in the field and be awarded the certification without taking the courses. There will be an application cost and other fees to take the certificate evaluation process.

You are the instructional design team lead for the college and have been assigned not only the new courses in the program but also the process of creating a competency-based evaluation of mastery for the certificate. You will have no problem with the course designs since your team is constantly designing new courses. However, no one at the college has ever created competency-based evaluation before.

Where will you start? How will you make sure that each applicant for the certificate is evaluated for mastery? Will you have only a written evaluation, or will you also require observed performance-based evaluations of mastery in certain areas like sanitation and disinfection methods?

CASE STUDY 3

A consortium of regional transit organizations and organized labor representing railroad workers has a need for a certification process for railroad signal technicians. This certification will be used to increase reliability of the signal systems and assure the riding public that regional transit is safer because of this program. At the present time, all signal technicians must complete a five-year apprenticeship, and this will be used as the prerequisite for taking the certification exam once in place.

The question has been raised that there are presently hundreds of journeyperson signal technicians who have already been through the apprenticeship who need to have a way to apply for and complete the exam process. Both labor and management want this exam to be more than just a written exam since there are certain elements of the field that rely on the operation of sophisticated equipment for the installation and repair of vital track-signaling systems.

Your ISD firm has been hired to bring this plan to fruition, and you have been asked to prepare a report to be given to the national consortium quarterly meeting on how you propose to address the issues associated with already-working signal technicians and their ability to take the exam for certification.

Where will you start developing an approach to the competency-based evaluation process? What will you tell the consortium to build confidence in your approach?

CHAPTER 17

Migrating Classroom to Digital Learning

KEY CONCEPTS

- Migrating courses from classroom to online
- Advantages to moving courses online
- Process for migrating courses online
- Instructional design solution to challenges
- Challenge of evaluating courses after migration

CHAPTER OBJECTIVES

At the end of this chapter, the learner should be able to:

- Define the process for migrating classroom courses to online courses.
- List at least three advantages for migrating courses.
- List at least five of the steps to migrate a course.
- Discuss at least two challenges to migrating a course.
- Discuss at least two challenges in providing evaluation with migrated courses.

One of the biggest challenges instructional designers face is migrating courses from analog to digital. This is not just about taking a classroom course and videotaping it to show to students. This is a complex process of making sure that the original content is reimagined in a way that not only is distributable online but also respects the original content and intent.

The recent rush to move courses online is certainly not a new phenomenon. Since the advent of learning management systems and the internet, instructional designers have been perfecting the process to make the magic happen. Lessons learned over this time have shown the way for some of the best practices in this process. This chapter examines the process for migrating courses from the classroom to online and the advantages and challenges for the instructional designer.

Before digging into the specifics of how to manage this process, let's look at some reasons this is taking place:
- Cost savings
- Dispersed learning populations
- Health or safety facility closures
- Expand potential learner pool
- Visibility
- Learner demand

Each situation is different, and as the instructional designer you will often have to discuss these issues with the client to make sure that you have a clear appreciation for their goals. This information will vary from situation to situation, and making sure everyone is on the same page early in the process is important in getting started on the course-migration process.

Course-Migration Process

Instructional designers need to make sure they have at least thought about the process and the workflow they will want to follow as they move courses online. The uniqueness of each situation aside, the process is more laborious than difficult. Here are the general steps to the process:
- Assemble all available course materials.
- Secure the most recent course syllabus.
- Meet with the most recent instructor for each course.
- Review and edit course objectives.
- Determine and review the specifications for the delivery system.

REFLECTION

Many teachers who are facing having their courses migrated to online will argue that their relationships with their students will be negatively affected. Other teachers who have taught online for a long period of time will say that they have better relationships with students in their online courses.

As an instructional designer, how does the impact of designing these courses with all the ISD parameters like interaction, ease of navigation, and building community affect the relationship between teachers and students?

- Prepare a design plan for the new implementation modality.
- Storyboard the course within the guidelines and limitations of the delivery software.
- Prepare the lesson plan for the new implementation modality.
- Pilot test the course.
- Train the instructional staff on the new software and applications being used.
- Provide practice shells and sections for instructional staff to review and use prior to actual implementation.
- Go live with the course.
- Evaluate at Level 1 with both instructors and learners.
- Plan Level 3 evaluation process.

General Challenges to Migrating Courses

As with any instructional design process, there are always challenges to moving courses to digital. Some are technical, while some challenges spring from learners' and instructors' reluctance to change. Here are some of the most common challenges to migrating courses:

- Instructors do not want to move their courses online.
- Instructors do not want to teach online.
- Learners do not feel comfortable online and miss the classroom.
- A new mindset needs to be created for teaching and administering courses.
- There is a technical skills vacuum among instructors and learners.
- Evaluation is different and sometimes more difficult.
- There are unanticipated cost increases for learning infrastructure.

Instructional Design Challenges to Migrating Courses

Instructional designers need to consider a number of critical aspects related to course design and learner-specific challenges when moving courses online. These are several of the most important instructional design issues to consider:

- Learners require more attention.
- Learners require more interaction.
- Instructor involvement and requirements increase exponentially.
- Evaluation can be more difficult for both learners and instructors.
- Learners require a more complex participation structure.
- Materials must be digital ready.
- Interface must be inviting for learners.

- Pre-course communications with learners is required.
- Training on software and the interface may be required for both learners and instructors.

Evaluation Challenges and Differences

You will often hear from instructors and designers that one of the biggest design challenges in migrating to digital is evaluation. Instructors are familiar with in-person evaluation methods like quizzes, tests, assignments, group work, and peer-to-peer evaluations that involve discussions, role plays, and simulations. While some of these can be easily migrated to online, there are some that are either more difficult or perhaps nearly impossible to implement.

Designers and instructors always worry about the increased risk for cheating on evaluations that are delivered digitally since the evaluation can be both asynchronous and taken at any location, making it difficult to verify that it's the registered learner who's taking the evaluation. Some designs and organizations choose the honor system. Others, becaues of either regulation or lack of confidence in a population, decide to evaluate in a way that minimizes the opportunities for dishonesty. This is an important element of evaluation that a designer should discuss with clients or decide for themselves as an instructor also designing their courses.

These are some of the more common evaluation-related questions that designers need to consider:

- What types of evaluations are required for a course?
- What is the ability of the applications, software, or LMS to allow evaluations?
- What is the ability of the applications, software, or LMS to allow secure and monitored participation?
- Is there availability for use of chat, blog, vlog, and journal apps?
- Is it possible to have synchronous instructor and learner-to-learner activities, both audio and video?
- Will proctored exams be required (third party or in person)?
- Is group work possible?
- How will grading take place for participation and other learner activities besides formal quizzes and exams?

Let's answer each of these questions.

REFLECTION

The migration of traditional classroom-based courses to online is now the norm in most academic learning environments. Both learners and teachers accept that the learning environment changes with this process.

As an instructional designer, do you feel that well-designed migrated courses are as instructionally sound as the courses they are replacing?

Course Evaluation Requirements

From a design perspective, when considering required evaluations for a course, it is the perfect time to think about whether what has happened in the past is really the best choice for the new digital environment. Instructors may not want to think about this if the past system worked well for them. Designers should be looking at what works best for the new course. Evaluations from the past might easily be placed online; some may need to be reconfigured for the new interface; others might be better off dropped. And, there is always the possibility that a new evaluation approach will work better with the new course.

The best way to work through this is to list all of the existing evaluations and work with the instructor to see if they are all still required for mastery determination and grading. It is not unusual to find that some of the existing quizzes and tests were more busywork than necessary and can be eliminated. If there are academic requirements for midterm and final exams, these can usually be migrated without too much effort if they are simply a standard exam.

Evaluations that require single and group presentations or peer review, or contain real-time elements, will probably have to be reimagined for the new interface. There are solutions for all of the challenges, but they will be based on availability of apps and software that allow group participation and the learners' ability to show slides, talk, and discuss assignments. Each of these will require organization and resources specific for each design.

Ability of Interface to Allow Evaluations

Once you decide what you will need for the evaluations in the new digital format, you have to determine if the applications and software available to you offer what you need. Many LMSs have a separate evaluation function, and you should be able to work through those options. If you are not using an LMS, will you be able to have evaluations either emailed or dropped to the instructor with available systems? Applications like Dropbox or Microsoft Docs are options if you can use them.

Security of Interface to Allow Evaluations

If you are going to use something other than an embedded application in an LMS, you will need to make sure that the security and privacy requirements for your courses are being met. In an academic environment, you will need to make sure that the documents and communications between instructor and learner are guaranteed to be private and that no grades, comments, or other student-specific information is shared with anyone else. In organizational environments, these rules may vary.

Availability of Chats, Blogs, Vlogs, and Journals

If your redesign to digital includes a requirement for a chat function, as well as learner and instructor blogs, vlogs, and journals, you will need to make sure that these are available in one form or another. LMSs generally have some version of these, which you will typically find in the Tools section. If you don't have easy access to these as part of your interface, you can always fall back on email for the blog, vlog, and journaling requirements for evaluation. Chat can also be arranged with other applications like Messenger and Messages in iOS. It may take a little research to find the best fit for each set of circumstances.

Using Synchronous Interfaces for Instructor and Learner Participation

Many, if not most, synchronous course design elements will require some way to offer directional or bi-directional video and audio interfaces. Here are several options:

- Zoom
- GoToMeeting
- Google Classroom
- Microsoft Teams
- Cisco Webex Meetings
- BlueJeans
- ClickMeeting
- Intermedia AnyMeeting

Remember that most of these are considered videoconferencing applications and may need to have limitations on bi-directionality, visual content presentation, attendance, and other features your design may anticipate. These will generally be separate from your online courses because they are often stand-alone applications and would need to be accessed independently from your course shell.

The other obvious consideration is cost. Some of these are free; however, the term *free* often means something different to a software company. The free platforms may be missing some of the options you consider necessary, and they may require an upgrade to a paid level of use for what you want. It is also possible that there are academic discounts and programs that might make the use of one or more of these more economical. You will have to do the research.

Proctored Exams for Online Courses

The challenge of having learners take exams while participating in an online course is often one of the biggest concerns to both designers and instructors. Without some level of confidence that evaluations are being completed by the learner, there are problems not only internally but also with state, regional, and other accrediting bodies. There are several options for you to consider:

- Require students to appear at a designated place and complete exams under the supervision of the instructor.
- Require students to complete the exam using an in-person, independent organization.
- Require students to complete the exam using an online, independent organization.

The first option is obvious and not generally any different than final exams with classroom courses. At a set day and time, students take the exam with the instructor in the room as the administrator and observer.

The second option requires students to make an appointment with the outside vendor to visit a testing facility and take the exam. These are usually online tests, but other options are available depending on the vendor. The results are then forwarded to the instructor and organization as arranged before the testing.

The third option is more complicated and requires students to make an appointment to take an exam using their computer. Almost all of these external examination vendors require learners to have a video camera and microphone operating during the actual implementation of the exam. There are vendors that have software that actually locks a student's computer and does not allow them to access any other software or applications on their computer during the testing. This eliminates the opportunity for accessing search engines, notes, or other prohibited information. The exam is almost always online in these situations. Evaluation results are then forwarded to the organization. If there were observable violations of the testing process by the student, the information is also forwarded with the evaluation results.

Group Work Options

The use of group activities in these scenarios takes a little thought and some sound design approaches. To simply duplicate the group work seen in a classroom is not as easy as it may seem. Then, there is the issue of how to grade these exercises and projects from a distance. Here are some ideas.

If you are using an LMS and it has a group function, you are set. Just set it up and add the necessary information for the students. There will be an option for the instructor to assign groups, or they can self-select partners in most LMSs. Grading is then the same as any other course element.

If you are not using an LMS and you have a widely dispersed group of students, you are going to have to be creative. It may be necessary to fall back on email, texting, or messaging for the teams to work on projects. They can also use the conferencing software mentioned earlier, which can include group members and the instructor. The fallback option is simply having students use smartphones to join a conference call so they can work collaboratively in a more analog mode.

Grading

While most LMSs have an integrated grading module, it still takes a fair amount of design work to migrate an existing classroom-grading process to the new environment. The challenge is to assign grading percentages and points to every aspect of a course that requires a grade. For example, if an eight-week course has 12 assignments, each of these will have to have points assigned for each grading element. The same is true for discussion board posts and other assignments. For an instructor who has never had to break down grades in this way, it can be a daunting process.

Let's say an assignment is to post a process that contains six distinctive elements. To grade the assignment, each of the elements will have to be assigned a value. So, if the entire post is worth 10 points, it is now necessary to assign a specific value to each of those elements. It might look like Table 17-1.

Table 17-1. Grading Rubric Example

Element 1	2 points
Element 2	1 point
Element 3	2 points
Element 4	1 point
Element 5	2 points
Element 6	2 points
Total	10 possible points

It is also usually an option to post specific comments for each assignment and grading group. Extra credit is also an option with most systems. Once the instructor enters the numeric grades, they are available to the learner through the grading link in the course, which is visible to them on their home screen in the LMS.

Once you have assigned points for each gradable course element, there will also be a points total for the entire course. The LMS will do the math, but it can be complicated and it is not something that can be done quickly the first time. Instructors are generally not fond of this process. However, it is a great time to review the evaluations for a course and see where things might be made more efficient or representative of the content.

Summary

Migrating traditional classroom courses to online has become a common task for instructional designers. While the process might seem daunting at first, using some guidelines, like those in this chapter, will assist in planning and implementing course migrations.

CASE STUDY 1

The leaders of a small community college have decided that they need to make all for-credit courses available online. They may continue to offer in-class sections of courses in programs that are related to the building trades and auto mechanics programs, but the focus will be to offer as many courses as possible online, even in these programs.

The administration is somewhat hesitant about this process and many faculty are expressing reservations about both their ability to teach online and the effectiveness of online courses compared with their present classroom courses. The migration to online is being encouraged by the board of trustees and the state board of education.

Specifics:
- 17 associate degree programs
- 10 certificate programs
- 122 individual courses
- 202 sections, on average, per fall and spring term
- 48 full-time and 72 adjunct faculty
- LMS is in place and being used for less than 20 sections a term
- Goal is to have the process completed in 24 months

As the senior instructional designer and manager of the department, you have been tasked with presenting some basic ideas for getting started with the planning process.

How will you start thinking about this process and what preliminary ideas will you have for the project?

CASE STUDY 2

A local school district's leaders have made the decision to offer their high-school honors programs and courses online. They believe that most learners in these programs will be attending college and will be taking courses online as part of their programs there.

As the district's instructional design manager, you correctly view this as a huge task. You and your team have been given three months to make this happen for the upcoming school year.

For the first group of honors courses, they have chosen biology, chemistry, math, and history. Two of these, biology and chemistry, usually involve lab instruction and subsequent lab time for students.

What ideas do you have for designing and implementing the migration of these four courses? What approach will you use for the lab-dependent courses? How will you approach the scheduling of the courses using synchronous or asynchronous approaches?

CASE STUDY 3

An MBA graduate program at a university has decided to take the entire program online using the university's LMS. One of the major features of the courses for the MBA is group projects and activities. At this point, they are facilitated in the traditional classroom meeting design approach, with some allowances for email and chat interactions between group members and the professor.

While the course migration process is already well established at the school, the program faculty are really concerned about how to migrate the group activities to the LMS. While the LMS has options for group work, the faculty is unfamiliar with them because up to this point most have not taught using the system.

You are the school's instructional design manager and you have been assigned the responsibility to explore options for group work and communications that will address the concerns expressed by faculty.

How will you work with the faculty on the migration issues?

What will you share as the advantages and disadvantages of teaching and group work online?

Acknowledgments

First, I want to acknowledge the partners that I am privileged to work with at ATD. For more than 25 years I have been a proud member of this family, and each book and article renders me more in their debt. Specifically, I want to thank Melissa Jones, Kay Hechler, Kathryn Stafford, Hannah Sternberg, Eliza Blanchard, Erin Strider, and Suzy Felchlin.

To all of my students throughout the years. Rest assured I learn more from each of you than you could ever hope to learn from me. This volume is a reflection of what you told me you wanted and needed to know about ISD. Thanks to my grad student Tina Butcher for allowing me to use her terrific pre-course lesson plan element in chapter 8.

To my many UMBC faculty colleagues and coconspirators, including Greg Williams and Stu Weinstein, and my grad-students-turned-faculty Jeannette Munroe, Catherine Zaranis, Paul Kellermann, and Keith Curran.

To my colleagues at the University of Maryland School of Pharmacy especially my partner and role model for limitless energy, dedication to students, and academic excellence, Lynn McPherson.

To Sivasailam "Thiagi" Thiagarajan for sharing his incredible work for this publication.

To my colleagues at the International Masonry Training and Education Foundation for allowing me to give back to my sisters and brothers in the union skilled trades and apprenticeship community around the world through the Instructor Certification Program.

To my best bud and better angel Jeannette Munroe.

To my incredible family that have always supported me in my various endeavors, including Heather and Alex Herrig, Nick Ransom, David and Jess Hodell, Savannah Ransom, and Joe Hodell.

To my wife, partner, and best friend Karen. Without her, this publication would have never been completed.

Chuck Hodell
Third Hill Mountain, West Virginia

Glossary of ISD Terms

Defined in the context of instructional design

Accumulation of Advantages: A chess term that references the fact that no chess game can be won in one move, but must be the result of many successful moves. In ISD it means that all elements of ISD must be followed to ensure successful course development.

ADDIE: The generic ISD model that contains the elements of analysis, design, development, implementation, and evaluation.

Adulthood: In the practice of ISD, this is the period when a learner is beyond the age of usual participation in high school.

Analysis: The first element in the ADDIE model.

Andragogy: The study of adults as learners.

Application Feedback 1: The first of the interactive elements in the nine events of instruction.

Application Feedback 2: The second of the interactive elements in the nine events of instruction.

Application Feedback 3: The third of the interactive elements in the nine events of instruction.

Asynchronous: When online learning does not take place synchronously and learners are not participating at the same time.

Audience: The first element in the A-B-C-D format for writing behavioral objectives; refers to the learner.

Behavior: The second element of an objective that details the expected observable and measurable actions of a learner to reach mastery.

Behavioral Objective: see *Objective*

Behaviorism: The learning theory that reflects the belief that conditioning impacts behavior and learning to the exclusion of thought and emotion.

Bloom's Taxonomy: A hierarchical approach to clustering learning behaviors by relative difficulty.

Chaos Theory: In ISD, the concept that every variable in a project is in some way related to all other project elements.

Chat Room: The area within an online course that is used for synchronous discussion.

Closure: The last of the Nine Events of Instruction and the element that closes a learning event.

Cognitive Domain: An objective domain that relates to objectives primarily mastered by a student speaking or writing.

Cognitivism: The learning theory that suggests that human cognition is at the center of learning and mastery.

Cohort: A group of learners taking one or more courses together as a single group.

Condition: The element of an objective that describes the conditions of learning given to support mastery. Usually starts with wording such as "given . . . ".

Constructivism: The learning theory that views learning as a construct of each learner's individual approach to learning specific content.

Content: The fourth element of the Nine Events of Instruction; contains most of the original material or content within a lesson.

Content Mastery Continuum: The way to measure learner mastery on a continuum from novice to expert.

Content Tipping Point: The point in a lesson or group of lessons that the objective domain and evaluation domain "tip" or change from one to another.

Continuing Education Unit: A measure of non-credit hours generally associated with continuing education programs.

Course: A unit of learning consisting of one or more modules.

Course Description: The design plan element that contains all of the specific requirements for a course to be implemented, such as delivery time, materials, room setup, and audiovisual requirements.

Criticality: A purposeful process for content inclusion guided by criteria that contextually define objectives into four areas of criticality: critical, essential, prerequisite, and unnecessary.

Degree of Difficulty: The term that refers to the relative level of mastery as related to the mastery continuum.

Deliverables: The tangible items required during the design process.

Delivery System: The instructional system used to deliver learning to a student.

Demographics: In analysis, the census-like data that is related to variables like age, gender, education level, and occupation.

Design: The element in the ADDIE model that relates to the design function.

Design Plan: The working document developed and used by instructional designers in ISD.

Development: The element in the ADDIE model that relates to the development function.

Direction: The second element in the Nine Events of Instruction; contains the behavioral objectives for a learning unit.

Discussion Board: The asynchronous element of online learning where assignments and messages are posted within the learning management system.

Distance Learning: A generic term for any learning that takes place when the teacher and student are not in the same location.

Enabling Objective: Objectives which combine to allow for the accomplishment of a terminal objective.

Evaluation: Fifth element in the ADDIE ISD model; responsible for determining learner mastery.

Evaluation Strategy: The design philosophy and intent for any evaluation process or product.

Evaluation Tasks: The specific evaluation tools used to determine mastery and performance agreement.

Facilitator Prerequisites: The specific skills and knowledge required to facilitate a course.

Focus Group: A group that represents or includes learners for a specific course or program that is asked specific questions related to the intended content or course.

Formative Evaluation: The evaluation for mastery of a specific segment of a unit of learning.

Functional SME: A subject matter expert that is involved in the non-design aspects of a course project, including programmers, photographers, artists, writers, and other professional fields.

Fuzzy Logic: In ISD, the concept that there is no definable beginning or end to a project.

Gagné's Nine Events of Instruction: The sequential elements of learning used in some fashion in most lesson plans.

Gaining Attention: The first element in the Nine Events of Instruction; used to gain a learner's attention before new material is presented.

Generational Learning: The theory that suggests that age-separated generations of learners approach learning in different ways.

Generations of Learning Transfer: The eight distinct periods of time identified by a specific influence in the process of learning transfer.

Goals: Generalized and nonspecific objectives.

Half-Life: Term used to describe the time until content or other course design features like technology must be reviewed and revised.

Hybrid SME: A subject matter expert who also facilitates courses.

Implementation: The element of the ADDIE model that represents the time when a course is actually delivered to the intended population.

Instructional Method: The way in which a specific segment of a unit of instruction is presented; examples are lecture, role play, and case study.

Instructional SME: A subject matter expert who is an experienced teacher and brings that knowledge to the design process.

Instructional System: Any group of diverse elements that work together to make the development of curriculum more efficient based on systems theory.

Interpersonal Domain: An objective domain that relates to objectives primarily mastered by a student communicating in some way with another person or group.

ISD: Instructional systems development, a systems approach to developing curriculum; also called instructional systems design.

ISD Model: Any of a number of theoretical models that represent the way instructional design is structured.

Job Task Analysis: Analysis of a specific skill or task for the purpose of designing training.

Kirkpatrick's Four Levels of Evaluation: A model for evaluation that includes four separate areas of concentration, including reaction, learning, behavior, and results.

Learner Ownership Level: In a lesson plan, the amount of responsibility a learner should assume in one of the three application feedback levels.

Learner Prerequisites: Requirements necessary for a learner to participate in a course.

Learning: The act of storing information and data in long-term memory.

Learning Management System: Any of a variety of online software programs and apps that serve as the interface between learners, facilitators, and the content of a course.

Learning Styles: The neuromyth that proposes that a course design approach must reflect a learner's favored learning style to be successful.

Learning Transfer: The act of passing knowledge and skills from a source to a learner.

Lesson: A unit of instruction, also called a module or unit of instruction.

Lesson Plan: A detailed guide to the implementation of a lesson, usually written in the nine-events format.

Level 1 Evaluation: A Level 1 evaluation is based on the reaction of the learner to the experience; sometimes called "smile sheets."

Level 2 Evaluation: A Level 2 evaluation measures if a learner achieved mastery of objectives at the end of the lesson.

Level 3 Evaluation: A Level 3 evaluation is based on a learner's behavior after a course; did the learning impact post-learning behavior?

Level 4 Evaluation: A Level 4 evaluation is based on results and is sometimes referenced as return on investment or ROI.

LCMS: Learning content management system.

LMS: See *Learning Management System*

Long-Form Objective: Four-part behavioral objective with the elements of audience, behavior, condition, and degree.

Mandated Training: Any training that is required by legislation, regulation, or policy.

Mastery: The ability of a learner to complete a behavioral objective to the required specifications of proficiency.

Module: A single unit of instruction containing a terminal objective and supporting enabling objectives; see also *Unit of Instruction*

Neo-Behaviorism: The learning theory that suggests that non-behavioral actions influence learning; originated in the work of Hull and Tolman in the 1930s.

Objective: The formal definition of the audience, behavior, condition, and degree required for mastery of knowledge, skill, or other definable behavior.

Objective Domain: A classification of objectives referring to the predominant learning focus of either cognitive, psychomotor, interpersonal, or affective.

Online Learning: Generally refers to lessons requiring learners to use internet or intranet technology to access and participate.

Packet: A single unit of instruction.

Participant Prerequisites: The requirements for a learner to participate in a course.

Pedagogy: The study of pre-adults as learners.

Performance Agreement: Refers to the relationship between an objective and an evaluation task; the principle requires them to match in behavior, condition, and degree.

Pilot Testing: A term for the presentation of a course for the purpose of review and revision prior to general implementation.

Population: A group of learners, generally for a specific course or program.

Population Analysis: The process of gathering and analyzing data related to a specific population during an instructional design project.

Posting: The act of a learner placing data in a course for review in online learning.

Prerequisites: The knowledge, skills, or abilities required before participating in, or facilitating, a unit of instruction.

Pro Bono: A professional service performed without compensation.

Process Objective: A less formal objective used in the early stages of the design process.

Programmed Learning: A design approach that emphasizes logical sequencing of content and frequent evaluation.

Project: The design and development of learning units using the ISD process.

Psychometrics: The psychological measuring of skills and knowledge.

Psychomotor Domain: An objective domain that relates to objectives primarily mastered by a student completing a task requiring physical activity.

QRDP: Quality rating for design plans; a quality review instrument.

QRLP: Quality rating for lesson plans; a quality review instrument.

QRO: Quality rating for objectives; a quality review instrument.

Rationale: In a design plan, the element that serves as the overview of a project.

Reaction: That level of evaluation that represents a learner's immediate feelings related to an instructional event.

Recall: The third of the Nine Events of Instruction; requires the recall of previous learned information for the purpose of building a foundation for new content.

Return on Investment: A form of evaluation that refers to monetary or other benefits derived from a project.

ROI: See *Return on Investment*

Role Conflict: When a designer tries to play more than one key role in a design project, like being both instructional designer and SME.

SAM: Successive Approximation Model of ISD.

SCORM: Sharable Content Object Reference Model.

Section 508: Law requiring access to and purposeful navigation for all populations to federal websites.

See One, Do One: An approach to train-the-trainer course design that involves first observing, then facilitating a learning event.

Short-Form Objective: A informal objective used prior to writing a formal four-part long-form objective.

SME: See *Subject Matter Expert*

Social Media: Any of a variety of software that allows interpersonal communications in either synchronous or asynchronous environments.

Subject Matter Expert: Any of a variety of professionals who provide subject-specific data and support to the instructional design process.

Summative Evaluation: A term used to describe a lesson-end or total content evaluation.

Survey: An analysis and evaluation tool used to gather data; usually a formal written document that may be either online or printed for distribution.

Synchronous: In online learning, this refers to learners being in communication at the same time without any delay, such as in a chat room.

Systems Approach: Instructional design process based on systems theory and the relationship of all variables to each other in a course design project.

Target Population: The learners designated as the end user for any instructional design project.

Task Analysis: The process of gathering data related to mastery of a specific task or skill for the purpose of designing a unit of instruction.

Technical SME: A subject matter expert who provides detailed content information to the design process.

Terminal Objective: The objective that reflects the end or terminal behavior for a lesson, course, or program.

Train-the-Trainer Course: A course that instructs facilitators in the implementation of a specific unit of learning.

Unit of Instruction: A single content element defined as having a terminal objective and supporting enabling objectives.

Workflow: The process followed by an instructional designer to complete a course design project.

References

Chapter 1

"Johann Gutenberg." 2019. *Columbia Electronic Encyclopedia*, 6th ed.

"Sumerian Language." 2018. *Funk & Wagnalls New World Encyclopedia*.

Allen, J.P. 2012. *The Ancient Egyptian Language: An Historical Study*. Cambridge: Cambridge University Press.

Congressional Digest. 2007. "Internet History from ARPANET to Broadband." *Congressional Digest* 86(2): 35.

Cordall, M. 2020. "Which Word Is History Derived From?" History—Movements of Ancient Peoples and Development of Language, Quora, September 30. quora.com/Which-word-is-history-derived-from.

Day, R.K., B.F. Skinner, and S.M. Markle. 2016. "The Beginnings." *Performance Improvement* 55(1): 39–47. doi:10.1002/pfi.21549.

Drack, M. 2009. "Ludwig von Bertalanffy's Early System Approach." *Systems Research and Behavioral Science* 26:563–572. doi:10.1002/sres.992.

Glaser, R. 1963. "Instructional Technology and the Measurement of Learning Outcomes: Some Questions." *American Psychologist* 18:519–521.

Gray, P. 2008. "A Brief History of Education." *Psychology Today*, August.

Guarino, B. 2018. "Oldest Known Drawing Discovered in African Cave." *Washington Post*, September 15.

Miranda, F. 2014. *Systems Theory: Perspectives, Applications and Developments*. Hauppauge, New York: Nova Science Publishers.

Nye, D.E. 2013. *America's Assembly Line*. Cambridge, MA: MIT Press.

Oppenheimer, O. 1958. "Toward a New Instinct Theory." *The Journal of Social Psychology* 47:21–31.

Pressey, S.L. 1960. "A Machine for Automatic Teaching of Drill Material." In *Teaching Machines and Programmed Learning: A Source Book*, edited by A.A. Lumsdaine and R. Glaser, 42–46. Washington, DC: National Education Association of the United States.

Reiser, R.A. 2001. "A History of Instructional Design and Technology: Part II: A History of Instructional Design." *Educational Technology Research and Development* 49(2): 57–67.

Richardson, M., and B. Slife. 2013. "A 'Narrowing of Inquiry' in American Moral Psychology and Education." *Journal of Moral Education* 42(2): 193–208.

Schoenfeld, J., and Z.L. Berge. 2004. "Emerging ISD Models for Distance Training Programs." *Journal of Educational Technology Systems* 33(1): 29–37.

Simonson, M., and D.J. Seepersaud. 2019. *Distance Education: Definition and Glossary of Terms*, 4th ed. Charlotte, NC: Information Age Publishing.

Thorndike, E.L. 1916. *Educational Psychology: Briefer Course.* New York: Teachers College, Columbia University.

Tomasello, M. 2014. *A Natural History of Human Thinking.* Cambridge, MA: Harvard University Press.

Von Bertalanffy, L. 1968. *General System Theory: Foundations, Development, Application.* New York: George Braziller.

Chapter 2

Armstrong, T., and Association for Supervision and Curriculum Development. 2018. *Multiple Intelligences in the Classroom*, 4th ed. Alexandria, VA: ASCD.

Barrouillet, P. 2015. "Theories of Cognitive Development: From Piaget to Today." *Developmental Review* 38:1–12.

Boitel, C.R., and L.R. Fromm. 2014. "Defining Signature Pedagogy in Social Work Education: Learning Theory and the Learning Contract." *Journal of Social Work Education* 50(4): 608–622.

Bolisani, E., E. Scarso, and A. Padova. 2018. "Cognitive Overload in Organizational Knowledge Management: Case Study Research." *Knowledge and Process Management* 25(4): 223–231.

Bouzenita, A.I., and A.W. Boulanouar. 2016. "Maslow's Hierarchy of Needs: An Islamic Critique." *Intellectual Discourse* 24(1): 59–81.

Clark, K.R. 2018a. "Learning Theories: Behaviorism." *Radiologic Technology* 90(2): 172–175.

Clark, K.R. 2018b. "Learning Theories: Cognitivism." *Radiologic Technology* 90(2): 176–179.

Clark, K.R. 2018c. "Learning Theories: Constructivism." *Radiologic Technology* 90(2): 180–182.

Dąbrowska, I. 2019. "Diverse Nature of Literacy: The Sociocultural Perspective." *Lublin Studies in Modern Languages & Literature / Lubelskie Materialy Neofilologiczne* 43(3): 33–43.

Faruji, L.F. 2012. "Neobehaviorism and Second Language Acquisition." *BRAIN: Broad Research in Artificial Intelligence & Neuroscience* 3(4): 46–50.

Gagné, R.M. 1972. "Domains of Learning." *Interchange* 3(1): 1–8.

Gardner, H. 1983. *Frames of Mind: The Theory of Multiple Intelligences.* New York: Basic Books.

Gardner, H. 2013. "Multiple Intelligences Are Not Learning Styles." *Washington Post*, October 16.

Gellatly, A., and N. Braisby. 2012. *Cognitive Psychology*, 2nd ed. Oxford: Oxford University Press.

Ghazi, S.R., and K. Ullah. 2016. "Concrete Operational Stage of Piaget's Cognitive Development Theory: An Implication in Learning Mathematics." *Gomal University Journal of Research* 32(1): 9–20.

Goldie, J.G.S. 2016. "Connectivism: A Knowledge Learning Theory for the Digital Age?" *Medical Teacher* 38(10): 1064–1069. doi:10.3109/0142159X.2016 .1173661.

Huang, L. 2020. "Unit of Visual Working Memory: A Boolean Map Provides a Better Account Than an Object Does." *Journal of Experimental Psychology: General* 149(1): 1–30.

İnankul, H. 2016. "Behavioral Learning Theories and a Review for Police Basic Training." *Journal of International Social Research* 9(42): 1540–1551.

Knoll, A.R., H. Otani, R.L. Skeel, and K.R. Van Horn. 2017. "Learning Style, Judgements of Learning, and Learning of Verbal and Visual Information." *British Journal of Psychology* 108(3): 544–563.

Knowles, M.S. 1968. "Andragogy, Not Pedagogy." *Adult Leadership* 16(10): 350–352, 386.

Koltko-Rivera, M. 2006. "Rediscovering the Later Version of Maslow's Hierarchy of Needs: Self-Transcendence and Opportunities for Theory, Research, and Unification." *Review of General Psychology* 10(4): 302–317.

Kropf, D.C. 2013. "Connectivism: 21st Century's New Learning Theory." *European Journal of Open, Distance and E-Learning* 16(2): 13–24.

Larson, C.B. 2009. *Metacognition: New Research Developments.* New York: Nova Science Publishers.

Lawson, T.E. 1974. "Gagné's Learning Theory Applied to Technical Instruction." *Training and Development Journal* 28(4): 32.

Lee, S.A., and D.M. Edget. 2012. *Cognitive Behavioral Therapy: Applications, Methods and Outcomes.* Hauppauge, NY: Nova Science Publishers.

Malerstein, A.J., and M.M. Ahern. 1979. "Piaget's Stages of Cognitive Development and Adult Character Structure." *American Journal of Psychotherapy* 33(1): 107.

Maslow, A. 1982. *The Journals of Abraham Maslow.* Lexington, MA: Lewis Publishers.

Murphy, E. 1997. "Constructivism: From Philosophy to Practice." Lanham, MD: ERIC Processing and Reference Facility.

Nancekivell, S.E., P. Shah, and S.A. Gelman. 2020. "Maybe They're Born With It, or Maybe It's Experience: Toward a Deeper Understanding of the Learning Style Myth." *Journal of Educational Psychology* 112(2): 221–235.

Nguyen, M.A. 2017. "Liberal Education and the Connection With Vygotsky's Theory of the Zone of Proximal Development." *Cultural-Historical Psychology* 13(1): 81–88.

Olson, M.H., and B.R. Hergenhahn. 2016. *Introduction to Theories of Learning*, 9th ed. New York: Routledge.

Piaget, J. 1964. "Development and Learning." *Journal of Research in Science Teaching* 3.

Pugsley, L. 2011. "How to Begin to Get to Grips With Educational Theory." *Education for Primary Care* 22(4): 266–268.

Saeedinejad, S., H. Nazafarin, R. Parvin, and H. Marziyeh. 2018. "Investigating the Relationship Between Academic Innovation and Organizational Identity With Higher-Order Thinking Skills Among Students at Yasuj University of Medical Sciences." *Middle East Journal of Family Medicine* 16(4): 126–131.

Schreurs, J., and R. Dumbraveanu. 2014. "A Shift From Teacher Centered to Learner Centered Approach." *International Journal of Engineering Pedagogy* 4(3): 36–41.

Scotton, B.W. 1996. "Introduction and Definition of Transpersonal Psychiatry." In *Textbook of Transpersonal Psychiatry and Psychology*, edited by B.W. Scotton, A.B. Chinen, and J.R. Battista. New York: Basic Books.

Siemens, G. 2004. "Connectivism: A Learning Theory for the Digital Age." Elearnspace. elearnspace.org/Articles/connectivism.htm.

Steffens K. 2015. "Competences, Learning Theories and MOOCs: Recent Developments in Lifelong Learning." *European Journal of Education* 50(1): 41–59. doi:10.1111/ejed.12102.

Thiagi, S. 2020. "The Thiagi Group: Improving Performance, Playfully." thiagi.com.

Thomas, M., M. Wieser, and D. Fittipaldi. 2019. "Utilizing Bloom's Taxonomy for Facilitating Effective and Meaningful Online Classroom Discussions." Marketing Management Association Annual Conference Proceedings, 1–9.

Utecht, J., and D. Keller. 2019. "Becoming Relevant Again: Applying Connectivism Learning Theory to Today's Classrooms." *Critical Questions in Education* 10(2): 107–119.

Vygotsky, L. 1978. *Mind in Society: The Development of Higher Psychological Processes.* Cambridge, MA: Harvard University Press.

Welsh, M.J. 2017. "Assist Student Learning through Scaffolding." *Pennsylvania CPA Journal* 88(1): 10–11.

Westby, C. 2019. "The Myth of Learning Styles." *Word of Mouth* 31(2): 4–7.

Chapter 3

American Psychiatric Association. 2013. *Diagnostic and Statistical Manual of Mental Disorders*, 5th ed. (DSM-5). American Psychiatric Association.

Aro, T., K. Eklund, and E. Korhonen. 2019. "Associations Between Childhood Learning Disabilities and Adult-Age Mental Health Problems, Lack of Education, and Unemployment." *Journal of Learning Disabilities* 52(1), 71–83.

Burns, A., M. Irvine, and K. Woodcock. 2019. "Self-Focused Attention and Depressive Symptoms in Adults With Autistic Spectrum Disorder (ASD)." *Journal of Autism and Developmental Disorders* 49:692–703.

Burriss, L., E. Ayers, J. Ginsberg, and D.A. Powell. 2008. "Learning and Memory Impairment in PTSD: Relationship to Depression." *Depression & Anxiety* 25(2): 149–157.

Eloranta, A., V.M. Närhi, K.M. Eklund, T.P.S. Ahonen, T.I. Aro, and A.K. Eloranta. 2019. "Resolving Reading Disability—Childhood Predictors and Adult-Age Outcomes." *Dyslexia* 25(1): 20–37.

Emerson, E., S. Baines, L. Allerton, and V. Welch. 2012. "Health Inequalities and People With Learning Disabilities in the UK." *Tizard Learning Disability Review* 16(1): 42–48.

Erickson, W., C. Lee, and S. von Schrader. 2012. *2010 Disability Status Report: United States.* Ithaca, NY: Cornell University Employment and Disability Institute (EDI).

Hagland, C., and Z. Webb. 2009. *Working With Adults With Asperger Syndrome: A Practical Toolkit.* London: Jessica Kingsley Publishers.

Hartree, A. 1984. "Malcolm Knowles' Theory of Andragogy: A Critique." *International Journal of Lifelong Education* 3(3): 203–210.

Harvey, J., K.J. Johnson, K. Roloff, and A. Edmondson. 2019. "From Orientation to Behavior: The Interplay Between Learning Orientation, Open-Mindedness, and Psychological Safety in Team Learning." *Human Relations* 72:1726–1751.

Horwitz, A.V. 2018. *PTSD: A Short History.* Baltimore: Johns Hopkins University Press.

Johnston, K., K. Murray, D. Spain, I. Walker, and A. Russell. 2019. "Executive Function: Cognition and Behaviour in Adults With Autism Spectrum Disorders (ASD)." *Journal of Autism and Developmental Disorders* 49:4181–4192.

Knowles, M.S. 1980. *The Modern Practice of Adult Education: From Pedagogy to Andragogy,* 2nd ed. New York: Cambridge Books.

Knowles, M.S., R.A. Swanson, and E.F. Holton. 2005. *The Adult Learner,* 6th ed. Amsterdam: Routledge.

Lai, K.W., and K.S. Hong. 2015. "Technology Use and Learning Characteristics of Students in Higher Education: Do Generational Differences Exist?" *British Journal of Educational Technology* 46(4): 725–738.

Learning Disabilities Association of America. 2020. "Support and Resources for Adults With LD." LDA. ldaamerica.org/audience/adults.

McGough, J.J. 2014. *ADHD.* Oxford: Oxford University Press.

Merriam, S.B. 2002. "Andragogy and Self-Directed Learning: Pillars of Adult Learning Theory." *New Directions for Adult & Continuing Education* 2001 (89): 3–14.

Parsons, R. 2016. *Learning Disabilities: Assessment, Management and Challenges.* New York: Nova Science Publishers.

Ring, M., C.L.T. Derwent, S.B. Gaigg, and D.M. Bowler. 2017. "Structural Learning Difficulties Implicate Altered Hippocampal Functioning in Adults With Autism Spectrum Disorder." *Journal of Abnormal Psychology* 126(6): 793–804.

Rogers, J. 2007. *Adults Learning,* 5th ed. Maidenhead: McGraw-Hill Education.

Swartz, T.T., D. Hartmann, and R.G. Rumbaut. 2017. *Crossings to Adulthood: How Diverse Young Americans Understand and Navigate Their Lives.* Leiden, Netherlands: Brill.

Trent, K. 2019. "Motivating and Educating Millennials." *Military Review* 99(6): 40.

Webb, J., and S. Whitaker. 2012. "Defining Learning Disability." *Psychologist* 25(6): 440–443.

Wlodkowski, R.J. 2003. "Fostering Motivation in Professional Development Programs." *New Directions for Adult & Continuing Education* 2003(98): 39.

Yingling, M.P. 2011. "Learning Disabilities and the ADA: Licensing Exam Accommodations in the Wake of the Ada Amendments Act of 2008." *Cleveland State Law Review* 59(3): 291–313.

Chapter 4

Akbulut, Y. 2007. *Implications of Two Well-known Models for Instructional Designers in Distance Education: Dick-Carey Versus Morrison-Ross-Kemp.* Eskisehir, Turkey: Anadolu University.

Cardey, S. 2013. *Modelling Language.* Amsterdam: John Benjamins Publishing Company.

Daugherty, J., Y-T. Teng, and E. Cornachione. 2007. "Rapid Prototyping Instructional Design: Revisiting the ISD Model." Paper presented at the International Research Conference in The Americas of the Academy of Human Resource Development, Indianapolis, IN, February 28–March 4.

Dick, W., and L. Carey. 1985. *The Systematic Design of Instruction*, 2nd ed. Glenview, IL: Scott, Foresman.

Gentilhomme, Y. 1985. *Essai d'approche systémique, Théorie et pratique. Application dans le domaine des sciences du langage.* Berne, Francfort/main, New York: Peter Lang.

Gustafson, K.I. 1991. *Survey of Instructional Design Models.* Washington, DC; US Department of Education.

Jablonski, A. 2017. *Business Models: Strategies, Impacts and Challenges.* Hauppauge, NY: Nova Science Publishers.

Tripp, S.D., and B. Bichelmeyer. 1990. "Rapid Prototyping: An Alternative Instructional Design Strategy." *Educational Technology Research and Development* 38(1): 31–44.

Chapter 5

Baum, N. 2018. "Problem Solving in the Medical Practice: Use the Five Whys to Get to the Root of the Problem." *The Journal of Medical Practice Management*, Nov/Dec: 170–177.

Hill, L.H., and S.C.O. Conceição. 2020. "Program and Instructional Strategies Supportive of Doctoral Students' Degree Completion." *Adult Learning* 31(1): 36–44.

Okes, D. 2019. *Root Cause Analysis: The Core of Problem Solving and Corrective Action.* Milwaukee: ASQ Quality Press.

Parker, J. 2017. "The Root of the Matter." *Internal Auditor* 74(4): 53.

Price, S. 2011. *Worst-Case Scenario? Governance, Mediation and the Security Regime.* London: Zed Books.

Reed, A. 2016. *Chaos Theory: Origins, Applications, and Limitations.* Hauppauge, NY: Nova Science Publishers.

Chapter 8

Robinson, S. 2019. "L&D's Struggle With Learning Evaluation." *ATD Insights,* December 6. td.org/insights/l-ds-struggle-with-learning-evaluation.

Chapter 11

Anderson, T., and J. Dron. 2011. "Three Generations of Distance Education Pedagogy." *The International Review of Research in Open and Distributed Learning* 12(3): 80–97.

Martínez-Cerdá, J.-F., J. Torrent-Sellens, and I. González-González. 2018. "Promoting Collaborative Skills in Online University: Comparing Effects of Games, Mixed Reality, Social Media, and Other Tools for ICT-Supported Pedagogical Practices." *Behaviour & Information Technology* 37(10/11): 1055–1071.

Vorbach, S., E.M. Poandl, and I. Korajman. 2019. "Digital Entrepreneurship Education: The Role of MOOCs." *International Journal of Engineering Pedagogy* 9(3): 99–111.

Xu, D., and Y. Xu. 2019. *The Promises and Limits of Online Higher Education: Understanding How Distance Education Affects Access, Cost, and Quality.* Washington, DC: American Enterprise Institute.

Chapter 12

Bagustari, B.A., and H.B. Santoso. 2019. "Adaptive User Interface of Learning Management Systems for Education 4.0: A Research Perspective." *Journal of Physics: Conference Series* 1235(012033).

Kolekar, S.V., R.M. Pai, and M.M. Manhora Pai. 2019. "Rule Based Adaptive User Interface for Adaptive E-Learning System." *Education and Information Technologies* 24:613–641.

Chapter 13

Gramlich, J. 2019. "10 Facts About Americans and Facebook." FactTank: News in the Numbers, May 16. pewresearch.org/fact-tank/2019/05/16/facts-about-americans-and-facebook.

Greenhow, C., J. Sonnevend, and C. Agur. 2016. *Education and Social Media: Toward a Digital Future.* Boston: MIT Press.

Jensen, L.J. 2019. "Integrating Social Media Into Online Education." *Library Technology Reports* 55(4): 27.

Li, Y., and Y. Xie. 2020. "Is a Picture Worth a Thousand Words? An Empirical Study of Image Content and Social Media Engagement." *Journal of Marketing Research* 57(1): 1–19.

Mistry, N., M. Carter, J. Seltzer, A. Dichiara, E. Cowan, and A.A. Gubi. 2018. "Social Media Guidelines Within University-Based Professional Psychology Training Programs: Ethical Challenges and Professional Considerations With Graduate Students." *Ethical Human Psychology & Psychiatry* 20(1): 43–55.

Sayce, D. 2020. "Digital Marketing Consultant." David Sayce. dsayce.com.

Vie, S. 2017. "Training Online Technical Communication Educators to Teach With Social Media: Best Practices and Professional Recommendations." *Technical Communication Quarterly* 26(3): 344–359.

Index

Page numbers followed by *f* and *t*, respectively, refer to figures and tables.

About the Author

Chuck Hodell has been writing about, practicing, and teaching ISD for many years. His books and articles have earned him the title of "The Man Who Wrote the Book on ISD." His bestselling four editions of *ISD From the Ground Up* and his *SMEs From the Ground Up* books are used internationally in both academic and workplace settings. He is also the author of many issues of *TD at Work*, *TD* magazine articles, and Best on ISD pieces, and is an *ATD Handbook for Training Development* contributor. He has appeared in ATD videos and participated in numerous online and ATD international conferences, including teaching pre-conference programs in ISD. Chuck has designed thousands of training programs for the White House, major corporations, nonprofits, and numerous apprenticeship programs as well as assisting clients in Egypt, Africa, Europe, and other locations around the world. He presently serves as affiliate professor at the University of Maryland School of Pharmacy, and associate director and faculty of the Learning and Performance Technology master's program at The University of Maryland Baltimore County; he has served as deputy provost at The National Labor College as well as holding faculty positions at Antioch University and other institutions. He presently serves as the academic advisor for the Instructor Certification Program at the International Masonry Training and Education Foundation. Chuck holds a PhD in language, literacy and culture from UMBC, a master's in ISD from UMBC, and an undergraduate degree from Antioch University. Chuck encourages conversations and questions raised by his work at hodell@me.com and on LinkedIn.